WILLFUL BLINDNESS:
A MEMOIR OF THE JIHAD

WILLFUL BLINDNESS:

A Memoir of the Jihad

Andrew C. McCarthy

ENCOUNTER BOOKS
New York and London

First edition published in 2008 by Encounter Books, an activity of Encounter for Culture and Education, Inc., a nonprofit, tax exempt corporation.

Encounter Books website address: www.encounterbooks.com

Manufactured in the United States and printed on acid-free paper.

Text design and composition by Wesley B. Tanner / Passim Editions, Ann Arbor.

∞ The paper used in this publication meets the minimum requirements of ANSI/ NISO Z39.48-1992 (R 1997) (Permanence of Paper).

FIRST EDITION

Library of Congress Cataloging-in-Publication Data

McCarthy, Andrew C.
      Willful blindness : a memoir of the Jihad / by Andrew C. McCarthy.
            p. cm.
      ISBN-13: 978-1-59403-213-4 (hardcover : alk. paper)
      ISBN-10: 1-59403-213-0 (hardcover : alk. paper) 1. Terrorism—New York
(State)—New York. 2. Terrorism—Psychological aspects. 3. Jihad. I. Title.
      HV6432.44.N7M33 2008
      363.32509747'1—dc22   2008001914

Contents

For Alexandra, my two sons, and Mom

WILLFUL BLINDNESS:
A MEMOIR OF THE JIHAD

⌛ Chapter 1

"Imagine the Liability!"

"IMAGINE THE LIABILITY!"

We were squinting in a new dawn's first glimmers. A terrifying new dawn. Law enforcement's visionaries–and, yes, there really were a few–could not yet see how profoundly things had changed, how the very notion of *law enforcement* would have to change. Already, though, there was reason enough to blanch at the insouciant idiocy of that reedy sigh of relief.

Imagine the liability! The words spilled from the lips of the FBI's top foreign counterintelligence agent in New York City. Fifteen years later, the plea is as jarring as when first I heard it. For all the sober resolutions about new enforcement "paradigms," it endures: endogenous, invariant, maybe immutable. By July 1993, I'd already been in government for well over a decade, so the ethos was far from unknown to me. Still, the thud I was sure I heard had to be the sound of my jaw striking the war room floor.

War room. There was an irony. There was a war on, alright. But not in that room. The war was right outside the window that looked out on the frenetic majesty of lower Manhattan. It may be impossible to clap with one hand, but a war can be fought by one side. Radical Islam was proving it. Inside the "war room," however, there was no war. There was legal strategizing.

Just a few blocks away, not five months before, the most brazen attack against the American homeland since Pearl Harbor had taken place, the bombing of the World Trade Center. Hard on it had followed an even more ambitious–though unsuccessful–mass-murder plot against other New York City landmarks. Yet the vigorous government counterattack being planned in that room involved no military personnel, no intelligence officers, no maps or grids or pins.

We were writing an indictment.

In 1993, the United States Department of Justice was not merely the point of America's counterterrorist spear. It was *the spear*. Period. The enemy was at war. Jihadists had made that exquisitely clear, in word as well as deed. Our response was to call in not the marines, but the prosecutors. And here in the war room, by the battle's frontline, I would be the field commander.

My chief qualification? Why, I was a lawyer, of course.

It had to be that way, at least for a time. We'd been struck a stunning blow. But, unlike Pearl Harbor, we didn't yet know exactly where it had come from, or why. Well, better to say, "We didn't yet know exactly what we knew," because, as it turned out, we had reason to know plenty. In any event, it is now patent that the bombing and its aftermath marked a liminal moment in American history: An offensive executed by sub-sovereign, transnational enemies, embedded and operating not only from inaccessible safe-havens but also within friendly nations. This was to be the era of asymmetric warfare, fueled by a chiliastic ideology, barbarously capitalizing on civilization's once-settled assumptions about the limits of deviancy.

The war was on, but we didn't see it yet. It was still dawn and we were playing catch-up. That we couldn't see was a problem easily rectified by information. That we *wouldn't* see even upon informing ourselves–that was a problem within us. One that hasn't changed. The enemy's declaration of war would be complemented by a campaign of murder and mayhem, culminating in the same place, eight years later, when this first strike would be dwarfed. In the interim, the United States would respond with law. And so, while the enemy prosecuted the war, we prosecuted the enemy–er, the defendants.

No surprise there. For government, "Terror" was the new "Drugs," which themselves had been the new "Poverty"–the trendy nuisance sure to register at the ballot box. There was no stomach and, it was supposed back then, no cause, to wage a real war. When the public is roused, though, high officials must always be seen as *doing something!* So, urgently flipping to page one of the High Official Playbook, they declared "war" and put the lawyers in charge. In terms of actual national commitment, such wars translate into a somewhat higher priority than the dogged pursuit of tax cheats and corporate fraudsters. To be sure, jihad differs from Wars on Drugs, Poverty, Disease, Incivility, Intolerance, Greenhouse Gases, or whatever the next Flavor of the Month may be. Jihad, after all, actually does involve warfare: real bombs, real victims, and real death. But the distinction is lost when the side that declares only rhetorical war is exclusively on the receiving end of the blows and reacts by installing its lawyers at the helm.

As a class, baby-boom attorneys know nothing of war. Prosecutors included. The vast majority (I am no exception) has never donned the uniform. In our formative years, unparalleled American might provided the luxury of paying scant mind to matters martial. Except, that is, in those airy precincts of academe that churn out our swelling nomiocracy—there, the rich variety of scholarly nuance runs from barely concealed contempt to outright revulsion.

Yet lawyers, and most of all trial lawyers, are peerlessly grandiose when it comes to slaying such dragons as there are. The witness who must be impeached–*destroyed!*–so that the breach of some humdrum supply contract can be proved–*and victory won!*–becomes the megalo-mind's personal Iwo Jima. Or so he thinks as he imagines the liability.

It was only natural, then, that we should be standing in what, without a trace of embarrassment, was called a "war room." The designation is crisis-headquarters cachet for an otherwise nondescript file-strewn government office, nestled in an impractical, seventies-style government office building. A "war room" is the portentous Central Command for game-planning litigation in the criminal justice system. And this particular war room was thus cachet within cachet. Not only was it dedicated to a litigation like no other; the building it was inside breathed a sense of purpose belying its prosaic appearance.

One Saint Andrews Plaza is the inevitable mismatch of bulging mission and shrinking space. Its anterior assault on the eyes is government's standard-issue monstrosity of incompatible "art"–in this instance, a statue of gargantuan coins. But the building has character nonetheless, for it houses the nation's prosecutorial Mecca: The United States Attorney's Office for the Southern District of New York. Steeped in the lore of its top-shelf talent pool, its fierce independence from Washington, and its trailblazing giants from Henry Stimson through J. Edward Lumbard, Robert Morgenthau, Rudy Giuliani, and, we were about to learn, Mary Jo White, the Southern District is known with affectionate hauteur to denizens past and present as the "Sovereign District." Naturally, this prompts an equal measure of envious disdain from the halls of Main Justice to the shores of . . . well, of wherever in America there are shores–or, for that matter, mountains, prairies, and, most of all, other prosecutors.

I was meeting in the war room that morning with members of New York's legendary Joint Terrorism Task Force (JTTF), an amalgam of federal agents and NYPD detectives which, under the FBI's leadership, investigates terrorist activity. Feds and cops notoriously do not work and play well together. The JTTF's legend thus lay in its *esprit de corps*, which is refreshingly genuine. It sprang to life in 1980, in reaction to the wave of domestic terrorism propelled by the Weather Underground–Leftist "revolutionaries" who teamed with the like-minded Black Liberation Army to carry out the infamous 1981 Brinks Robbery, mowing down a security guard and a Nyack police officer. Matters of life and death–terrorists waging war against America by killing its peace officers–have a way of pushing people past the petty jealousies inbred by their competing institutions.

Rule One: Avoid Accountable Failure

My presence and purpose among the JTTF made our war room confab unusual. Countering international terrorism is principally a federal responsibility, but prior to 1993 it had not been deemed a law enforcement mission. To the contrary, national security investigations have historically been handled strictly as intelligence matters. Information was amassed and analyzed primarily to inform policy makers in the executive branch, who would then attempt to stanch foreign threats via diplomatic channels, intelligence operations, or, if dire enough, military measures.

Criminal prosecutions were rare. In fact, before the World Trade Center bombing, there was so little international terrorist activity in the United States–at least as met the eye–that most federal prosecutors, despite daily contact with the FBI, could be excused for not knowing about the Bureau's double-life. In addition to being America's leading law enforcement agency, the FBI is the nation's domestic intelligence service–sort of a CIA for internal security, though a much more rigorously regulated one, since its activities, unlike the CIA's, target people inside the United States.

The FBI agents assigned to the JTTF as part of this internal security apparatus were based in the New York Field Office's Foreign Counterintelligence Division (FCI). Though terrorism had suddenly become the nation's top priority, it had been but a small part of the FCI's portfolio. Countering intelligence was, instead, mostly about countering espionage: monitoring the spying and other unwelcome activities of traditional foreign powers. New York, an international city called home by both the UN and the diplomatic missions of over 180 member nations, was an obvious hotbed.

Given their primary mission, it was unsurprising that FCI agents virtually never dealt with government attorneys. And it showed. For agents schooled to regard their very thoughts, never mind their reports, as "top secret" information, it had to be unnerving suddenly to be saddled with prosecutors–attorneys depicted by even the criminal investigators who liked them as defense lawyers in training, entirely too ready, under the rubric of "due process," to reveal sensitive information to the bad guys. For my part, I came to think the *Foreign* in "Foreign Counterintelligence" must have referred not to the nature of the threat but to elementary procedures for safeguarding evidence and handling witnesses. Though rooted more in common sense than due process, these procedures seemed alien to much of this crew, despite being so ingrained in their Criminal Division counterparts as to be part of the drinking water.

Many young agents were assigned to FCI early in their careers and, we found out, had never produced discovery in a criminal case. Others, grizzled FCI veterans, had been removed from criminal investigations so long they were startled by the burden due process had become–just as I would be startled by the high costs of their non-acquaintance with basic protocols. In sum, things were not off to a flying start. International terrorism had become a law enforcement concern by virtue of events, not planning. For what was now the nation's most important crime, our agents–those with crucial historical knowledge of the subject matter–were lacking in rudimentary know-how. We were learning, moreover, that our pre-Terror Era laws failed to contemplate the possibility of religiously motivated mass-murder plots.

These, however, were not raising my anxiety level at the moment. Nor was 1993's unusually oppressive summer heat. Instead, the temperature was rising because I found myself in a depressingly familiar spot: The infernal space between the sociopaths besieging our society and the FBI's oddly arrogant diffidence.

Four months earlier, during the late morning of Friday, February 26, 1993, Islamic militants had driven a Ryder van containing a 1400-pound urea nitrate bomb into the underground parking garage of the World Trade Center. At a few minutes after noon, the explosive detonated. The hyperintensive shockwave bored a six-story canyon into the bowels of the complex. Seven people were killed (one of the six officially listed murder victims having been well along in her pregnancy), over a thousand were injured, and the structural damage–from a device that had cost only a few thousand dollars to build–would cost nearly a billion dollars to repair.

The bombing had not been a one-off. The jihadists were laboring toward more spectacular exploits. As Americans struggled to come to terms with what the audacious Twin Towers attack implied about their safety, members of the same cabal, far from resting on their laurels, conducted surveillance on their next targets: the United Nations complex along the East River; the Lincoln and Holland Tunnels through which, each day, hundreds of thousands of commuters cross the Hudson River between New Jersey and the West Side; and the Jacob K. Javits Federal Building, home to the FBI's New York headquarters. For these, Islamic radicals planned simultaneous bombings.

That plan had been thwarted. It stands as the only one of the many jihadist conspiracies in the pre-9/11 years to be foiled by anything other than dumb luck. Why? Because of human intelligence. The government had been fortunate enough to have the help of a confidential informant, an enigmatic former Egyptian army officer named Emad Salem. He had infiltrated the organization, enabling the JTTF to catch the terrorists *in flagrante delicto*: on videotape, mixing bomb components in a dank Queens safehouse. This was the investigative coup that brought us to the war room on that steamy July morning, drawing up subpoenas, poring over transcripts of startling recorded conversations, and envisioning an indictment that would tie it all together.

That, though, was the problem: There was a lot more to tie together than the atrocities–real and contemplated–that had Americans reeling in the early months of 1993.

The FBI and the JTTF, it turned out, had been well aware of the jihad organization for a half-decade, long before the 1993. The aspiring holy warriors had been active in the United States since at least 1988, preparing and training for a global jihad, including domestic strikes against American economic, political, and military targets. They were led by a firebrand cleric named Omar Abdel Rahman, better known as "the Blind Sheikh," who'd memorized the Quran after falling sightless at age four, going on to renown as a scholar of Islam and the international *"emir* of jihad." In 1990, Abdel Rahman was issued a visa despite appearing on the State Department's terrorist watch list. He relocated to Brooklyn and, later, to Jersey City, bringing his holy war directly into the heart of its ultimate target.

Ironically, this should have been a boon. As long as he was inside the United States, the government had a chance to monitor this master terrorist in a way it could not in militant haunts like Cairo, Khartoum, and Peshawar. On our own turf, Abdel Rahman and his acolytes could be spied on. The government could identify their associates, map their network, and thwart their violent intentions. And that, indeed, is what happened.

Salem's infiltration of Abdel Rahman's organization had not begun with the stunning events of 1993. It had started much earlier, in 1991. In fact, Salem's penetration had been so thoroughly successful that he'd had intimate access to Abdel Rahman himself, almost from the start. He had, furthermore, been taken into the confidence of the Blind Sheik's circle—radicals who were talking about, and training for, bombings and political assassinations.

It is not enough to say the federal government should have seen the World Trade Center attack coming. We *did* see it coming—if not the target then, at the very least, the strong potential for a bombing. We had, moreover, been in a decent position to stop it. But we failed. And we failed precisely because the tools and assumptions of law enforcement are not suitable for religiously motivated war.

Law enforcement is most comfortable, and most effective, solving completed crimes. When it comes to preventing future crimes, especially mass-slaughter attacks that are better understood as acts of war, the cynosure of law enforcement culture is not success. It is the avoidance of accountable failure. And now that the time was past due for decisive action, that culture was front and center.

Our North Star

To make the case that cried out to be made, to ensure that we were neutralizing the ringleaders, not just the pawns, we had to abandon any pretense that time had begun a few minutes after noon on February 26, 1993. We would have to go back. We would have to lay bare the history, the radicals' menacing ideological bond, and the years of methodical planning that had culminated in their snaking a bomb-laden rental van into an awesome symbol of American economic might. Necessarily, that would mean also laying bare the gory details of government awareness, timidity and incompetence in the face of a gathering threat.

Though one might imagine otherwise, the inevitable caricature of America as Frankenstein, besieged by a mujahid monster of government's own creation, was not much of a concern for us. Sure, we'd have to endure defense arguments and media critiques about how our nation had underwritten the jihad in Afghanistan. But there seemed to be a sensible answer to that complaint: The Afghan mujahideen had been the lesser evil bolstered for the greater good of consigning the execrable Soviet Union to history's ash heap. And, besides, we were domestic law enforcement–Afghanistan was the CIA's problem, right?

But how could we possibly explain that the FBI had spent months nestling a confidential informant into the inner sanctum of radical Islam, that he'd reported discussions underway to carry out bombings and other attacks . . . and that the Bureau had terminated him, only months before the World Trade Center attack, out of sheer stubbornness and without any Plan B? What would we tell Americans whose world had been rocked by a brazen but perhaps preventable strike?

"Imagine the liability!"

That was it. I first heard the rationale in the war room that morning, offered by Carson Dunbar, the Assistant Special Agent in Charge of the New York Bureau's FCI. It was not the last time, nor was Carson the last official who'd frame the party line for me. But his was the first and most bracingly unadorned articulation of the prevalent mindset. And it is the one that still reverberates today, every time we elevate the soaring majesty of law over the nitty-gritty of safeguarding Americans–while telling ourselves, in all earnestness, that this is somehow the path to winning.

"Imagine the liability": Just think of what would have happened if we'd left Salem in place and–*Bureau ethos-alert: high*–the bombing had happened anyway. The FBI wasn't thinking: Just think what would have happened if we'd left Salem in place and, maybe, just maybe, stopped it. There was no sense that we could have saved lives, demoralized rather than energized our enemies, and prevented homicidal maniacs like Ramzi Yousef, the bomb-builder, from fleeing the country to kill again . . . as he would soon do.

The FBI's default position was that an unruly informant would not have empowered government but left it vulnerable. Agents would have been involved enough to be aware of events but powerless to control them. They'd have been blamed. There would be nothing like the victory lap the Bureau had enjoyed in the week after the bombing. A week of well-executed, well-choreographed, law enforcement bread-and-butter. A week during which the FBI was seen, with justification, as performing brilliantly: Solving a sudden, shocking crime with lightning speed through its nonpareil forensic expertise; apprehending the culprits (only some of them, as it later emerged) by following leads from a vehicle identification number engraved in a shard, unearthed from the hellish wreckage and expertly traced to the Ryder van.

How brilliant, though, could that have been, the public naturally would ask, if the FBI had actually known about these very terrorists for years?

The most infuriating thing about Carson's observation was this: He was right. He was reflecting not merely FBI culture but the broader law enforcement approach to international terrorism. Unwittingly, he was speaking to our exercise in national self-immolation—now fifteen years running and still going strong—which regards alien security threats as if they were legal issues to be spotted and adjudicated rather than enemies to be smoked out and defeated before they can kill.

Clearly, the FBI had made galactic gaffes in handling Salem. But the fear of failure had not been the Bureau's alone. Not by a long shot. Before the messy divorce with its informant, the FBI had contemplated keeping Salem in place. In 1992, when the informant was recruited to build bombs for the jihadists, the Bureau had consulted extensively with the U.S. attorney's office. And as reliably happens when a national security challenge is treated as if it were a mere legal problem, the result was absurd: A set of protocols was proposed, designed to shield the government from responsibility for a bombing rather than empower it to prevent a bombing and to amass intelligence about the plotters—counseling, for example, that the informant could talk about explosives, but should avoid handling or, most certainly, assembling them.

Perhaps somewhere there was a law school exam in which such parsing made sense. Down here on Planet Earth, it was insanity. By 1992, the terrorists were already talking about bombs. They didn't need Salem—whose cover was highly-trained Egyptian explosives expert—for more talk. What they needed him for was hands-on bomb construction. How long the lawyers figured Salem would have remained welcome in jihadist circles the first time he declined to touch components he'd been specifically recruited to assemble was never very clearly explained to me when I was assigned to take over the investigation the following year.

But if, in the tragic blunder of ejecting Salem from the investigation, the FBI and JTTF were convinced that the Justice Department's advice did not hold out much hope of success—if the FBI had taken away the lesson that it was more important to imagine the liability than take the risks necessary to protect a nation from determined savages—one could hardly blame them.

Law is our North Star. The lawsuit has replaced baseball as the national pastime—such that court proceedings routinely edge out last night's scores for the coveted space above the sports-page fold. When Americans are not suing each other, they are reading Scott Turow, watching courtroom dramas, or listening as jurisprudential talking-heads flood the airwaves, expounding on matters great and small. Need a 9/11 Commission to study intelligence "failure"? Why fill the panel with intelligence professionals, historians, economists, military analysts, or experts from other related disciplines when passels of lawyer/politicians are available? Need an Iraq Study Group to explore a way forward amid the strife of war and insurgency? Surely Sandra Day O'Connor, a former Supreme Court Justice with no military, intelligence, or foreign policy experience would be a valuable contributor—after all, she's a very fine lawyer.

The Law is our noble, all-purpose abstraction. Reason, free from passion, said Aristotle. Who could argue with that? To doubt the fitness of law to resolve all our problems, including the most intractable, is to invite ostracism from polite society. Yet, doubt it we must. The law's majesty lies in the consent of the governed to abide by it, and the capacity of the governed to compel adherence to it. Outside their body politic, in the international arena, it is a fantasy. In the hands of barbarians, it is an offensive weapon.

In the war against radical Islam, the great calling of our generation, what was true when the enemy declared war fifteen years ago remains true today. If we are too obsessed with law, and liability, we are shrinking from our highest duty: to protect lives.

▣ Chapter 2

Battalions and Illusions

IN EARLY MARCH 1993, while searching the offices of a Morristown, New Jersey, scientific research company called Allied Signal, JTTF agents seized the hard drive of a computer assigned to a man named Nidal Ayyad. A week earlier, Ayyad and his confederates had bombed the World Trade Center.

Rutgers-educated with a chemical engineering degree, the ostensibly Americanized Ayyad was widely regarded as an unlikely terrorist.[1] JTTF agents knew better. In 1993, they were not so much discovering as *rediscovering* the Kuwaiti-born Palestinian. They'd first encountered him four years earlier among a fanatical group of young Muslim men engaged in paramilitary training at a remote shooting range in Calverton, Long Island.

The group was a budding jihadist militia—a "battalion of Islam" as their inspirational leader, Sheikh Omar Abdel Rahman, liked to put it. The Blind Sheikh taught that the happenstance of being vastly out-numbered and under-armed was no justification for refraining from the duty of jihad. "The individual work and the jihad done by the individuals whether separately or in groups, is work Islam has approved and legitimized," he explained. Fighting could not be reduced to a clash of two armies, "[b]ecause, if we said, 'Let us wait til the establishment of an Islamic army,' then we have eliminated jihad, then jihad does not exist." The solemn duty to render Islam triumphant would go unfulfilled. After all, he explained, the infidel rulers who needed toppling were "agents for" and "employees of America." "If it is an army which should do the jihad," he reasoned, "then there will never be jihad."

No, the battles would have to be carried out by small "battalions"—

embedded jihadist cells which understood that "power is in the guerrilla warfare. There is power in city battles." Shiite Hezbollah had already proved it in 1983 by killing 241 United States marines who were on a peace-keeping mission in Beirut. Thus, Abdel Rahman brayed to a throng of supporters at a 1990 rally in Denmark, "If Muslim battalions were to do five or six operations to the Americans in surprise attacks like the one that was done against them in Lebanon, the Americans would have exited [the Persian Gulf] and gathered their armies and gone back . . . to their country."

The Blind Sheikh's sentiments were far from unknown to the JTTF. And the men being surveilled in Calverton in 1989 were just the type of battalion Abdel Rahman had in mind. They were already planning terrorist operations against the United States. Like Ayyad, several of the men who made the weekend training trips–men like Mohammed Salameh, Mahmud Abouhalima, and Sayyid Nosair–would carry out radical Islam's declaration of war against the United States by striking the Twin Towers in 1993. And in so doing, they would take pains to foreshadow the cataclysmic attack to come on September 11, 2001.

That adumbral warning was right there on the hard-drive agents grabbed at Allied Signal. It was framed in a claim-of-responsibility letter which, unlike the first one mailed by the bombers to the *New York Times*, had been left unsent, interrupted by Ayyad's arrest:

> We are, the Liberation Army fifth battalion, again.
>
> Unfortunately, our calculations were not very accurate this time.
>
> However, we promise you that next time it will be very precise and World Trade Center will continue to be one our [sic] targets unless our [*space*] demands have been met.

Ayyad's monstrously rueful damage assessment was spot on: Belying the apocalyptic scene at Ground Zero, the battalion had failed. An absolute miracle had occurred, one that has been overlooked ever since. Reminiscent of the dog that didn't bark, the mass-murder that didn't happen proved more consequential than any other terror-related development in the tumultuous 1990s.

The Miracle

It had been the intention of the World Trade Center bombers to annihilate tens of thousands of Americans, in addition to rendering the world's most significant financial district uninhabitable. Detonation was consciously timed for maximum carnage: high noon on a Friday, when as many as 120,000 business professionals, laborers, diners, tourists, and area residents typically swarmed the Twin Towers and their immediate Wall Street environs. More diabolically, not content with their sophisticated, powerfully combustible urea-nitrate mixture, the jihadists laced the compound with deadly sodium cyanide and attempted to boost the explosion with hydrogen tanks. The aim was a horror virtually unimaginable back then (though it is, today, an omnipresent fear): wide dispersal of a lethal, aerated chemical, killing the thousands too distant to be obliterated by the sheer force of the blast.

The battalion, however, miscalculated. They'd hoped to place the bomb close enough to primary support structures that one tower, in its decimation, might topple into the second. The van, though, had been parked many yards away from the ideal location. Yes, the aftermath resembled the ninth ring of hell, but the devastation was orders of magnitude less than it could have been. Added to this good fortune, the hydrogen tanks had been destroyed upon detonation, adding nothing but shards to the impact. And another break: the cyanide failed to vaporize—simply burning away like the rest of the bomb components.

Thus the miracle: Only seven lives were lost in the attack. No one then, or since, has had a good explanation for why. Hundreds of people were injured, mainly due to smoke inhalation during their frantic flight down scores of narrow staircases—harrowing, but a coup compared to being gassed, as the jihadists planned. It makes no sense, however, that the death toll was not geometrically higher given the time of day, the lethal combination of bursting pipes and shredded power lines, as well as wintry weather that shuttered indoors many who would otherwise have been out for lunch or a leisurely stroll. All loss of life to terror is an outrage, but with tens of thousands of people in and around the complex at zero-hour, that there were only seven deaths surely qualifies as a suspension of nature's laws.

Every silver lining, though, has its dark cloud.

The miracle kept America's guard down. As shocking as the World Trade Center bombing was to the national psyche, the finite casualties and relatively modest damage (estimated at less than a billion dollars, comparative chump change) proved crucial to our perception of, and response to, the radical Islam. Ayyad's letter conjured visions of a next time, but what consumes human beings is *this time*. The strike haughtily announced the global jihad with a dagger aimed at the Western economy's beating heart. Fright aside, though, the dagger was a pin-prick.

The enemy's ambitious reach had far outstripped its grasp. Seven deaths just is not Armageddon. Absent much more information about the murderers, it was easy to see such a bombing as a violent crime. Undoubtedly among the most heinous in history, yet, in cold numbers, less deadly than many a street-gang case or a hot weekend in one of America's urban flash-points. Declaration of war or not, without wartime casualty levels there would be no hue and cry for a wartime response or a new type of enforcement paradigm. Not then. From the get-go, the attack was regarded as a crime, investigated as a crime, and prosecuted as a crime.

Had the carnage been of 9/11 dimensions, there would unquestionably have been a searching inquiry into who had attacked the United States, who had abetted the attack, and how the nation should respond. Instead, the wheels of rote reaction began to spin. Law enforcement has its rhythms and protocols, including for emergencies. Back in 1993, it was really the only sector, public or private, that regularly trained for and responded to critical domestic incidents. Notwithstanding the military's considerable presence here, *posse comitatus* principles complicate its capacity to plan and operate inside the U.S.–a flaw made painfully patent after the initial 9/11 strikes, when military and aviation authorities had to improvise a response because their training assumed any aerial attack against the continental U.S. would come from overseas (resulting in scrambled fighter aircraft under confusing rules of engagement mangling response routes).[2]

Catharsis on Stage

The modest death toll helped bring another foible of human nature into play.

Unlike 9/11, the 1993 World Trade Center bombing was not a suicide attack. The terrorists hoped to live to fight another day. They did, but some of them of course, were captured. When the public is roused, what it most wants is catharsis. Its sense of justice demands that the guilty be identified, seen openly, and called to account. The legal system is our default center-stage for such dramas.

By contrast, the 9/11 hijackers self-immolated. That, however, did not mean Americans would be denied their catharsis. The focus simply shifted from the culpable parties who had committed the atrocity to the politically useful public officials who "allowed" it to happen, and who were ceremonially flayed by sundry blue-ribbon investigations. That these officials were exponentially less culpable mattered little in our public drama. With the jihadists off to Allah's promised orgiastic paradise, someone had to take the heat.

Admittedly, our operating assumptions about radical Islam's intentions and capabilities called for less wariness before the 1993 World Trade Center bombing than after. The performance of law enforcement and the intelligence community, however, was at least as abysmal, if not worse, in the run-up to that attack than in the years just prior to 9/11. Why is the earlier event remembered as a government triumph but the latter as a failure of such monumental proportions that a wholesale restructuring of the intelligence community was warranted? Very simply, because the 1993 bombing, unlike 9/11, featured captured defendants. Core participants were available to satisfy our craving for a public accounting.

This fact-of-life had a variety of negative ramifications. First, with minimal fatalities and a bullet-dodging perception that things could have been much worse, the public was content to let events unfold and information trickle out through the long and winding road of court proceedings. The quick arrests of five suspects a week after the bombing provided both a comforting image of law enforcement efficiency and some worthy objects for the public's wrath. The arrests of another fourteen terrorists just four months later, under circumstances where a frightful plot was snuffed out before it could become a catastrophe, underscored the sense that the threat was well-contained—a perception bolstered by the subsequent arrest of the Blind Sheikh, suggesting that the blight's catalyst had been neutralized. Unaware that there had been abundant reason for government to foresee radical Islam's bursting on the American scene, satisfied that the problem was now under control, the public—and a media dependably less curious with a Democratic administration in the White House—did not rise up in that shopworn mantra of scandal: *what did you know and when did you know it?*

Second, law enforcement is a very effective propaganda tool in the hands of policy makers who don't see the need, or who lack the will, to adopt more controversial, preemptive approaches to national security challenges. The criminal justice process presents limitless opportunities to choreograph the illusion of progress.

A successful non-suicide terrorist attack will typically feature an immediate post-event press conference to assure the public that an alphabet soup of enforcement bureaucracies is on red-alert, scouring the earth for clues. Next, typically soon afterwards, follows the press conference to announce that arrests have been made. Thereafter, court appearances present the accused terrorists and publicize the charges as well as some of the ghastly supporting evidence.

Within a few weeks, there will be an indictment with additional charges, attendant press releases, and, perhaps, another bells-and-whistles press conference—or even two, one by the district U.S. attorney and one by the Attorney General in Washington. Hard on that follows the arraignment, another closely scrutinized public appearance of the accused. Subsequently, a flurry of activity precedes the much-anticipated trial: motion practice, voluminous discovery, pretrial hearings, perhaps superseding indictments. All the while, defense counsel are talking to the media in an attempt to equal or outdo the Justice Department's earlier public announcements. Officially, the government tends not to speak to reporters after its initial flurry of announcements. Nonetheless, it constantly adds to the public record by court submissions, occasionally comments on that public record, and its agencies are well-known to leak investigative information and assessments (of wildly varying reliability) that are not part of the public record.

Then, at last, comes the trial, or, better, the "mega-trial." These are lengthy affairs, generally five months or more, and covered wall-to-wall. The end will feature days of tense jury deliberations and, finally, convictions prompting a blusterous wave of publicity, including celebratory press conferences. The denouement, about three months later, is imposition of sentence, attended by another spike of media intensity.

Start adding all that up, and four defendants with the seemingly interchangeable Arabic names that still ping oddly on Western ears, start to look like forty, or more. But there weren't forty. In fact, in the eight years between the World Trade Center's bombing and its destruction, the high-profile court cases that constituted the Clinton administration's counterterrorism strategy resulted in the convictions of exactly twenty-nine terrorists.[3] *Twenty-nine.* For a frame of reference, consider that since military hostilities began after 9/11, the United States forces have often killed and captured *in a single day of combat* more jihadists than were prosecuted throughout the 1990s.

Intelligence and Crime

A third consequence of treating the World Trade Center bombing solely as a crime rather than an act of war was the tunnel-vision self-imposed on our intelligence by reliance on the criminal process. Law enforcement has its time-honored methods, and they are geared to courtroom success. Adherence to them is why conviction rates soar, with well over 90 percent of those charged ultimately convicted of some offense. The rudiment of all investigative inquiry is, naturally, the crime. Clinically, it is a statutory offense comprised of certain "essential elements"–the component facts that must be established beyond a reasonable doubt to secure conviction.

Typically, some of these facts, though the *sine qua non* of conviction and thus requiring sharp investigative attention, have little or nothing to do with the big picture being probed. It is difficult, for example, to think of anything more elemental to Islamic terrorism than the radical Muslim ideology that fuels it. If intelligent people in anything but dire economic straits are inspired to sacrifice their lives as necessary to kill in further-ance of a doctrine–and many jihadists are people of means and educational accomplishment–one might think that doctrine rather important. Yet, from a purely legal standpoint–that is, using the prism through which we choose to analyze such things–it is much more critical to the case against an indicted bomber that his exertions have somehow affected interstate commerce than that he was motivated by a Salafist construction of Islam. Or that he may have been abetted by a rogue nation.

An effect on commerce is an essential element of a federal bombing prosecution. On the contrary, there is no requirement that either a defen-dant's motivation be proved or every conspirator identified. To be sure, motivation and accomplices do tend to play a role in the proof. Trials, after all, are conducted before juries. Unlike legal elites, jurors tend to be down-to-earth folk possessed of common sense, who want to be satisfied, before finding someone guilty of a serious crime, that they understand why and with whom the accused acted. Those facts and circumstances, nevertheless, are collateral to what makes the prosecutor's case legally "sufficient."

Imagine if, on a clean slate, you were tasked to design a security system for banks. Undoubtedly, you would consult experts, study diagrams, cata-logue the bank's vulnerabilities, marshal its protective assets, assess trends in security technology, and plan accordingly. You would not limit your study to the quirky details of a single bank robbery, or even a string of such rob-beries, no matter how infamous. You would not conclude that by address-ing whatever flaws had led to the robbery, you had perforce addressed the bank's overall security challenges.

Yet, that is precisely what we did with Islamic terrorism after the World

Trade Center bombing. The investigative energy was substantially channeled into designing cases that stood the best chance of convicting the operatives who were apprehended. Transcendent national security questions were subordinated to transient legal ones. What buildings were in interstate commerce? Which gun had an obliterated serial number? Were identification documents phony because they'd been stolen or forged? Were enough acts undertaken in a planned bombing to establish a legal "attempt," or were those acts "mere preparation" absent the "substantial step" necessary for conviction? These were the types of issues that got primo scrutiny–as they had to if prosecutions were going to be successful. Necessarily, though, that means resources–including some of the best, most knowledgeable minds, during an era when few such minds were engaged in the subject of radical Islam–were diverted from such issues as: How extensive was the terror network? What were its aims? What about rogue-state facilitation? And what do we do about the fact that, as a practical matter, most of an international terror network's hierarchy outside the United States simply cannot be reached by law enforcement?

The law can answer some of those questions, but not all of them. They are not the law's principal concern. In a terrorism trial, it is more important to demonstrate that a low-level jihadist has been adequately represented by the court-appointed lawyer with whom he has declined to cooperate than to prove who in Afghanistan might have covertly financed the purchase of the bomb components he was mixing. The jihadist, after all, is here. If you're going to try him in the criminal justice system, the Constitution's injunctions must be honored. It is the law. But it is not national security.

The criminal justice system's prestige, its algorithms, and its factitious parsing of even the irrelevant paint a tableau of law enforcement energy, attention, and competence. Its adversarial jousting, weighty burdens of proof and solemn, painstaking verdicts generate the final record, the definitive version of what happened and what is true. The process burnishes resulting convictions with not only a deserved aura of accomplishment but the veneer of security, the confirmation that public safety has truly been advanced.

Sometimes, it's an illusion. Sometimes there is a bigger picture that is obscured. The legal system's job is not to produce the definitive version of history. It is to produce a judgment about the provenance of facts the government chooses to put in dispute by leveling accusations. In crafting an indictment, moreover, the Justice Department—acutely aware of the warts in its investigation and the high burden of proof for serious crimes—mines the underlying scenario for the charges on which it is most likely to prevail. Those charges may not be reflective of the scenario's true significance. The reality of Al Capone, meta-racketeer, is not exactly captured by the conviction of Al Capone, tax cheat.

The 1993 World Trade Center bombing was not unpredictable. It shocked the public, but for law enforcement it was a case of evil people doing exactly what they'd been saying they were going to do: terrorize the American people by bombing attacks. Not taking them seriously, we averted our eyes. And when bomber Nidal Ayyad wrote, "we promise you that next time it will be very precise and World Trade Center will continue to be one [of] our targets," we averted them yet again.

⧗ Chapter 3

"We Are Terrorists!"

WASN'T THE "JIHAD" HE WAS CLAMORING FOR just a spiritual camouflage for *terrorism*? The Blind Sheikh didn't mince words:

> What kind of name is this? Why are we afraid of it? Why do we
> fear the word *terrorist*? If the terrorist is the person who defends
> his right, so we are terrorists. And if the terrorist is the one who
> struggles for the sake of God, then we are terrorists. We . . . have
> been ordered with terrorism because we must prepare what power
> we can to terrorize the enemy of Allah and your enemy. The Qur'an
> [said] "to strike terror." Therefore, we don't fear to be described
> with "terrorism." . . . They may say, "He is a terrorist, he uses vio-
> lence, he uses force." Let them say that. We are ordered to prepare
> whatever we can of power to terrorize the enemies of Islam.

Omar Abdel Rahman was indeed proud to be a terrorist. He was relentless in the cause of annealing his acolytes to this purpose. It was a cause
he traced to a centuries-old summons to revive the "true Islam" of the
founders. It was also the cause of a lifetime, ever since he'd lost his sight to
juvenile diabetes in 1942, at the age of four. Reared in the tiny Nile Delta
town of al-Gamalia, the sickly boy memorized the Qur'an and became a
stellar academic, earning renown as a scholar graduated from Cairo's ven-
erable al-Azhar University, where he earned a doctorate, with distinction,
in Qur'anic studies.

Trailing only Morocco's Al-Karaouine among the world's oldest institutions of higher learning, al-Azhar is the seat of the Sunni tradition vastly
predominant among the world's 1.4 billion Muslims. In terms of influence,

al-Azhar's Grand Imam is about as close a cognate as Islam has to the Roman Catholic papacy. The analogy, though, is far from perfect. Islam is bereft of a regimented clerical hierarchy, councils, or synods to provide standards of orthodoxy.[1] It relies, instead, on a venerated consensus of its greatest *mujtahids*, the masters of its four established schools of thought. That consensus was set in stone even before al-Azhar's doors first opened in the middle of the tenth century. Though early Islam had enjoyed a tradition of *ijtihad*, free and independent inquiry into Islamic scripture by believers seeking to discern Allah's intended meaning, those authoritative schools determined by about 900 A.D. that all essential questions had been settled with finality. From then on, no one would be deemed qualified for independent reasoning. "[A]ll future activity would have to be confined to the explanation, application, and, at the most, interpretation of the doctrine as it had been laid down once at for all."[2] The so-called "gates of *ijtihad*" were closed.

The Emir of Jihad

It was to this task of interpretation that Abdel Rahman set himself. Never reaching the high station of Grand Imam, Abdel Rahman's accomplishments did include a prestigious stint as an al-Azhar lecturer, as well as the leadership of a vicious Egyptian terror organization called *Gama'at al Islamia* (or the Islamic Group), and great influence over the so-called "Arab-Afghans," who joined the mujahideen resistance against the Soviet invasion of Afghanistan. This led him to be dubbed the "pope of jihad" by some of the few Western investigators who followed such things in the early 1990s. We would learn, though, that *"emir* of jihad," employing the Arab term for "prince" or "commander," was the more apt and widely used honorific among the faithful.

The Blind Sheikh was undeniably a *mufti*, a specialist in Islamic law authorized to opine on points of doctrine and to issue *fatwas* or binding legal opinions.[3] On the other hand, his status as an *emir*, a position of high operational authority, evoked occasional dissent, including from a feisty young Ayman al-Zawahiri—his ally and sometime rival who would rise years later to become al Qaeda's second-in-command—when the two, detained together in an Egyptian prison after the 1981 murder of President Anwar al-Sadat, squabbled about whether the sightless are qualified for command under sharia law.[4] Such dissent, however, was rare and muted, owing to the awe Abdel Rahman's religious erudition inspired and the practical impossibility of cleaving the spiritual from the operational in radical ideology.

Perhaps the most profound influence on Abdel Rahman's scholarship, and hence the intellectual font of radical Islam's modern iteration, was the fourteenth-century Sunni docent, Taqi al-Din Ahmad Ibn Taymiyyah. Born in what is now Turkey in 1268, Ibn Taymiyyah came of age in a tumultuous time. Just a decade earlier, invading Mongols had routed the empire of the Abbasid Caliphate, laying Baghdad to waste and depriving it ever after of its honored place as the center of the Islamic universe.[5] The upheaval prompted an era of soul-searching for the vanquished, not least Ibn Taymiyyah's clan. His father, a moderately well-known scholar and preacher of the Hanbali School, Sunni Islam's most fundamentalist, relocated the family to Damascus. There, Ibn Taymiyyah became an esteemed but controversial scholar in his own right, championing a literal interpretation of scripture and the notion that the original Islamic communities forged during the Prophet Mohammed's Medinan period were the ideal to which all humanity must aspire.[6]

Muslim reverence for the prophet is, of course, a given. The Qur'an endorses Mohammed as "an excellent model of conduct" (33:21) who exhibited an "exalted standard of character" (68:4); obedience to him is repeatedly adjured—made, in fact, just as essential as obedience to Allah Himself (4:80).[7] Ibn Taymiyyah's focus on the Medinan period, though, was of seismic significance. This was the phase of Islamic development when the Muslims were forced to flee from Mecca by powerful tribes, including the prophet's native Quraysh, which refused to accept the new religion. This flight, the *Hijra*, is Islam's groundbreaking moment, the event by which time is marked. As the scholar Robert Spencer observes, "[t]he beginning of Islam as a political and social entity is the beginning of [the religion's] calendar."[8]

In the preceding thirteen-year Meccan period, when Mohammed first endeavored to call converts to Islam, he had been highly solicitous of the existing tribes and their traditions—to the point of incorporating many of their beliefs and rituals into the rites of nascent Islam, notwithstanding the doctrine's airs about being the unmediated message of Allah Himself.[9] It should come as no surprise, then, that the more tolerant verses of the Qur'an trace to this early Meccan period, such as the injunction that there shall be "no compulsion in religion" (2:256)—the unparalleled favorite of self-styled "moderates" and Western elites who mulishly portray Islam as "the religion of peace" in the teeth of overwhelming counter-evidence.

In Medina, things changed drastically. It was from there that Islam was principally spread not by intellectual persuasion but by the sword. The scriptures tending toward ecumenism and tolerance were negated, superseded by divine commands that the prophet "make war on the unbelievers and the hypocrites and deal rigorously with them. Hell shall be their home: an evil fate" (9:73). This is not immediately apparent to the unschooled observer since the Qur'an is not arranged chronologically but according to the length of its suras (or chapters). It is reflective, however, of the Islamic doctrine of abrogation (*naskh*), the concept that, as He sees fit, Allah refines or repeals his prior instructions.[10] Abrogation is essential to a proper understanding of the Medinan period, and of the chasm between the Islam of Western fantasy and the one that actually exists.

The Mohammed of Medina—which is to say, the Mohammed of Ibn Taymiyyah—sought Islamic hegemony not ecumenical coexistence. Enemy tribes that had tormented him were savaged, their leaders slain and decapitated, their pleas for mercy ignored.[11] Rejection of Islam was construed as attack upon Islam, to be met with brutal retribution, meted out more than once by the Prophet himself. For example, as jihad historian Andrew Bostom relates,

> According to Muhammad's sacralized biography by Ibn Ishaq, Muhammad himself sanctioned the massacre of the Qurayza, a vanquished Jewish tribe. He appointed an "arbiter" who soon rendered this concise verdict: the men were to be put to death, the women

and children sold into slavery, the spoils to be divided among the Muslims. Muhammad ratified this judgment stating that it was a decree of God pronounced from above the Seven Heavens. Thus some 600 to 900 men from the Qurayza were [led] on Muhammad's order to the Market of Medina. Trenches were dug and the men were beheaded, and their decapitated corpses buried in the trenches while Muhammad watched in attendance. Women and children were sold into slavery, a number of them being distributed as gifts among Muhammad's companions, and Muhammad chose one of the Qurayza women (Rayhana) for himself. The Qurayza's property and other possessions (including weapons) were also divided up as additional "booty" among the Muslims, to support further jihad campaigns.[12]

Further jihad campaigns, indeed. For jihad was the catalyzing imperative of Medina's triumphalist Islam.

The Good Jihad and the Real Jihad

When I was a young organized-crime prosecutor, there was a fable, bolstered in the public mind by the iconic portrayal of the Corleone family in the fabulously successful *Godfather* movies, pitting the "good" mafia against the "bad" mafia. The former was a society for the protection of the weak, formed by "men of honor" who imposed order and protection on what would otherwise be chaos and exploitation; who had their own internal moral code, much of which was quite admirable; and who were rigorously opposed to such *infamia* as narcotics trafficking. They made their living, so the fable goes, on harmless vices like gambling and prostitution, and no one got rubbed out unless he really deserved it. The bad mafia, in contrast, was a lawless syndicate without regard for tradition and codes. Against the noble traditions of *Cosa Nostra*, it killed wantonly–thugs, in it only for the money and heedless of the dystopia wrought by high-profit crimes like drug-dealing. In reality, of course, there was no divide. There was just *the mafia*. The attributes of the "good" are either a total fiction or, at best, window-dressing to rationalize pursuit of the "bad"—the bad being what it's all about, no matter that there are some within the system who have deluded themselves into believing the fable.

The same dynamic is at work with jihad. Modern Islamic adherents, sympathizers and apologists grudgingly acknowledge that jihad is a tenet of Islam—although, they imply, not all that important a tenet since it is not one of the five so-called "pillars" of the faith.[13] But while Mohammed himself made jihad—militaristic jihad—Islam's doctrinal *ne plus ultra*, declaring that no deed on earth could equal it in God's favor, today's salons are determined to portray jihadists as heretics who have perverted the "true" faith—relieving us of any need to concern ourselves over Islam, the 800-pound gorilla that is somehow always in the middle of the room when terror strikes.

Thus is a narrative assiduously advanced—a fable, pitting the good (or "greater") jihad against the bad (or "lesser") jihad. This school of thought finds a fine exemplar in Dr. Marc Sageman, a forensic psychiatrist and former CIA case officer (from the late 1980s when the Agency was underwriting the Afghan mujahideen's jihad against the Soviets). A frequent advisor for various government agencies on how to think about terrorism issues, Dr. Sageman writes:

> Like other great, long established religions, Islam is full of contentious issues, especially about some of its core concepts, such as *jihad*, which translates roughly as "striving" but denotes any form of activity, either personal or communal, undertaken by Muslims in attempting to follow the path of God. No single doctrine is universally accepted.
>
> In a world full of iniquities, the greater jihad is the individual nonviolent striving to live a good Muslim life, following God's will. It includes adhering to the five pillars of Islam: profession of faith (*shahada*); praying regularly; fasting during Ramadan; being charitable; and performing the *hajj*, the pilgrimage to Mecca. It requires lifelong diligence and constant vigilance.[14]

How admirable, indeed. The "greater" jihad is the good jihad. That other jihad—he is too nuanced to suggest it is altogether bad—is the "lesser" jihad. Only this small, subordinate species of the genus involves "the violent struggle for Islam." It's a vestige of an antiquated *Weltanschauung* that simplistically divided the world into the land of Islam (*dar al-Islam*) and the land of conflict (*dar al-Harb*), "and saw jihad as the Muslim ummah's communal obligation "to expand dar al Islam throughout the world so that all humankind could benefit from living within a just political social order."[15]

That old world, Dr. Sageman would have us believe, is no more. The purportedly lesser jihad has been "diluted," he contends, by "one school of interpretation" which introduced the concept of a "land of treaty (*dar al-Suhl*)" in which jihad was forbidden in lands which had struck agreements with Muslims. Sageman conveniently glides by the rather obvious point that the existence of "one school of interpretation" implies that there are other schools, following different interpretations—to say nothing of the facts that the Qur'an limits treaties to ten years' duration and that Mohammed reserved the right to break them whenever it was expedient to do so (since "war," as the Prophet observed, "is deceit"). Instead, he plows ahead with the suggestion that this "lesser" jihad has been further marginalized by its division into "defensive" and "offensive" strivings. Individual Muslims are required to fight only in the former, which happens only if a Muslim land has been invaded and a competent authority has issued a fatwa declaring a "state of jihad."[16]

Self-defense, of course, is a natural right, a veritable bedrock of the natural-law basis for modern international law. Who, then, could argue with "defensive" jihad? It's so, well, Western. Indeed, in Sageman's telling, it is the very echo of Emmerich de Vattel. The Swiss philosopher, both a founder of international law and a contemporary of America's founders, opined:

> Every nation, as well as every man, has, therefore, a right to prevent
> other nations from obstructing her preservation, her perfection,
> and happiness, – that is, to preserve herself from all injuries. . . . [A]
> nd this right is a perfect one, since it is given to satisfy a natural and

indispensable obligation: for, when we cannot use constraint in order
to cause our rights to be respected, their effects are very uncertain.
It is this right to preserve herself from all injury that is called the
right to security.[17]

The right to security: that, we are benignly led to believe, is really all the
"lesser" jihad is about, at least in its "defensive" mode. But what about the
"offensive" version? This, Sageman concedes, involves Muslims invading
infidel lands to impose sharia and spread the faith. So, isn't that cause for
concern? Apparently not. According to Sageman, "offensive" jihad is a *collective* obligation—only for Islamic governments, not for individual believers, to involve themselves in.[18] No individuals, no terrorists; no terrorists,
no terrorism; terrorism, therefore, has no relation to jihad. *Q.E.D.*—it's
un-Islamic.

Dr. Sageman is far from alone. In their invaluable account of al Qaeda's
rise, *The Age of Sacred Terror*, former Clinton administration National
Security Council officials Daniel Benjamin and Steven Simon more accurately acknowledge that jihad grew up as "exclusively actual, physical
warfare." They argue, however, that "the concept of jihad took on a new
meaning" in the late eighteenth and early nineteenth centuries as Islam
was beleaguered by the rise of imperial Western European powers and the
decay of Ottoman Turkey. There was, they aver, a "domestication of jihad,"
rendering it "a struggle against evil impulses within the soul of a believer."
The "greater jihad" became the "internal battle" for personal betterment
waged through "[a]cts of charity, good works in society, and education."
"Military jihad" was "denigrated" to "lesser" status.[19] Alas, I'm afraid
many hundreds of millions of Muslims did not get the memo.

Benjamin and Simon forthrightly concede that this greater/lesser
divide is a "modern-day distinction" that would have been unrecognizable
to classical Muslim scholars such as Ibn Taymiyyah.[20] It is an evolving distinction, guiding contemporary efforts to reprogram jihad into an impulse
congenial to enlightened sensibilities, such that there are now jihads to rid
societies of blights like narcotics trafficking, hate-speech, intolerance, etc.

Coming soon: New York City Mayor Michael Bloomberg's jihad against trans-fats.

Yet, for all their energetic earnestness, the new constructions are most persuasive in the rarefied towers inhabited by elites desperate to be persuaded. Down here on Planet Earth, they are futile. The Muslim world is not populated by Western intellectuals hard-wired to nuance white into black by legalistic arcana and historical massaging. In large swaths of the ummah, there is rampant illiteracy, education consists of myopic focus on the Qur'an, and intolerance (especially anti-Semitism) is so rudimentary a part of everyday life that any jihad rooted in "good works in society" would not conceivably reflect what "progressive" Westerners mean by that well-intentioned term.

Progressive, moderate Muslims would doubtless like the concept of jihad to vanish. They are in a battle for authenticity with fundamentalists, and jihad would be far easier to omit than it is to explain away. Jihad, however, won't go away. There would be no Muslim world without it. When it comes to jihad, authenticity is simplicity, and, simply stated, jihad is and has always been about military conquest. As explicated by the West's pre-eminent scholar of Islam, Princeton's Bernard Lewis:

> Conventionally translated "holy war" [*jihad*] has the literal meaning of striving, more specifically, in the Qur'anic phrase "striving in the path of God" (*fi sabil Allah*). Some Muslim theologians, particularly in more modern times, have interpreted the duty of "striving in the path of God" in a spiritual and moral sense. The overwhelming majority of early authorities, however, citing relevant passages in the Qur'an and in the tradition, discuss jihad in military terms.[21]

In fact, the erudite former Muslim of the *nom de plume* Ibn Warraq points out that even

> [t]he celebrated *Dictionary of Islam* defines *jihad* as "a religious war with those who are unbelievers in the mission of Muhammad. It

is an incumbent religious duty, established in the Quran and in the Traditions as a divine institution, enjoined specially for the purpose of advancing Islam and of repelling evil from Muslims."[22]

It is no wonder that this should be so. The Qur'an repeatedly enjoins Muslims to fight and slay non-Muslims. "O ye who believe," commands Sura 9:123, "Fight those of the disbelievers who are near you, and let them find harshness in you, and know that Allah is with those who keep their duty unto him." It is difficult to spin that as a call to spiritual self-improvement. As it is, for another example, with Sura 9:5, which instructs, "But when the forbidden months are past, then fight and slay the pagans wherever ye find them. And seize them, beleaguer them, and lie in wait for them in every stratagem (of war)," relenting only if they have accepted Islam.[23] The *hadith*, lengthy volumes recording the words and traditions of the prophet, are even more explicit, as in Mohammed's teaching that "[a] single endeavor (of fighting) in Allah's cause in the afternoon or in the forenoon is better than all the world and whatever is in it."[24]

This is the jihad of Islamic scripture. It is the jihad on which Ibn Taymiyyah, a strict literalist, insisted. The Caliphate's defeat and the suddenly dire straits of thirteenth-century believers were caused by deviation from the true Islam: the Islam of conquest, whose calling, whose *command*, was to bring about universal submission to Allah– *submission* being the literal meaning of *Islam*. For Ibn Taymiyyah, this divine mandate required both imposing the penalties of *sharia* (Islamic law) on Muslims who strayed, and

> the punishment of recalcitrant groups, such as those that can only be brought under the sway of the Imam by a decisive fight. That then is the jihad against the unbelievers (*kuffar*), the enemies of God and his Messenger. For whoever has heard the summons of the Messenger of God, Peace be upon him, and has not responded to it, must be fought, "until there is no persecution and the religion is God's entirely."[25]

"[L]awful warfare," he elaborated, "is essentially jihad." Because its purpose is to eradicate all obstacles to the obligatory spread of Islam (so that *the religion is God's entirely*), "those who stand in the way of this aim must be fought." These include non-combatants, such as women and children, found to be assisting the resistance in any way–though it remained an option to enslave women and children who, as Mohammed's afore-described persecution of the Quraysh underscores, "constitute property for Muslims."[26] Famously, Ibn Taymiyyah further inferred from this a duty to overthrow rulers who failed to govern in accordance with a fundamentalist construction of sharia–including nominally Islamic rulers like the Mongols, who, though they converted to Islam, clung to legal codes promulgated by Genghis Khan. Refuting worries that this divine injunction to jihad would trap the faithful in unpleasant or seemingly hopeless predicaments, Ibn Taymiyyah's remonstrance drew directly from Allah's own admonition: "[W]hen a clear sura is sent down, and therein fighting is mentioned, thou seest those in whose heart is sickness looking at thee as one who swoons of death; but better for them would be obedience and words honourable. Then, when the matter is resolved, if they were true to God, it would be better for them" (47: 20-21).[27]

Freedom . . . to Submit

The heirs of Ibn Taymiyya's thought–those who "swoon of death" while their enemies, as Osama bin Laden scoffs, cling desperately to life–included Muhammad ibn Abd al-Wahhab, the eighteenth century fundamentalist whose atavistic Sunni Islam, familiar to us today as "Wahhabism," became the Saudi royal family's established creed . . . and, in the twentieth century, its second-best known export.[28] Ibn Taymiyya's influence, furthermore, was hardly peculiar to Sunnis. Iran's Grand Ayatollah Ali Khomeini, trailblazer of the most significant revolutionary movement in Shiite history–and, potentially, in all Islamic lore–echoed Ibn Taymiyya in this blistering critique of those who would bowdlerize the true jihad:

Islam makes it incumbent on all [able] adult males . . . to prepare themselves for the conquest of [other] countries so that the writ of Islam is obeyed in every country of the world. [T]hose who study Islamic Holy War will understand why Islam wants to conquer the whole world. . . . Those who know nothing of Islam pretend that Islam counsels against war. [They] are witless. Islam says: Kill all the unbelievers just as they would kill you all! Does this mean the Muslims should sit back until they are devoured? Islam says: Kill them, put them to the sword and scatter [their armies]. . . . Islam says: Whatever good there is exists thanks to the sword and in the shadow of the sword. People cannot be made obedient except with the sword! The sword is the key to Paradise, which can be opened only for Holy Warriors! There are hundreds of [scriptures] urging Muslims to value war and to fight. Does all that mean Islam is a religion that prevents men from waging war? I spit upon those foolish souls who make such a claim.[29]

From across the Arabian Peninsula and the Sunni/Shia divide, the Blind Sheikh admired the Grand Ayatollah, and harbored dreams of an Egyptian replication of his Iranian coup d'état. Still, for Abdel Rahman, coming of age in a boiling cauldron of dissidence, the most striking of Ibn Taymiyya's legatees was Sayyid Qutb. The intellectual father of modern jihadism and an iconic figure in the formidable Muslim Brotherhood, Qutb was "martyred" by Nasser's Egypt in 1966, when Abdel Rahman was twenty-eight years old.

Qutb was an education scholar who studied in the United States from 1948 until 1950, and was repulsed by what he saw as America's racism, debauchery, and vulgar materialism. Presaging Khomeini, he rejected the revisionism that limns jihad as a personal struggle, a purely "defensive" obligation, or an antiquated concept confined to the time and circumstances of the early Muslims—a revisionism more resonant with Pollyannaish Western intellectuals than contemporary Muslims. Islam, he explained, was not merely intended for Arabs and, plainly, there would not be what today is known as the "Islamic world" (*Dar al Islam*) unless

Muslims had fought and conquered the pre-existing regimes. "The religion," he wrote,

> is really a universal declaration of the freedom of man from servitude to other men and from servitude to his own desires, which is also a form of human servitude; it is a declaration that sovereignty belongs to God alone and that He is the Lord of all the worlds. It means a challenge to all kinds and forms of systems which are based on the concept of the sovereignty of man; in other words, where man has usurped the Divine attribute. . . [Thus it] addresses itself to the whole of mankind, and its sphere of work is the whole earth.[30]

It is crucial to grasp this Islamic notion of *freedom*, for it is the inverse of the Western conception, a fact reckless indifference to which has led to such follies as the grand project to democratize the Islamic world. *Islam* means *submission* to God. *Freedom* in Islam must be understood in this transcendent context. It is not, as we Westerners assume, free *choice*; it is the voluntary *surrendering of oneself* to Allah, unqualifiedly accepting the laws He has established–for, as Qutb instructed, "[l]egislation is a Divine attribute," so to concede it to other men is to "accept [them] as Divine," whether or not one actually considers them so, because the Qur'an equates obedience with worship.[31] When the Islam speaks of free will, as in Western intellectuals' much loved decree that there shall not be compulsion in religion, *this* is the sense of freedom it conveys. That freedom, Qutb taught, cannot be realized without establishment of the sharia system–the only system that removes all obstacles to the comprehension and, inexorably, the acceptance of the imperative to submit to Allah.

Qutb saw that supplanting man's dominion with God's could never "be achieved only through preaching." Incumbent infidel regimes were plainly "not going to give up their power merely through preaching."[32] Expelling them was the mission of jihad, highlighting its centrality as a core Islamic obligation, the *sine qua non* of, as Ibn Taymiyya put it, making the religion God's entirely–of cementing Islam as universally supreme. The purpose of jihad is "to wipe out tyranny and to introduce freedom to mankind."[33] Whenever Islam is obstructed by "the political system of the state, the socio-economic system based on races and classes, and behind all these, the military power of the government," the religion, according to Qutb, "has no recourse but to remove them by force so that when [Islam] is addressed to peoples' hearts and minds they are free to accept or reject it with an open mind."[34] All such impediments, hindering human beings from achieving their highest calling, are deemed to be persecution, implicating the Qur'anic injunction to "Fight in the cause of Allah those who fight you . . . and slay them whenever you catch them, and turn them out from where they have turned you out, for persecution is worse than slaughter."[35]

The logic of Qutb's construction is patently circular, and frightening. Sharia is the precondition necessary to ensure perfect "freedom," but sharia cannot be established without the violent overthrow of regimes that refuse to adopt it voluntarily. And–again foreshadowing Khomeini–the "freedom" extended by Islam is not liberty of conscience, for the purportedly "complete freedom to accept or reject" the religion's tenets "does not mean [people] can make their desires their gods, or that they can choose to remain in the servitude of other human beings, making some men lords over others."[36] No, the system in which this "choice" takes place must be based "on the authority of God, deriving its laws from him alone."[37]

Thus the "free" decision to submit occurs in an atmosphere of intimidation, where the Islamic battalions have supplanted their opposition and installed the sharia system in which the "choices" of nonbelievers are: to convert "voluntarily"; to remain infidels in the consciously humiliating status of *dhimmitude*, compelled to pay a tribute, the *jizya* tax, the primary purpose of which was to sear into *dhimmis* a constant reminder of their subjugation; or to die.

While obsessed with establishing sharia societies, moreover, Islam is never content with them. Islamic history is an inevitable progression. There have been times when Muslims refrained from jihad for tactical reasons (such as when Mohammed was first attracting converts in Mecca). And there have been times when Muslims employed jihad defensively because they actually were under armed attack. Nevertheless, none of that can obscure Islam's sacred quest for hegemony–to expand *Dar al Islam*, the realm of the Muslims, throughout the world. Qutb saw history as having reached this final phase of Islam's march, with war declared against all non-Muslims, in accordance with the command of Sura 9:29: "Fight those who do not believe in Allah nor the Last Day, nor hold that forbidden which hath been forbidden by Allah and His messenger, nor acknowledge the Religion of Truth from among the People of the Book, until they pay the *jizya* with willing submission, and feel themselves subdued."[38]

Echoing Ibn Taymiyyah, Qutb's jihad targeted not only declared non-believers but also those rulers who professed to be Muslim but did not adhere to the commands of the faith–the commands divinely required for the furtherance of "freedom." In many ways, such Muslims, particularly those in authority positions, were more responsible than declared infidels for the ummah's descent into the dystopian condition of *jahiliyya*. This term, drawn from the Qur'an and Ibn Tamiyyah's theology, denoted the pre-Islamic phase of history, the dark pagan ignorance overcome by the incandescence of the Prophet's Message. "While the Unbelievers got up in their hearts heat and cant–the heat and cant of *jahiliyya*," says Sura 48:26, "Allah sent down His Tranquility to His Messenger and to the Believers, and made them stick close to the command of self-restraint."[39]

Qutb infused the concept with a connotation of oppressive, anti-Islamic corruption. The *jahiliyya* included all people, including Muslims, who failed to comport unflinchingly with sharia. There was but a single true Islam, which Allah had commanded His adherents to establish through jihad. Everyone and everything else was *jahiliyya*. By nature, they could not co-exist with Islam. Therefore, in this the final phase of Islam's history, there was a positive duty to eradicate them–not to wait for them to attack so the jihad could be spun as "defensive," for their very existence was an affront to Allah.[40]

Qutb's fundamentalist brand of Islam dovetailed comfortably with the principles of the Muslim Brotherhood (formally, the Society of the Muslim Brothers or *Ikhwān al-Muslimūn*). The Brotherhood was, and remains, a revolutionary movement begun in 1928 by Hassan al-Banna in the Egyptian town of Ismalia on the west bank of the Suez Canal. Remarkably like Qutb, whom he never actually met, al-Banna had been born in 1906 and was a Cairo-trained educator.[41] Al-Banna, however, was the far more charismatic personality, and within two decades, membership in the Brotherhood he'd established with just a handful of activists swelled into millions of members, with branches opened in several Arab countries. Its goal was to establish a transnational caliphate imposing a fundamentalist sharia system, and its now well-known principles were succinctly stated: "Allah is our objective; the Qur'an is our constitution, the Prophet is our leader; Jihad is our way; and death for the sake of Allah is the highest of our aspirations."[42] This philosophy was irresistibly attractive to someone of Qutb's bent of mind, and to an up-and-comer like Abdel Rahman. As journalist Lawrence Wright relates in his engaging history of al Qaeda, *The Looming Tower*, "Banna completely rejected the Western model of secular, democratic government, which was opposed to his notion of universal Islamic rule," expressly declaring it "the nature of Islam to dominate, not to be dominated, to impose its law on all nations, and to extend its power to the entire planet."[43]

At the close of 1948, a member of the Brotherhood murdered Egypt's prime minister, Mahmud Fahmi Nokrashi. In the aftermath, al-Banna was killed. The organization was outlawed and went underground. Qutb, meanwhile, officially joined the Brotherhood upon his return to Egypt in 1950. He was already the intellectual engine of the movement when it was relegitimated in 1952, after the Egyptian monarchy was deposed in a military coup by the so-called "Free Officers," led by Gamal Abdel Nasser and other veterans of "the *Nakba*"–or "the Catastrophe," as the 1948 war establishing Israel's existence is known in Arab circles.

Free Officers, including such Nasser intimates as Anwar al-Sadat, had made a point of cultivating the Islamic radicals. Some surface commonalities between their muscular Arab nationalism and the Brotherhood's hegemonic vision were permitted, for a time, to paper over the elemental incompatibility between Nasserite secularism and Qutb's jihadism. But long it could not last. The increasingly frayed *modus vivendi* was decisively rent in October 1954 when the Brotherhood, having carped at various regime policies (especially the Egyptian-Anglo accord on evacuation of the Suez Canal), attempted to assassinate Nasser in Alexandria very shortly after he had formally taken control of the government.[44] In a scenario that would repeat itself throughout the ensuing decades, the secular regime reacted with an iron fist. The Brotherhood was once again banned, thousands of radicals were rounded up and tormented in Egypt's brutal prisons, and six of the main culprits were swiftly executed.

Among those imprisoned was Qutb, charged with membership in an ambitious Brotherhood conspiracy to topple the government and establish a sharia state. He was tried before a special court, presided over by Sadat and two other Nasser loyalists, and sentenced to life-imprisonment.[45] The sickly scholar served much of his time in a hospital ward, writing an influential eight-volume series of scriptural commentaries called *In the Shade of the Qur'an*. Due to the intercession of Iraq's president, Nasser directed Qutb's release in 1964, after fifteen years' incarceration. Within months, though, he was back in prison, charged with leading another vast conspiracy to overthrow the regime. This time, conviction brought the sentence of death. Qutb was hanged on August 29, 1966.

The "martyr's" demise was set in motion by the 1964 publication, soon after his parole from prison, of his jihadist philippic, *Milestones*. It brazenly called for violent revolution against governments which failed to adhere to sharia, including the elimination of nominally Muslim rulers whose betrayal of Islamic principles Qutb construed as an unforgivable affront to Allah. This summons was drawn straight from Allah's revelations to His prophet and the exegetical trailblazing of Ibn Taymiyyah. It was the torch the Blind Sheikh, so proud call himself a "terrorist," would carry forward, from Egypt . . . to America.

⧗ Chapter 4

The Blind Sheikh Emerges

HARD ON SAYYID QUTB'S EXECUTION followed the tumult of 1967: The humiliation of Egypt, as well as its Arab-Muslim allies Syria and Jordan, in the Six Day War. For Qutb devotee Omar Abdel Rahman, completing his master's degree that year at Cairo University's School of Theology, the swift decisiveness of Israel's victory–the *Nakba* reprised, only worse–was beyond painful.

Again building on Ibn Taymiyyah's thought, Qutb had reinvigorated a hermeneutical anti-Semitism. To the settled conviction that Muslims had been foiled by Jewish treachery from the beginning of their history, he added the innovation that "anyone"–Jew or non-Jew–"who leads the community away from its religion and its Quran can only be a Jewish agent." As Benjamin and Simon trenchantly observe, the Jews thus became for Qutb and his cohort "the incarnation of all that is anti-Islamic, and such is their supposed animosity that they will never relent 'because the Jews will be satisfied only with destruction of [Islam].'"[1] For his part, Abdel Rahman– more deeply grounded in Islamic scripture than Qutb–would offer a proselytism at least as rife with Jew-hatred.

Now a true *sheikh* or religious scholar, Abdel Rahman would go on from Cairo to al-Azhar for the completion of his doctoral studies. By the time that occurred, in 1971, he had already accrued a devoted following of foam-flecked jihadists. In fact, he had twice been imprisoned (once in solitary confinement at the infamous Qala prison) as a rabble-rouser known to demagogue President Nasser as "Pharaoh," "infidel," and "apostate"–the last a particularly serious accusation, especially when leveled by a recognized religious scholar. Unlike the duty to eliminate wayward rulers contro-

41

versially posited by Qutb and Ibn Taymiyyah, apostasy is almost universally regarded as a capital offense in Islam.[2]

The academic institutions were deeply and necessarily involved in the ferment of Egyptian politics. Even before Qutb's death, Nasser's relentless crack-down on religious radicals had rocked storied al-Azhar. Pious instructors and students bitterly protested the regime's increasingly authoritarian policies, and Nasser responded with ever tighter controls. These included a decree that the government would henceforth hand-pick the Grand Imam rather than have him chosen by al-Azhar's scholars, as had long been the tradition—a policy that backfired over the long haul, increasing the radicals' cachet as Islam's authentic voices while the scholars (*ulema*) who might otherwise have marginalized them were discredited as the cat's paw of an increasingly hostile regime.

The Forgotten Duty

In the short term, the fundamentalists' prospects improved, however fleetingly, on October 28, 1970, when Nasser finally succumbed to various illnesses. Vice President Anwar al-Sadat immediately acceded to power. Long a loyal Nasserite, he stunned former allies by embarking within months on his "Corrective Revolution," and by pulling Egypt back from the sharp Left turn by which Nasser had socialized the economy, nationalized businesses, and bonded with the Soviets as the crises of the 1950s and 1960s elucidated the West's generally solid support for Israel.

In Sadat's strategy, religious radicals were thought highly useful. Instinctively opposed to atheistic Communism, they would be fierce competition in universities and in the public square against Leftist intellectuals and Nasserite socialists targeted for purging.[3] Thus was Sadat's regime seduced by the same folly bedeviling the United States to this day: The notion that one can cultivate fundamentalist Islam, loose it on one's enemies, implicitly endorse its savagery, and maintain such control that, against all its hegemonic logic, the beast won't inevitably bite the hand that once fed it.

Abdel Rahman was a beneficiary of this sea-change. Despite his gadfly reputation, and over the prescient objections of Egypt's internal security service, the regime permitted him to resume teaching, initially in upper Egypt's Fayoum region, and then, in 1973, as an instructor at al-Azhar's campus in Asyut.[4]

The flame was now free to find the moths. And so he did, advancing as the Muslim Brotherhood receded. The Brotherhood had been cowed as Nasser's choke-hold snuffed out Qutb and scores of its like-minded members. In the aftermath, it timidly committed—ostensibly, at least—to seek its sharia utopia through peaceful persuasion. The cognitive dissonance in that stance infuriated jihadists whose passions had first been stirred by Brotherhood ideology—an ideology obsessed with destroying the same execrable order the Brotherhood was now accommodating. Therefore, alienated Brothers created new outlets to resuscitate the cause, with the Blind Sheikh providing both inspiration and the shroud of religious legitimacy. The new "Pharaoh" would pay with his life.

The first of the Brotherhood spin-offs was *Gama'at al Islamia*, the Islamic Group. Originally formed in the universities in 1973, its student activists were galvanized by the fiery cleric who had withstood Nasser's indignities and obligingly issued fatwas blessing the robberies of Coptic Christians by which they supported themselves.[5] In this, the Blind Sheikh was relying on a rich heritage of Muslim plunder. As Robert Spencer relates, the Prophet's very first military strikes against Quraysh caravans, many of which he led personally, were not merely vengeful acts against those who had scorned Islam; they further "served a key economic purpose, keeping the Muslim movement solvent."[6] Booty was just as central to the viability of twentieth-century Islamic militancy as it had been in the Seventh, when rules were developed (or, of course, divinely revealed) for its division—such as setting a fifth of the haul aside for the Prophet's use, and distributing female slaves as concubines.[7]

The Islamic Group first grew as a loosely organized umbrella organization for jihadist malcontents. Among those to whom it had ties were remnants of a movement spawned in the mid-Seventies by an agronomist named Shuqri Mustafa. Invoking both his mentor, Sayyid Qutb, and the *Hijra*, the original Muslims' flight to Medina from rejectionist Mecca, Shuqri taught that true Muslims must withdraw themselves from the corruption of the *jahili* society all around them. His followers made their eremitical quietus to caves and desert in Upper Egypt, determined to purify and strengthen themselves until they grew sufficiently robust in number and resolve to overthrow the regime and establish a new caliphate, much as Mohammed had done in his triumphant return to Mecca.

Because of this, the movement was popularly labeled *Takfir wal-Hijra*, Arabic terms for "excommunication" and "migration"; but members actually referred to themselves as the "Islamic Group" or the "Muslim Group," *Gama'at al-Muslimun*.[8] Many dispersed due to government pressure and the eccentric harshness of Shuqri. In desperation, he kidnapped and killed a former al-Azhar dean who was among the government's complaisant clerics. Shuqri's final emulation of his hero, Qutb, was his execution in 1978, after a spectacle of a trial at which he scalded the establishment ulema for their deviancy and their coziness with the secular regime.[9]

Wedded to a more top-down revolutionary approach was Islamic Jihad, whose formative figure was Muhammad Abd al-Salam Faraj, and whose hub was Asyuit, where Abdel Rahman was teaching and met Faraj through other Islamic Group leaders. Faraj authored a famous manifesto, *The Forgotten Duty*, which became the textbook for jihadist strategic thinking well into the 1990s. Its echoes of Qutb—the rejection of the notion that jihad was merely a defensive obligation, the stress on the individual obligation to oppose a government that failed to enforce sharia—were to be expected. It was in his emphasis on the "near" over the "far" jihad that Faraj distinguished himself, lasering on the need to overthrow apostate Muslim regimes before moving on to territories occupied by infidels, such as Israel.[10] When Ayman Zawahiri later rose to become Islamic Jihad's emir, he continued Faraj's myopic focus on Egypt for years—finally abandoning it upon merging the group into al Qaeda and its global jihad in 1998.

Given Zawahiri's preponderant influence on Osama bin Laden, it is little surprise that Islamic Jihad was the microcosm of what al Qaeda would eventually become. It attracted well-educated, well-connected recruits, was organized into operational components, and emphasized training and intelligence craft while biding its time for surgical strikes aimed to decapitate the regime and impose a fundamentalist caliphate. The best chance came in 1981.

The Pharaoh and the Fatwa

Jihadists were by then seething over the ultimate betrayal: Sadat's decision to strike a formal peace treaty with Israel.

Years earlier, Sadat had thrilled his countrymen by launching a surprise attack against Israel to start the Yom Kippur War of October 1973, an effort to liberate Sinai territories lost in 1967 (with Syria simultaneously attacking in an effort to reclaim the Golan Heights). The military is prominent in Egyptian society, and the thrashing it had received six years earlier weighed heavily. Much later, I would be taken aback at the depth to what had been its desire for redemption: In months of debriefing Emad Salem, a former Egyptian army officer and the informant who eventually proved to be Abdel Rahman's undoing, I'd find him often returning, with a patriotic pride bordering on delirium, to the "great victory" of 1973. But that, in truth, is how many Egyptians choose to remember it—notwithstanding that Israel had quickly reversed virtually all of Egypt's gains and been poised to rout its encircled Third Army when a U.S./Soviet-brokered ceasefire mercifully ended the fighting after less than three weeks. In Egyptian lore, the war stood as a triumph and Sadat was hailed as the "Hero of the Crossing."

He was not a hero for long. Once he consolidated his power, the jihadists were no longer as useful to him, and the security forces began cracking down, provoking deep resentment. Then Sadat began diplomatic overtures that resulted in a rapprochement with America and peace negotiations with Israel—abhorred in the Islamic world as the perfidious, illegitimate occupier Muslims are obliged to destroy. The diplomacy culminated in sins unforgivable by jihadist lights: Sadat's remarkably warm 1977 visit to Israel to address the Knesset, and, finally, the Camp David peace accord of 1978.

In the interim, the Blind Sheikh managed to avoid the regime's renewed crack-downs against his avid followers by enjoying a three-year hiatus in

Saudi Arabia, where he joined the theology faculty at a prestigious Islamic university in Riyadh. From his Saudi perch, he courted significant political and financial benefactors. These included two of his most important friends and allies in the beckoning Afghan jihad against the Soviets: Gulbuddin Hekmatyar, the powerful Afghan warlord who would twice emerge as prime minister in the bloody civil wars that followed the Soviets' ouster, and Sheikh Abdullah Azzam, the charismatic Palestinian leader of the Arab fighters who flocked to the jihad.[11] Azzam, like Abdel Rahman, was an Ibn Taymiyyah scholar, held a Ph.D. in Islamic jurisprudence from al-Azhar University, and took a prestigious Saudi professorship (at the King Adul Azziz University Jeddah). He would go on to become a founder of the Hamas terrorist organization, and, ultimately, the mentor and partner of Osama bin Laden—a student in Saudi Arabia during the years Abdel Rahman and Azzam taught there.[12] The Blind Sheikh also had contact in Saudi Arabia with Hassan al-Turabi, the worldly leader of Sudan's jihadist movement.[13] In the early 1990s, Turabi would loom large with Abdel Rahman's several Sudanese followers in the United States, in addition to hosting Osama bin Laden's burgeoning al Qaeda.

His reputation duly enhanced, the Blind Sheikh returned to Egypt in 1980 as the recognized emir of the Islamic Group and a figure revered by members of Islamic Jihad. By then, furor over Sadat was boiling.[14] But killing a Muslim president is no small matter, and as the jihadist movement's most influential and accommodating religious authority, it was only natural that Abdel Rahman would be asked for a fatwa. The wily sheikh addressed the matter—just as he would later address similarly delicate questions about terror plots in the United States—ever suspicious that police spies were working to infiltrate his disciples and catch him conspiring.

It was his wont, in matters of serious criminality, to couch responses in a way that left him some deniability: Keeping exchanges abstract and hypothetical, and growing positively Delphic when questioners tried to pin him down, yet—like a Henry II bewailing Thomas à Becket without exactly ordering that the "meddlesome priest" be eliminated—leaving no real doubt about where he stood.[15] It was thus circulated that Abdel Rahman had been asked, "Is it lawful to shed the blood of a ruler who does not obey the laws of God," and had opined in the affirmative. Though the circumstances rendered the meaning pluperfectly obvious, note that neither the question nor the answer explicitly referred to Sadat. But asked more precisely about Sadat, the Blind Sheikh declined to say whether the president had "crossed the line into infidelity"–that is, when concrete mention of Sadat was made, the answer carefully avoided the subject of murder and was ambiguous even on the crucial issue of apostasy.[16]

This was the Blind Sheikh's deadly methodology–the same one he had used in approving robberies and extortions against the Copts: Cite the religious principle validating attacks on Christians in jihad, refrain from addressing specific plans to attack specific Christians, and leave it to his underlings to connect the dots.[17] His most unmistakable commands to slaughter were transmitted in the language of scripture–who, after all, would dare take issue with the words of Allah and the dictates of His Prophet? But when it got down to brass tacks, the firebrand switched on a dime to nod-and-wink caginess. In the case of Sadat, that caginess would serve him well. Plots were in motion, and in a fitting irony, Egypt's hubristic limning of the 1973 War as a "victory" would be its "hero's" undoing.

An Islamic Jihad member and Abdel Rahman admirer, Khalid Ahmed Shawki al-Islambouli, was a first lieutenant in the Egyptian army. He learned in September 1981 that he had been assigned to participate in the parade held annually on October 6–marking, of course, the start, not the end, of the war. This meant he would have access to the presidential reviewing stand. Sensing their opportunity, Islambouli, Faraj and other jihadists concocted an ambitious scheme to murder Sadat and seize control of the government. Phase I went swimmingly: Islambouli strafed Sadat and his guests with bullets, gleefully braying: "My name is Khalid Islambouli, I have slain Pharaoh, and I do not fear death!" But the rest of the plan was botched.[18] The Vice President, Hosni Mubarak, seamlessly assumed power and the regime's reaction was sweeping and brutal. Thousands, including Abdel Rahman and Zawahiri, were rounded up and tortured. Islambouli, Faraj and four others were executed the following spring.[19]

The Word of Truth

"One of the greatest forms of jihad," a Hadith famously teaches, "is to utter a word of truth in the presence of a tyrannical ruler."[20] When he was finally brought to trial after nearly three years in prison, the Blind Sheikh resolved to make this lesson the leitmotif of his defense before the courts of Egypt, a nation which purports, above all else, to honor Islamic law. Betting that his incontestable mastery of that corpus would transform him from a feeble prisoner into an intimidating presence, Abdel Rahman delivered an unflinching tour de force: flaying the regime and its craven, compliant *ulema*. Tactically exploiting the paltriness of proof that he had specifically authorized the murder of Sadat (as opposed to rhetorically condemning all unfaithful leaders) or that he had taken—or, indeed, was physically capable of taking—and operational role in the plot, the *emir* of jihad embarked on a brazen defense of the conspirators, as if he were a professor objectifying a historic event remote from himself. If they had acted honorably, how dare the tribunal accuse them, much less condemn him?

Jihad is not merely a duty. It is, as Abdel Rahman ceaselessly counseled his disciples, "the peak of a full [embrace] of Islam . . . . [T]here is no work that equals jihad." Acts of jihad could not be condemned. What were condemnable were efforts by cowardly clerics and corrupt rulers—using the prestige of their positions to distort jihad's true meaning—to divert Muslims from this sacred striving. For fourteen centuries, the Sheikh admonished, jihad had unambiguously and unapologetically called for the aggressive application of military force against oppressors and infidels. It "means fighting the enemies." Jihad was not about internal betterment, other efforts at peaceful achievement, or to be accomplished by such quotidian practices as prayer, mosque attendance, alms giving, or living a virtuous life. At such nonsensical suggestions, he often scoffed (as in this recording from his American trial):

> Jihad is jihad. . . . There is no such thing as commerce, industry

and science in jihad. This is calling things . . . other than by [their] own name. If God . . . says, "Do jihad," it means do jihad with the sword, with the cannon, with the grenades and with the missile. This is jihad. Jihad against God's enemies for God's cause and his word.

The nature of jihad, like the strictures of Islamic law, were unchanging. They *could not change* for they had been enunciated by Allah Himself. His injunctions were eternal, not confined to the time and place in which they were revealed. Mere men had no power to modify them for changing times or expedience. These commands held that society must be governed by sharia; if it is not, it becomes the individual duty of every Muslim to perform jihad against the regime until it is either overthrown or enforces God's law as God decreed it. This self-evident truth, Abdel Rahman thundered, required no scholar to interpret and no fatwa to vindicate. Thus, Sadat's slayers were performing a sacred duty, and it was pointless to quibble over whether it had been authorized by him or by any man; it was dictated by the Qur'an, which Muslims can read for themselves.[21]

It was a strategy as brilliant as it was frightening. The core of the regime's case against him, the Sheikh's equivocal fatwas, was reduced to a side issue. The main event was God's law, which it was a cleric's duty to interpret when asked, and which Egypt claimed to venerate but was plainly not enforcing. Muslims, especially those presiding over court proceedings involving other Muslims, are required to acknowledge the binding force of divinely prescribed obligations even if they are not themselves adhering to those obligations.[22] And, as Abdel Rahman well knew, acknowledgment by the court of the scriptural commands he had explicated would have seemingly little practical consequence beyond his own case: The plotters who actually killed Sadat had already been executed; conceding the Blind Sheikh's logic and erudition would not bring them back.

And so he was acquitted.

The proceedings burnished his legend. He was lionized not for being innocent but because he had staked his life on the unshakable conceit that

God approved his actions, and he had been delivered. He had spoken *a word of truth* to the tyrant. Through all his sightlessness and infirmities, he had stared his accusers down through the sheer force of his will. A few years later, he would write a book based largely on his browbeating of the court. He called it *A Word of Truth*. The phrase thereafter became his insufferable signature, right down to the last will and testament he issued twenty years later from his American prison cell, imploring followers: "Do not have my blood [be] in vain. Seek for me my revenge, the most violent revenge. And remember a brother of yours who said a word of truth and was killed in the sake of God." *A word of truth*, the maxim he feigned to personify in all his crafty deceitfulness. Jihad, after all, is war, and "[w]ar," said the Prophet, "is deceit."[23]

Most of all, Abdel Rahman's star blazed in the jihadist firmament precisely because he had been guilty, yet he'd won. The Pharaoh had been slain, the Blind Sheikh had fortified the murderers, and now he would be permitted to move on to the next jihad. Years later, safely out of Egypt and stoking new recruits, he would reflect that, of the "many jihad operations" carried out by his Islamic Group, the "most famous" one was "killing . . . the atheist, the oppressor and the profligate . . . Anwar Al-Sadat."

But what about the result, someone asked. Hadn't getting rid of Sadat only given Muslims Mubarak, who was worse? Abdel Rahman would hear none of it. God "ordered us to eliminate" Sadat, he insisted, "even if this had to be done by killing him[,]" and even though Mubarak proved to be worse. Yes, following Nasser and Sadat, Mubarak was indeed "the third traitor, backstabber who became the loyal dog to America, . . . and was at the forefront of the treachery caravan to give to Israel and then America everything." That, though, would be dealt with in time.

The Islamic Group, the Blind Sheikh assured his audience, was "now. . . hoping for another operation."

⌛ Chapter 5

Afghanistan? Who Needs to Know?

WE'RE HAPPY TO COME TALK TO *you* about Afghanistan, the politely professional voice from Langley deadpanned. But the FBI was not to be in the room.

The phone call in late 1993 was my first ever encounter with the CIA– at least, to my knowledge. By then, however, I'd been involved for over a dozen years in the most sensitive aspect of law enforcement: the life and death issues of people who put themselves and their loved ones at grave risk by providing the government with intelligence. Now, I had reached the point of having a very high security clearance, but I had long fully grasped what "need to know" meant. I knew the FBI understood it too. So naturally, I was floored–which I was beginning to fear was the permanent condition of a terrorism prosecutor.

Before becoming an attorney, I'd served as a deputy United States marshal in the federal witness-protection program. For a twenty-year-old kid from the Bronx, there was an air of James Bond to it–especially talking to my friends about not being able to talk to friends about what I did most days. The reality was decidedly unglamorous, but it was important. While attending Columbia College and later New York Law School mostly by night, I would by day traipse through the dingy basement of New York City's vital statistics bureau, along row upon row of binders, thumbing through stack after stack of birth certificates. My mission: the execution of sealed court orders that altered the identities of protected witnesses and their families. Without a clean slate, there would be no hope of relocating them safely. Keeping that slate clean, and them alive, depended at every stage on the integrity and competence of government agents. One slip-up, corruptly or by inadvertence compromising some small detail–a phone number, a cherished keepsake, an old nickname, a child's birthday–could give mafia hitmen or drug cartel killers just the hot lead needed to track down an undercover operative or a turncoat.

By the time I passed the bar exam in 1985, I had already been working at the U.S. attorney's office for two years as a full-time paralegal. Plunged into organized crime investigations and trials, I'd been schooled by America's the finest prosecutors and FBI agents–including my immediate boss and the eventual FBI Director, Louis Freeh, who had been among the best of both. The lesson, time and again, was that discretion was vital to our duties. The failure to hold sensitive information closely destroyed investigations, allowed the most insulated crime bosses to slip the noose, and endangered lives.

Protecting intelligence was the rule we lived by. It was a rule I enforced rigidly when I started running my own cases. Not that much vigor was required. With exceedingly rare exceptions, and regardless of what tactical disagreements we had, the investigators I worked with–including hundreds of FBI agents–were beyond honorable. Besides reflecting how they'd been brought up, honor and discretion were indispensable to winning the allegiance of extremely reluctant sources. That, singularly, was the prerequisite to wheedling out the information we needed to make cases.

Now it was late 1993, and the CIA seemed to be saying we law-enforcement types, particularly the FBI, couldn't be trusted.

The Sovereign District had filed an ambitious indictment against the Blind Sheikh and thirteen underlings–an indictment that promised to lay bare the history of radical Islam's growing U.S. hub. The jihadist road to New York City, it was clear, had passed through Afghanistan. To do my job, I would need to understand intimately something of which I'd been only dimly aware: the Central Intelligence Agency's shadowy but certain role in helping the rag-tag, poly-factional Afghan Mujahideen defeat the mighty Red Army–the king-has-no-clothes feat that was followed, in a few whirlwind months, by the razing of the Berlin Wall and the collapse of the Soviet Union itself.

Coming unexpectedly upon any fracas between local rivals, the Irish are apt to ask: "Is this a private fight, or can anyone join?" The FBI/CIA scrap I had inadvertently waded into, though, had been ongoing for five decades, ever since J. Edgar Hoover and "Wild Bill" Donovan first leered at each in the wake of Pearl Harbor's intelligence lapses. I was not anxious for the fray. These contretemps were of little concern to us in law enforcement. Outside the occasional ruinous independent counsel probe into some executive branch farrago, prosecutors had no need before 1993 to deal with the U.S. intelligence community and barely knew the FBI had a night-job in the domestic national security business. Now, suddenly, that had changed. Government's national security mission was being merged, on the fly, with its criminal investigation functions, and it was suddenly my problem that these guys didn't seem to get on very well.

Intelligence v. Law Enforcement

On that score, I'd eventually come round to the view of the Manhattan Institute's Mark Riebling that a full half-century's worth of national disasters—from Pearl Harbor through the Bay of Pigs, the Kennedy assassination, Watergate, and Iran-Contra (and, ultimately, 9/11)—had been enabled or exacerbated by turf-battling between the FBI and CIA.[1] In the here and now, though, I peremptorily dismissed the CIA's stance as petty and ignorant. Assuming for argument's sake that the Agency had some plausible rationale for its intransigence besides "we don't want to be in the same room with them," I figured—in my own presumptuous ignorance— that even intelligence agents must know the elementary rule that prosecutors don't meet by themselves with sources of information. But, of course, that's a *litigation* rule. The CIA wasn't in the litigation business, and—as I was learning daily in my maiden voyage with the Joint Terrorism Task Force—even at the FBI, which presumably was in the litigation business, the Foreign Counterintelligence Division had apparently been absent the semester they taught Investigation & Prosecution 101.

Any human source of information is a potential witness. It is not unknown for people to say one thing when being informally interviewed in a prosecutor's office and then something the polar opposite on the witness stand. When that happens, the prosecutor has to be able to summon someone who can testify to the contrary version. He can't do it himself. Trial lawyers are advocates. The integrity of the truth-seeking process carves a bright line between advocacy and testimony. It forbids prosecutors and defense attorneys from acting as witnesses in the cases they try–such that disqualification occasionally results if they have foolishly allowed themselves to be the only person to see or hear something of palpable relevance to the case.

There was no way I was going to meet alone with a CIA briefer. Federal prosecutors preparing for trial don't meet with any witness unless an observer is present. In a high-profile case, that observer is typically an FBI agent. That agent, who is usually the "case agent"–the investigator whom the FBI has assigned as the lead agent on the matter–is supposed to know the facts, have a feel for the legal issues that prompted the need to speak with the witness in the first place, and participate in, or primarily conduct, the questioning. Obviously, the FBI had to be present when the CIA briefed the prosecutors.

Had I been more savvy, though, I'd have disconnected my law enforcement synapses. This was not, as I thought, just another pointless scrap between agencies whose mutual distaste seemed chiseled into their DNA. The problem was galactically more complex. Yet it was indiscernible, as problems that should be patent always are when they challenge one's whole framework for perceiving a phenomenon. At that poin t, I was not ready to transcend the lawman's ingrained regard for his discipline as *the* algorithm for resolving all life's challenges. I failed to appreciate that we were trying to impose our system and all its procedural mandates on national security operatives who inhabit a very different realm–one which was every bit as important, and more. The "rule of law" was our trust. But the very phrase implies that everyone being ruled is bound by the same law. That's not true outside our country where the CIA operates. American lives and freedoms depended on the intelligence community's ability to obtain information and conduct operations in ways that would be inconceivable for law enforcement.

Indeed, if I'd taken an occasional time-out from the aggravation that had thrummed through my first months of dealing with JTTF agents, I might have figured out that their unfamiliarity with some basic law enforcement protocols wasn't so inexplicable. It was not excusable. After all, we *were* inside the United States. Everyone *was* bound by our law whether they acknowledged it or not. We *did* have remedies–unavailable to the CIA overseas–for dealing with outlaws. But it was explicable. JTTF agents weren't dealing with mere criminals. Their quarry, much like the CIA's, was not just in it for a quick buck or the other motives that drive run-of-the-mill crooks. The people they were investigating were enemies of the United States. We were now abruptly asking domestic national security agents to apply the settled rules for investigating crimes, a job in many ways incompatible with what they had been tasked to do before the World Trade Center bombing: gather whatever intelligence could be reaped against foreign threats to the American people. To be sure, they had not done a very good job of that–in fact, their performance had been appalling. That, however, was a separate concern.

Much of the CIA's knowledge, particularly that drawn from its covert operations, is top-secret intelligence. When an Agency analyst gives the kind of briefing I needed on Afghanistan, it is certain to be based on at least some classified information, including intelligence from deep-cover operatives, from foreign countries, and from electronic surveillance the CIA was lucky enough to set up on just the right telephone or meeting place. Such intelligence is sometimes confined to a circle so tight its revelation would effectively blow the source. Let's say, for example, you're an insulated terrorist leader, and you've told something to only two subordinates in a safehouse in Pakistan. If you somehow learn the Americans know about it, it is not a matter of quantum physics to deduce that either one of your subordinates is a mole or the safehouse is bugged–and that the Pakistanis are probably cooperating with the CIA. You stop using the safehouse and maybe kill both the subordinates just to make sure–terrorists not being especially finicky about the presumption of innocence.

That compromise of such precious insider intelligence is almost certain to render the informant, country, or eavesdropping coup endangered, uncooperative, or useless for future purposes. That's why such information is never meant to see the light of day. It is not obtained to prove legal cases. There are—hard as this may be to believe—things more important than legal cases. That kind of intelligence is collected to anticipate the next moves of dangerous actors who mean us harm and can't be reached by law. It must be accessible only to those who need to know it in order to protect the United States.

As the CIA official who spoke to me understood, FBI agents operating inside the United States are, to the contrary, trained to have the courtroom always in mind. When they collect information, it is often not solely for intelligence consumption. Everyone inside the United States, except an infinitesimal few with diplomatic immunity, is reachable by law. We can collect intelligence on them, but they can also be indicted for any statutory violations—and even if a person can't be prosecuted due to diplomatic immunity, evidence of law-breaking can result in his being expelled by the State Department as *persona non grata*. FBI agents, therefore, take copious notes and write reports. After all, if a matter does end up in litigation, it may take months or years to get to court. Those notes and reports are key if fresh memories are to be preserved and seized evidence is to be authenticated for trial. There is, nonetheless, a significant intelligence cost: If charges do get filed, many of those reports become "discoverable"—they have to be turned over to the defense. Agents, in fact, are trained to presume that whatever they write will someday be scrutinized by experienced defense lawyers whose job is to pick it apart.

Thus, to the CIA, the specter of briefing people who didn't absolutely need to know the subject matter—people who *might even take notes*, for God's sake—spawned visions of precious intelligence and confidential relationships not only being exposed but actually handed directly to the nation's enemies—who, thanks to our prosecution, were now "defendants" vested with an extraordinary array of due process rights. The Agency was not enthusiastic about the prospect of telling me things, but it understood this was where its interests lay. Like it or not, this case was going to happen. It's the prosecutor who choreographs the government's trial presentation and who is responsible for positing any legal arguments that might persuade the court to preserve state secrets. Given advance warning, prosecutors can usually steer the case away from Pandora's boxes that might trigger unwelcome disclosure obligations. In this sense, I'd be the intelligence community's lawyer, and that was reason enough to play ball with me.

But that didn't mean the FBI needed to know.

The Left Hand and the Right Hand

Of course, the FBI *did* need to know what the CIA knew. And ironically, the FBI needed to know for the very reason the CIA was reluctant to tell them: because, though we hadn't yet grasped it, the great cause we were about to embark on, the terrorism trial of Islamic radicals, was not nearly as important to the United States as the need for all our national security officials—whether stationed at home or overseas—to understand the jihadist threat. We weren't at the end. We were at the beginning. The legal case, our current obsession, was crucial . . . but secondary. We couldn't save the lives that had been lost, but to save lives in the future the left hand would have to know what the right hand was doing. If such coordination triggered disclosures that might compromise valuable intelligence and sources—if, in sum, disclosure might harm the country more than prosecuting particular terrorists would help the country—then that was an argument for exploring counterterrorism weapons other than prosecution in the criminal justice system. It was not an argument against the coordination.

We didn't see it. Wouldn't see it.

Of course, as one might imagine, this storm passed. Concerns were allayed about the scope and purpose of the Afghanistan briefing. Not only did the CIA give it to us, in my office with the FBI present, but the Agency was also exceedingly helpful thereafter in answering our questions, allowing me to review relevant files, and agreeing—without compromising intelligence methods and sources—to declassify the information necessary to satisfy the court's due process concerns. In the years that followed, moreover, day-to-day cooperation between our two top intelligence agencies seemed to improve noticeably.

Still, we were far from perceiving that information-sharing was our paramount defense against enemies who told us and showed us, again and again, that they were bent on slaughtering our citizens. The Justice Department actually, and quite deliberately, *increased* the structural barriers against information-sharing and fostered an ethos of non-cooperation–the better, it claimed, to protect a counterterrorism strategy reliant on criminal prosecution that netted fewer and fewer jihadists even as the nation was attacked with greater frequency and audacity after 1993.

That was on the horizon. For now, though, the issue was Afghanistan. And this being the FBI and the CIA, there were, inevitably, reasons beyond institutional tension for the usual inter-agency tetchiness.

From the late 1980s into the early 1990s, the two had worked in the field at cross-purposes. The FBI had been roused to investigate the U.S. stirrings of jihadists galvanized by a war which, it turned out, the CIA was underwriting. From an intelligence-gathering perspective, this might not have been so bad had it not been done with such staggering inattention and flat-out incompetence: the Agency empowering Islamic fighters to addle the Soviets in conscious avoidance of the virulently anti-American radicals feeding at the trough; the Bureau collecting scads of valuable information but, as was too often the case, failing to internalize it.

Consequently, both at home and abroad, U.S. intelligence missed blazing augurs of radical Islam's rising threat to America.

⌛ Chapter 6

Feeding the Beast

For radical Islam, life under President Hosni Mubarak was indeed worse, as the Blind Sheikh conceded. Encouraged to leave Egypt after years of imprisonment and his acquittal, Abdel Rahman made his way in 1985 to a warm reception in the fundamentalist hotbed of Peshawar, Pakistan. Just west of the Khyber Pass, this hardscrabble proving ground for aspiring warriors was the gangplank to the jihad in Afghanistan, and became the gateway to the jihad against the world.

In Peshawar, both in 1985 and several times thereafter, Abdel Rahman would enjoy the august company of his former student Mohammed Shawky al-Islambouli, a fixture there. A rising jihadist star in his own right, Shawky's prominence owed much to his mythogenic brother, Lieutenant Khalid al-Islambouli, who had so audaciously murdered Sadat and, soon after, been "martyred" by the Mubarak regime. Like the Blind Sheikh, Shawky would ultimately seek his revenge against Mubarak–in 1992, he was tried and sentenced to death in absentia for plotting the president's murder and the regime's overthrow, escaping execution, his brother's fate, by finding safe-haven in Pakistan and elsewhere.[1]

On this first trip, the emir of jihad was escorted into Afghanistan by both Islambouli and another heavyweight, Gulbuddin Hekmatyar, who, with 800,000 of his countrymen under his command, was the most important of the Afghan chieftains.[2] The Blind Sheikh later described for the journalist Mary Anne Weaver how he swelled with pride and certainty "that Allah would aid these people and this religion, and that Islam would be victorious in the end." A Hekmatyar aide recalled the sightless man weeping near a makeshift encampment, sandbags stacked at his sides, artillery exploding in the distance, until at last he confided to the warlord, "I have never asked Allah for anything, but I am under a great disadvantage now. If only Allah could give me eyes for a couple of years, or for a couple of hours, so I could fight in the jihad!"[3]

To fight in the jihad, which the revered Abdel Rahman described as the unequalled "peak" of Islam's "full embrace," was the passion of those who became known as the "Afghan mujahideen." This motley collection of warriors was comprised mostly of hundreds of thousands of indigenous fighters from Afghan tribes, supplemented by a much smaller contingent of non-Afghan Muslims, mostly Arab. Tens of thousands of the latter poured in from the Islamic countries and territories of the Near East and North Africa, as well as from outside the Islamic world—including a smattering from Southeast Asia, Europe, and the United States. By far, the more regimented and capable jihadists were the native Afghans, fighting for their homeland against the Soviets, who had invaded in 1979. But amongst themselves, they agreed on little else besides the necessity to drive out the occupying Communists.

Sensing an opportunity to bleed the Soviets, the CIA, throughout the Reagan administration and well into the term of President George H.W. Bush, backed the mujahideen with money and arms, most famously "stinger" anti-aircraft missiles that were critical to neutralizing the Russians' control of the skies. By the time the Red Army went home in early 1989, the United States had contributed about $3 billion to the jihadists' cause.

American aid was matched, dollar-for-dollar and beyond, by the Saudis. The Soviets' imperialist gambit had been just as alarming to the House of Saud, due to both geopolitical calculations and Wahhabist principles, which regard communism as an affront to Islam and Afghanistan as a Muslim land from which the faithful were adjured to expel occupiers. Initially, there were six major Afghan recipients of the international aid. A seventh faction, *Ittihad-e-Islami* (the Islamic Union), was cobbled together under Abdurrab Rasul Sayyaf, an Afghan and yet another al-Azhar doctor of Islamic jurisprudence who subscribed to Sunni Islam's Wahhabist strain.[4]

For the most part, the U.S. aid went to the indigenous Afghan warlords, who fielded the most effective forces. The Saudis funded them too, but concentrated much of their effort on subsidizing Sayyaf and the so-called "Arab-Afghans,"the non-Aghan mujahideen who answered the global call to join the jihad against the Godless communist occupiers and who fought alongside Sayyaf and Hekmatyar, among other warlords.[5]

See No Evil

There has been great misunderstanding about how American aid was funneled, leading to misinformed claims that top jihadists like Abdel Rahman were covert CIA operatives. Such speculation is understandable in light of the Agency's mind-boggling ineptitude in letting the infamous (and hard to miss) cleric enter the United States multiple times. He was, however, no American operative. The stubborn facts won't retreat: besides the CIA's denial of any relationship with him, Abdel Rahman, a dyed-in-the-wool America-hater who waged war against the United States, never claimed to be a U.S. spy while undergoing both American deportation proceedings and an American criminal prosecution that resulted in a sentence of life-imprisonment—when, that is, had there been any truth to the spy canard, it would have been greatly to his advantage to pipe up and say something.[6]

No, the real reason it sometimes looks so plausible that the CIA's covert roster could have included the likes of Abdel Rahman and such other jihadist luminaries as Osama bin Laden (whom the government has also vigorously and convincingly denied ever using as a spy[7]) is that radical Islam so profited from—essentially, came to life as a global phenomenon because of—the Afghanistan operation that the CIA lavishly abetted. The CIA can continue to pretend otherwise—and probably will until Hell freezes over. But the unrelenting fact is: We weren't careful about whom we were helping.

Pace the State Department and its cant about our burning desire to "support the Afghans fighting for their country's freedom," the truth is the United States was myopically consumed with the Soviets: with both miring the U.S.S.R. in as painful and costly a guerrilla war as possible, and maintaining deniability about the fact that we were doing just that—which, of course, is what makes a covert operation a covert operation.[8] Beyond those goals, the CIA didn't care about much else—including such unintended consequences as the anti-American juggernaut its largesse helped unleash. The Agency structured its assistance, and allowed other international financing efforts to be structured, in such a way as to turn a blind eye to where billions upon billions in funding and materiél went.

Further, all these years later, looking past overwhelming evidence of intimacy between some of the fiercest, most anti-American Afghan factions and the fierce, anti-American terror network that sprang from the jihad, the intelligence community persists in disavowing *any* contribution to the emergence of radical Islam as a global phenomenon. After all, the CIA mulishly maintains, its money went only to the Afghans, and the Afghans—notwithstanding the fact that they venerated Abdel Rahman, nursed the jihadist movement, and gave al Qaeda safe-haven for years—didn't really like the Arabs anyway.

Perhaps the best example of this preposterous story line is offered by the aforementioned Dr. Marc Sageman, who was a CIA officer dealing with the mujahideen in the late 1980s. In his book *Understanding Terror Networks*, widely touted in government circles, he asserts, "I am not aware of any major Afghan participant in the *global Salafi jihad* except for Wali Khan Amin Shah" (emphasis added), who was convicted in 1996 for participating in a plot to bomb American airliners in flight over the Pacific. Dr. Sageman further implies that the CIA ought to get a Mulligan for even this allegedly singular Afghan terrorist. After all, Shah's Salafism, Sageman deduces, is really less the result of his Afghan-Islamic heritage than the fact that he was a close personal friend of bin Laden—evidently Wali Khan and Osama, like Sheikh Omar and Hekmatyar, managed somehow to bridge this chasm of enmity that supposedly divides Afghans and Arabs.[9]

Sageman repeatedly stresses that the Arab Muslims who formed al Qaeda comprise a global *Salafi* jihad from which Afghanistan—and thus the

CIA's role in Afghanistan–can be neatly compartmentalized. Fresh from his tooth-pulling Shah exception to the supposed general rule that Afghans and Arabs have no use for each other, the mantra comes round again: "Afghans," he chants, "are conspicuous by their absence from the global Salafi jihad." [10]

The term *Salafi* denotes a veneration of the first Muslim generations. Though often used interchangeably with the more pejorative term *Wahhabism*–the eighteenth-century theology of Muhammad ibn Abd al-Wahhab which, as we have seen, became the official Islam of Saudi Arabia–*Salafism* has a broader constituency.[11] Sageman's focus on it is no accident. Salafijihadism is the fundamentalist Islam adhered to by today's Sunni militants, who are predominantly Arab. Ignoring prodigious evidence to the contrary, Sageman, a forensic psychiatrist, diagnoses that Afghans monolithically prefer a relaxed Sufi version of Islam that is repellant to these Salafists. Since the two are so theologically and temperamentally incompatible, so the theory goes, it's just plain silly for anyone to suggest that by funding and arming the noble Afghans the CIA might derivatively have improved the lot of those awful Salafist, Wahhabist jihadis.

With due respect to Dr. Sageman, whose book contains some valuable insights, this fustian is of a piece with the absurd mental prism through which, even today, it is not difficult to find some current or former intelligence official ready and willing to opine that Sunnis would never cooperate with secularists or Shiites–overlooking abundant evidence of the Ba'athist Saddam Hussein coddling Sunni jihadists and a years-long history of collaboration between al Qaeda and Shiite Hezbollah. Thus does Dr. Sageman find it "all the more surprising [that] al Qaeda kept training camps in Afghanistan for more than a decade." Why, yes . . . and who do you suppose let them do that? Real life can be full of surprises if we insist on rationalizing rather than observing it. Perhaps not as surprising is that, in weaving his yarn of loathing between the Arabs who came to fight besides their brother Muslims and the Afghans who made a home for them, Dr. Sageman finds room in his book for exactly one fleeting mention each of the Taliban and Hekmatyar.[12]

Endowing the Jihadist Harvard

In recent years, the government, finally, has officially acknowledged that the CIA's cut-out in Afghanistan was Pakistan's InterServices Intelligence Directorate (ISI). We prosecutors were forbidden from admitting as much at the Blind Shiekh's 1995 trial, even though U.S. aid to the Nicaraguan Contras was probably a better kept secret. The stipulation read to the jury–after endless negotiations, the review of countless top-secret files, and eighteen months of sealed litigation under the Classified Information Procedures Act–conceded only that the United States had provided economic and military support to the mujahideen "through a third country intermediary"; it did not identify our abettor.[13] This was as it should be. Even long after a covert operation is over, and even if the truth has been unofficially leaked and discussed so widely it has become common knowledge, the CIA properly fights like hell against fingering its accomplices–including when those trying to nudge the Agency into more openness are snooty young Justice Department lawyers who see their trials as paramount and bristle at being forced to defend a secret that's no longer much of a secret.

Years later, with the intelligence community under the public microscope of myriad investigations into its dismal pre-9/11 performance, it could no longer afford to be so stingy. The 9/11 Commission was thus able to disclose that "United States supplied billions of dollars worth of secret assistance to rebel groups in Afghanistan fighting the Soviet occupation. This assistance was funneled through Pakistan: the Pakistani military intelligence service ([ISI]), helped train the rebels and distribute the arms."[14]

Moreover, with the nation under considerable criticism for having allegedly reared the terror network that has now matured into a global threat, the State Department got into the act. In 2005, it issued a press release categorically denying that the United States had "created Osama bin Laden." That, though, answers the wrong question. It's not whether we "created" bin Laden; it's whether we materially helped him and his network grow and evolve into what they've become. The release's more glaring difficulty, moreover, was State's attempt to have it both ways: to hold the CIA blameless yet explain forthrightly what actually happened. That won't work.

State dutifully undertook to regurgitate the drivel about how Afghans and Arabs despised one another, such that our helping the former in no way facilitated the latter. Its impressive array of expert witnesses offering lengthy testimonials on this point included Dr. Sageman, of course, as well as his former boss, Milt Bearden, who ran the CIA's Afghan operation. State presents the latter's summation courtesy of a report by CNN's terrorism analyst Peter Bergen:

> CIA official Milt Bearden, who ran the Agency's Afghan operation in the late 1980s, says, "The CIA did not recruit Arabs," as there was no need to do so. There were hundreds of thousands of Afghans all too willing to fight, and the Arabs who did come for jihad were "very disruptive . . . the Afghans thought they were a pain in the ass."[15]

Yes, we've heard–they couldn't stand being in the same jihad together. On the more salient point, however, the question is not whether the CIA *recruited* Arabs. In fact, to listen to Dr. Sageman, *even al Qaeda doesn't recruit Arabs*. As terrorism expert Lorenzo Vidino observes:

> The studies on recruitment for jihad undertaken by Marc Sageman, a former CIA official and an adjunct professor of psychology at the University of Pennsylvania, have revealed that al Qaeda carries out no top-down recruitment; instead, spontaneously formed clusters of young radicals naturally team up with recruiters, who select those who have the skills and dedication that can be useful to the cause. "It's actually very much like applying to Harvard," says Sageman, pointing out that al Qaeda's problem is selection, not recruitment.[16]

Exactly. The issue, essentially, is did the CIA endow the jihadist Harvard? Was it like today's university donors who contribute huge sums but then disavow any responsibility for what's being taught in the schools? In that connection, it is worth pausing to observe that we are talking here about the Central *Intelligence* Agency. The "I had no idea" excuse is unconvincing enough when it comes from above-it-all donors; it is truly lame coming from the CIA. Did the Agency knowingly foster an atmosphere in which these spontaneously arriving clusters of Arab-Afghans could easily and quite foreseeably find the opportunities, the trainers, and the means to become more effective, more networked terrorists? Did the Agency do so knowing virulently anti-Western jihadists were finding each other? The answers to those questions are palpable, and neither counter-factual psycho-babble nor lists of all the things we didn't do—carefully eliding mention of the enormous thing we *did* do—suffices to paper the problem over.

The Cut-Out

Ironically, it's the State Department that gives up the ghost. Along with its remarkable candor in conceding that the CIA went through the ISI precisely in order to maintain deniability, State, in its angst to shift to Pakistan the blame for al Qaeda's rise, inadvertently destroys the CIA's fairy tale. Again, the Department's proffered expert source is Peter Bergen:

> The United States wanted to be able to deny that the CIA was funding the Afghan war, so its support was funneled through Pakistan's Inter Services Intelligence agency (ISI). ISI in turn made the decisions about *which Afghan factions to arm and train, tending to favor the most Islamist and pro-Pakistan. The Afghan Arabs generally fought alongside those factions*, which is how the charge arose that they were creatures of the CIA." [Emphasis added.]

Well, I'll be darned. You mean to tell me some of those rigorously Sufi Afghans turn out to have been . . . Islamist? *Islamist* being today's term-of-art for *Salafi jihadist*—we wouldn't, after all, want to call someone an "Islamic terrorist"; that might suggest terror may have a teensy bit to do with Islam. In any event, there you have it. We well knew the Pakistanis favored the Salafi-oriented Afghan factions. Armed with this knowledge, we funded and armed the Pakistanis, knowing they'd get a goodly share of that funding and matériel to those Afghans, like Hekmatyar, who were intimate with the Arabs.[17]

Hekmatyar, as Bergen relates, was (and is) an "Islamist zealot"; yet his

Hizb party received fully 20 percent of the U.S. contribution–about $600 million, and that's before the considerable Saudi aid that came his way is factored in.[18] It is perfectly reasonable, and no doubt true, that our main reason for doing what we did was to get the assistance into the hands of the factions that would be most effective in combating the Soviets–although how effective Hekmatyar's was in that regard is hotly disputed. It is simply inane, however, to insist that the easily foreseeable fallout–the fueling of jihadism–didn't happen. It happened in spades and we did nothing meaningful to account for it. We simply didn't much care that Hekmatyar and some of the other Afghan warlords themselves hated America and the West.

My good friend Michael A. Ledeen, the American Enterprise Institute scholar who advised the State Department and the National Security Council during the Reagan administration, is characteristically more clear-eyed:

> In the late eighties and early nineties, there were precious few Americans on the ground in Pakistan, let alone in Afghanistan, where virtually no one from the Pentagon or the CIA was permitted to operate. The Islamic forces were mostly funded by the Saudis and mostly trained by the Pakistanis. The really telling American failure in Afghanistan was not an excess of zeal but a lack of engagement and follow-through. If we had been more fully involved in the war against the Soviets in Afghanistan, we might have taken steps to dismantle the Mujahideen networks, or penetrate them, or at least remove the most dangerous weapons, like Stinger missiles. This never happened.[19]

Amen.

I've always gotten a queasy feeling on hearing unqualified assurances from intelligence community that this or that mujahid was never a CIA operative. Prosecutors, and anyone who has ever worked in the United States government for more than about ten minutes, become wary to the point of squeamishness about any agency's categorical claims that "we would *never* do this," or that something "*could not possibly* have happened." The unwieldy federal Leviathan has too many people working too many contradictory agendas. It implements too many policies before their likely consequences are thought through. No one could sensibly be comfortable with such assurances. (Hence the tiresome propensity of us lawyers to swaddle our representations in weasel-words like "generally speaking," "virtually," "more or less," and the like–as in, "Generally speaking, two plus two virtually always make four, more or less.") Still, we can be fairly confident here. This insular arrangement, with the Pakistanis as intercessor between the CIA and radical Islam, allows our government to assert confidently that the people fighting us today were not on our payroll yesterday.[20] That, however, is very far from the end of the matter. A Frankenstein monster came to life in Afghanistan, and we had a hand in it despite the self-delusive comfort of psychological distance the CIA has drawn from its cut-out.

That distance, moreover, is actually much shorter than appears on first blush. By training the spotlight on Afghan-Arab relations, the State Department and the Agency conveniently skip past an even more blatant instance of see-no-evil: our chosen intermediary, Pakistan.

As Bergen pointed out, the Afghan mujahideen factions that were allied with the Arab jihadists also happened to be the most pro-Pakistani, which, naturally, is why the Pakistanis steered so much U.S. aid their way. Indeed, the CIA well knew that Hekmatyar had been a Pakistani agent in the 1970s.[21] It's not a very gigantic leap of logic to conclude from this that the Salafi-jihadists and our chosen intermediary, the Pakistanis, were also quite favorably disposed toward one another. That is, wholly apart from our awareness that there were Afghans who were more than willing to work with anti-Western Salafists, we had very good reason to know *the Pakistanis themselves*–the direct recipients of U.S. aid given for the specific purpose of being dispensed, *at their discretion*, to Muslim fighters–would train and provide other logistical assistance for these Arab jihadis.

Therein lay perhaps the most suicidal feature in the see-no-evil structure. The ISI, reflecting Pakistan itself, has long been rife with Islamic radicals. No Pakistani leader, including its present strongman, the tepidly pro-

American President Pervez Musharraf (who has been the subject of several unsuccessful assassination attempts, some redolent of insider-treachery), has been able to purge them. Thanks to the ISI, for example, the Clinton administration decided in early 1999, after al Qaeda's bombing of two U.S. embassies in east Africa the previous summer, that it would be pointless to try to kill Osama bin Laden by a U-2 strike against his Afghan redoubt. Such an operation would require a heads-up to Pakistan, whose air-space would be traversed, and Clinton's counterterrorism coordinator, Richard Clarke, advised that the ISI would alert bin Laden, guaranteeing failure.[22]

As this is written, over six years after 9/11, with the Pakistani government our assertedly committed ally against radical Islam, not much has changed. Radicals, probably with the help from sympathetic elements in the Pakistani government, murdered Benazir Bhutto in December 2007 as she campaigned for democratic reform. Al Qaeda, meanwhile, has been permitted to reconstitute itself in Pakistan's lawless Afghan border region, again under the umbrella of the Taliban, which is resurgent there.[23] In July 2007, U.S. counterterrorism officials presented the House Armed Services Committee a classified estimate entitled "al Qaeda Better Positioned to Strike the West." The report bleakly related that the terror network had reassembled and revitalized itself in Pakistan's ungovernable tribal areas.[24] Despite six years of American military operations in Afghanistan and Iraq, and billions in aid to the Musharraf regime, the jihadists have nevertheless restored their operating capabilities to a level not seen since the months just prior to the 9/11 attacks. "They seem to be fairly well settled into the safe haven and the ungoverned spaces of Pakistan," John A. Kringen, the CIA's Director for Intelligence told the Committee. "We see more training. We see more money. We see more communications. We see that activity rising."[25] In addition, Thomas Fingar, the Deputy Director for Analysis at the new National Intelligence Directorate, conceded that al Qaeda's "core elements . . . continue to plot attacks against our Homeland and other targets with the objective of inflicting mass casualties. They continue to maintain active connections and relationships from their leaders hiding in Pakistan to affiliates throughout the Middle East, North and East Africa, and Europe."[26] An unidentified counterterrorism official familiar with the top-secret report further explained to the Associated Press that al Qaeda is "considerably operationally stronger than a year ago" and was "showing greater and greater ability to plan attacks in Europe and the United States."[27]

How could such a thing happen? Pakistan, after all, is now the world's fifth largest recipient of U.S. foreign aid[28]– it has received even more in U.S. billions since 9/11 than the considerable skim it took from U.S. aid to the anti-Soviet mujahideen. President George W. Bush, echoing the CIA of the 1980s, maintains that Pakistan is a "strong" and "valuable" ally against our worst enemies,[29] and our current intelligence community insists that the Musharraf regime has taken "aggressive military action against extremists [that] has been costly for that government's security forces."[30] Yet, Musharraf's regime chose *to strike a treaty* in 2006 with al Qaeda's top benefactor, the Taliban, ceding sovereignty over its South Waziristan no-man's land under the hallucination that jihadists would somehow behave better, rather than be emboldened, if they were just left alone.[31] That agreement, which– like so much in the Pakistani/Jihadi dynamic–seemed to catch the United States by surprise,[32] "allows Taliban and al-Qaeda operatives to move across the border with impunity and establish and run training centers," according to the counterterrorism official who briefed the Associated Press. An American military official in Afghanistan admitted in late 2006, "The strong belief is that recruiting, training and provision of technical equipment for [improvised explosive devices (IEDs)] in the main takes place outside Afghanistan." Like the Bush administration, he pulled up short of uttering the P-word for fear of giving offense to our allegedly staunch allies; an Afghan intelligence official, however, was not so reticent: "Every single bomber or I.E.D. in one way or another is linked to Pakistan."[33]

In the United Kingdom, the target of a slew of al Qaeda-inspired attacks and plots in the last three years, intelligence officials fear that as many as 4,000 operatives currently embedded throughout England have been trained in Pakistan's al Qaeda camps.[34] British intelligence officials now believe al Qaeda commanders "in Pakistan . . . planned all of the recent terrorist incidents in Britain, including the suicide attacks in London on July

7, [2005,] the thwarted fertiliser bomb plot to blow up shopping centres and the alleged conspiracy to destroy transatlantic airliners."[35]

And to bring matters full circle from over two decades ago, when Pakistan first emerged as the launch-pad for the Wahhabist, Salafist, stridently anti-American jihad in Afghanistan–while the CIA looked around and managed to see nothing but pleasant, patriotic Afghan Sufis who had as much contempt for Arabs as they did for Russians–the Blind Sheikh's good friend Gulbuddin Hekmatyar is again ascendant in tribal Pakistan. He has formally joined forces with al Qaeda and his fighters now dominate north-west frontier pockets in Chitral and Dir, where one loyalist bragged to the *Washington Times* that "They have weapons stocks that remain from the fight against the Russians, but they are also buying up new weapons and have anti-aircraft guns."[36] In early summer 2007, Pakistani soldiers in the area seized explosives components from four jihadists–three Pakistanis and an Afghan–as they were en route to plant mines aimed at American and NATO convoys fighting in Afghanistan, just over the border.[37] It's an everyday occurrence. Yet, compare Dr. Sageman, the former CIA official, still towing the party line as late as 2004: "The Pakistanis favored the fundamentalist mujahedin, but there is no evidence that they later exported jihad and terrorism around the world."[38] Right.

Significant Pakistani governmental components have always had a warm spot for fundamentalist Islam, ensuring that the country remains a willing safe-haven for jihadists to train and plot attacks against the West. The frontier remains ungovernable, and, as Deputy Director Fingar conceded to Congress in his July 2007 testimony, the threat of "tribal rebellion and a backlash by sympathetic Islamic political parties" persists in staying the hand of a regime that is, at least superficially, pro-American.[39] The problem, moreover, has more to do with the Pakistani people than their hapless government: half or more support the installation of sharia, and bin Laden is far more popular than Musharraf.[40] When it comes to Pakistan, we don't seem to have come very far in the fifteen years since its then-President, Nawaz Sharif, bluntly told Egypt's President Hosni Mubarak, "We cannot control Peshawar."[41]

⌛ Chapter 7

Jihad in America

MANY OF THE ARAB-AFGHANS FLOCKED unsolicited to Afghanistan. For the most part, though, aspiring jihadists had to be recruited. And solicited or recruited, virtually all of them had to be trained. That required serious money and rigorous international outreach. The principal organization established toward just that end was called *Mektab al-Khidmat* (MAK), the Bureau of Services. MAK was founded in Peshawar and Afghanistan in 1984 by Osama bin Laden, the scion of a wealthy and extraordinarily well-connected Saudi construction empire, and his Palestinian mentor, Sheikh Abdullah Azzam, a long-time friend and ally of the Blind Sheikh (and, later, a founder of the Hamas terrorist organization). MAK was the seed from which would sprout the international jihadist terror network we now know as al Qaeda.[1]

In addition to millions in Saudi underwriting, MAK needed nodes all over the world to facilitate jihadist recruitment and training. By the late 1980s, it had them, including lucrative ones throughout the United States and Europe. The main catalyst for this outreach effort was Azzam, who, unlike bin Laden, traveled frequently and widely. A spellbinding speaker, Azzam galvanized Muslims worldwide with the call to jihad–traditional, unreservedly violent jihad, to be fought not just in Afghanistan, but in "Palestine" and, he urged, "in any place you can get."[2]

Since his death in 1989, there have been assiduous efforts to airbrush Azzam's legend, suggesting that he limited his jihadist summons to the reclamation of former Islamic lands enslaved by occupying, non-Islamic governments–such as Afghanistan and that part of "Palestine" we like to refer to as Israel. This was, for example, key to the defense strategy of

Sayyid Nosair, a co-defendant in the Blind Sheikh's eventual American prosecution. It is also echoed by such former CIA Afghanistan operatives as the aforementioned Dr. Marc Sageman.[3] Nosair needed to tidy up Azzam as part of a risible defense that he could not have conspired with Abdel Rahman to wage war against the United States because he was an Azzam follower and, perforce, that somehow meant he was pro-American. Much the same motive doubtless drives the CIA, which, having disclaimed any responsibility for the ongoing global jihad, is clearly mindful that the phenomenon grew out of the Afghanistan operations it so zealously backed and that Azzam was that phenomenon's progenitor.

Such posturing, however, deliquesces in the heat of Azzam's blistering rhetoric. As elucidated by my friend Steven Emerson, the nonpareil investigator of Islamic extremism, Azzam unabashedly preached that jihad was every bit as much and more a Muslim obligation as any of the religion's other requirements. Like his fellow al-Azhar scholar, the Blind Sheikh, Azzam urged jihad as the *sine qua non* of bringing about Islam's dominance—not just in Afghanistan or Palestine but universally. In a rousing 1988 Oklahoma City speech, for example, Azzam declared: "The jihad, the fighting, is obligatory on you whenever you can perform it. And just as when you are in America you must fast . . . so, too, must you wage jihad. The word *jihad* means fighting only, fighting with the sword."[4]

Blindness at the Border

Sheikh Abdel Rahman, again like Sheikh Azzam, proved invaluable to the MAK efforts, globetrotting to raise funds and recruits. In this, he was helped immeasurably by the CIA's astounding indifference to the wanderings of an unabashed—and hard to miss—terrorist, widely known to have approved the murder of a head-of-state and to harbor deep disdain for America. Between 1986 and 1990, the Blind Sheikh applied for visas to enter the United States (including multiple entry visas) on at least four occasions. Only once did the State Department deny a request.[5] On each occasion, CIA officials were responsible for reviewing the applications. This should come as no surprise given the practice of assigning Agency officers to official cover roles at U.S. embassies. Diplomatic immunity, which this practice affords, is a valuable shield since espionage is universally a serious crime, and often a capital offense.[6] Consular desk work, however, has little to do with the CIA officer's principal task of unearthing vital intelligence, and the fact that the cover makes sense is no guarantee that the work will be done well.

In any event, critics have deduced that the CIA must have been in cahoots with Abdel Rahman, the more industrious ones even finding anonymous government officials to parrot their theories.[7] Nevertheless, in 1993, after it surfaced publicly that the cleric was closely associated with several accused World Trade Center bombers, the Clinton administration's State Department—with every political incentive to be suspicious of the CIA's motives for admitting the Sheikh during the Reagan and Bush-41 eras—concluded that misfeasance, not malfeasance, had been the cause.[8] The 9/11 Commission Staff, moreover, conducted a second searching inquiry and issued a monograph in August 2004, with detailed findings that largely confirmed the State Department investigation from a decade earlier.[9] The astonishing failures to keep this avowed terrorist out of our country were the result of government culture: sprawling, multi-layered bureaucracy; compartmentalized information-gathering and -hoarding; utter lack of communication on both the sending and receiving ends (in government, "cover your ass" often means writing memos, but rarely includes reading memos); and an oddly defiant ostrich ethos—especially at the State and Justice Departments—which eschews the possibility that when it comes to Islam, our usual indifference about (or mindless lauding of) religious and political convictions is irresponsible . . . to the point of suicidal.

Abdel Rahman received his first U.S. visa in 1986. At the time, he was extremely well known to American diplomats and intelligence officials in Egypt for urging the imposition of sharia law, relentlessly opposing the secular regime, and almost certainly issuing the fatwa authorizing Sadat's assassination. The Blind Sheikh, however, applied for the visa in Khartoum—having been encouraged to leave Egypt after his acquittal, and thereafter making his way to Sudan, Pakistan, Afghanistan, and elsewhere. Despite everything they knew about Abdel Rahman, U.S. officials in Egypt had refrained from including him on the State Department's terrorist watchlist–that wasn't finally done until August 7, 1987. To complete the circle, the CIA officers in Sudan, where jihadists were even then trying to wrest control of the country, failed to review the application carefully before issuing the visa.[10]

Essentially, the CIA of the 1980s was just as studiously uncurious about which jihadist was getting a U.S. visa as it was about which jihadist was on the ultimate receiving end of U.S.-backed arms, military training, and subsidies. Moreover, although most big businesses had by the mid-to-late 1980s automated to electronic databases, many of State's consular offices were still maintaining their indices on microfiche or index cards. Consular officials often relied on host country staffers to process visa applications. And, to the extent State did keep an electronic database of terrorists, it was riddled with omissions and detection-defeating spelling errors–a commonplace when English confronts a language that must not only be translated but transliterated. The failure to enter the Blind Sheikh into the system, and, later, to recognize him once he was in it, was hardly singular, recurring as it did with a depressing number of known terrorists.[11]

By 1987, the American embassy in Cairo had completed an extensive biographical profile on Abdel Rahman, providing a rich bounty of justification to deny him entry into the United States. But it proved to be of little use in April of that year, when Abdel Rahman applied for another visa. It had been compiled, you see, by the embassy's "political section," which evidently saw no need to share it with the "consular section." State had its priorities: terrorist intelligence was for the benefit of diplomats who had to interact with the Mubarak government, not for the officials whose job was to be an outer perimeter defending the American people against incoming hostiles.

Those latter officials, meanwhile, wore their special-issue government blinkers when evaluating potential hostiles. The Blind Sheikh had benignly explained in his 1987 application that he was a Muslim cleric and that the good folks at "Islamic Brotherhood Inc." of Brooklyn, New York, were asking him to spend Ramadan ministering to their, er, spiritual needs. Of course, the Sheikh's métier was the theology of jihad against secular governments, and the Brooklyn congregation was the potent seed of jihad in America. No matter. It would, after all, have been an affront to Islam, not to mention to diplomats from Muslim countries, were we to start asking whether we really needed to import *that* into our country. Certainly, it would make for some very nerve-wracking dinner parties within the vaunted "International Community." So the visa was issued, even though the application on which it was based had been rife with incomplete and misleading information–a ground all by itself for rejection.[12]

Abdel Rahman applied for another visa in Egypt in 1988, and it was originally granted. Although he was by then finally on the terrorist watchlist, the consular officials missed that. Fortuitously, though, one of the embassy's Egyptian staffers learned of the application and pointed out that the Blind Sheikh was one of the country's most famous hell-raisers. This induced the consular staff to reconsider and cancel the visa. But, again, every silver lining has a dark cloud. For reasons that defy explanation, back in those days the Immigration and Naturalization Service did not include on its watchlist everyone who was on State's watchlist.[13] To make it into INS's database, an alien would actually have to attempt to get a visa and be rejected *specifically because of his inclusion on State's watchlist.*

The Blind Sheikh had been ferreted out by luck, not by the system. One might think that once the staffer had called the Blind Sheikh's infamy to everyone's attention, someone might have double-checked the watchlist, found that he was already included, and treated the matter as if the watchlist had been a factor in the visas denial. Alas, it was not to be, and the INS was not alerted. That meant there was no fail-safe measure in place. In national security, mistakes are not supposed to be the only redundancy. Had Abdel Rahman been placed in the INS system, there was a decent chance he'd have been denied entry even if State again erroneously issued a visa . . . which it would soon do.[14]

Bottom line: the woeful tale of Abdel Rahman's breathtakingly unrestricted travel in and out of the United States, even as he urged Muslim radicals to attack and destroy our country, is not sinister. It is, instead, a story of inefficiency, political correctness, and incompetence. Why that should make anyone feel better, I don't know: Malfeasance is a lot easier to remedy than structure, culture, and human nature. But it bears underscoring that, in 1993, the CIA told the *New York Times* that it had "never sought in any way to facilitate the entry of Sheik Omar Abdel Rahman into the United States," and that its records showed "no indication that the C.I.A. ever employed or used Sheik Omar Abdel Rahman in any capacity whatsoever."[15] I looked hard and never found anything to contradict these assertions.

The Head of the Snake

Contrary to concerted efforts at Azzam revisionism, there is no real dispute about the Blind Shiekh's focus when it came to spreading jihad. He was convinced that the main culprit for Muslims, the "head of the snake," was the United States. For Abdel Rahman, America, through its support of Israel and secular Muslim regimes, as well as what he (somewhat amusingly) regarded as its control of the United Nations, was responsible for "the humiliation, degradation and filth" that Muslims faced in Egypt, elsewhere in the Middle East, and throughout the world—including in the former Yugoslavia, where, notwithstanding U.S. military efforts on behalf of Bosnian Muslims, he maintained in the early nineties that Americans were responsible for the Serbian atrocities.

The Blind Sheikh found especially contemptible American peace initiatives. Each, for him, was

> nothing but a conference for surrender and humiliation in which
> Israel can impose its conditions as it wishes. Then, those betrayers,
> dishonest, vicious Islamic rulers agree to all the conditions imposed
> by Israel. . . . Then, a secret document is negotiated between Israel
> and America in order for the United Nations resolutions to be inter-
> preted as Israel wishes. America will approve the Israeli interpreta-
> tion, and the Arab nations will abide by the Israeli interpretation

of the UN resolutions. The result is that Israel's demands will be imposed by those dishonest Muslim rulers who are running breathlessly behind America just like a dog that runs breathlessly behind you whether you call him or not.

Would that it were true. In any event, while he reviled and avidly plotted the demise of the secular regime in his native Egypt, the Blind Sheikh portrayed its president as a mere puppet who led the "surrendering [peace] conferences," and was "against Islam in every aspect of life." For Abdel Rahman, Mubarak personified the "rotten and unworthy Egyptian regime running behind America, fighting and killing Muslims on the streets and squares." The only response, he inveighed, was jihad: "A duty from God," which could not be abandoned lest the United States and Egypt accomplish their design to destroy Islam. Consequently, Abdel Rahman preached that it was a duty to perform jihad against the United States and its allies, an obligation that the "battalions of Islam . . . be in a state of continuous readiness," prepared to strike the United States at every opportunity, in the Middle East–where U.S. troops, the "enemies of God, and enemies of Islam" were stationed–or inside America herself.

Al-Kifah's Heroes

While the CIA fortified radical Islam in Afghanistan, the FBI investigated it in the United States. The Bureau and the JTTF collected mounds of intelligence on New York-based jihadists. It is fair to ask, though: toward what end? The trove should have provided powerful confirmation of an informant's insistence, in the critical months prior to the World Trade Center attack, that militants had established a New York operations base and were hatching bomb plots. Instead, the Bureau would tragically shut its sole window on the conspiracy, purporting that it could not independently corroborate such alarmist claims–even though it had duly regarded those claims as deadly serious immediately before its piqued expulsion of the high-maintenance informant.

In 1988, radical Islam had put down roots in New York City. There, at the al-Farooq Mosque on Atlantic Avenue in Brooklyn, a pair of Azzam followers—a spirited Egyptian redhead and Afghan jihad veteran named Mustafa Shalabi, and the mosque's Palestinian imam, Fawaz Damra—set up an MAK branch that became known as the al-Kifah Refugee Center, and was commonly called the "jihad office."[16] This was fitting: One of bin Laden's primary training camps, near the Afghan city of Khost, was called al-Farooq, and many prominent terrorists would pass through it over the years, including John Walker Lindh, the so-called "American Taliban" who was captured fighting alongside his fellow jihadists against U.S. forces in 2001, and Wali Mohammed al-Shehri, one of the suicide hijackers who plowed American Airlines Flight 11 into the World Trade Center on the morning of September 11, 2001.[17]

Ostensibly, al-Kifah was a Muslim charitable organization with an on-site house of worship. In the twenty years since, such arrangements have continued to prove a sound jihadist strategy. Muslim radicals grasp that, contrary to Islamic culture, freedom of conscience is part of the American character. Though they themselves tolerate no creeds outside their own fundamentalist breed of Islam, jihadists bank on our ur-toleration. Communal prayer is strongly encouraged for Muslims, and even if performed privately, ritual prayer (*salat*) shares an exalted station with alms-giving (*zakat*) among the five so-called "Pillars of Islam."[18] Instinctively, Americans are loath to comment on, much less judge, the tenets to which believers hew. This self-restraint, in our obeisance to political correctness, becomes a blindfold when minority religions are involved—even, it turns out, when the minority religion in question has a dynamic faction that would like to kill us. The wide berth Americans reflexively grant religious practices creates immense opportunities for Islamic terrorists to meet and plan in the safety of mosques. It also allows for funds, raised under the auspices of Muslim charity, to be channeled to warriors and mass-murderers. Al-Kifah created the model.

Beginning in the mid-eighties, Sheikhs Abdullah Azzam and Omar Abdel Rahman made global MAK recruiting and fundraising tours to dozens of U.S. cities.[19] It was at al-Kifah, though, that Azzam established MAK's

American headquarters, and at the al-Farooq Mosque where he convened its first "Conference of Jihad" in 1988. Among Steve Emerson's singular Azzam collection is a recording of the event, in which the firebrand cleric thundered, yet again, that the jihadist agenda was far from confined to the Near East:

> Every Muslim on earth should unsheathe his sword and fight to liberate Palestine.... The jihad is not limited to Afghanistan.... Jihad means fighting.... You must fight anyplace you can get.... Whenever jihad is mentioned in the Holy Book, it means the obligation to fight. It does not mean to fight with the pen or to write books or articles in the press, or to fight by holding lectures.[20]

At al-Kifah, this message was heard loud and clear. Young Muslim men began organizing themselves into a paramilitary force. Afghanistan was a valuable cover for these activities. The mujahideen's grit against the Soviets was much admired by those Americans who paid attention to such things, and whose familiarity with jihadist philosophy was scant. Plus, al-Kifah truly did recruit a relative handful of young Muslims who made the trek to Afghanistan. Indeed, two other veterans of the jihad were among the leaders of the rising jihad army.

The first was Mahmud Abouhalima. Like Shalabi, a tall, feisty Egyptian redhead, Abouhalima was singularly devoted to the Blind Sheikh, providing housing and protection for the cleric when he journeyed to the United States and, ultimately, when he relocated here. Besides building America's first jihad army, Abouhalima drove a cab—which, given the rigor with which our government then (as now) enforced its immigration laws, naturally qualified him for a residency visa as an "agricultural worker," tending the fecund fields of Brooklyn. Eventually, Abouhalima would join another "agricultural worker" friend of his, a Jersey City-based Palestinian named Mohammed Salameh, in doing one of those jobs Americans won't do: bombing the World Trade Center.

The other mujahid was Clement Hampton-El, who would eventually be a co-defendant in the Blind Sheikh's trial after laboring to provide explosive detonators for the spring 1993 plot to bomb New York City landmarks. A revered African-American elder statesman, and a hustler of the first order, Hampton-El had taken the Muslim name Abdul Rashid Abdullah, and was popularly known as "Doctor Rashid," though he never finished high school. At seventeen, he had joined the United States Army. There, he recalled in 1995 during five excruciating days testifying in his own defense, he'd first begun cultivating the no-nonsense, tell-it-like-it-is persona that, he indicated, was at all times his trademark—except on those occasions when the government caught him on tape maybe, possibly talking about blowing up half of lower Manhattan . . . when, of course, he was simply slinging "bullshit."

The American military was just a cesspool of racism and discrimination, incensing Hampton-El, who was moved to write complaints to the president, senators, and the inspector general. "People got a little pissed off" over his flinty propensity to Speak Truth to Power—and Power, Hampton-El recalled, tended to respond with trumped-up charges, the stockade, and, finally, a dishonorable discharge. That made it difficult to find work, so this soul of rectitude naturally began misrepresenting his service record on employment applications. He landed a job as a hospital messenger, though, as a side-line, Hampton-El recalled performing "counseling" services for end-stage polio patients.

Subsequently, he moved on to Brooklyn's Long Island College Hospital, but after a time was confronted with the lies on his employment application. Doctor Rashid took the occasion to prove himself a harbinger for what has since become the lucrative and hugely effective Muslim Grievance Industry: He accused the hospital of trying to push him into criminality and deny him "honest employment." The hospital, stunning as it may seem, caved.

It's a good thing, too. Emergency room doctors, you see, tend to become paralyzed by "shock" upon seeing traumatic injuries, so Hampton-El remembered being singled out for his ability to remain unfazed and minister to "my patients." Indeed, he related one occasion when a woman tried to commit suicide by inhaling gas in her locked apartment. First, he had to stop a foolish member of the response team from shooting the lock, which

Hampton-El (who later said he knew nothing about explosives) admonished could make the "whole place blow up." Then, thinking quickly, he leapt out an upstairs window onto the terrace below, and, despite having thus broken his "foot in like five places," let the emergency team into the apartment–and that was before he carried the woman down the stairs so she could be hospitalized!

Hampton-El became a community activist, working with the police and setting up "patrols" to keep his neighborhood free of muggers and drug dealers–"No Mugging Through Hugging," was their motto, the jihadist recalled. But, since hugging, on occasion, can be less than effective, Hampton-El also opened a martial arts do-jo and, later, a paramilitary training camp. It was in Afghanistan in 1988, though, that he truly became "Doctor Rashid." Outraged by the Soviet siege, he resolved to join the battle. After contributing $500 to Imam Damra "for the orphans and the widows and the women and children," Hampton-El experienced his first "miracle": He was bodily transported, in a space of ten minutes, from his home in Flatbush to Kennedy Airport for a flight to Peshawar. Not surprisingly, he took this as "a sign to me and myself that this was Allah making something manifest."

Eleven days after arriving in Afghanistan, stricken with malaria, Hampton-El was assigned to go out on a mission. By the time he regaled the jury with this tale many years later, it was greatly in the interest of Doctor Rashid (under indictment for waging a terrorist war against the United States) to portray himself as a healer, not a jihadi. How, after all, could anyone think an army veteran and martial arts trainer who voluntarily left his job to join an overseas war could possibly be capable of violence? Thus, Hampton-El qualified that his war mission was to accompany a team of fighters strictly "to treat the ill". . . though he conceded toting along an AK-47 and a rocket-propelled grenade launcher–you know, just in case. He now walked with a noticeable limp because, he explained, he'd stepped on a landmine (although all those broken bones from the heroic derring-do at the apartment couldn't have helped).

Triumphantly returning to New York, Doctor Rashid began making celebrity appearances and inspirational videos chortling over yet another miracle: thanks to his dedication to jihad (without fighting, of course), Allah had empowered him to walk again. Having met Shalabi in Afghanistan, he became a fixture at al-Kifah. There, he met several "beautiful people," including Abouhalima, who, Hampton-El believed, simply wanted to meet and pray with the renowned Doctor Rashid, thinking "perhaps he would get some blessings because he figured I was blessed."

Training the Jihad Army

The growing al-Kifah group used the mosque as its rendezvous point for firearms training sessions as well as more intense weekend-long field-combat exercises held in rural outposts of the tri-state area. At the latter, the jihadists-in-training experimented with a variety of explosives, including bombs fueled by propane tanks and triggered by remote detonators.

Quickly emerging as the group's most aggressive member was the aforementioned Sayyid Nosair, a naturalized American, native of Egypt, who was another of the "beautiful people" to whom Hampton-El grew attached. Though he had graduated with an engineering degree from Egypt's Hilwan University, Nosair found mostly menial jobs in the United States, settling in as a maintenance worker in the New York State court system. A dedicated student of both Abdel Rahman and Azzam, management of the new al-Kifah branch near his house in New Jersey was more tailored to his skills and enthusiasm.

Dubbed the emir of marksmanship (*remaia*) for his love of guns, Nosair would occasionally bring along his own personal swinging target to firing sessions. He even practiced shooting handguns in the attic of his home, where he kept used bull's-eyes and live handgun rounds. That home, shared with his wife and three young children, was littered with combat manuals on the preferred techniques for short-range assassinations, and the like. *Booby Traps and Explosive Traps*, for example, demonstrated how common household items could provide "imaginative methods aimed at planting charges against personnel or against equipment or bombs against the enemy." *Hand Grenades*, which he'd extensively annotated with diagrams and Arabic translations, was an account of the properties of short-range explosives. *Hidden Handguns* described the tribulations of the covert pistol assassin, ever on the look-out for a "short gun . . . that conceals with comfort but performs with a punch." In The *Tactical Edge–Surviving High Risk Patrol*, Nosair had underscored a passage in the "Rapid Assault" section, advising: "You want the situation to be one where one second there is nothing happening and the next all hell breaks loose and your goal is accomplished before the confused suspect realizes what has happened." *Storming Buildings* recommended techniques for matters such as "Room Storming," "How To Land On Roofs," and "Storming An Airplane," as well as the optimal equipment for these activities, like "explosives to open the doors outside" and "bombs that blind people temporarily." A publication entitled *Afghan Refugee Service Inc.* contained diagrams with handwritten notations on matters such as "the manufacture of primary ingredients needed to demolish any building"–describing, for example, "the construction of a small explosive device utilizing common items such as a tuna can, a nail, a wooden rod, aluminum metal shavings and a blasting cap." Interestingly, as we would learn a decade later during the post-9/11 Patriot Act debate, today's librarians and civil libertarians see no reason why we should be at all curious about what jihadists might be reading.

Nosair and Abouhalima would report to the Blind Sheikh during overseas phone calls in which each of the two furtively referred to himself as "Abu Abdallah"–*Abu* means "father of" and it is used often by Arabic speakers as either a nickname or a handy way not to use one's real name when doing so would be unwise . . . like when the police may be listening. Thus would the pair convey the progress of paramilitary training and seek the Great Man's intercession in resolving intra-jihad disputes. Nosair recorded some of these calls for later broadcast at Farooq and other area mosques where militants were recruited and funds were raised.

"Do you have any instructions for us, Sheikh," the emir of marksmanship asked in one such call.

The emir of jihad cut directly to his main interest, paramilitary training, inquiring, "How was the camp that you held?"

Nosair explained that it had run from Friday night through Monday,

and that the results had been "very good." Mindful that the weekend sessions held wider opportunities for explosives experimentation, Abdel Rahman asked, "Did you have a good agenda?"

"Yes," Nosair countered, "God willing, there will be very good
results."

In time, there would.

Nosair, meanwhile, asked if his leader had "any instructions," and
agreed to heed the Blind Sheikh's responsive admonition to "call me more
often. . . . Once a week or so, so we know what is going on with you all." And
so he did, well into 1990 when Abdel Rahman finally relocated to New York.
Keeping his eye on the ball, Nosair would assure the cleric that the al-Kifah
group had "organized an encampment, we are concentrating here."

As time proves again and again, this stress on paramilitary training
was enormously important. Estimates on the size of al Qaeda vary widely–
necessarily, because it is a highly atomized, transnational network; alarm-
ingly, because the variance underscores how little of what we need to know
has been mastered in the past two decades. Some estimates put the number
of members in the mere hundreds; others–more realistically–peg it in the
tens of thousands.[21]

The variance is due to the elusiveness of *membership* as a concept:
Should it be limited to formal inductees or expanded to account for loose
affiliation, ideological sympathy, and tactical cooperation? For example,
Mohamed Rashed Daoud al-`Owhali declined to swear *bayat*, the oath of
allegiance to Osama bin Laden taken by al Qaeda members.[22] He believed
pledging fealty to human beings transgressed Islamic principles. Yet he
met with bin Laden and other al Qaeda big-wigs, conspired with their
subordinates, and, in 1998, bombed the U.S. embassy in Nairobi, Kenya,
killing 213 people. Was he any less a "member" of al Qaeda because he
declined to take an oath? I don't think so–any more than the mafia "associate" who extorts or kills is less a part of the "family" just because he has
not experienced the thrill of the blood-drawing, holy-card-burning induction ritual reserved for "members" only. Of more moment than whether
al-`Owhali was a "member" of al Qaeda, though, is that he received para-

military training—in his case, at bin Laden's Camp Khalden in Afghanistan's Khost region.

Training is a more reliable barometer of radical Islam's strength than membership, again because of a terror network's atomized structure. Trained jihadists go back to their homelands (and elsewhere) as competent militants—able to recruit and train others, and to carry out operations, even if they have not gotten specific guidance from central command. Indeed, as we have seen since the United States began military operations against al Qaeda after the 9/11 attacks, training is the conveyor belt which produces small cells of capable operatives—what Abdel Rahman called "the battalions of Islam"—which are able to spread out and embed in target areas. It is what allows a sophisticated terror network to continue operating at a reasonable level of efficiency—for example, executing attacks in Bali, Madrid, and London; fomenting sectarian and civil strife in Iraq, Somalia, Pakistan, and Afghanistan—even when central command has been on the run and must devote much of its energy to surviving rather than plotting.[23] Al Qaeda, in fact, has put such a premium on training that, beginning in the mid-1990s, it sent its already quite capable operatives to the Bekka Valley in Lebanon where they could receive additional deadly instruction from the real pros at Hezbollah.[24]

So how many potential terrorists have been trained? Here again, our information is sketchier than anything we can take comfort in. Radical Islam has typically maintained camps in remote, lawless regions of Pakistan, Afghanistan, Somalia, and Sudan—places where our access and intelligence are sparse.[25] Al Qaeda and Hezbollah, to take the top two examples, are disciplined, compartmentalized networks, so wringing cooperation from captured low- and mid-ranking members does not necessarily give us the big picture—and even when high-ranking members are apprehended, they may lie or their information may quickly become stale.[26] Terror networks are also hyper-secretive entities—Islamic militants have maintained training camps covertly inside the United States, Western Europe, and other places where their existence may go largely undetected absent an investigation or prosecution that brings them to the fore. There is a consensus, however, that some large number of young Muslim men, no doubt in the high tens of thousands, and probably into the hundreds of thousands, have been through jihadist paramilitary training since the mid-1980s.[27] Training—including classes on bomb-construction and detonation, poison chemicals, improvised explosive devices (IEDs), assassination techniques, close-order combat, hijacking, hostage-taking, and attacking specific targets (prominently including potential American targets)—tends to be the difference between successful (or, at least, truly threatening) terrorist attacks and ambitious plans that falter because jihadist fervor is not matched by competence.

Calverton

What we now know as the imperative of training had already been internalized at al-Kifah by the summer of 1989, when some of the jihad office stirrings first came to the FBI's attention.

As a major part of its domestic security mission, the Bureau collects intelligence on "foreign powers." This is a legal term-of-art. It can denote a traditional sovereign country. It can also refer to a sub-national foreign entity (a militia or terror organization—say, the PLO, the IRA, or the Tamil Tigers—which seeks to oust or break away from the ruling regime) or a transnational terror network (such as al Qaeda or Hezbollah). In foreign counterintelligence parlance, the Afghan mujahideen were a "foreign power," which meant anyone in the U.S. appearing to abet them was potentially an "agent of a foreign power"—the term-of-art for targets of domestic national-security surveillance.

Things, though, are never so cut-and-dried with intelligence collection inside the United States. Many activities in which foreign agents are known to engage, such as espionage and terrorism, are also criminal offenses. The FBI's national security division also has law-enforcement powers, rendering it critically different from the CIA or internal-security agencies like Britain's MI-5, which are strictly in the intelligence business. The Bureau might start out an investigation intending no more than intelligence collection only to have the probe "go criminal" if indictable conduct is uncovered—and if (a *big* "if") the cost of prosecuting that conduct is not

outweighed by competing national security concerns, like the public exposure of critical intelligence sources and collection methods.

It is a fact of human life that the most valuable informant–the source
who can reveal the activities and plans of dangerous people because he
is one of the dangerous people–does not tend to cooperate out of sudden
patriotic fervor. Such people become informants because they have been
caught breaking the law. That is what gives government agents leverage to
squeeze them for information: the unpleasant prospect of lengthy imprisonment. Consequently, the American domestic security structure–syner-
gistically housing both criminal prosecution and intelligence collection
under the FBI's single roof–should be an enormous advantage. But, as we
shall see, in the 1990s it was calamitously converted into a disadvantage
by–*what else?*–the criminal justice system.

Back in 1989, though, the dual missions gave the FBI both intelligence
and law-enforcement reasons to monitor the al-Kifah jihad office. First, its
members made no secret of their affinity and fund-raising for the Afghan
mujahideen–ostensibly supporting displaced war refugees, but actually
supporting whatever was necessary to advance the jihad. Second, by assisting the mujahideen, the Brooklyn activists were potentially violating the
federal neutrality statutes. These provisions make it illegal for persons in
the United States to take up arms in or against a nation with which the U.S.
is officially at peace–as was the technical American state of play *vis-à-vis*
both Afghanistan and the Soviet Union.[28] The theory behind the law is
sound: We don't want vigilante or mercenary activities by individual Americans (or aliens under our dominion and control) to propel the nation into
international conflicts. Yet here, of course, the U.S. "peace" with the Soviets was a fig-leaf at best. It was not for nothing that they called it the "Cold
War," and besides, the CIA was actively–though indirectly and covertly–
encouraging and equipping the jihad in Afghanistan.

The al-Kifah center, the FBI soon learned, was encouraging and equipping the jihad in America. In July 1989, the JTTF set up surveillance on
the jihad office and soon discovered that, in addition to fostering Muslim
prayer and charity, it was serving as a weapons depot. On several summer

weekends, as agents covertly looked on, groups of young, mostly Arab men carried boxes of equipment out of the Farooq mosque, loaded them into vehicles, and drove them to a firing range on Calverton, Long Island. The boxes contained all manner of guns, which the men spent hours shooting in various practice drills.

The participants were a Who's Who of the budding jihad army. What's more, though there is nothing inherently illegal about honing marksmanship skills at a firing range, these men evinced every sign that they were up to no good and knew perfectly well that their activities would be of interest to police.

On July 2, for example, Nosair, Abouhalima, and Salameh joined several others loading up the cars near the mosque. At 7 a.m., the traffic was light, but the men drove slowly and evasively, obviously trying to detect whether they were being followed. Finally, they made way to Calverton, stopping en route to pray on the side of a road. Upon reaching the range, they spent the day firing at targets with an array of weapons, from high-powered AK-47 rifles to nine-millimeter semi-automatic pistols.

A nearly identical trip occurred the following weekend. As agents again snapped dozens of photographs, mujahideen veterans Abouhalima and Hampton-El led a dozen young men through an afternoon of shooting long guns and firearms with collapsible stocks.

The Bureau's surveillance initiative, however, came to an abrupt end on July 23, 1989. That sunny afternoon, Nosair and Abouhalima led a group of sixteen men through shooting drills. Among them was Nidal Ayyad, the young chemist who would later brag about his enlistment in the "Liberation Army fifth battalion" in the letter claiming responsibility for the World Trade Center bombing. As the training session continued, Nosair and Abouhalima's counter-surveillance antennae were pinging. After withdrawing from the group and huddling together inside a blue van, they dispatched one of their charges to check out a van, windows darkened, parked nearby—the perch from which FBI agents were watching and taking pictures. Abouhalima then led a group to the van, pounding on it until an agent finally responded. Consistent with Hampton-El's best-defense-is-a-good-offense approach, the jihadists bloviated about being victims of harassment based on religious bias.

"Islamophobia" had not yet come into vogue as a grievance-industry rally cry—that would be several years and several Islamic terror attacks later. But, as is reliably the case today, the posturing worked to a fare-thee-well. The Bureau and JTTF had been curious, and they had been right: Dangerous men were readying themselves to be more dangerous. They were highly worth monitoring. Nevertheless, they maintained their innocence with defiant confidence: they were legally bearing their firearms from the mosque where they legally worshipped to the shooting range where they legally blasted away. The FBI is sensitive to even the emptiest allegation that it has violated someone's civil rights. The effort was thus aborted since, as a practical matter, additional surveillance would have been much more difficult now that the agents had been "made" by their subjects.

Government is enormous, bureaucratic, and lethargic. Too often, "much more difficult" quickly becomes "not worth doing." So, in 1989, when the surveillance dried up, the investigation dried up. The *investigation*, mind you. Not the *subjects* of the investigation. They continued merrily along, scheming to execute, and then finally executing, murder, and mayhem.

The year after Calverton, Nosair would commit one of the most notorious murders in the modern history of New York City. Four years after Calverton, Abouhalima, Salameh, and Ayyad bombed the World Trade Center—an attack planned in part from Nosair's jail cell in New York's Attica State Prison; and a plot during which the jihadists consulted with Hampton-El about mixing explosives. It was cold comfort, when that finally happened, that the FBI was able to dig out vivid action photos depicting all of them.

Chapter 8

The Real Deal . . . Under Our Nose

THE BLIND SHEIKH IS THE MOST FAMOUS international terrorist ever tried in the United States, and among the most dangerous ever prosecuted anywhere. More due to these circumstances than any particular merit of my own, I've derived a certain prosecutorial sheen over the years.

After all, Osama bin Laden credits Abdel Rahman with having issued that fatwa approving the 9/11 attacks, the most horrific acts of terrorism in American history, direct from the federal penitentiary I helped put him in.[1] And every few months, it seems, jihad-world's *capi di tutti terrori* threaten new savagery if and when the Sheikh dies in American custody–as bin Laden and Zawahiri did in late September 2000, when they were joined by the Islamic Group's current leader, Rifa'i Ahmad Taha Musa, and the Blind Sheikh's son, Mohammed, at the "Convention to Support Honorable Omar Abdel Rahman." Because al Jazeera was good enough to broadcast the event, the Arab world was treated to Mohammed's plea to "avenge your Sheikh" and "go to the spilling of blood."[2] Perhaps not so coincidentally, by the way, al Qaeda bombed the U.S.S. *Cole* in Aden, Yemen, three weeks later, killing seventeen members of the United States Navy.

Occasionally, just in case we've missed the point, the Blind Sheikh's global loyalists actually do commit some massacre aimed at extorting his release. In 1997, for example, in Luxor, six Islamic Group assassins viciously shot and sliced to death fifty-eight tourists and four Egyptian police officers, for good measure inserting into one split torso a leaflet foretelling more bloodlettings unless American authorities freed their esteemed leader. The next day, the organization issued a statement explaining that one of its "unit[s] tried to take prisoner the largest number of foreign tourists possible . . . with the aim of securing the release of the general *emir* of the *Gama'at al Islamia*, Dr. Abdel-Rahman." As one would expect, the Islamic Group blamed the regrettably "high number of fatalities" not on its own Sheikh-inculcated barbarism but on "the rash behavior and irresponsibility of government security forces." Evidently, it figured more such rashness would not be difficult to prompt since additional "military operations" were promised unless the Mubarak regime agreed to "the establishment of God's law, cutting relations with the Zionist entity . . . and the return of our sheik and *emir* to his land."[3]

In March 2000, moreover, Abu Sayyaf jihadists in the Philippines kidnapped twenty-nine hostages and demanded, as part of the ransom, the Blind Sheikh's freedom, warning they would behead the hostages if their demands were not met. Authorities later found two decapitated bodies left to decompose in the place where the hostages had been held–consistent, Abdel Rahman would no doubt tell you, with the injunction of Sura 47:4 that Muslims should, upon "meet[ing] the Unbelievers in fight, smite at their necks." Four other hostages have never been accounted for.[4]

Even today, out of government for several years, I still get an occasional free publicity blast, for doing absolutely nothing, whenever stories circulate (as they did throughout 2007) that Sheikh Omar is on death's doorstep because of his failing health–health the sickly but tough-as-nails cleric has been known to manipulate into failure by prison hunger or medicine strikes launched over this or that indignity (such as being served generic tea–his Excellency prefers Lipton). And I was suddenly much in media "expert" demand for a couple of years when Abdel Rahman's self-styled "radical civil rights lawyer," Lynne Stewart, was indicted, tried, and convicted for materially supporting terrorism by helping him communicate with the Islamic Group from jail.[5]

The minor celebrity I've passively accumulated by association with the jihad's grand maestro obscures an irony: Most of the terrorists I prosecuted were not exactly the A-Team. Don't get me wrong, they were still quite dangerous. As I told our jury, one needn't be a genius to kill massively since terrorism is not exactly brain surgery–a line I got lots of mileage out of until the summer of 2007, when British authorities arrested an actual neurosurgeon, in addition to several other trained medical practitioners, in a jihadist plot to bomb targets in London and Scotland.[6]

Still, what can one say, for example, about the young Puerto Rican named Victor Alvarez? Also known (of course) as "Mohammed the Spanish," Alvarez was a bulb so dim his fellow jihadists poked fun at him—in Arabic—as they sat right next to him, amazed at his inability to keep straight which infidels were to be annihilated at which times. Upon reviewing the evidence of his complicity in the 1993 plot to bomb New York City landmarks, "Mohammed's" counsel unsurprisingly opted to argue that his client was a "borderline retard," incapable of forming the legally required "specific intent" to wage war with the United States. Now, common sense says individuals willing to commit indiscriminate mass homicide in homage to a deity they incessantly call "Allah the Most Merciful" may not be among the most well-adjusted, but I did actually worry that this defense might gain some traction in Alvarez's case. At least, that is, until Alvarez, a former Santeria devotee, opted to take the stand in his own defense, testifying that he was one of those rare borderline retards who watched the History Channel on cable television, whence he had discovered Islam. Would that he had surfed, instead, to the Cooking Channel.

When you're immersed in the battle, it's hard not to snicker knowingly at the comic blunders of the jihad's second stringers. Like Mohammed Salameh, grabbed for bombing the World Trade Center because he saw no risk in trying to reclaim the deposit he'd put down for the rental van in which the bomb had exploded. Or the Sudanese wannabe terrorists in the Landmarks plot. Determined to avoid Salameh's mistake, they resolved—in the Queens safehouse where they were mixing explosives—to use stolen, rather than rental, cars to get their bombs to the UN and the Lincoln and Holland Tunnels. That sage strategy, however, ended up delaying their operation prohibitively: it turned out that these cold-blooded jihadists were afraid to purchase hot-wired wheels on the black market—the South Bronx, you know, being a very bad neighborhood.

Why roll my eyes, though? However inept or idiosyncratic they may be, what can really be amusing about sadistic killers and their senseless attacks? Nothing really. It's not that the B-Team amused me. It didn't. Salameh, after all, *did* bomb the Twin Towers. The Sudanese would have blown the tunnels to smithereens had we given them the time to work out the kinks. Alvarez would surely have helped them . . . perhaps with the AK-47 semi-automatic rifle he contributed to the plot. Senseless attacks don't happen without low-level players. Plus, these low-level players had the benefit of significant A-Team guidance.

No, it's not that they weren't deadly serious. They were. It's just that I sat in court with them for nine months without feeling frightened. To be sure, we had impressive security. And even his royal jihadist majesty, the Blind Sheikh, seemed a less-than-dynamic figure in cuffs, whatever charisma he is said to exude for the Arabic faithful lost in translation–and perhaps because he was genial enough, in his paltry English, to call me "Sheikh Andy," with a wry, resigned smirk that always sounded like, "Man, would this ever be a different game on my home court, insha Allah!"

Face to Face with Terror

I'd love to be able to con you, like I conned myself, into believing they didn't really frighten me because I had grown up in the Bronx and just couldn't be all that impressed by terrorists who were fraidy-scared to come up to the old neighborhood. The truth, though, is they didn't frighten me because they didn't measure up . . . to one of their own. One who had frightened me plenty.

For several hours on a December day in 1994, I sat eyeball-to-eyeball across a narrow table in a Santa Barbara conference room with the real deal: Ali Abdelseoud Mohamed. He had been pitched to me as an engaging friendly by his handlers–FBI agents in Northern California with whom he was purportedly cooperating, though it quickly became clear who was picking whose pocket. By the time I got to that conference room, though, I already knew better. And if I'd needed any confirmation, it was right there in the steady glare of eyes that didn't smile as he finessed his best cordial greeting, extending a hand that, when I shook it, cooly conveyed his taut, wiry strength. Ali Mohamed was a committed, highly capable, dyed-in-the-wool Islamic terrorist. I couldn't prove it yet. But I was sure it was true—and in that moment, I understood that he knew I knew.

I couldn't prove it yet because Mohamed's astounding past was shrouded in mystery. I hadn't gotten to the bottom of it. I never did—not completely. But in small compass, he is the story of American intelligence and radical Islam in the eighties and nineties: the left hand oblivious not only to the right but to its own fingers . . . while jihadists played the system from within, with impunity, scheming to kill us all.

Of all the Islamic radicals we have come to know over the last three decades, Mohamed is easily the most intriguing. He has nonetheless been difficult for me to discuss, a happenstance that has led the writer Peter Lance to speculate that I am stonewalling to cover up egregious behavior by myself and some of my colleagues. In point of fact, I have stonewalled only Lance, with whom I declined to cooperate upon concluding, after reading some of his oeuvre, that he's an irresponsible journalist—an impression more than vindicated by the publication of his loopy book about the government's investigations of radical Islam.[7]

Actually, I have been dying for years to tell the story. I have an instinctual loathing for shameless self-promotion, of which there is more than a little in government service. I learned long ago that the stars, unlike the empty suits, don't need to tell you they're stars—you'll know it when you see it. I am very proud, however, of my role in Ali Mohamed's downfall, both because my apoplexy helped put a stop to the government's insane dalliance with one of the most dangerous people ever to come on our radar screen, and because that ultimately led to Mohamed's finally being brought to justice by two of the best prosecutors in the history of the United States—my friends Patrick Fitzgerald and Mary Jo White, who have collectively done more and sacrificed more to fight the jihadist menace plaguing our country than any combination of Americans outside our heroic armed forces.

Nevertheless, Mohamed's lurid tale has been hard to recount faithfully because key details have been classified, including, most saliently, the seminal episode critical to understanding the rest of the story: Mohamed's brief involvement with the CIA in the mid-eighties. I was surprised to learn after Lance's book was published, however, that government officials had revealed the details in 1998 (a year during which I was largely out of government[8]), and that a chatty though erratic FBI agent named Jack Cloonan had more recently given the story to Lance.[9] Though some important matters remain sealed, enough information is now in the public domain, thanks to energetic reporting by Benjamin Weiser and James Risen of the *New York Times*, to do the narrative justice. There is no way to sugarcoat it: Ali Mohamed is a window on breathtaking government incompetence.

Mohamed was born in Nasserite Egypt, in a town called Kafr El Sheik, in 1952, the year Sayyid Qutb returned and Egypt, still reeling from Israel's triumphant 1948 war for independence, churned with fundamentalist passion. A pious and clever youngster, he eventually became fluent in four languages (Hebrew, English, and French, in addition to his native Arabic) and, at seventeen, entered Cairo's military academy.[10] From there, he enlisted in the army. Drawn irresistibly to the martial life and gifted with speed, stamina and strength, Mohamed was an extraordinarily capable soldier, soaking up intelligence training and distinguishing himself in Egypt's special forces.[11] His performance led him, in the early eighties, to accompany a team of elite soldiers to the U.S. military base at Fort Bragg, North Carolina, for joint training with American forces in an annual exercise known as "Bright Star"—begun after Sadat signed the Camp David accords and began receiving U.S. aid.

Little did the Americans know that within their midst was, in fact, a member of the Egyptian Islamic Jihad terrorist organization. EIJ had extensively infiltrated the Egyptian army, as evidenced by such radicals as Lieutenant Khalid Islambouli and his confederates, who had murdered Sadat at the military parade a few years earlier. Ayman Zawahiri, by then an EIJ majordomo, had recruited members of the armed forces into secret cells since the 1970s.[12] Mohamed, a rabid fundamentalist, joined EIJ in the early eighties, became a trusted Zawahiri underling, and eventually served as a bodyguard and special projects operative for Osama bin Laden himself.[13] It is doubtless true that Zawahiri, who had an eye for talent and its uses, encouraged him to attempt the penetration of U.S. intelligence.[14] For his part, Mohamed shrewdly grasped that there was no more perilous enemy for a government than one who, like Islambouli, burrows into the system, enabling him to master its structure, understand its weaknesses, and strike when and where it is most vulnerable–all the while operating with the patina of legitimacy and exploiting the very real fact that, in government, your closest colleagues are generally the least apt to suspect you of treachery and the most likely to defend you against the suspicions of others.

In 1984, Mohamed retired from the Egyptian army as a major and took a job as a security adviser at Egyptair.[15] Around this time, he walked into the CIA's station in Cairo and offered himself as a covert agent.[16] It was a propitious time to make the approach. Though our intelligence community was in league with Sunni jihadists (like Mohamed) in Afghanistan, our nation was under siege by Shiite jihadists in Lebanon. After humiliating the United States in 1979 by storming our embassy in Tehran and detaining hostages, Ayatollah Ruhollah Khomeini's Islamic Republic of Iran created Hezbollah (the "Party of God," or Hizb Allah) in 1982. It became the world's most ruthlessly proficient terror organization–a professorate for others, including al Qaeda. A spate of kidnapping, torture, and bombing rapidly followed its formation.[17] Most infamous is the October 1983 barracks attacks in Beirut that killed 241 U.S. marines and fifty-eight French soldiers–the atrocity so often urged by Abdel Rahman as the jihadist gold standard. But the massacres actually began six months earlier, when a Hezbollah car bomb, also in Beirut, killed sixty-three people, including eight CIA officials at the U.S. embassy. By the end of 1983, the U.S. embassy in Kuwait had been struck, killing six and wounding scores of others. And by the time Ali Mohamed walked through the CIA's door in 1984, Hezbollah had followed these strikes up by bombing both the U.S. embassy annex in Beirut (killing two) and a restaurant near the U.S. Air Force base in Torrejon, Spain (killing eighteen American servicemen). That March, furthermore, Hezbollah operatives kidnapped William Francis Buckley, the CIA's station chief in Lebanon. He was whisked to Damascus and on to Tehran, where, after 15 months of torture, he succumbed to a heart attack.

Infiltration, Betrayal and Silence

Obviously, the Agency was desperate for help—the kind of help it could only get from someone like Mohamed. Interestingly, the same CIA that often pooh-poohs the notion that militant Iranian Shiites just might cooperate with militant al Qaeda Sunnis in the common goal of killing Americans, instantly recognized that, if so disposed, Mohamed, the Egytian Sunni, could blend in comfortably with Hezbollah fundamentalists. Yet the Agency was appropriately cautious. Given Mohamed's background and militant leanings, the CIA understood his approach could very well have been a set-up—by Egypt or any of several anti-American terror groups. Mohamed was thanked for coming in and told the Agency might be back to him.

Cloonan, the FBI's case agent in the investigation of Mohamed during the mid-1990s, told him the CIA in Cairo put out feelers to other stations and got a nibble of interest from Bonn. Mohamed was thus contacted and dispatched to Germany, where the Agency tasked him to penetrate a mosque in Hamburg that was a suspected Hezbollah outpost.[18] What Mohamed did not know—and the main reason I've declined to speak about him publicly—is that the tasking was, in part, a test. The Agency, Cloonan elaborated, had at least one other source (human or otherwise) providing it with information on Hezbollah's Hamburg activities.[19]

Mohamed failed the test. In classic double-agent fashion, he advised the suspected terrorist operatives that the Americans had sent him. In other circumstances, this would have given the terrorists an opportunity to use Mohamed as a channel to run a misinformation game. But because the Agency had an independent channel of its own, Mohamed's chicanery quickly became known.[20] Herein, however, lies the shadowy world of intelligence and counterintelligence—a world of deception, shifting loyalties, desperation to protect one's few truly reliable sources, and extremely restricted "need-to-know" access to information.

CIA officials now knew Ali Mohamed was not only a betrayer but at least

ENCOUNTER BOOKS

900 Broadway

Suite 400

New York, New York 10003-1239

www.encounterbooks.com
Please add me to your mailing list.

Name

Company

Address

City, State, Zip

E-mail

Book Title

a terrorist sympathizer, if not a terrorist in his own right. But did they tell him they knew? Certainly not.

Fourteen years later, after Mohamed was arrested in connection with al Qaeda's 1998 bombing of the U.S. embassies in east Africa, the *Times* tellingly reported that the embarrassed Agency–which had mind-bogglingly failed to prevent Mohamed from emigrating the United States–was "*now* say[ing] Mr. Mohamed knew he had been cut off by the agency, which never gave him a reason" (emphasis added).[21] But if the CIA was intimating that Mohamed knew because the CIA had *told* him so, that seems incredible. There would have been no upside to telling him such a thing–it would have been more valuable to monitor him without raising him up. More importantly, alerting him might have endangered their obviously valuable alternative source(s) in Germany.

From Mohamed's perspective, furthermore, had he suspected he was a hot number, the very last thing he'd have done is what he in fact did do next: seek a visa to relocate to the United States. Plus, as the *Times* elaborates, Mohamed told people in the United States that he had worked for the CIA and hoped to do so again.[22] And, once he got here, Mohamed sought government jobs–including with the CIA. Now, given that I grew up in this country, it might be understandable that I go about my days assuming federal agencies keep each other in the dark to a degree that raises what little hair I have left after a quarter-century of working closely with them. But there's no reason to think Mohamed, raised in a police state, would have known such a thing about the United States.

No, the Agency dropped Mohamed like a hot potato as a potential source, but it plainly did not *tell him* it was doing so. Now, there is no legal requirement to speak truthfully to the *New York Times*, but it is ethically wrong and tactically dumb not to do so. Assuming, as I do, that the CIA maintained a cordial tone with Mohammed but simply didn't task him to do anything further, that would allow government officials colorably to opine to the *Times* in 1998 that Mohamed "knew" he had been cut off: Not because he had *been told* the CIA was cutting him off but because–the officials would now conveniently suppose– he must have *gotten the hint* when no new assignments were forthcoming. From Mohamed's perspective, moreover, it would also make sense for him to proceed all those years just as he seems to have proceeded: in ignorance that the CIA had found him out. After all, he left Egypt for America soon after his brush with the Agency, the Agency obviously did not prevent him from doing so, and, as the CIA does not operate inside the United States, there would have been no reason for Mohamed to wonder why the Agency did not ask him for further assistance once he was here. In any event, all the dodgy misdirection would affect future calculations on both sides.

What happened next beggars credulity. Just as it had done with Abdel Rahman–and would do with two of the 9/11 hijackers many years later–the CIA failed to put Mohamed's name in the State Department's suspected terrorist database as soon as it learned he had betrayed the Agency to Hezbollah. Instead, it waited until 1985–after it learned Mohamed was already in the process of seeking the visa. The Agency made some meager preventive efforts at that point, but given the deep systemic flaws, it was too little too late. Mohamed got his visa and arrived in the United States on September 6, 1985, settling in California where he married an American citizen–a flight attendant he had met on the trip from Egypt.[23] Worse, though the CIA claims to have issued warnings to various government agencies to be wary of Mohamed, he was permitted in 1986–as a thirty-four-year-old Egyptian–to enlist as a private in the United States Army.

As it happens, I had the privilege in 2004 of working for several months at the Pentagon as a consultant to Deputy Secretary of Defense Paul Wolfowitz. I can thus attest first-hand that the United States military, while it is surely the most awesome entity in the world when it gets all its innumerable parts moving in the same direction, is the rest of the time a behemoth of such sprawl, redundancy, and infighting that the FBI, by comparison, seems a well-oiled machine. Hence, it is not remotely impossible for me to believe that a highly trained Egyptian, well beyond the normal peacetime enlistment age, who had attempted to betray the United States to Hezbollah and who made no secret of his fundamentalist Islamic leanings, was somehow able to join our armed forces at a very low level without setting off all kinds of alarms. Nonetheless, the mind reels at Mohamed's American military career, engulfed by a thick fog of confusion, unexplained gaps, and war–for the United States may have been at peace but Ali Mohamed surely was not.

Mohamed spent three years in the American army before being honorably discharged in 1989. Along with his marriage, this paved the way for his naturalization as a U.S. citizen that year. There is a considerable misinformation about his American military career, largely thanks to Sayyid Nosair and Peter Lance, who for different purposes–Nosair trying unsuccessfully to get acquitted, Lance trying unsuccessfully to sell books–have portrayed Mohamed as a top-secret, special operations commando. In truth, he enlisted in America as a lowly private, climbed no higher than E-5 sergeant, should have been discharged for serious misconduct, and never held a security clearance of any kind.

As already noted, Mohamed had managed, while a stand-out Egyptian military officer, to get himself sent to Fort Bragg, North Carolina, for joint training with American counterparts. Now in the U.S. Army, he badly wanted to get back there. Fort Bragg, locus of the John F. Kennedy Special Warfare Center to which Mohamed was soon assigned, is a home-base for our Special Operations Command which is dedicated to so-called "low-intensity combat": gritty, bloody, no-holds-barred fighting characteristic not of full-blown multi-national wars but of guerrilla insurgencies and urban terrorism.[24] The army's top anti-terrorism warriors, the Delta Force, train there. Delta had just been formed in the late 1970s and its ethos–small teams of highly independent, uniquely capable operatives who prepare for difficult, behind-enemy-lines missions, and eschew uniforms and the outward demeanor of soldiers–would have been hugely attractive to Mohamed, an alien terrorist fully capable of such physical demands who wanted to blend in and learn.

Government officials told the *New York Times* that Mohamed never became a Delta Force member; in reality, he was a mere supply sergeant. At Fort Bragg, however, he received specialized instruction, including paratrooper drills, and, as in Egypt, his performance was superior. "You have separated yourself from your peers, and I have taken notice," one senior officer, Captain Brian R. Layer, wrote of Mohamed in a 1987 commendation.[25] Yet other American soldiers, a tad more grounded in the real world, took notice that on the long runs he would go on to maintain his peak conditioning, Mohamed would listen to recitations of the Qur'an on his Walkman.[26] Though his more credulous peers—of which there were distressingly many—regarded Mohamed as an American, and one who seemed as patriotic as any volunteer soldier, a more intuitive official later told the *Times* the Egyptian's devotion to Muslim fundamentalism was palpable. "You could sit and have lunch with him, and he'd be as nice as pie," the official recalled. "But if the call came in to blow you up, there is no question in my mind that Ali would blow you up."[27] A decade later, Mohamed would tell us law-enforcement types that attacks against the United States do not even require a fatwa, so "obvious" is it that America is the enemy of Islam.[28]

I believe, though I don't know, that Mohamed may have been under consideration for induction into our special forces. He certainly had a number of attributes that would have come in handy: skill, endurance, language proficiency, cultural awareness, and, out of uniform, he would not at first blush have appeared as an American military operative. But whatever Mohamed's hopes and the army's intentions may have been, it was not to be. His brief American military career was tinged by the bizarre. For example, Mohamed now got to experience the Bright Star exercises from the other perspective: as one of the American soldiers assigned to joint training in Egypt—sent, no doubt, because he spoke the language. Except, alas, the Egyptian police state does not look kindly on its citizens' enlisting in the military of a foreign country. Mohamed had to be put on a plane and high-tailed back to the United States to prevent an embarrassing international incident.

Jihad in the American Army — Is That a Problem?

Stranger still, in 1988, due to go on leave for several weeks, Mohamed requested permission to travel to Pakistan, making no bones about the fact that his true intention was to make his way to Afghanistan to fight with the mujahideen–raising the specter of an active-duty American soldier engaging in combat against Soviet forces, and the hair-raising storm his capture or killing would have caused. Take your pick about what is more insane here, I have never been able to make up my mind: The fact that Mohamed told his superiors what he was planning to do, the fact that after being told not to go he went anyway, the fact that he bragged about doing so upon returning, or the fact that he was not court-martialed.

Mohamed had clearly gotten comfortable with his commander, Lieutenant Colonel Robert C. Anderson–to the point, Anderson later reminisced to the *Times*, that they had argued about the famously murdered Egyptian president whom Anderson thought a great patriot only to hear Mohamed counter, "Anwar Sadat was a traitor and had to go."[29] Anderson, now retired and available to complain about the failings of every other governmental arm (especially the CIA) when it comes to the bumbling that allowed Mohamed to infiltrate, actually bragged, according to Lance, about being the brain behind the decision to keep Mohamed around at the JFK Special Warfare Center. I'm sort of surprised that the Bush State Department has not yet grabbed him for a spot in its energetic Muslim Outreach programs. Astonishingly, Anderson believed Mohamed "was a little afraid of me" because "I had the power to remove him at any time I so desired." The kindly commander, overlooking the Egyptian's unconcealed Islamic radicalism, decided instead that it would be useful to retain Mohamed as a "training aid" for personnel who might eventually be assigned to Middle East hotspots.[30] Perhaps this provides an inkling as to why Mohamed felt confident enough to inform Anderson in 1988 that he was going to Afghanistan–to "kill Russians," as he told other friends–and that he planned to do it, in contravention of military protocols, by flying to Paris and then using fraudulent documentation to get to the fighting.[31]

Anderson related to the *Times* that he told Mohamed not to go. Mohamed was so afraid of Anderson that . . . he went anyway. Anderson was sufficiently concerned that he and another officer shot a memorandum up the intelligence chain, but no action seems ever to have been taken. Mohamed, nevertheless, returned from his trip after about a month, shorn of several pounds and trumpeting that he had killed several Soviets, including two special forces members whose belts he readily displayed to Anderson—mementos from the jihad. Government officials subsequently conceded to the *Times* that Mohamed had gone to Afghanistan, taking pains to caution the Gray Lady that "there is no specific evidence that he killed Russian soldiers," and dismissing the belts as souvenirs probably purchased at an Afghan bazaar. We are, of course, without "specific evidence" of a good many things in life we can nonetheless be fairly certain have occurred.[32]

One thing surely did happen in Afghanistan: Ali Mohamed conducted low-intensity warfare training for Arab-Afghan jihadists, the recruits drawn to the fray by Abdullah Azzam and Omar Abdel Rahman, and bankrolled by Osama bin Laden's personal fortune and impressive fundraising. Mohamed also appears to have had contact with Afghan tribal leaders—the kind with whom Azzam, Abdel Rahman, and bin Laden often rubbed elbows but who, the CIA figures, wanted nothing to do with Arabs. Upon returning to Fort Bragg, Mohamed thanked Captain Michael W. Asimos for giving him unclassified maps of Afghanistan; they had, Mohamed cheerily recounted, been greatly appreciated by Ahmed Shah Massoud—the Afghan icon who later led Northern Alliance forces against the Taliban until being killed by al Qaeda just two days before 9/11.[33]

Anderson, flabbergasted by Mohamed's brazen defiance, recounted for Lance that he both wrote a lengthy memo complaining about the Egyptian's self-proclaimed jihadist exploits and inquired whether an American soldier might not rate a court-martial for engaging in unauthorized armed combat with Soviet forces during what then seemed like the height (but turned out to be the sunset) of the Cold War.[34] Whatever stir his outrage may have caused was short-lived. Mohamed was retained at the JFK Special Warfare Center well into 1989, no small thanks to the good graces of Norville de Atkine, a retired colonel who was a top instructor at the Center.

Jihad Professor . . . for Infidels and Jihadis

As I found upon interviewing and briefly cross-examining him in 1995, Colonel de Atkine is a pleasant, engaging man, and a scholar of Middle

Eastern warfare.[35] The last place on earth he ever expected to find himself was on the stand in a packed courtroom, summoned as a defense witness for an accused terrorist like Sayyid Nosair. But there he was because, like Lieutenant Colonel Anderson, he had figured the unabashed Islamic fundamentalist hiding in plain sight 'neath his nose would be a marvelous specimen for exposing special warfare trainees to the militant mind—as if Mohamed were a clinical exercise who shut off the role once class was over rather than a full-time terrorist using his access to an inner sanctum of America's defenses to advance his cause.

As the journalist Lawrence Wright perceptively observes, "The secret to preserving [Mohamed's] double identity was that he never disguised his beliefs." "The American army," Wright adds, "was so respectful of [Mohamed's] views that it asked him to help teach a class on Middle East politics and culture and to make a series of videotapes explaining Islam to his fellow soldiers."[36] This, naturally, was an exercise in hallowed exposition, not critical inquiry. Then, as now, our government recoiled at the notion that we might actually want to scrutinize an ideology that was fueling anti-American militarism. With the hair-splitting so emblematic of academics (and which is still gospel in government circles), de Atkine rejected the notion that convictions rooted in a literalist interpretation of Islamic scripture correlated to terrorism committed by Muslim militants. "I don't think he was anti-American," de Atkine told the *Times* in a 1998 interview about Mohamed. "He was what I would call a Muslim fundamentalist, which isn't a bomb thrower."[37] Sure.

Well, de Atkine was correct about one thing: Mohamed didn't throw bombs. He planned them with sedulous exactitude. We eventually learned that he had helped establish al Qaeda's Nairobi cell beginning in 1993, conducting elaborate target surveillance that bin Laden would use four years later to execute the bombing of the United States embassy in Kenya.

Back at Fort Bragg in 1989, though, Colonel de Atkine took Sergeant Mohamed under his wing as a clerical assistant at the JFK Special Warfare school. As part of the job, Mohamed was indeed featured in a series of televised roundtable discussions in which he answered questions about Islam and the Muslim world for high-ranking officers. Without hesitation, he explained such concepts as how Islam by nature had to be politically dominant in order to survive; that Muslims eschewed nation-states, seeing themselves, rather, as a worldwide community, the ummah, obliged to spread Islam's dominion; that places not governed by sharia law were deemed *dar al-harb*, the realm of war; and that Muslims had a religious duty—they were commanded—to establish Allah's law wherever on earth it did not reign.[38]

When the army wasn't having him play himself on TV, Mohamed used the access provided by his clerical position to rifle through the school's files, pilfering old internal Defense Department communiqués (including one from the Joint Chiefs of Staff) and documents pertaining to outdated training exercises. On some weekends that spring and early summer, he would haul some of the materials, festooned by his Arabic translations and annotations, from Fort Bragg up to New York. That was where his close friend and fellow veteran of the Arab-Afghan mujahideen, Mustafa Shalabi, was running the al-Kifah Refugee Center, home of the MAK's jihad office.

In the metropolitan area, the jihadists were spreading out. Besides the al-Farooq mosque in Brooklyn, they were now also hubbed west of the Hudson River, where small mosques and companion Islamic Centers had sprouted in a section of Jersey City that teemed with Muslim immigrants from the Near East and parts of Africa. So when Mohamed came up for the weekend, Shalabi would arrange for him to teach military tactics classes in Brooklyn and Jersey City apartments. Among the jihadist recruits in attendance were Sayyid Nosair and Mahmud Abouhalima, as well as their friend Khalid Ibrahim—one of the Calverton shooting students who would eventually relocate his family to Afghanistan, though not before providing another friend, World Trade Center bomber Mohammed Salameh, with a false affidavit to help Salameh seek American citizenship.

Ali Mohamed: Fact and Fiction

To state the obvious, the sordid story of Ali Mohamed—which is not yet done—is embarrassing enough for the government. Nosair would eventually, albeit speciously, attempt to capitalize on it in his defense. It is worth pausing here, though, to note that Peter Lance, picking up the ball from Nosair, has run with it to a place no one who actually cared about the truth, much less needed to face a jury, would ever go.

Ludicrously, Lance asserts that Ali Mohamed, as a CIA double-agent, ran al Qaeda's New York cell; that he oversaw the cell's firearms training at Calverton and elsewhere; and that he was aided in these efforts by having "gained access to *top secret* training manuals and other communiqués on U.S. troop strength from the highest levels of the Pentagon" (emphasis added)–his presence at Fort Bragg providing "Zawahiri and Egyptian Islamic Jihad inside access to an array of military tactics, not to mention a keen sense of U.S. military readiness."[39] Naturally, the story wouldn't be complete without the assertion that I, along with my colleagues, knew all these things and spent years covering them up. His tome, to the extent one can slog through it, reads like a series of bad acid trips.

Of course, he might have noticed that he only had access to the Calverton paramilitary training evidence and the documents Ali Mohamed stole from Fort Bragg because the prosecution team I led *disclosed them to the defense fifteen years ago*. No one had to tell us to do so, by the way. Criminal prosecutions proceed in accordance with rules. Like most prosecutors all over America, we honored them. The proud legacy of the Justice Department and the Southern District is that no one expects a medal for doing his job.

Nonetheless, if you want to get a sense of how on top of things American counterterrorism investigators were in the early-to-mid-nineties when radical Islam was beginning its jihad against America, just consider Lance's top source: the FBI's Jack Cloonan, a study in the absorption of the self to the exclusion of the world around him–in fact, to the exclusion of the desk next to him. Lance says Cloonan explained in a 2006 interview that he "began building a profile of Ali in 1996," and was surprised that "even he"–as one of the Bureau's top New York counterterrorism investigators and the lead agent on Ali Mohamed–"didn't become aware of the 1989 Calverton training until [Cloonan's] bin Laden squad went back 'and did the data mining' seven years later."[40]

Perhaps Cloonan should have tapped one of his fellow agents on the shoulder. He might then have learned that in the Blind Sheikh trial–which was officially carried by the government as an *FBI case*–the Calverton training was publicly alleged in 1993 when we filed the grand jury's indictment. I then spent some very public trial days in February 1995 proving the training to the jury. This was not all that difficult to do given that *it was FBI agents who had taken photographs and written reports about Calverton in 1989*, the same FBI agents I put on the stand to testify about it six years later . . . a year before Cloonan claims to have unearthed it through his undoubtedly groundbreaking data-mining processes.

One might have thought that Lance, who likes to brag about how heavily footnoted his books are (as if footnoted nonsense were any less nonsense), would have realized that. Apparently, though, talking about footnotes is preferable to reading them. Just a few paragraphs before the Cloonan blather, his description of the Calverton training I was supposedly covering up is supported by a footnote which refers the reader to a court proceeding held on February 7, 1995. Well, what do you know? That turns out to be a session of the Blind Sheikh trial: One of the days I examined FBI witnesses and showed the jury the scores of Calverton pictures snapped by the Bureau to memorialize the birth of jihad in America.[41] Now, it wouldn't stun me to learn that, as late as 1996, the FBI's crack Ali Mohamed sleuth thought he needed to "data-mine" a "profile" of his subject–and yes, many agents who prize process over knowledge really do talk that way. But I can assure you that the good citizens who sat on the Blind Sheikh's jury had already mined the data and developed a profile more than a year earlier. Ali Mohamed was the plinth of Nosair's defense. He was, in fact, the subject of elaborate testimony and evidence–including painful courtroom hours spent viewing his logorrheic disquisitions on Islamic fundamentalism and Middle East politics, videotaped courtesy of Colonel de Atkine and preserved for posterity by Sayyid Nosair.

The Calverton photos would be worth a look by Lance for another reason: Ali Mohamed isn't in them. Far from overseeing the training, there is no evidence that Mohamed was even at it. What he was able to accomplish–convening classroom military studies for murderers-in-waiting because a lot of people in government dropped the ball by letting him come here—is quite bad enough without exaggerating it. But it is revisionism to the point of fiction to speak of a New York al Qaeda cell in 1989. Al Qaeda formed in 1988, but in its larval stage it was not the extensive transnational network we know it as today.[42] For example, Egyptian Islamic Jihad, of which Mohamed was a member, had a different relationship with al Qaeda in 1989 than it did, say, in 1991, when bin Laden moved his headquarters to Sudan; and a different relationship still in 1998, when Zawahiri, by then EIJ's emir, folded his organization into bin Laden's. Al Qaeda's existence, in any event, was not a prerequisite for radical Islam to plan attacks in the 1980s—just ask the family of Anwar Sadat. Al Qaeda is a product of jihadism, not the other way around.

To be clear, there was a radical jihadist cell in New York under the direction of people like Abdel Rahman, Azzam, Shalabi, Abouhalima and Nosair, who had extremely close, operational ties to what, in the late eighties, was evolving into the global al Qaeda network we know today. Ali Mohamed was a fleeting participant on the New York scene, but not a leader. He appears to have played no part in forming the group and, but for a spate of weekend classroom sessions in 1989, had little more to do with it. That's not to say he wasn't important—as already noted, training is critical for jihadists. No, Mohamed was far away from New York because he happened to have more important things to do for radical Islam. There is, for example, not a shred of evidence that he even knew about the plot to bomb the World Trade Center, much less participated in it, or, still less, orchestrated it.

I am not minimizing him. I am putting him, and what was happening in New York, in the real context of what was a global jihad in its infancy. From the time he got out of the army in 1989 until the World Trade Center was bombed four years later, when Ali Mohamed wasn't home in California, he was busy building al Qaeda's capacity in Afghanistan, Somalia, and Kenya, among other places. The meeting I had with him in 1994 was not in my home base of New York because he was nowhere near New York. I had to travel across the country to the vicinity of his U.S. domicile; he needed to fly in from halfway across the globe because he had been in Sudan with bin Laden.

There is, moreover, one small detail to mention about Lance's "top secret" training manuals and communiqués: They weren't top secret. Had they been, Ali Mohamed could not have acquired them. Lance's secret agent didn't have access to actual classified information. He was a top operative for Zawahiri, but as far as the U.S. army was officially concerned in 1989, he was a low-level clerk who didn't rate a security clearance.

Don't get me wrong: The documents he took were not inconsequential. They were not the sorts of things the military would want publicized, let alone shared with jihadists. At the same time, however, they did not, as Lance claims, reflect current deliberations at the "highest levels of the Pentagon," nor provide a contemporary "sense of U.S. military readiness." Far from being "top secret," they were not classified at all. Some of them were labeled with the word "secret" because, when first generated, they had been secret. But by the time Mohamed laid his eyes and grubby paws on them, they had been declassified. If they hadn't been, he couldn't have gotten physical access to them. Further, if they hadn't been, I couldn't have freely disclosed them (along with the Ali Mohamed videotapes) to lawyers for Nosair in 1993–when, Lance bizarrely claims, I began covering up Ali Mohamed's existence.

As it happens, Mohamed's preternatural interest in national defense secrets did finally rub some people at Fort Bragg the wrong way. Captain Asimos, not thrilled by the Egyptian's disclosure that he had shared U.S. Army maps with the Afghan mujahideen, recalled that Mohamed frequently tried to sell himself as someone whose talents made him suitable for inclusion in intelligence operations. Asimos later recounted for the *Times* that, during a 1988 classified war game, he was moved to tell participants to be careful what they said in front of Mohamed, who had no clearance and was not read into the exercise.[43]

Finally, just before being discharged from the service in 1989, Mohamed sought an introduction to the CIA representative at the base, something that would have been irrational–and Ali Mohamed was very far from irrational–if, as the CIA later claimed, Mohamed knew he had been burned by the Agency back in 1984. As Ben Weiser and James Risen related in the *Times*, their source, an unidentified army officer who was "unaware that

Mr. Mohamed already had a history with the agency," told a CIA official:

> Mohamed "has this burning desire to be utilized as an intelligence operative, and you're the logical guy to look at him." The meeting [between Mohamed and the CIA official] lasted about an hour, the Army officer recalled. Afterward, he said, the C.I.A. official joked that Mr. Mohamed might already be a "spook," using the slang term for a foreign espionage agent. "I just kind of laughed," the officer said. "How ridiculous that this guy could possibly be a spook matriculating in this sort of bastion of special operations activity."[44]

How ridiculous indeed. How ridiculous that a militant with Egyptian intelligence training who covertly worked for a terrorist organization would seek twice to infiltrate the CIA, then enlist in the U.S. Army, at age thirty-four, wending his way to the JFK Special Warfare Center, filching his way through the files, and trying to worm his way into classified operations. No doubt it was equally ridiculous that, upon leaving the military, Mohamed eventually applied to become an FBI language specialist—that is, a staffer fluent in Arabic, brought in by English-speaking agents to help interview sensitive sources, monitor secret wiretaps, and translate critical documents seized in ongoing investigations. Mohamed, moreover, later applied for a security clearance so he could be hired as a security guard for the classified operations of a Defense Department contractor.[45]

Those applications were unsuccessful. But Mohamed did, of course, manage to infiltrate the FBI as an "informant." That occurred in 1993. A great deal had happened in the interim.

⧗ Chapter 9

Upheaval

THE SOVIET UNION, SHOCKINGLY ON ITS LAST LEGS, announced in the spring of 1988 that it would pull its forces out of Afghanistan by the following February. The iron curtain first recognized by Winston Churchill in 1946, totemic of a bipolar divide that ruled the world for over four decades, was lifting. The stunning concession of superpower failure ushered in a period of triumph, tension, and upheaval for radical Islam. Recrudescent in the victory jihadists believed that they, that *Allah*, had won was a bipolar order of a much older vintage: The clash of Islam against *dar al-Harb*, the "realm of war" as they, like their Prophet, depicted the non-Islamic world– the *jahiliyya* reviled by Qutb and Ibn Tamiyyah that had yet to submit to Allah's law.

On the ground in Afghanistan, victory was far from complete. The Russians had left a puppet regime in place, and thanks largely to infighting spearheaded by Gulbuddin Hekmatyar, it would be three years before that government was toppled–and even that would lead to more internecine Afghan bloodshed. From the Arab jihadist perspective, however, the Russian withdrawal was the best of all worlds. The Afghans had done the bulk of the fighting, bolstered by American and Saudi aid. Radical Islam, however, claimed and *branded* the victory: The slaying of a hegemon, possible only through the intercession of Allah, but inevitable, they believed, because Allah's intercession, His *conquest*, is assured to those willing to fight for His cause.

Rhetorically, defeating the U.S.S.R. was a powerful recruiting tool. Jihadist enterprises are unique in many ways, but they feature a group dynamic very similar to other revolutionary movements. The catalyst is a core group of true believers—leaders and theorists like bin Laden, Abdel Rahman, Azzam, and Zawahiri. Drawn to this fire are the mayhem makers, savages like Ramzi Yousef and Mohamed Atta whose attachment to principles (other, perhaps, than anti-Semitism) is more superficial, and who are most attracted by the opportunity to swaddle in a noble cause the brutality to which they naturally incline and would, as night follows day, have found some other pretext to unleash had jihadism not first caught their eye. Then come the followers, committed to the cause but lacking the vision and the creative savagery to do anything but the necessary scut-work of terror. The rest, the vast majority, are the fence-sitters: potential recruits who, to varying degrees, are sympathetic to the cause but unsure about the risk of jumping in with both feet.

The magnet that lures them is ideology. What seals the deal for their active participation, though, is success. They need to believe the movement can win. It's a case of the strong horse and the weak horse, to borrow bin Laden's famously apt metaphor. People want to be with the strong horse. If you tell them fidelity to Allah will make them victorious no matter the odds, their religious conviction and a general awareness of Islam's once dominant history of military conquest suggests intriguing possibilities. But convince them that you've just knocked off a superpower, and you're no longer just an intriguing possibility. You're a winner. The fence-sitters want to be with the winner.

For Arab jihadists, being a winner against the Soviets was a double-boon. The victory allowed them to beat their chests and profit handsomely; yet they continued to reap benefits from the aftermath—the civil war—without enduring the bloody downsides the Afghans had to bear. The ongoing plight of the latter, the jihad to rid a Muslim land of the Godless Communists' proxy government, was a worthy cause and a great justification to persist in recruitment and fundraising. Yet, with the Soviets themselves gone, that struggle no longer so clearly preponderated over other "fields of jihad," as the Blind Sheikh called them. The Soviets had been the cement congealing the mujahideen. With the Soviets gone, Muhammad Najibullah, whom the Russians had installed in Kabul in 1986, was, by jihadist lights, not much different from any other puppet or oppressor—Mubarak in Egypt, the Zionist entity in Palestine, or, as Abdel Rahman repeatedly stressed, the head of the snake in America, the "source" of "every conspiracy against Islam."

Fracture in Afghanistan

Consequently, fractures began to develop in the very core of the jihadist alliance. At the moment of his greatest victory, Sheikh Abdullah Azzam's stock was rapidly falling as his protégé, bin Laden, surpassed him in influence—money, in jihadist circles as in most circles, being more prized than charisma. Azzam yearned to tack toward his native Palestine, where he had helped found Hamas as a counterpoint to Yasser Arafat's more secular-socialist Palestine Liberation Organization.[1] He found himself, however, on the wrong side of the struggle for the direction of the movement. The Egyptian rivals, Abdel Rahman and Zawahiri, were intent on a more diffuse approach, the imperative of toppling Mubarak never far from their minds.[2] Abdel Rahman, in fact, returned to Egypt in 1989 and, inexorably, incited a riot in Fayoum, resulting in still another stint in the regime's vicious prisons.[3] Azzam, meanwhile, also edged to the wrong side of the Afghan civil war, looking with increasing favor on Ahmed Shah Massoud while other Arab jihadists like the Blind Sheikh and bin Laden favored their old stand-by, Hekmatyar.[4]

With the Soviets leaving Afghanistan, American aid was scaled back, meaning the global fundraising took on added significance. Toward that end, Azzam and Abdel Rahman continued their tours. The old unity of purpose, though, was no longer as strong. Toward the end of 1988, Azzam made an American swing that took him to the usual New York area mosques, including al-Farooq. By now, the Blind Sheikh had very different ideas about how the funds collected should be distributed. Further, with his relocation to the United States on the horizon and his designs on the al-Kifah operation patent, he also had a well-entrenched coterie of Egyptian followers like Abouhalima and Nosair in a position to exert his influence, making life especially difficult for Shalabi, who, though Egyptian, was seen as Azzam's guy.[5]

On January 3, 1989, Shalabi, Damra (the al-Farooq imam), and several others from the al-Kifah contingent escorted Azzam to JFK International Airport in New York City for his flight back to Pakistan. While they waited at the terminal, an argument broke out. The commotion was such that airport security guards responded. When one of them had the temerity to touch Azzam's garments, a brawl ensued—with one of the jihadists using a pair of pliers he happened to have on hand to assault the guards. When order was finally restored, several of the jihadists were placed under arrest.[6]

The incident is interesting to look back on today. In 2006, with the 9/11 attacks still a fresh memory for air travelers hassled by ramped-up security, six Muslim imams, in the course of boarding a flight in Minneapolis, reportedly carried on in a manner transparently aimed at putting passengers in fear of a hijacking. The ploy laid the groundwork for claims of Islamophobic harassment and unconstitutional "profiling" (in a war against Muslim terrorists, Americans are expected to overlook the Muslim part). And it worked: Passengers were horrified by the scene, airport security responded, and the imams—aided by the execrable Islamic "civil rights" group CAIR (the Council on American-Islamic Relations—a Hamas spin-off with a history to terror ties)—sued U.S. Airways and the "John Doe" passengers who had quite properly reported their behavior to police.[7]

Once again, they were taking a page out of Hampton-El's playbook.

"Doctor Rashid" had been nowhere near JFK Airport the day of the Azzam scuffle. But that didn't stop him from springing into action. Upon being informed by Damra and Shalabi about the brouhaha and the possibility that his "brothers" could be prosecuted, Hampton-El submitted to the authorities a false affidavit, averring that he had "witnessed what seemed to be unfair treatment" inflicted by airport security and police during the incident. With the air of a detached bystander, Hampton-El described how he had just been dropped off by a friend at the airport when he "witnessed" a large contingent of security personnel following a group of men whom Hampton-El pretended not to know. He watched in horror, he said, as one of the security guards "attacked the other men with what seemed to be very large pliers, hitting and beating them about the face and head."

Worse, when the police showed up, the renowned straight-shooter pined that although, unlike himself of course, they had "not been there from the start of things," they nonetheless "seemed to favor airport security without knowing what had happened." Fully warmed to the task, the good "Doctor" summed up with a crescendo:

> My reason for this document is because these men seem to be Arab from the language they were speaking, and I feel injustice here in America is important, and the incident I witnessed didn't seem fair and the men attacked appeared to be mistreated. . . . I think we should set an example for other people of fair play and justice. If I am needed, I will speak in court.

Years later, cornered with his perjury during the Blind Sheikh trial, Hampton-El sputtered that he had just been kidding about offering to appear in court. After all, unlike swearing out an affidavit, "stepping up in court and standing on the witness stand" to give false testimony was not something he could see himself doing. Not at all. Anyway, he needn't have worried. Several other outraged "witnesses" submitted remarkably similar testimonials of anti-Muslim bias. The authorities imagined the liability . . . and the charges were dropped.

Azzam returned to Pakistan, but his days were numbered. Aside from the growing divergence of interests with his old ally, Abdel Rahman, by late 1989 he had lost much of his influence with bin Laden. As Lawrence Wright recounts, with al Qaeda now formed but its agenda the subject of bitter infighting, its new emir came increasingly under the sway of Zawahiri—the EIJ heavyweight fast transforming into Azzam's mortal enemy was, in addition, a medical doctor who took advantage of opportunities to bend the new boss's ear while treating illnesses bin Laden was then fighting off. And as if matters were not precarious enough, Azzam's drift toward Massoud infuriated the mercurial and savage Hekmatyar.[8]

On November 24, 1989, Azzam and two of his sons were killed by a roadside bomb in Peshawar. In death, he was lauded as a legend and a "martyr" by Zawahiri and several others who'd had every incentive to kill him.[9] After all, lionizing him was good business. For example, through the early nineties, the Blind Sheikh's Islamic Group maintained a lucrative fundraising presence in Denmark, in the same office as the "Martyr Azzam Information Center," which encouraged believers to send contributions to the "Islamic Jihad Fund" at the same address. And when Ahmed Ajaj, one of the World Trade Center bombing plotters, attempted to enter the United States in 1992, he was carrying a letter addressed to "The Martyr Abdallah Azzam Hostel" in Pakistan.

Fracture in America

Also feeling the heat now were Shalabi and Damra at al-Kifah. In their division of labor, Shalabi had always concentrated his fundraising efforts on Afghanistan, while Damra was the "emir" for what had been the less pressing but still essential jihad in Palestine, regarding which he railed in a 1989 speech that "terrorism and terrorism alone is the path to liberation."[10] A Brooklyn vignette thus unfolded in the global jihadist drama.

Abdel Rahman, aligned with bin Laden and with tentacles in al-Kifah, wanted more control over the disposition of jihad funds. This had spilled into contentious disputes by early 1990, as tempers flared openly between the Blind Sheikh's disciples and Shalabi. On one occasion, moreover, Abdel Rahman's point-man, Mahmud Abouhalima, had even punched Damra during an argument over money Abouhalima insisted should be routed to Palestinian Islamic Jihad.

Fed up, on March 24, 1990, Abouhalima and others called Abdel Rahman, who had been released from prison but was still under house arrest in Egypt.[11] Nosair recorded the conversation, in which interlocutors again used pseudonyms in addressing their emir. They whined that Shalabi was too headstrong and refused to cooperate. Having laid out the situation, a man who identified himself as "Mohammed" asked, "What are your orders, Mr. Sheikh?"

Abdel Rahman directed that Shalabi and Damra should be told, "The Sheikh orders you to meet and sort out your problems and end them, and the Islamic work should not have this type of problems."

Mohammed interjected that Shalabi had already been asked to convene just such a meeting and had refused.

"He refused?" the cleric responded, enraged. "Tell him that this is an order from the Sheikh. If he refuses then I take a different stand with him."

Abdel Rahman repeated that Shalabi should be told, "That's what the Sheikh orders us to do." In fact, he added, "Tell him that the Sheikh orders you to open your door to anyone who wants to sit with you."

"Mohammed" said he would convey those instructions, and recalled that there had been some confusion about whether Abdel Rahman had already "ordered the punishment of" Shalabi. Abdel Rahman mulled and finally opined that, for the moment, "Mustafa's" awareness that "the Sheikh [would] know" about his behavior would be punishment enough.

Abouhalima then took the phone, again calling himself "Abu Abdallah." After lamenting the difficulties that had made it impossible to speak with Abdel Rahman for so long, Abouhalima apprised his emir of the latest paramilitary developments: "We were at the camp last week with the brothers and the results are very good." Palpably concerned about government wiretaps, "Abu Abdallah" furtively added, "When we get the opportunity, we are going to tell you the results."

Abdel Rahman was clearly pleased, but stressed to Abouhalima that he must "work hard . . . and end these problems."

"These problems," Abouhalima, agreed, were limiting the New York group's effectiveness. Cryptically, he added, "I want to tell you . . . we are living here in America, Sheikh Omar. I do not want to further explain to you. You are aware of the society that we are living with."

When his emir registered a knowing concurrence, Abouhalima responded with a plea:

> If you talk to Mustafa, Sheikh Omar, and tell him to take care of us
> and tell him there is no need for disputes and problems. . . . When
> Mustafa knows that somebody talked to Sheikh Omar, he gets
> upset, very upset and never forgets. So I told him . . . even if some

of the brothers talked to Sheikh Omar, he is his emir and leader and everything at the start or at the end is going to go to Sheikh Omar.

Before ending the call, Abouhalima confessed that he had struck "Fawaz" in a dispute over money Damra had failed to turn over to "Sheikh Udah of the Islamic Jihad of Palestine." Adducing that Abouhalima had done it because it "was right," the satisfied Sheikh pronounced, "Okay. Then it is over with."

It was actually just beginning.

America's Sentries Sleep as Jihad's Emir Enters

A couple of years later, when he sought asylum in the Great Satan, Abdel Rahman plausibly claimed to the immigration service that, sometime in April 1990, Egyptian authorities had ended his house arrest and escorted him to an airport, whence he made his way to Sudan.[12] On May 2 and 3, 1990, the American embassy in Cairo alerted the embassy in Khartoum that Abdel Rahman, Egypt's "leading radical" had, in fact, left the country for Sudan. The Khartoum embassy was asked to provide any information it learned about the Blind Sheikh's activities and was warned that his plan might be to seek exile in the United States.

By this time, in addition to the fact that Abdel Rahman had been on the State Department's terrorist watch list for nearly three years, U.S. officials further knew, as the 9/11 Commission Staff later found, that he "had been arrested repeatedly in Egypt between 1985 and 1989 for attempting to take over mosques, inciting violence, attacking police officers, and demonstrating illegally, and that he had been imprisoned and placed under house arrest until he left Egypt for Sudan." Yet, astoundingly, when Abdel Rahman, as foretold, immediately made an application at the American embassy upon arriving in Sudan, a multiple-entry visa was issued to him on May 10. It turned out that a Sudanese staffer at the embassy falsely told the CIA officer working under official cover as a State Department official that Abdel Rahman was not watch-listed. The staffer had decided not to check, he later confessed, because the Blind Sheikh seemed old and infirm, and had successfully applied for nonimmigrant visas on several prior occasions—none of which, of course, should have been authorized. In turn, the CIA officer failed to check the watch list, did not scrutinize the application carefully, and was personally unaware of who the Blind Sheikh was and what warnings the embassy had received only a few days earlier.[13]

Visa in hand, Abdel Rahman left Sudan. After making brief stops in Pakistan and Saudi Arabia, he relocated to the United States on July 18, 1990, taking up residence in a home Shalabi leased for him in Bay Ridge, with Abouhalima, his oft-time companion.[14]

Eventually, he would settle in a Jersey City apartment. Ever on the ball, the State Department, six months after first learning that it had issued the visa in error, revoked it on December 10, 1990. By then, the Blind Sheikh had used it to come into our country not only on July 18 but yet again on November 15. Worse, if worse there can be, he actually used the visa to enter again on December 16, *six days after its revocation*. How? Well, although the visa revocation resulted in Abdel Rahman's being entered into the INS database for excludable aliens (the National Automated Immigrant Lookout System, or NAILS), the Blind Sheikh had avoided detection by using a slight variation on the spelling of his name. As the 9/11 Commission Staff ruefully concluded, "to identify potential terrorists, the INS watchlist needed an almost exact name match."[15] Is that a problem? Well, since I started writing this chapter I have spelled al-Kifah three different ways (spellcheck will eventually fix it, *insha Allah*). That's after about fifteen years of immersion in Arabic names—and I can tell you we make many fewer mistakes now than we did in 1990.

But wait, it gets more infuriating. The INS in New York began an investigation at the start of 1991 to determine whether grounds existed to deport Abdel Rahman for fraud in the acquisition of the visa. By midsummer, they finally had grounds. Officials told the *New York Times* that "on July 31, 1991, [investigators] found indications in a computer file that Mr. Abdel Rahman had falsified a check in Egypt and was a polygamist"; he'd made contrary representations in his visa application, meaning it had been fraudulent.[16]

Unfortunately, at that point, the visa was no longer the half of it. Six months earlier, on January 31, 1991, Abdel Rahman had sought permanent resident alien status as a "Special Immigrant, Religious Teacher." Thus, far from being bounced because of the terror watch list, the visa revocation, and the ongoing investigation, the INS responded by *granting him permanent residency* on April 8.[17]

How could such a thing happen? Well, the INS office in New York City may have been put in charge of investigating Abdel Rahman, but the Blind Sheikh sought the adjustment of status a few miles to the west, at the INS office in Newark, New Jersey. Consequently, when Abdel Rahman once again tried to come into the United States on July 31—the same day the INS discovered evidence of fraud—the authorities could detain him only briefly and let him enter: After all, he was now a green-card holder.[18]

Soft Landings and Consolidation

The Blind Sheikh's relocation to America coincided with tumult in the Near East. In August 1990, Saddam Hussein's forces invaded Kuwait, claiming it as part of Iraq and sending existential shivers down the spines of Saudi royalty. Bin Laden decried Iraq's secular Ba'athists as infidels—at the time, that is; he would later come around where Saddam was concerned. But in 1990, the Iraqi invasion represented an opportunity for the nascent al Qaeda to reassemble the mujahideen for a jihad against Iraq, to liberate Kuwait and defend Saudi Arabia against Saddam's encroachments. The Kingdom, instead, after mulling it over for what must have been at least a nanosecond, opted to cast its lot with the Americans. It permitted (indeed, pleaded with) the United States to lead a coalition that would mass forces—hundreds of thousands strong—in Saudi Arabia.

For jihadists this was too bitter a pill to swallow. Not only had they been spurned by the Saudis, their primary benefactor during the Afghan jihad. The regime's decision raised the specter of a permanent presence in the most sacred Muslim land for the planet's greatest infidel power—the power Abdel Rahman, bin Laden, and other Salafist jihadis were convinced was out to destroy Islam. This was anathema. So, even as the Americans quickly accomplished what al Qaeda had itself dreamed implausibly of attempting—the ejection of Saddam's forces from Kuwait in February 1991, after just six weeks of combat—militant Islam's leading Sunni voices blasted what they perceived as the far greater outrage: Americans ensconced in the heart of the Muslim world. Abdel Rahman summoned the "battalions of Islam" to strike the U.S. forces in the Gulf, just as Hezbollah had in Lebanon a decade earlier. Bin Laden turned on the Saudi regime—the very font of his family's enormous wealth.

The United States may have been hapless when it came to Abdel Rahman's shenanigans, but the Saudis, by contrast, would have none of bin Laden's insolence. He was stripped of his citizenship and barred from the Kingdom. And his life was in very real danger. Though al Qaeda would maintain its long established training camps in the Afghan/Pakistani border region, hostility from the Saudis—still a crucial funding source for jihadists fighting the Soviet puppet regime—meant the area was no longer safe for bin Laden. He needed to shift his base of operations, post haste.

As luck would have it, he had a soft place to land: Sudan, where Abdel Rahman's old friend and benefactor Hassan al-Turabi, was the most influential leader of the governing National Islamic Front and an intellectual powerhouse in the global jihadist movement. Turabi had helped lead a coup that swept a sharia regime into power in 1989, at which point Khartoum became an open door to jihadists the world over.[19] So a new home awaited al Qaeda's emir. All he needed to do was get there. That was no small trick. His full command structure would need to be transported, and a safe-haven designed, suitable as a home-base for a global jihad network with a growing number of targets and a commensurate number of enemies.

One man in particular was well suited for that task: Ali Mohamed.

Following his discharge from the United States Army in 1989, Mohamed had returned to his home in Santa Clara, California, splitting time among the U.S., the Near East, and eastern Africa, helping build al Qaeda's military and intelligence capabilities. He cloaked his travel in legitimacy by working in the import/export business, purchasing cars in the Persian Gulf for resale in Kenya and Tanzania, and leather products in Africa for resale in the Gulf.[20] Now, he was needed once again. Years later, Mohamed would describe the trying journey for a federal grand jury. Though bin Laden had "his own personal jet," he had to get to Pakistan from Afghanistan. Then the "tough part," Mohamed recounted, was how to move him "from Peshawar to Karachi. . . . It's a thousand miles away in very hard terrain. How to disguise him? How to get him outside the country?"[21] Nevertheless, Mohamed managed the trip, transporting bin Laden through Pakistan into India, and finally on to his new home, near Khartoum—acting, he later said, "because he loved bin Laden and believed in him."[22]

How had Mohamed learned in early 1991 that bin Laden desperately needed his help? As we sat eye-to-eye in that Santa Barbara conference room in 1994, Mohamed told me he'd received a call from his old friend Mustafa Shalabi. If Mohamed was telling the truth, he is probably one of the last people who ever spoke with Shalabi.

Under the strain of tremendous pressure from Abdel Rahman and his supporters, Shalabi feared for himself and his family. Once the Blind Sheikh was in New York, the ramifications suggested by the ominous overseas phone call the previous spring materialized in the worst way. Abdel Rahman and Shalabi clashed over al-Kifah's funds and direction. The Sheikh began bad-mouthing Shalabi. Threatened by Abdel Rahman loyalists, Shalabi moved his wife and young daughter out of the country, and began making plans for his own imminent departure.[23] Alone at home in Brooklyn on February 26, 1991, the tall, robust, and quite physically capable Egyptian opened his door to company plainly familiar to him—subsequent investigation produced no signs of forced entry. It was five days later before anyone thought to check on him. New York City police found him brutally murdered in his apartment—shot assassination-style in the head, bludgeoned, and stabbed multiple times.[24] The homicide has never been solved.

Such drastic measures would be unnecessary in the case of Fawaz Damra. Right around the time of Shalabi's killing, he abruptly decided that New York was no longer his kind of town. He left al-Kifah for more tranquil surroundings, becoming imam of the Islamic Center of Cleveland, where he raised money for Palestinian jihadists, inveighed at Jews as the "sons of monkeys and pigs," and was, it goes without saying, widely regarded in media and "civil rights" circles as an exemplary Muslim moderate right up until he was deported in 2005.[25]

Interestingly, bin Laden had already made his move, dispatching his close aide Wadih el-Hage to replace Shalabi at the Brooklyn operation. A native Palestinian, naturalized American, and convert to Islam, el-Hage had become active in the al-Kifah office in Tucson after moving to Arizona in 1987. He had visited the New York area al-Kifah offices many times, befriending Abouhalima, Nosair, Shalabi, and others. As luck would have it, he arrived at the Brooklyn jihad office on the very day Shalabi's body was discovered. Rather than taking over, though, he seems only to have used the premises for a few days before being summoned to Sudan to become bin Laden's personal secretary.[26]

The Blind Sheikh was now firmly in command. For his part, though, el-Hage did make one final stop before leaving for Khartoum. On March 11, 1991, he went to Riker's Island prison in New York City. His friend Sayyid Nosair was in custody there, awaiting trial for the murder of Rabbi Meir Kahane.

⚱ Chapter 10

Conspiracy? What Conspiracy?

ABDEL RAHMAN'S ARRIVAL IN NEW YORK was a pressure-cooker for others beyond Shalabi and Damra. It lit a fuse to the jihadist community. It was time, the emir exhorted, to stop pretending the problem for Muslims was over there someplace. The United States itself, he reiterated, was "the big evil," the "fiercest enemy of Islam," and the "puppet[eer]" behind Mubarak, other secular Islamic governments, and interloping Israel.

The Blind Sheikh's power-wielding at al-Kifah and elsewhere has been grossly oversimplified. Received wisdom has it that, with the Soviets pulling out of Afghanistan, a conflict arose over the immense fundraising pot, with Azzam and other Palestinians like Damra wanting it channeled to the struggle against Israel, mujahideen vets like Shalabi single-mindedly determined to see the jihad in Afghanistan through to the establishment of a new caliphate, and Abdel Rahman myopically trained on Mubarak, hoping to pull off the Sunni version of the Khomeini triumph in Iran that he so admired. The truth is more complex.

The Blind Sheikh went global long before there was an al Qaeda. Because he was a native of Egypt, the regime there always held a special place in his attentions. For him, though, that was a function of Egypt's special place in the ummah as the most populous Arab Muslim country, home to al-Azhar, the intellectual center of Islamic life. It was not about Egypt qua Egypt. Abdel Rahman was the mold of the modern jihadist. Nation-states, political boundaries wrought by men, were significant only insofar as they demarcated territory identifiable as part of the current Muslim heritage . . . as opposed to the eventual Muslim entitlement. If a nation had ever been under Muslim rule, it was because Allah had willed it. The triumph was Allah's and so was the nation. Muslims therefore had a duty to defend its territory and take it back from any other occupiers. This was a facile distinction, of course: Abdel Rahman also believed Allah's law was compulsory and intended by its Author to rule everywhere; therefore, if a nation was not currently under Muslim rule, it could only be due to the suppression of Islam. This is why it is foolish to draw distinctions between purportedly "defensive" (good) and "offensive" (bad) jihad—as we have seen modern apologists do in rationalizing jihad's doctrinal centrality in Islam. For fundamentalists, "defense" is in the eye of the beholder.

Tracing motivation to nationalism is the wrong way to analyze the Blind Sheikh. His frame of reference was the Muslim nation—the ummah—not Muslim (or infidel) nation-states. Like Afghanistan, Egypt was the site of a historic jihadist triumph. The elimination of Sadat did not so much decide the direction of the Egyptian nation as testify to the capacity of the ummah. Even Abdel Rahman's credible claims of being tortured in the regime's notorious prisons were not grounds for merely vindictive focus on Egypt—though there was clearly some of that. They were a reification of the Qur'an's teaching about the ummah's proper response to tyrants. For the Blind Sheikh the jihad transcended Cairo, Nasser, Sadat, and Mubarak. He didn't want to control the funds so that they'd flow to Egypt. He wanted to control the funds, period. He wanted to control *the movement*, not just the movement in Egypt.

Abdel Rahman was a tireless booster of Hamas, he supported Abouhalima in an effort to target disputed funds to Palestinian Islamic Jihad, he traveled the world to raise lucre and fighters for the Afghan mujahideen, he primed the pump for a gush of money to Bosnian Muslims, and he thundered that Muslims were bound to perform jihad not just in Egypt but wherever on earth it was necessary to establish Allah's law. It blinks reality to assume—as his unsuccessful American trial defense would later argue—that he was consumed by Egypt. He had other, and bigger, fish to fry.

Getting the Message in New York

With a quite justifiable self-image as a renowned catalyst of dynamic action, Sheikh Omar pilloried his new flock for embarrassing him by their shallow talk, talk, talk. He wanted jihad, not talk about jihad. He wasn't urging recklessness. This was, after all, the leader who targeted heads of state, and whose favorite example of an effective operation, after the Sadat murder, was Hezbollah's strike against United States Marines in Lebanon. "Child's play," he counseled, was to be avoided. Resources should be marshaled for strikes of greater impact, like bombs at army bases—although, as he had in Egypt, he agreed that bank robberies in America were permissible for the purpose of underwriting more aggression. One way or another, however, it was time to stop shying away from jihad in, and against, America.

Sayyid Nosair was listening. He continued spearheading the training activities at al-Kifah. He and several associates who had attended the Calverton firearms training—including the eventual World Trade Center bombers Mohammed Salameh and Nidal Ayyad, as well as their friend, Bilal Alkaisi—considered bombings and robberies that could further the jihadist cause.

In *America Alone*, the brilliant commentator Mark Steyn offers a compelling thesis on the disappearance of Europe as we know it.[1] It's all about demography: European nations, for a variety of reasons, encouraged uncontrolled immigration from the Near East and Northern Africa. Now, as Europeans reproduce only at, or below, the replacement rate, Muslims are breeding them into submission. Mark would have been impressed by the Blind Sheikh, who was shrewdly arguing demography a quarter-century ago.

It was, not atypically, a subject of conversation when he spoke on the phone with Nosair shortly before moving to America. The two commiserated over the Mubarak regime's programmatic encouragement of birth control in Egypt, a swelling Muslim nation where economic growth is stagnant. This initiative, they complained, was poorly timed since Eastern European Jews were stepping up the pace of emigration to Palestine. The regime, they concluded, was shoring up Jewish control of the region, not only abiding "the Jewish migration" but actually abetting it by permitting settlers "to pass through Egypt" on their way to Israel.

The most radical proponent of Jewish migration to Israel was Rabbi Meir David Kahane, founder of the Jewish Defense League (JDL) in New

York in the late 1960s. The JDL was responsible for several terrorist attacks, including a bombing campaign against Soviet targets in the United States, aimed at freeing Russian Jews to move to Israel. After emigrating to Israel himself, Kahane was elected to the Knesset, occupying a seat until the late 1980s when the party he'd started, Kach, was expelled for anti-Arab racism. (By contrast, anti-Semitism seems to be a requirement for membership in what passes for the legislature in most Muslim countries.) Kahane called, among other things, for an unapologetically expansionist "Greater Israel," which would expel non-Jews from the West Bank (Judea and Samaria) and the Gaza Strip.

During October and November 1990, Kahane embarked on a speaking tour of the United States. On the evening of November 5, he appeared in the Morgan D ballroom at the New York Marriott East Side Hotel in midtown Manhattan. His two-hour lecture called for Jews to resettle in Israel. Fifty or sixty people were in attendance. Spread out among them were Nosair, Salameh, and Alkaisi.

At the conclusion of the speech, Kahane mingled with stray audience members near the podium. Nosair approached, concealing a .357 magnum Sturm Ruger revolver, fully loaded with hollow-point rounds, its barrel shortened, the sight filed down (to avoid inadvertent hooking on clothing at the moment of truth), and the serial number obliterated—the trademarks of an assassin. Worming into a small knot of people, Nosair suddenly drew from about seven feet away, pumping two shots into Kahane, who was instantly killed.

As onlookers recoiled, Nosair began to flee, trailed by one of Kahane's coterie. At the rear door, however, he ran into a plucky septuagenarian, Irving Franklin, who struggled briefly with the murderer until Nosair again fired, striking him in the leg. As Franklin, who would survive, fell bleeding to the floor, Nosair skipped away, running out of the hotel and into the frenzied city night.

Murderers don't generally bank on hailing a cab. As he raced out to 49th Street, Nosair was almost certainly looking for a very particular yellow taxi, the one usually driven by Mahmud Abouhalima. But if Abouhalima was out there, Nosair failed to find him. The panicked, adrenalized jihadi randomly picked out a taxi, dove into the rear passenger seat, and ordered the driver to step on it, jabbing him in back of the head with the magnum. Nosair lay across the back seat, but his pursuers closed, having seen him plunge in. At a traffic light, the terrified cabby alighted, gesturing to the back seat. Nosair, magnum in hand, bolted, waving the gun to ward off a pursuer.

As he sprinted south toward 47th Street, the clock struck 9 p.m. That meant it was time for United States Postal Police Officer Carlos Acosta, fully garbed in his blue uniform, to close the Lexington Avenue post office. Acosta heard the commotion and noticed Nosair, brandishing a gun and running in Acosta's direction as others gave chase. The officer's training took over. He shifted to present a smaller target while simultaneously drawing his service revolver and identifying himself. Nosair, however, blasted from about eight feet away, his first shot striking Acosta in the chest, a second whizzing within inches of his head. Fortunately, the officer was wearing a bullet-proof vest, which deflected the first shot into his right shoulder, causing severe pain and profuse hemorrhaging, but nothing worse. Acosta retained enough control to return fire, catching the assailant with a shot to the neck. Nosair fell to the ground, blood pooling at his back, the magnum lying at his side. He was rushed to Bellevue Hospital. Though critically wounded, he survived.

In murdering Kahane, Nosair patently did not act alone—this was a jihadist plot through and through, the first the Blind Sheikh's followers executed in the United States. Cagey as ever, Abdel Rahman would not flatly say he had authorized it, but he boldly declared that to have issued a fatwa calling for Kahane's death would have been "an honor. . . . We ask Allah . . . that we be worthy to issue a fatwa to kill tyrants, oppressors and infidels." Salameh had been in constant telephone contact with Nosair prior to the assassination, and, along with Alkaisi, accompanied Nosair to the Marriott. Abouhalima very likely botched the getaway role. This dereliction, Hampton-El later told a confidante, had been responsible for Nosair's capture, and the group had considered killing Abouhalima over it.[2] Three years later, in a conversation secretly recorded by an informant, Hampton-

El explained that he, too, should have been a participant—and that Abdel Rahman counseled him to avoid calling attention to himself by visiting Nosair in prison.

It was also quickly apparent that someone other than Nosair had moved his 1983 Oldsmobile. In the aftermath of the shooting, the car was nowhere in the vicinity during a police canvass. Nevertheless, in a transparent effort to make the murder appear as a solo effort, it was parked early the next morning in a no-stopping zone near the hotel.

If, as is likely, Salameh is the one who moved the car, he was displaying the same superb judgment that led him, in 1993, to claim his deposit for the rental van into which he'd put the World Trade Center bomb. His fingerprints, and Alkaisi's, had been found in several places on the interior. More interestingly, police who searched the car found a notebook, replete with the prints of Salameh, Alkaisi, and Nidal Ayyad, in which were scribbled chemical compounds for bomb-making, an Arabic notation describing a "devil" who "want[ed] to contact the American police," and an elaborate plan to carry out an assault or robbery at a store—a plan that included a sketch and instructions: "1—When he exits from the car to the store, 2—Block him between two cars front and back and approach him while in his car. 3—Standing beside him in the car and firing upon him, one of the brothers advancing towards [illegible]. 4—Create an accident; one brother hit him from the back and when he goes down to see what happened to his car; he carries out the job."

Consciously Avoiding the Jihad

The authorities quickly realized they had a powder keg on their hands. Kahane had been a lightning rod. Nosair, it was quickly became clear, was a fanatical Muslim. Within four days of the murder, the *New York Times* was describing him as "a 34-year-old Egyptian-born immigrant devoted to strict Muslim religious practices." Remember this was 1990. Today, the Gray Lady would doubtless describe him as an "American born in North Africa" or some such. But eighteen years ago, in a news article geared at probing why Nosair might have killed Kahane, the *Times* did not flinch from the relevance of his religion, elaborating that he was a voracious consumer of Middle East news who, while at work at the criminal court in lower Manhattan, "would not listen to music and . . . spread out a rug or a piece of plastic twice a day . . . to perform his prayers at the appointed hour, . . . often read[ing] the Koran during breaks."[3]

It required no intensive scrutiny, moreover, to grasp that Nosair was part of something much bigger than himself. It was palpable from the movement of his car, the evidence in it implicating other militants, and the way the murder galvanized Muslims who flocked instantly to Nosair's defense. As if all that did not signal a broad conspiracy, other proof left no doubt–the forty-seven boxes of documents, photographs, ballistics, and other items police seized in executing warrants to search Nosair's home and work locker. Sure, it would take time to translate much of the Arabic evidence that had been recovered. But you would have to go out of your way–far out of your way–to miss that Nosair was anything but an independent actor.

The authorities decided to go out of their way.

Almost immediately, before anything approaching a competent investigation could conceivably have gotten to the bottom of things, Joseph Borelli, Chief of Detectives for the New York City Police Department (during the era of Mayor David Dinkins, coiner of the phrase "Gorgeous Mosaic"), publicly announced that the shooting had been carried out by a "lone, deranged gunman." For the FBI's part, an unidentified official told the *New York Times*, "There are three possibilities. Either the man is a lone nut. Or he's a lone nut and someone whispered something in his ear knowing he'd do it. Or there's an enormous international conspiracy."[4]

With the enormous international conspiracy staring them in the face, the federal investigators, just like Chief Borelli, went with the "lone nut" view.

Not surprisingly, a dozen years later, once radical Islam had finally destroyed the World Trade Center after eight years of anti-American attacks, the embarrassed FBI party line was finger-pointing: The "international conspiracy" angle on the Kahane homicide had stalled, the Bureau maintained, because of the New York City Police Department and the office of Manhattan District Attorney Robert Morgenthau. In 2002, FBI officials told a congressional inquiry, that the DA and the NYPD resisted attempts to label the Kahane assassination a "conspiracy" despite the apparent links to a broader network of radicals. Instead, these organizations reportedly wanted the appearance of speedy justice and a quick resolution to a volatile situation. By arresting Nosair, they felt they had accomplished both.[5]

This is revisionist claptrap. Federal authorities *never* allow themselves to be hemmed in by New York State law enforcement officials. They investigate what they choose to investigate, and they are not in the slightest bound by state theories of prosecution. If a federal probe collides with a state investigation and a turf battle develops, there are often efforts to cooperate, but just as often the competitors plough ahead separately. The feds, moreover, proceed very much aware that they hold the trump card: federal law is prosecutor-friendly while New York's state constitution is a criminal's dream come true. If federal authorities bring charges, any related state prosecution is stopped cold under New York's double-jeopardy rules. The reverse is not true: a state case does not tie the feds' hands at all because the U.S. Constitution recognizes a "dual sovereignty" exception to double-jeopardy.

Nothing prevented the FBI from pursuing a broader conspiracy angle against Nosair and his fellow jihadists. The Bureau simply decided it wasn't worth the effort. Had it been, the mountain of evidence seized from Nosair's home would not have gone ignored for three years. The reality is that in December 1990, after six weeks of investigating the possibility of a larger conspiracy, the FBI let the *Times* know it believed "more strongly than ever that Mr. Nosair had acted alone in shooting Rabbi Kahane." Indeed, investigators said "they regarded the presence of the sheik [i.e., Abdel Rahman] in New York as a tantalizing but possibly meaningless footnote," for there was, they claimed, "no evidence that the sheik had known Mr. Nosair or had ever spoken with him in private."[6] Yes indeed, no evidence . . . other than the cassette tapes seized from Nosair's home that no one had troubled themselves to analyze—recordings of Nosair bantering with Abdel Rahman about Egyptian breeding habits and paramilitary training for jihad.

Post-9/11, the similarly revisionist Borelli vigorously denied that he had ever instructed any of his subordinates "not to look at the conspiracy angle."[7] Well, it certainly seemed that way at the time. Back then, Borelli painted Nosair as a solitary ne'er-do-well who "was taking a prescription drug for . . . depression." Specifically for media consumption, he added, "The impression we're getting is that he had menial jobs here. . . . He couldn't fulfill his potential. He had a serious accident at work that crippled up his legs. He didn't see any future."[8] Taking its cue from the Chief of D's, the *Times* dutifully pointed out that manufacturers of Prozac, the antidepressant Nosair was said to be taking, "are facing many lawsuits charging that patients became far more hostile, despairing and uncontrollable than they had ever been before, mutilating themselves, attempting suicide or developing homicidal tendencies."

Prozac was not the force driving Abdel Rahman's battalions of Islam.

"Exploding . . . Their High World Buildings"

The trove removed from Nosair's house, in addition to the bullets, targets, and assassination manuals, included sheaves of handwritten notes, mostly in Arabic. Some detailed tactics and formulae for the manufacture of explosives. One notebook expounded, in a section entitled "Goals," that in "guerrilla wars"—the kind Abdel Rahman frequently urged—it made better sense to use home-made ammunition than "military ammunition that the police forces use." Other notes described an organizational structure—mirroring al Qaeda's—which made an "Advisory Council" responsible for "Training, Supplies, Housing, Foreign Affairs [and] Finance."

Most significant, however, was the extensive notebook Nosair kept, with running entries couching plans and philosophy in the argot of war. He recorded that "To those against whom war is made, permission is given to fight because they are wronged and verily Allah is most powerful in their aid." He described the "counter-psychological war against God's enemies for their attempt to demonstrate their might." He detailed the "punishment of those who wage war against Allah and his messenger: That they should be murdered or crucified or . . . their feet should be cut off . . . or they shall be exiled from the land." And chillingly, three years before radical Islam bombed the World Trade Center, and more than a decade before it annihilated that complex while also attacking the Pentagon and endeavoring to destroy the Capitol or the White House, Nosair had written:

> Before announcing the establishing of the state of Abraham in our holy land (immediately before that) to break and to destroy the morale of the enemies of Allah. (And this is by means of destroying) (exploding) the structure of their civilized pillars. Such as the touristic infrastructure which they are proud of and their high world buildings which they are proud of and their statues which they endear and the buildings in which gather their heads (their leaders).

> And without any announcement of our responsibility as Muslims for what had been done. And therefore, the enemies of God will be busy in rebuilding their infrastructure and rebuilding their morales. And they will not care much about what goes on around them more than their care about rebuilding their morale; and therefore, the chance will be available for the Muslims to repossess their sacred lands from the enemies of God, the traitors and hyprocrites who will be at this moment in a very psychological weakness from what they see around them. (And this is because the forces on which they were depending were crushed into pieces and are in a tragic collapse). [Parentheticals in original.]

For all who had eyes to see, the Kahane murder propelled this "lone, deranged gunman" into the pantheon of iconic jihad warriors. Not only Wadih el-Hage but countless members of the Abdel Rahman's budding New York militia beat a path to Riker's Island, and, later, upstate to Attica Prison, for audiences with Nosair. From the moment in late November 1990, when Nosair was moved from the hospital to the prison, he was in continuous contact with his associates, particularly his cousin and chief confidant Ibrahim El-Gabrowny (who had been on the phone with him several times in the days before the murder). El-Gabrowny not only became the coordinator for all jailhouse visits; he also formed the Nosair Defense Committee, raising funds internationally–including a $20,000 contribution from Osama bin Laden.

Though he pled not guilty when the Manhattan District Attorney charged him with murder, attempted murder and weapons offenses, Nosair brazenly used his newfound prominence to promote fundraising and recruitment for the jihad. He made rousing audiotapes, distributed by El-Gabrowny, such as one in which he brayed:

> What is happening now in Palestine is exactly what happened back in 1948. Jews' immigration to Palestine with the knowledge of all the leaders and kings of Arab countries at that time, and under the guidance of the superpowers of that time, Britain and America. The same is happening now . . . but with greater . . . numbers. . . . God the Almighty commanded us to fight. . . . We cannot establish God's rules on earth except by fighting.

Nosair also sought to stiffen his listeners' resolve with a glorious rendition of his sneak attack on Kahane:

> God the Almighty . . . will facilitate for the believers to penetrate the lines no matter how strong they are, and the greatest proof of that [is] what happened in New York. God the Almighty enabled His extremely brave people, with His great power, to destroy one of the top infidels. They were preparing him to dominate, to be the Prime Minister, someday. They were preparing him despite their assertion that they reject his agenda . . . and that he is a racist. . . . That is why [God] promised to send unto them His people of terrible warfare, until the day of resurrection. . . . So, brothers, begin the jihad! Begin the jihad! Begin the jihad! There is no honor without al-jihad.

Meanwhile, among his confederates, Nosair used the prestige with which Kahane's slaying had imbued him to spur others. He rebuked the

United States and the Jews he said controlled its government, justice system, and foreign policy. He chided those who made the Attica pilgrimage for "doing nothing," adding the incessant refrain, "I did my part, what are you doing?" Visitors seemed reticent about some of his proposals, particularly that they shoot the judge on his case. Countering the concern that such an operation would require a sharpshooter, Nosair mimicked an assassin—imaginary pistol held close to the belt while pointed upward—and inveighed, "I didn't need to be a sharpshooter."

As he said it, he looked straight into the eyes of Emad Salem. It was 1992, and he had no idea this fellow Egyptian explosives expert, a friend of his cousin Ibrahim El-Gabrowny and a sometime escort and bodyguard for the Blind Sheikh, was an FBI informant.

⌛ Chapter 11

The Informant

"ANDY, I CAN'T COME TOMORROW. I'm having an autopsy."

It was Emad. He was going into a doctor's office to have a biopsy. A *biopsy* is a minor medical procedure the patient schedules when he doesn't feel like meeting with a federal prosecutor.

In a way, I didn't blame him. It was 1994, and, for both of us, it felt like the millionth time, preparing for what would end up being six grueling weeks of testimony which would make or break our little nine-month trial of the century. So I patiently explained to my famous Egyptian witness (who mangled the odd word but spoke fluent English), that an *autopsy* was, well, what I wanted to give him at the moment. It was also, I thought upon hanging up the phone, what I was sure he was going to give me.

Emad Salem is one of the bravest men I've ever known. He was a breathtakingly effective confidential informant. Many, many people in New York City are alive today because of his heroism. He was as good a witness as I ever put on the stand or heard testify during twenty-five years of protecting, preparing, and examining witnesses. He is also, beyond a doubt, the strangest, wiliest, most impossible, most infuriating pain in the ass I ever will know if I live to be a thousand.

The FBI and JTTF agents who were responsible for "handling" him—as if such a thing were possible—often did so incompetently. For the most part, once I understood the full story, I was as empathetic as I was angry—and I was *really* angry. There was no book on how to deal with such a person: He mined singularly good intelligence from people who wanted to mass-murder Americans, and he was a high-wire act who thrived on tension and caused everyone who came into his orbit to make mistakes—including me. My blunder, like many of the agents' blunders, arose out of an effort to appease him. In a time when prosecution in the criminal justice system was our national strategy against terrorists, it gave the jihadists a valuable due process defense and could have cost us the case. That is how thin the margins are when you hand your mortal enemies the presumption that they are innocent.

Creeping Doubts about the Party Line

Like Ali Mohamed, Salem had been an officer in the Egyptian army for many years. Grand cunning is also among their shared attributes. There, however, the similarities end. Salem, who was forty-two when I met him in 1993, had received a good education by the standards of mid-to-upper class Egypt, leaving him well enough versed in Islam to function among fundamentalists. But he was by no means one of them.

I observed that Emad was a practicing Muslim, not a pious one, nor a deep thinker about Islamic doctrine. Our prep sessions would be peppered by prayer breaks . . . except when they weren't. At times, I wondered if it was passion or fashion—with him, you could never be sure of anything other than that his wheels were spinning. Terrorism, he would tell me again and again, was antithetical to Islam; so was anti-Semitism, some of his best friends being Jews. I believed him, mainly because I wanted to believe him. As it conveniently happened, what he was saying echoed my employer's party line—which is still, all these years and deaths later, the federal government's party line. He was saying it out of raw emotion which, as raw emotion tends to do, hardened into unshakable conviction.

Nevertheless, as we spent many weeks together over the course of two years, I was unsettled to find that there was not much depth in his conviction. This was in stark and disturbing contrast to the other major focus of my attention, the Blind Sheikh. Abdel Rahman had made what I instinctively considered to be lunatic assertions: The Qur'an and Hadith command Muslims to terrorize, to wage war against non-Muslims, to decapitate; they regard Muslims as superior beings and women as chattel, etc. The only problem was: When I dug deeper, I found he certainly was not twisting or perverting the scriptures as our public pronouncements blithely and hopefully assumed. The scriptures said what he said they said. To be sure, there were other scriptures, too, and they were more benign–though I did not find them "beautiful" or "moving" as the Qur'an, for example, was typically, rapturously described by Western elites (for whom hostility had, in my experience, been the default position on religion). In any event, it gnawed at me that the Blind Sheikh, whom I so wanted to see as a shallow, manipulative, homicidal maniac, had what appeared to be a deep and very coherent–albeit chilling–understanding of his faith, the faith in which he was an internationally recognized authority.

Compared to him, the self-styled "moderates" appeared to be the ones dancing on the head of a pin. When you tried to press them about the Sheikh's exegesis, there seemed to be an awful lot of argument ad hominem, and very little deconstruction of substance. For me, dealing with Emad Salem was another side of this. Emad was not a scholar and I didn't expect scholarly interpretations. But he was a very smart guy with a good Islamic education. I am no George Weigel, the brilliant Catholic theologian, but I figured, "I'm a reasonably intelligent guy with a good Catholic education, and I can relate to you the major tenets of the faith and explain how they are rationally defended against the familiar broadsides. I may not convince you. I'm not sure I'm convinced. But it would be a cogent conversation." I expected that much out of Emad, and never got it–an experience that has recurred too many times with too many other bright Muslims for me to cast it aside as an aberration.[1]

Salem's syllogism was: He was a Muslim, he was personally repulsed by terrorism and anti-Semitism; therefore, violence was not the true jihad and Jew-hatred not the true Islam, end of story. As a gesture of friendship and faith, he once gave me a beautifully bound and illustrated English translation of the Qur'an, annotated with extensive commentary and officially published by the Kingdom of Saudi Arabia. I believe I read it more closely than he did.

In the summer of 1993, I was too focused on proving my case to spend much time pondering the cosmic questions. It nettled me, though, that we ignoramuses kept talking about who was a "true Muslim" and who was "distorting the true Islam." It was, after all, unnecessary in light of our other nonsensical position that religious doctrine was none of our business—we were concerned only with those bent on slaughter, as if, somehow, there were no patent correlation between the two. Nevertheless, since we were obviously presuming to make such pronouncements about Sheikh Omar, who knew a hell of a lot more about Islam than we did, I wanted to feel like we were right not just emotionally but intellectually. As time went on, I was less confident. And since there was already a battle raging over the leadership and direction of the Muslim world, I didn't think it boded well that fundamentalists like Abdel Rahman could not honestly be dismissed as the fringe crazies I wanted them to be.

Fabulist

Salem was from that side of the Egyptian street that cherishes the secular nature of the regime and reveres Anwar Sadat as a hero, patriot, and martyr for peace. That *was* a subject on which he'd thought deeply—and in a way that created great trouble for him and even bigger headaches for me as the lawyer for the United States. As a distinguished colonel, he recounted, he had been by the reviewing stand when Lieutenant Islambouli and his accomplices rushed and opened fire. He had valiantly but vainly tried to save the President, and been wounded in the process. A spellbinding story.

If only it had been true.

Salem had been at the parade. He may even have banged his knee in the chaos when the shooting started. But he hadn't even been in uniform. He was a spectator, just one among the throng, and he hadn't come anywhere close to, shall we say, taking one for the team. Perhaps everyone is entitled to the stray fish-story. But not if you're telling it to the FBI while sitting for a background interview to become a paid informant. And not if you're repeating it, under oath, while testifying in a criminal trial.

Salem had done both. Part incorrigible braggart, part Walter Mitty, he'd rehearsed his gallant tale to credulous agents, who'd dutifully regurgitated it in their reports. Worse, he'd been involved in a traffic mishap that ended up in court when the other driver was charged with recklessness. Summoned to testify as the complainant, he'd once again spun his Sadat yarn for a New York State jury. It was, in some ways, the worst kind of perjury: Completely gratuitous. Whether he'd been an Egyptian hero, an Egyptian bystander or, for that matter, an Egyptian god was utterly irrelevant to what had happened when a couple of cars got gnarled on the streets of New York City a decade later.

When a person testifies falsely about a critical fact, there is almost always a logic to it. It is not a good thing, but it can be understood. That's critical because once you figure out why someone has lied, you can be fairly confident about when he has told you the truth—you don't have to reject everything he has said.

On the other hand, when a person falsely testifies not about a fact central to some transaction but in an ancillary and bizarre effort to misrepresent the essence of who he is, that smacks of pathology and an inability to grasp the distinction in gravity between barroom jabber and trial testimony. It calls into question not only his relation of reality but his ability to perceive reality. Every other word he tells you may be true. Indeed, I never caught Salem in a lie regarding any detail of our investigations under circumstances where—whether he knew it or not—I had independent means (such as a tape or another witness) of verifying his version of events. His lies were all about himself. But his deep personality flaw meant we could never have a comfort level about anything he said unless there was corroboration.

Happily . . . and unhappily, there was almost always corroboration. That was because Salem, a super-sleuth legend in his own mind, liked to tape things—*everything*: the investigative subjects with whom he met; the JTTF agents to whom he reported; the media people with whom he enjoyed bantering; his old colleagues in Egypt's Military Intelligence Division, whom he would regale with details of his adventures; Bill Kunstler, the famous radical lawyer who represented Sayyid Nosair; Salem's own children; his ex-wife; even his psychic (yes, his psychic). He recorded each and every one. Salem had installed a home recording system that would have made the Nixon White House blush. He would sometimes wear amateur body wires to meetings with FBI agents and cops. He was not systematic about it. When he was out of tape and wanted to make new recordings, he would haphazardly grab an old tape and record over it. But what tapes he had, he maintained–here, there and everywhere in the clutter of his home. All sixty-seven of them, capturing well over two-thousand conversations which I was just thrilled beyond words to have to share with over a dozen salivating defense lawyers.

In the end, the substance of the Salem tapes was more good than bad for the government. And yet, the fact that he had made them was a near cataclysm.

Infiltration and the Seeds of Disaster

All that, however, would not unfold until almost two years after Salem's stormy relationship with the FBI began. In April 1991, four years after emigrating to the United States, he became a confidential informant for the FBI's Foreign Counterintelligence Division when he was approached for help by an agent named Nancy Floyd. Like most FCI agents in those days, Floyd's principal concentration was the Soviet Union. Suspected Russian spies periodically stayed in a New York City hotel where Salem was working as an assistant manager. He agreed to help the FBI monitor his guests, and continued to do so over the ensuing months.

Floyd took an instant liking to Salem. As the U.S.S.R. collapsed, it no longer seemed as pressing a matter by autumn 1991 to fuss over the KGB, but Floyd sensed that Salem could be useful to the Bureau in other ways. She introduced him to her FCI colleague, Agent John Anticev of the Joint Terrorism Task Force, who, along with his partner, NYPD Detective Louie Napoli, was assigned to investigate the suspected terrorist group that appeared to be operating in the United States under the direction of the newly arrived Sheikh Omar Abdel Rahman. In particular, Anticev and Napoli were working the Nosair angle: looking at how the Kahane homicide–the murder the brass had told the press was the work of a lone gunman–fit into what little they currently knew about Nosair, Abouhalima,

Ibrahim El-Gabrowny, and others gravitating around the Blind Sheikh.

Salem was excited by the prospect. Though he'd never met the Blind Sheikh, he regarded the cleric as the archenemy of his native country, which he could now serve by helping protect his adopted country. Salem, however, had major concerns. His two children had come with him from Egypt and were now living with him in New York. He had family in Egypt who could be easy targets for Abdel Rahman's Islamic Group and other militants if it ever publicly emerged that he had helped American authorities investigate the emir of jihad. This was not like snooping around Russians. The lives of many people Salem cared about would be gravely endangered if it were ever revealed publicly that he had helped the FBI spy on the Blind Sheikh. In Egypt, the Americans could do nothing to protect his family and Mubarak's regime might be angry with him, an Egyptian citizen, if it learned he had worked for American intelligence without permission.

Salem wanted to help the FBI and, in his supreme self-confidence, believed he could infiltrate the jihad group. He would not try it, however, unless he was given iron-clad assurance that he was involved only in intelligence-gathering, just as it had been with the Russians, and not in an investigation regarding which his public testimony might one day be required. Anticev, Napoli, and Floyd gave him that promise.

That was a grievous error. It also goes to the heart of the problem with using the criminal justice system as the primary weapon against international terrorism. There are many, many circumstances in which it is more important for government to *have information* than to be able to *use that information in court*. Nevertheless, because we are a litigious society, oriented more toward individual rights than communal security, the possession of information by the government has significant legal consequences. Once it has charged any person anywhere with a crime, the government is generally required to disclose to that defendant any information it has learned—even from a confidential informant immersed in a crucial undercover operation—if that information might be helpful to the defense.

Not only, mind you, "helpful" in the sense of proving the defendant is innocent. If that were the limit of the duty, things would be simple: The government could simply dismiss the charges rather than reveal the information. That's no big deal—we shouldn't be prosecuting innocent people anyway. No, the problem is that *helpful* in this context is shades of gray. Depending on the presiding judge's subjective sense of justice, it might mean anything a clever defense lawyer could conceivably use to suggest—not *prove* but merely *suggest*—that a defendant, even a clearly guilty one, is innocent. *Helpful* also includes any documentary evidence in the government's possession that a court might deem "material to preparing the defense"—whether that information is exculpatory or not.[2]

Think of how this plays out in practice. The best intelligence is the kind that reveals the secrets of the highest-ranking players in a criminal enterprise, a terrorist organization, or a foreign power. Such secrets are held extremely close. Rank has its privileges in the underworld, as everyplace else. The main privilege is that high-ranking operatives are insulated. They deal with very few insiders. If it emerges that the government has acquired information from those dealings, it is usually not hard to figure out who the informant must have been. As a practical matter, that is, the government often cannot disclose its information without implicitly revealing its source.

Consequently, an agent could not properly promise that a source will never be exposed as a cooperator unless the agent were both empowered and prepared to commit to dismissing any case, no matter how guilty and dangerous the defendant, in which a legal obligation to disclose the cooperator's information might be triggered. No agent is ever in the position to make that promise. Decisions about whether to bring or dismiss charges are made by supervisory prosecutors in the Justice Department, not street agents in the FBI. The agent doesn't have the necessary authority. More basically, no one can predict the future with certainty. Therefore, no one—certainly no agent or prosecutor—is in a position to assure an informant that his cooperation is so much more vital to the public interest than any case that may ever be brought in the future that the United States, right now, can commit to dismissing the case rather than outing the cooperator.

You can promise to do your best. You can solemnly swear that you will make every legitimate effort to preserve confidentiality. You can say we've had a very, very high rate of success protecting our informants from disclosure. But you cannot promise that someone will never, ever be revealed or called as a witness. It's neither in your power nor legally enforceable. It's also dumb. Civilian witnesses do not know the law as well as agents presumably do—though, in Salem's case, the agents simply didn't know the law. An informant working in the incredibly tense straits of an active, undercover investigation is often an emotional wreck. He has to be able to trust, confide in, rage at, and pour his soul out to his handling agents. If the agent has to go back on a promise, it can destroy the relationship, and the investigation.

That's what happened. The agents misled Salem, Salem lied to the agents, and it ended in a disastrous parting of the ways. But it is fair to describe the parting as a disaster only if one acknowledges that the union had been a coup: The agents guessed right and Salem, on the whole, performed superbly. More's the pity.

Anticev and Napoli realized that Nosair's 1991 state murder trial for the Kahane homicide and related charges had become radical Islam's *cause célèbre*. Militants were coming out of the woodwork. The fence-sitters were being drawn to them. The movement was a gathering storm, its swirl intensified by outrage in the Jewish community. Kahane was not a hero to many American Jews, but he had his cadre of followers. More to the point, the reality-blinking effort by local authorities to pretend the attack had been the handiwork of a deranged loner insulted their intelligence as they looked out at the ranks upon anti-Semitic ranks of ardent Nosair apologists. The trial resembled a Hatfield-McCoy wedding, the bride's relatives on one side of the courtroom, the groom's on the other, and everyone waiting for breaks in the proceedings so they could have at each other again.

But the agents realized the charged atmosphere presented a golden opportunity for intelligence penetration of the jihad organization, if the forty-year-old Salem could play a part tailored to his strengths: a career Egyptian soldier, explosives and martial arts expert, who had fought against Israel, wanted to support Nosair, and was in a position to do so since he ran a jewelry business and could thus control his schedule.

It worked like a charm. Salem began attending the trial on November 4, 1991, soon introducing himself to El-Gabrowny, who devoured the cover story, especially when he saw Salem in attendance on nearly a daily basis and came to rely on him for both physical protection and the tedious menial tasks of fundraising. Quicker than anyone could have hoped, Salem was in El-Gabrowny's orbit, meeting Abouhalima, Ali Shinawy (who was the group's elder statesman), a young Sudanese up-and-comer named Siddig Ibrahim Siddig Ali (who, in 1993, would recruit Salem for the plot to bomb New York City landmarks), and the Blind Sheikh's top aide, Ahmed Abdel Sattar (whom El-Gabrowny referred to as "our next champ"–an impressive label given that the current champ was Nosair).

"Turn Your Gun on Mubarak"

Infiltrating El-Gabrowny's circle so quickly was impressive. It was nothing, however, compared with Salem's simultaneous feat: direct meetings with the Blind Sheikh himself. By late 1991, Abdel Rahman had moved to Jersey City, and at the suggestion of El-Gabrowny's associates, Salem began attending the Salaam Mosque, the Sheikh's new base of operations. He attended Abdel Rahman's lectures there, and was introduced. He also happened into a Sudanese representative of Hassan al-Turabi's National Islamic Front who was promoting an upcoming confab in Detroit, the "Conference on a Global Islamic Economy," at which Abdel Rahman was to be the featured speaker. With the El-Gabrowny association as his entree, Salem–in a forward way that could easily have backfired–offered to accompany the cleric and help provide security. It worked. He was told the Blind Sheikh was favorably disposed . . . provided that Salem would rent a van large enough for a contingent of six.

The JTTF agents jumped at the opportunity. In a government-rented van, Salem picked up Abdel Rahman and five aides, driving them from Jersey City to Detroit. On the long ride, Sheikh Omar grilled Salem about his background in Egypt, trying to trip him up on the dates of his military service. Salem rationalized his time in the Pharaoh's forces, maintaining that fighting against Jews in the 1973 War made him "a good mujahid." Abdel

Rahman would have none of it. Salem, he countered, had neither been a mujahid nor performed jihad at all since his services had been bought and paid for by an "infidel government." When Salem pretended to be upset, the Blind Sheikh explained that the best way for him to make up for the lost time would be to "turn your gun on Mubarak"–to use the shooting skills he had learned to kill Egypt's president.

Abdel Rahman elaborated that Mubarak was a tyrant and a loyal dog to the American government. The U.S., he said, was a snake's head, with Egypt and Israel as its tail. Salem, by nature aggressive and cool as a cucumber among the jihadists, was thrown for a tongue-tied loop. He may have thought he was prepared for anything, but the fiery cleric's brazenness unnerved him. In his often-paranoid, fanciful perspective, he wondered whether any of the Sheikh's other ostensible aides was, like Salem himself, a mole–but for Egypt. Did he want to be appear ready and willing to kill Mubarak?

As was his wont, Salem later "solved" this problem by further complicating it–telling his friends in Egyptian Military Intelligence what had happened, which, of course, violated the secrecy of the American investigation. Realizing this, he later explained to his American handlers that he was talking to the Egyptians. They reacted with characteristic ham-handedness: instructing him that he shouldn't do that, yet asking him, on occasion, to consult his Egyptian sources regarding issues that arose during the investigation's course. Ultimately, this would result in a classic Bureau fiasco: Though Salem had openly told his handling agents that he was consulting with Egyptian intelligence, the agents' supervisors demanded that he be polygraphed . . . to find out if he had a relationship with Egyptian intelligence.

But that was still to come. Back in the van cruising toward Detroit, Salem's noncommittal silence in the face of Abdel Rahman's proposal had not been his only faux pas. To break the tension, he thought it would be a good idea to find a music station on the radio–a major no-no with the mirthless jihadis, who think music is a tool of Satan. To make matters worse, the party's growing chariness about Salem sharply increased when, upon disembarking in Detroit, an Abdel Rahman aide discovered that Salem had brought a camera along.

The Blind Sheikh, with a long history of fending off Egypt's agents, was much more discerning than the credulous El-Gabrowny. Like a good cross-examiner, he had rattled Salem and adduced grounds to suspect him. Still, what a boon for the investigation to have captured so explosive a conversation: an unambiguous solicitation to murder a head of state!

Except . . . we didn't really *have* the conversation. We had *Salem's account* of the conversation.

How could that be? After all, the government had approved the van rental—surely, anticipating that the Blind Sheikh would be holding forth for hours on a long trip, provisions must have been made to monitor him, right? Wrong.

No Tape, No Witness

At the start of the investigation, after he so quickly won El-Gabrowny's confidence, Salem had told his handling agents he thought there was a great opportunity to record conversations. The jihadists seemed to trust him. They were not patting him down. Surprisingly, they were speaking freely. The agents, however, rejected the idea out of hand. Anticev and Napoli told Salem that if he taped subjects, those recordings would have to be treated as evidence—the JTTF would have to take them and maintain them in the official file. Evidence, they explained, is what turns intelligence into criminal charges; charges then turn confidential informants into public witnesses—exactly what Salem didn't want, and exactly what the agents said they didn't want.

Incongruously, the agents understood that it was vital to investigate radical Islam because of the danger jihadists posed, but somehow thought the danger could be managed and would never get serious enough that the government might actually want to prosecute, say, a bombing conspiracy. They envisioned continuing to use Salem as a valuable intelligence source . . . but didn't want the resulting evidence to get too good. Of course, even with a witness of unimpeachable rectitude, an electronic recording is always better than human recollection—and the more shaky the source, the less reliable the recollection. But for the JTTF, the best intelligence was the worst intelligence. Agent Floyd, in fact, went so far as to tell Salem that taping conversations was illegal—something she knew wasn't true but figured was simpler to convey and more likely to have the desired effect. As such lies often do, this one would come back to haunt.

So, there was no recording of the emir of jihad telling Salem to kill Mubarak. But there is no reason to doubt Salem's account. Abdel Rahman hadn't gone much further in the van than he typically did in pubic. He told *everyone* that Mubarak had to be eliminated. His speech in Detroit was a diatribe against Mubarak—largely a repetition of what he'd told Salem in the van. When it came to the new "Pharaoh," the Blind Sheikh was nothing if not consistent. Indeed, during his later American immigration proceedings, when Abdel Rahman faced the possibility of deportation and had every incentive to soft-peddle his belligerence, the judge, the *New York Times* reported, was jarred by both his candid testimony that "'the people' should 'rise' up against governments and leaders that do not apply Islamic law," and his stubborn refusal "to rule out 'assassination or murder' as a way to remove such leaders."[3] Maybe the cleric figured this "word of truth" had worked in Egypt, but in a non-Islamic country that frowns on assassination as a political strategy, it was probably not the best tack. In any event, by the time the United States finally filed charges that included soliciting the Egyptian president's murder, Salem's testimony about Detroit was as a drop in Sheikh Omar's ocean of anti-Mubarak vitriol.

Salem's handlers, meanwhile, compounded the hash they were making of things. Although he was now meeting with the likes of Abdel Rahman, El-Gabrowny, and Abouhalima on a nearly daily basis, Anticev and Napoli debriefed him only once or twice a week. Moreover, because Floyd had initially recruited Salem and wanted to remain in the loop, it was decided that she would write the official FBI reports (though Anticev took notes occasionally). Floyd, however, worked Soviets. She didn't know from Islamic radicals. She wasn't familiar with the players Salem talked to and lacked Anticev's and Napoli's grasp of how they tied together. The reports, consequently, were a mess. If the point was to gather intelligence, this was not exactly the way to go about it.

To add to the debacle, Salem had a poor memory. If you debriefed him right after an event, he could give you a good account. If you waited a week, as the agents often did, and five other things had happened in the interim, his recitations were spotty unless you had markers to help reconstruct his recollection . . . which, of course, his handlers didn't because they had told him not to make tapes. So, to further confuse things, the agents gave him tapes but told him he was still not to record conversations—just make notes to himself so the debriefings would go smoother.

This was foolish on a host of levels. First, Salem hardly needed the agents to give him tapes; blank tapes are cheap and he had plenty—he, after all, had been the one who suggested making tapes in the first place. By giving him tapes after they'd told him not to make them, the agents should have realized they could be misconstrued, in a nod-and-a-wink way, to be encouraging him to record conversations—an impression underscored when Salem later admitted to the agents that he had made a couple of tapes and the agents responded by . . . doing nothing—no effort to collect them, despite having lectured him about how they were duty-bound to safe-keep any recordings he made. Second, if the real problem was making the debriefings go more smoothly, the way to remedy that was to debrief Salem more often. Nothing these national security agents were doing was remotely as important as staying current on an informant who had been asked by a renowned international terrorist—the main focus of their investigation—to kill a head of state. Yet, the sporadic interview pace persisted.

Finally, if the agents' goal in discouraging the type of recording that would have been most useful—namely, the taping of actual conversations with terrorists—was to reduce the creation of evidence that might lead to Salem's becoming a public witness, encouraging him to dictate notes to himself was a lamebrain idea. Federal law requires the government to provide criminal defendants with any prior recorded statement by a witness pertaining to the subject matter of his testimony. In addition, as already noted, arguably exculpatory evidence must also be disclosed. Implicitly, that means if the government encourages a witness to record summaries, due process requires those summaries to be preserved for potential disclosure. Maddeningly, the agents were creating the worst of all worlds. They were encouraging both the creation and destruction of evidence. The created evidence was essentially useless because dictated notes are hearsay and generally inadmissible to prove a case in court—they are preserved only for memory-jogging and impeachment purposes. Once destroyed, on the contrary, the dictated notes could be extremely useful . . . to terrorists. Intentionally destroyed evidence, no matter how inconsequential it may be in the greater scheme of things, is always a catastrophe for the government. It becomes the convenient phantom of defense counsel's imagination, casting a pall of doubt and impropriety over the government's whole case.

To add to this already perfect storm, Salem decided to disregard all the contrary instructions and mixed signals: He began taping anyway. Mindful of how the Blind Sheikh's aides had reacted when he merely brought a camera to a public conference in Detroit, Salem was leery of carrying a body recorder to tape face-to-face conversations. But he rigged up the system in his home to record phone calls—figuring this would be just as good as making notes. The system, naturally, did not have a jihad-sensor. It recorded *everyone* who called, including the agents.

"We Need High-Power Explosives"

Back from the Detroit trip that had started so well but ended with Salem raising the Blind Sheikh's suspicions, Salem redoubled his efforts to remain in the jihadists' good graces. He shrewdly told El-Gabrowny what had happened in Detroit and that he was concerned Sheikh Omar and his aides—all well known to El-Gabrowny—might suspect him. El-Gabrowny was appreciative and sympathetic, advising Salem that the paranoia would pass. Meantime, Salem continued to attend Nosair's trial and made himself indirectly useful to Abdel Rahman. The Blind Sheikh was monitoring the proceedings by having an aide sit in and phone him during breaks in the action. But the aide, Emad Abdou, was not as fluent in English as Salem. Sensing an opportunity, Salem would coyly sidle up to Abdou and translate the goings-on for him. Abdou would then impress his emir with more informative reports. The Blind Sheikh had figured out a way to get regular, solid debriefings out of Salem even if the agents hadn't.

On occasion, Detective Napoli and Agent Anticev would show up at the trial even though their informant was there, an odd tactic that made for awkward moments. The agents had been poking around for over a year, especially since Nosair murdered Kahane. They were well known to the community, which took a wary but generally respectful tone with them. In role, Salem was "introduced" to Napoli and Anticev, as El-Gabrowny and Abouhalima looked on. In the chit-chat that followed, Salem foolishly bragged that he was a former Egyptian army officer and explosives expert. El-Gabrowny and Abouhalima bristled. Once the agents had moved on, they chastised Salem for running off at the mouth, drawing the wrong kind of attention to himself, and perhaps compromising his future usefulness to the group. Amusingly, this unwitting episode clearly helped Salem's credibility: El-Gabrowny and Abouhalima had to figure no real informant would do something so stupid. Thus, as time and the trial wore on, Salem became increasingly friendly with Abouhalima, who asked him many questions about explosives and complained about the fence-sitters who let worries about their loved ones deter them from jihad.

El-Gabrowny was so taken by Salem that he invited the informant to supper at his Brooklyn home one evening, treating him as if he were an uncle to the El-Gabrowny children. He raised the volume on a nearby television set as he moved Salem to the dinner table, grumbling that the FBI, surely, was bugging him. "See this tyrant lying down like a dog," he exclaimed as he showed Salem post-mortem photos of Kahane he'd gotten from Nosair's lawyers–photos seized from El-Gabrowny's home a year later when agents searched it after the World Trade Center bombing.

As the evening unfolded, Nosair's cousin consulted Salem about bomb-building. Salem began by describing how Molotov cocktails were made, but El-Gabrowny cut him off. "No," he interjected, "We need high-power explosives." More sophisticated bomb construction required explosive substances and detonators, Salem explained. Access to explosives was not the problem, El-Gabrowny countered; the problem was police surveillance. El-Gabrowny was being watched and couldn't risk keeping bomb components in his home–though he speculated that the roof of his building might be an appropriate stash.

Bombing, always an undercurrent of El-Gabrowny's intense interest in Salem, was now out in the open, and it became a frequent topic of their conversations. El-Gabrowny also encouraged Salem to get involved in paramilitary training, observing that his expertise would be a real asset and suggesting that Salem look into becoming certified as a firearms instructor since, he believed, the certification's air of legitimacy would deter law enforcement attention. Soon, the pair attended a firearms training session together, and El-Gabrowny noticed that the instructor had a machine for pressing powder into newly manufactured bullets. This inspired El-Gabrowny, who was in the construction business, to wonder whether it was worth extracting the powder in carpenter's nails for bomb-making–impractical since the goal was high-explosive impact, but a telling barometer of jihadist determination.

In the interim, Nosair's contentious trial was winding toward its stunning conclusion. A few days before it ended, Salem once again hit the bigtime. El-Gabrowny brought him, along with an Afghan mujahid named Tarek Khaterria, to Rikers Island. Salem was presented to Nosair as "a new member of the family." With El-Gabrowny's warm introduction, Nosair accepted the informant into the fold. It was a brief meeting but, unlike the Detroit trip, Salem hadn't choked. He'd been in top aspiring terrorist form. It meant there would be several more sessions with the killer who, from jailhouse sanctums, now held court in a manner befitting jihadist royalty.

⧖ Chapter 12

The Jihadist Way:
Victory and Vengeance

TRIALS, THE LATE BILL KUNSTLER ONCE TOLD ME, are won and lost in jury selection. Like much of what he said, it was a good sound-bite and a vast oversimplification. But I had to hand it to him: It was certainly true of the murder trial he won in New York state court on December 21, 1991.

To anyone of a political and legal bent of mind growing up as I did in the sixties and seventies, Kunstler was a flamboyant legend . . . or rogue. For me, he was in the latter category: the "movement lawyer"—basically, a radical Leftist with a law degree for whom laws apply only to the government—who had represented Abbie Hoffman and others in the famous 1969 "Chicago Seven" trial. But, at least when court was not in session, I found him a most charming rogue. When I met Bill, I was in my mid-thirties—around the same age as his partner and protégé, the whip-smart Ron Kuby. It was 1993, and Bill, then seventy-four and in declining health, had lost a lot off his fastball. He'd clearly had it, though, the last time he needed it: While hurling bombast for his client, Sayyid Nosair.

In one of the most outrageous injustices in modern New York history, Nosair—who had killed Meir Kahane in front of several people before shooting two others in flight—was acquitted of murdering the rabbi as well as attempting to murder Irving Franklin and Carlos Acosta. The State had thought its case so overwhelming it could afford to paint Nosair as a deranged loner whose motives were irrelevant. Kunstler had used the opening to turn the trial into precisely the political spectacle the State was trying to avoid. In selecting the jury, he had made no bones about the fact that he and Nosair "want[ed] a third world jury of non-whites, or anyone who's been pushed down by a white society."[1] The State, moreover, had called no witness who could clearly say he saw Nosair fire the shot that killed Kahane (Nosair, as he told his comrades, had fired quickly from close to his body), and, though Kahane had clearly been shot to death, the jurors wondered why one of the bullets had not been recovered.[2]

On December 21, after five tendentious weeks, the jury Kunstler had so carefully selected brought unbridled glee to the courtroom throng of Islamic activists, returning a verdict that was incontestably irrational. The jurors somehow acquitted Nosair of both the homicide and attempted murders even though they found him guilty of all the lesser charges: assault and coercion in the course of the shootings for which it had exonerated him, and unlawful possession of the firearm proved beyond cavil to have fired at all three victims—as if the .357 magnum had had a mind of its own, there being no NRA spokesman on hand to remind us that "guns don't kill people, *terrorists* kill people."

The verdict was a transparent compromise. . . unless you were a jihadist. In the latter case, it was the intervention of Allah's miraculous hand. Nosair had been delivered just as the Prophet had been delivered against impossible odds during the "Battle of the Trench," when God sent a "piercing blast of northeast wind" that caused the enemy Quraysh tribe to retreat in confusion just as they had Muslim fighters trapped in Medina.[3]

As Abouhalima and others rejoiced with Kunstler outside the courthouse, an ebullient El-Gabrowny invited Salem to a victory celebration the following day at the Abu Bakr Mosque in Brooklyn. The revelers were feeling invincible, so no one seemed to mind that Salem had taken the opportunity to videotape the festivities, like a wedding photographer capturing their glee for posterity. Thus were Mohammed Salameh, Nidal Ayyad, Ahmed Abdel Sattar, Ali Shinawi, and dozens of others videotaped in full coo as El-Gabrowny and then Siddig Ali triumphantly addressed them. Nosair wasn't quite out of the woods yet. The weapons offenses carried potentially serious penalties. Given the acquittals on the major charges, though, the judge would have to go light on Nosair. America had a jury system, and the jury had spoken. The "champion" would soon be back in the fold.

"I Did My Part"

Or so they thought. Now, it was their turn to be stunned. Judge Alvin Schlesinger, who had presided over the circus of a trial, threw the book at Nosair, castigating the acquittals as "against the overwhelming weight of evidence and . . . devoid of common sense and logic."[4] On January 29, 1992, he imposed the maximum sentence, seven-and-one-third to twenty-two years' imprisonment. Further, in a blatant message to the parole board, he made it quite clear that if there were a legal way to lock the cell door and throw away the key, he would do so. Nosair, the jurist added, had "conducted a rape of this country, of our Constitution and of our laws, and of people seeking to exist peacefully together."[5]

Miserable and enraged, the champion was banished to the wasteland of Attica Prison in upstate New York to serve what promised to be a very long stretch. It was a bitter pill for the jihad. In the not so linear logic of Islamic radicals, Nosair was now a hero for killing Kahane, touched by Allah for being acquitted of the murder he had unquestionably committed, and yet . . . the victim of a despicably unjust sentence.

Salem adroitly capitalized on the fever pervading the spectacle. He was indispensable to El-Gabrowny in setting up security for the rambunctious sentencing that again pitted rival activists at close range. His efforts even thawed the previously icy Blind Sheikh. Salem was now welcomed into Abdel Rahman's New Jersey home, where the emir made a point of noting his pleasure that Salem was helping restart the paramilitary training, dormant since Nosair's arrest. The time was coming, Sheikh Omar pregnantly added, "when all would need to be trained."

As he grew further entrenched, the informant became enmeshed in ever more harrowing plots. He attended a security meeting at which several jihadists railed about a Kahane partisan named Leon who had provoked Muslims during the trial. Sattar and a Nosair friend, Mohammed Saad, were trying to find out where he lived, and Saad suggested that Salem build a small bomb that could be placed under his car.

They continued talking as meeting ended, and Saad explained that he had also been thinking about breaking Nosair out of jail. If they could get hired by Attica's sanitation or food services contractors, he proposed, Nosair could then push for a prison job that would situate him to be snatched and spirited away. They could then hide him at a nearby apartment until it became safe to move him. El-Gabrowny, however, threw cold water on the idea, opining that everyone should just "slow down" since he believed the case could be reversed on appeal–an option preferable to risking a botched jail-break.

Stuck doing the time, though, Nosair was not nearly so patient. The prospects of redress in the courts were iffy. The courts, after all, had landed him in the slammer, and they, like the rest of America, were controlled by Jews. Moreover, being a hero was not all it was cracked up to be. His stream of visitors was less steady. Unlike Rikers Island, the trip to Attica required his comrades to invest more than sixteen hours of round-trip road travel. Still, when not meeting with Nosair himself, El-Gabrowny dutifully arranged visits by others. On May 5, 1992, he dispatched Salem to Attica, accompanied again by the mujahid, Tarek Khaterria, and El-Gabrowny's brother, Mohammed.

It was Salem's first trip to the facility, and the visitors' lounge meeting lasted five long hours, throughout much of which the agitated Nosair inveighed against the evils of the United States, upbraiding his guests for "sitting doing nothing" while he sat in jail for "doing my part" in the jihad. Salem decided to bring up Saad's jail-break scheme, prompting Nosair to observe ruefully that there had only recently been a great escape opportunity: He had been escorted off campus to the prison hospital by only two lightly armed guards who could easily have been overtaken by well-trained jihadists. An invention by Salem? No, his report was easy to corroborate and proved to be true: Nosair had in fact been taken to Erie County Medical Center a few days before by two guards armed only with service revolvers.

Nosair was nevertheless unimpressed by the other plan in motion, the one to bomb Leon's car. Leon, Nosair observed, was just "a little kid." If the group actually wanted to accomplish something meaningful, they should be targeting "the big heads," like Judge Schlesinger and New York City Assemblyman Dov Hikind, who was active in Jewish causes. Nosair was not picky as far as his sentencing judge was concerned: Schlesinger should either be kidnapped and held as a bargaining chip to trade for Nosair's release, or simply killed.

On the latter, and on killing in general, Nosair had some considered views. Engaging Salem in some explosives shop-talk, he offered that there were a variety of ways in which bombs could be assembled using readily available items. Many of these, like timers and fuse, could be purchased on Canal Street in lower Manhattan. Echoing the Blind Sheikh, the crucial thing, Nosair repeatedly stressed, was for the jihadists to quit talking and get down to business.

Bombs and Guns

"He's hot right now," El-Gabrowny said dismissively on hearing Salem's report. He persisted in the view that drastic measures for freeing Nosair should be put off until the appeal was done–they were not yet at the point where the risk was worth running. But Nosair continued to badger him. Under this pressure, in the safety of the Abu Bakr Mosque, El-Gabrowny finally confided in the informant that there were "underground people," whom Salem would not be permitted to meet until "the right time," but who would soon be brought forward to help him build bombs.

Salem, meanwhile, went to Canal Street and was able to find fuse and a simple timer, just as Nosair had said. But El-Gabrowny scoffed that such items were obsolete. Explosives, instead, should be detonated by remote-control. Such devices, El-Gabrowny explained, were also available on Canal Street and would "give you 100 to 150 feet, and that's sufficient for our purpose." He also provided a helpful example as he and Salem drove through a predominantly Jewish neighborhood in Brooklyn. Pointing to one of the houses, he hypothesized, "If we want[ed] to kill Dov Hikind" with a bomb, and used a timer instead of a remote detonator, the bomb might go off before Hikind reached the kill zone. "We lose, we don't accomplish the mission. We make noise, and that's it."

The mercurial Nosair browbeat his cousin yet again on June 6, 1992. When El-Gabrowny returned, he related that Nosair had summoned both Salem and Ali Shinawy. A week later, on June 14, they made the trek to Attica.

Nosair was fulminating. "You told us that you going to do something," he vented, glaring at the informant. "You said that you want to be a good mujahid. You said you want to do something for jihad. And here you sit, doing nothing."

Salem had come a long way since allowing the Blind Sheikh to rattle him on the drive to Detroit seven months earlier. He met Nosair's eyes and firmly countered that he had not been idle. It was Nosair and others who had failed to bring forward the mujahids–the "underground people"–they'd said were ready for action. "One hand," Salem pointed out, "can't clap."

To underscore that it wasn't he who was shirking, he pulled out a small piece of the fuse he had purchased on Canal Street. Nosair was impressed, but Shinawy, alarmed by the informant's recklessness–jailers were all around them, and they'd had to pass through prison security to get to the visitors room–grabbed the fuse and stashed it in a soda can.

Obviously appeased by Salem's apparent earnestness, Nosair told him both Shinawy and Emad Abdou (the aide who'd given the Blind Sheikh reports from the murder trial) would help construct explosives for what would be a series of bombings. The plan was still unfolding. At least two bombs, Nosair said, would be set aside to kill Hikind and Schlesinger. Other targets would be identified in due course.

Turning to Shinawy, Nosair took pains to remind him that it was essential to seek a fatwa from Abdel Rahman, approving the plan. Shinawy agreed.

On the long bus trip back to New York City, Shinawy informed Salem that the plan ultimately called for the construction of twelve bombs. The elder statesman was worried, though, about security. It was important that Salem be armed. After all, if police or anyone else tried to stop them during the deployment of the bombs, they had to be able to defend themselves. Shinawy said he would check with his good friend and fellow Afghan mujahid Doctor Rashid (Hampton-El) about getting a gun for the informant.

Salem advised him that he'd need pipes, powder, fuses, and timers to build the bombs. Shinawy replied that they'd get the help they needed. Besides Abdou, he said he would call on Mustafa Assad—a good friend of Hampton-El whom Salem had seen at the trial and the victory celebration.

The wheels were moving now. When Salem went to El-Gabrowny's Brooklyn apartment to make his report the next day, he found Shinawy there. Already up to speed, El-Gabrowny related that they were working on securing a "safehouse" for bomb construction. The other challenge: determining whether there was a way to bring detonators into the country from Afghanistan.

Shinawy, meanwhile, moved forward on the matter of getting Salem a gun. Two days later, on June 19, he summoned the informant to the Abu Bakr Mosque, where he introduced Salem to the celebrated Doctor Rashid. In the seeming safety of Allah's house, they huddled in a corner. In hushed tones, Shinawy explained that Hampton-El was "a very good mujahid," a warrior from the Afghan jihad. The nodding Hampton-El proudly showed Salem his leg, the one that had been mangled by a land mine. Not to be outdone, Salem showed Hampton-El his timer.

Shinawy elaborated that they were in the process of making bombs. Salem cut to the chase: Detonators, the catalysts necessary to boost explosive compounds, were proving to be a big problem. Hampton-El responded that it was foolish to engage in the dangerous business of combining these components by hand. "Ready-made bombs" were available, for about $900 apiece.

Shinawy nodded. He wanted to think about it.

On to the pressing matter of a gun for Salem, Hampton-El said he had in stock AK-47 assault rifles, American rifles, and Uzi sub-machine guns, but not handguns. He doubted, though, that there would be a problem, and as he went on his way, he promised to see what he could do.

In no time, Hampton-El came through. Within a few days, Shinawy again called Salem over to the mosque. There, he presented the informant with a loaded .380 caliber Davis model pistol, with a box of additional bullets, both secreted in a cloth. Shinawy instructed Salem take it to the mosque's basement and inspect the contents. After complying, Salem reported that all seemed to be in order, but noted that the serial number on the handgun had been obliterated. "Of course," Shinawy responded. "That doesn't concern you in any way."

Salem reported to his handling agents that Shinawy had given him a gun, as promised.

⌛ Chapter 13

Divorce

THINGS WERE MOVING VERY QUICKLY, and the FBI was getting very worried.

The Bureau had commenced an investigation in the first place because there was good reason to think the men in their cross-hairs–many of whom they had known about since the Calverton training three years earlier– might be terrorists. Their suspicions, it was abundantly clear, were right. The men were, in fact, terrorists. The terrorists were, right now, plotting terrorism. Yet, the agents were in a bind.

Heinous plots were afoot, but the FBI and JTTF had no evidence. They had gone out of their way to avoid evidence. All they had was a witness to whom they had given a promise that he would never be a witness. If there really were bombings being planned, the bombers would obviously have to be stopped. That would mean making arrests and filing charges . . . except they had committed to their non-witness that his activities were only intelligence collection, that they were not doing a criminal case, and that his cooperation with them would never be revealed.

It was a spring of upheaval. While jihadists planned a bombing spree, new supervisors were put in place to oversee both the FBI's Foreign Counterintelligence Division and the squad directly responsible for the terrorism investigation. John Anticev, the lead FBI agent on the case, was stricken with a medical problem that put him out of action for several months. Salem was bouncing off the walls, frantically telling Detective Louie Napoli and Agent Nancy Floyd that a major terrorist operation was imminent. And right at that moment, the FBI had to inform him that everything he had previously been told was not true: This was now going to be a criminal case;

the agents needed him to be not just an intelligence source but a cooperating witness.

How Do We Corroborate Emad?

The new supervisors, Carson Dunbar running FCI and John Crouthamel taking over the case squad, justifiably strafed the line agents for the egregious error of promising an informant that he'd never be asked to testify. The damage done was substantial—Salem had been working, relying on these assurances and getting himself in ever deeper with jihadists, for eight months. He was not a criminal. He had voluntarily put himself in this situation not, as is the usual case with an informant, to get charges dismissed or reduced. He had done it out of a sense of duty and excitement, and for the few hundred dollars a week he was being paid—not substantial but nicely supplementing his income.

Had Salem been leveled with from the start, he'd almost certainly have declined to cooperate. And now, when a case had to be put together quickly, there could be no case without him. Sure, he could be subpoenaed and forced to testify, but the resulting eruption of hostility would surely end his cooperation. That would be a disaster: The agents had developed no other leads—Salem was it. If Salem refused to honor a subpoena, it would be both embarrassing and ineffective: embarrassing because it would inevitably publicize the betrayal of commitments made to the informant (which makes it more difficult to recruit informants); ineffective because the JTTF would then have no window into an emerging terrorist organization which might just go ahead and bomb New York City targets whether Salem was there or not.

What was needed was a soft touch—not always the Bureau's strong suit. Salem would have to be persuaded to become a witness. In the interim, if there were any way to build a case without him, the JTTF would have to try. That included obtaining court-authorized wiretaps that might permit the development of evidence without blowing Salem's cover. To get a wiretap, though, investigators need probable cause. Here, that would necessarily mean presenting Salem's information to a judge, which itself would be contrary to what the agents had promised—the affidavit given to a judge in support of an eavesdropping application in a criminal investigation is always disclosed to defendants once charges are finally filed. More paramount, though, the Bureau and the JTTF believed they needed to come up with any evidence that could independently confirm what Salem had been telling them. They needed more than his mere say-so.

So began the most gut-wrenching chapter in this tail of woe: The "How Do We Corroborate Emad?" debacle. If ever there was a monument to willful blindness, it was this.

In my mind's eye, I always see a room full of sleuths brainstorming. They ponder, "How do we corroborate him?" They are sitting around not on chairs but on boxes—the forty-plus boxes of evidence seized from Nosair after the Kahane murder. The boxes are able to support the weight of the reclining investigators because they are stuffed full. Emptying them, after all, would entail removing and, perhaps, analyzing the contents: reams of documents describing bomb construction and detonation; assassination techniques; the duty to perform jihad; the destruction of America's skyscrapers and political symbols; the recordings of Nosair, Abouhalima, and others reporting to the Blind Sheikh about paramilitary training and complaining to him about Mustafa Shalabi, who'd since been brutally murdered; the fingerprints and notebooks showing that Nosair, the purported "lone nut," had many confederates—something the agents could easily have confirmed, wholly independent of Salem, since the FBI had taken scores of pictures of those confederates, together with Nosair, conducting firearms training three years earlier.

There was, moreover, an *ideology* that was stirring this pot. These men were followers of Omar Abdel Rahman and his interpretation of Islam. You needn't have labeled all Muslims terrorists to see, already in 1992, the phenomenon of Islamic radicalism. The Qur'an and the Hadith command violence. Even if you were to conclude that this is a gross oversimplification that distorts the mythical "true Islam," that would be irrelevant. *Millions of Muslims believe it to be true.* Terror victims are not any less dead if those Muslims are mistaken. Hezbollah, so admired by Abdel Rahman, had been on the rampage for nearly a decade. Suicide bombing was in vogue–and when people can be convinced, against every natural impulse, to end their own lives in submission to a cause the goal of which is to kill the maximum number of non-believers, that is a cause worthy of notice. National security is not a theology exam. Motive evidence is not an ontological pronounce-ment; in the intelligence context it is a predictor of future behavior. We can't play ostrich just because accounting for it might hurt someone's feel-ings.

Well, actually, we can. We did. And we do.

The Calverton training, the wealth of Nosair search evidence, the preachings of the Blind Sheikh–these were all powerful corroboration of Salem's reporting. Indeed, they were the most convincing kind of corrob-oration: utterly unrelated to Salem. He hadn't arrived on the scene until long after most of the events established by this body of intelligence. He couldn't be accused of manipulating it in any way to support his account.

Yet, this information was treated as if it didn't exist. In the minds of those running the investigation, it was as if time started on November 4, 1991, the day Salem first walked into Nosair's trial. Everything before was a blank slate, and nothing after could be considered corroborated unless Salem himself would agree to play ball, ignore everything he had been promised, and make tapes–that is, do exactly the thing the agents had told him they didn't want him to do because it would endanger the lives of Salem and his family . . . including family the United States was in no position to protect because they were in Egypt, a hotbed of radical Islam.

Theater of the Absurd

Rather than diving into the trove at their fingertips, the first step the agents took was to determine whether Salem had recordings of his own. Salem's handlers confessed to the new supervisors that, several months back, the informant had told them about some tapes he'd made, tapes they had made no effort to retrieve–using the occasion only to discourage him from making any more. Agent Floyd was thus instructed to find out if Salem had tapes.

Of course Salem did have tapes because he was secretly taping every-one who called his home. That included Floyd when she phoned to prod him. Clueless that she was being recorded, Floyd also didn't know whether Salem actually had any tapes. And, to boot, she had previously misled him with the false monition that tape-recording was a crime. So she adopted a subtle strategy of non-confrontation and damage-repair. She didn't directly grill him about whether he'd made tapes. Instead, Floyd adopted a tone that assumed he'd made tapes, stressed that if he had done so there was really nothing criminal about that, and tried to gauge his reaction.

The agent recounted that she had not taken any tapes from Salem and knew Anticev and Napoli hadn't either. Matter-of-factly, she told the informant, "As long as you tape the conversations when you think it's safe to, on your own and we don't direct you to do so, you can do that without any prob-lem whatsoever." Any of those kinds of recordings, she emphasized, were Salem's own property, not the FBI's. Nothing to worry about. But then, the kicker: Come to think of it, though, the FBI would really appreciate any tapes Salem might happen to have lying around the house that could help prove the conspiracies he'd been telling the agents about.

Salem hadn't been born yesterday. He was conniving, surviving on guile and wits. His antennae were up. The blasé affect did not obscure the fact that Floyd was tugging on the rug underneath him. He wasn't fooled. Quick on his feet, he adopted his own non-confrontational strategy, at least while he tried to figure out what the FBI was up to. He liked Floyd better than the rest of the agents he'd met. She was, indeed, the best choice to make this pitch to him. But Salem wasn't giving. His tapes recorded not only subjects of the investigation but the agents themselves, in addition to Egyptian mili-tary officials, his children, squabbles with and about his ex-wife, and many other personal matters. He had no intention of handing them over to the FBI. Salem thanked Floyd for the clarification and carefully avoided saying whether he had tapes or not.

As Salem's handlers played cat-and-mouse with the informant, the brass was imagining the liability. Even assuming Salem could be convinced to become a witness, there was still what the Bureau, creature of our litigious society, saw as the enormous problem of an FBI informant neck-deep in a terrorist bombing plot. Salem did not know all the players; there were dangerous "underground people" out there who might be able to carry out a bombing with or without Salem's help; and Salem had no control over where El-Gabrowny would decide to set up the safehouse. Thus the concern: What if, as part of building a criminal case with sufficient evidence to satisfy courtroom due process standards, Salem helped terrorists make a bomb . . . but then the JTTF lost control of where the explosives were? What if, despite everyone's best efforts, an explosion happened anyway, people died, and the public learned that an FBI informant had been a key participant? The government, and in particular, the FBI would be blamed not only for allowing the bombing to happen but also for actually constructing the explosive device.[1]

The FBI, therefore, decided it was time to consult with the United States Attorney for the Southern District, Otto G. Obermaier. Given the highly secretive nature of the investigations, the discussions were tightly controlled. Only the top hierarchy was involved. No one in the Southern District was working terrorism in 1992. Neither I nor any of my colleagues who later prosecuted terrorism cases under U.S. Attorney Mary Jo White knew about or took any part in the consultation. To be fair to those who did, no jihadist conspiracy had ever executed a bombing in the United States before, although terrorist bombings were hardly unknown–that, of course, is why the FBI had a Joint Terrorism Task Force.

The result of these discussions was what the result always is when a national security challenge is framed as if it were a mere legal issue: a chimera. Completely unrealistic protocols–dos and don'ts–were designed to guide the informant. He'd be permitted to *talk* about how to build bombs, but actually *touching* bomb components was to be discouraged. And, naturally, *assembling* them–screwing rod "A" into flange "B"–was *verboten*. It was a perfect plan . . . if the goal was to get the jihadists to toss Salem out on his ass.

Salem's cover was bomb-*builder*. If he wasn't going to build bombs, what on earth would the terrorists need him for? As the Blind Sheikh and Nosair both repeatedly complained, they already had plenty of people willing to talk. Things were at a perilous juncture because the jihadists seemed to have gotten to the point of action. As an abstract legal proposition, the protocols may have seemed sound. If implemented in the real world, however, they'd only have jeopardized lives–the informant's and everyone else's. Salem would have been made to look at best like a reluctant jihadi, at worst like a probable mole, and in either event a useless liability–adding nothing to the plot but in a position to snitch on everyone else. Such people do not tend to have long careers inside terrorist organizations. Worse, the protocols would have increased the likelihood that the terrorists would shed the no-value-added informant, carry on without his knowledge, and leave the FBI with no practical way either to thwart the attack or build a case that would nab all the important players. The protocols were good for one thing and one thing only: If a bomb went off, the FBI couldn't be blamed . . . at least for *building* it.

The protocols also contemplated an unprecedentedly labor-intensive effort. They would have called for rigging any safehouse for video and sound, and dedicating scores of agents, round-the-clock, to monitor activity, ensuring that any explosive components could be accounted for at all times. The imperative for such a production was obvious, but sustaining it for any length of time would have been prohibitively expensive, while ending it prematurely would mean key plotters would not be identified–thus that the terror threat would not be quelled even after arrests were made. Although there is no excuse for the failure to analyze the bounteous corroborating evidence that was available, the Bureau's determination to press Salem hard becomes more understandable when one considers these strictures. The anticipated costs of this operation would have been exorbitant. They would have demanded that numerous agents be peeled away from other significant law enforcement and national security responsibilities to pitch in. It was not worth doing on a hunch. The Bureau can't be faulted for wanting to be sure. The problem, though, is that it had abundant reason to be sure.

As it happens, the protocols were never implemented. Regrettably, the urgency for them vanished.

Things came to a head because, as the government bureaucracy temporized, the serious business of bombing conspiracy continued apace. On June 28, El-Gabrowny told Salem that tight airport security was daunting the effort to import detonators from Afghanistan. He asked whether Salem could build detonators himself. No, the informant replied. He was stalling. For the kind of operation they were talking about, he said, detonators were out of his ken. El-Gabrowny indicated he would give the matter more thought.

The safehouse, meanwhile, was still in the works. As the calendar turned over to July, El-Gabrowny and Shinawy again told Salem that Nosair wanted to see him. This time, the Attica contingent would include Siddig Ali (who would later be the architect of the New York City landmarks plot), Mustafa Assad (the man Hampton-El consulted while trying to get Siddig detonators for that plot), and Emad Abdou (the Blind Sheikh's on-scene reporter at the Nosair trial, whom Shinawy had already described as someone who could be counted on for bomb-building).

Then came the explosion . . . between Salem and the FBI.

Shutdown . . . But Not for the Jihad

The subtle, non-confrontational strategy having gotten nowhere, the Bureau, with matters intensifying, reverted to its less appealing "Because we're the FBI, that's why" approach. This, however, tends mainly to move people over whom the government has leverage—people who have good reason to fear the FBI's machinery, which can be quite impressive to someone in its cross-hairs. The schtick is sheer effrontery to someone like Salem. There was no government anvil over his head, and he was sufficiently wily to realize the agents needed him a lot more than he them. Their lives weren't going to change, but they were asking him to turn his inside out, and there were no guarantees that he'd be compensated accordingly. Plus, they had lied to him—which, in his mind, was far more consequential than the fact that he was lying to them.

In early July, Salem was summoned to the FBI's New York headquarters for meetings with Dunbar, John Crouthamel, Floyd, and Napoli. The agents told him it was critical that he agree to become a cooperating witness. They needed him to testify against the terrorists in court, and they needed him to make undercover tapes so it wouldn't just be his word against the terrorists'. Salem was unmoved.

The agents tried a different tack. Maybe, they suggested, we could make do without your testimony . . . but we do need corroboration for what you've been telling us. So, the pitch went, how about recording a meeting with Nosair so we can be sure of what we're dealing with.

Now, Salem's back was up. They should already be sure, he countered, because he had been reporting it to them for eight months—it wasn't in his interest to lie and he'd given them no indication he was doing so. They had come to him for help with the jihadists because he had served them well with the Russians. It hadn't been his idea, but he volunteered his help, at great risk to himself. Yet, now they were making duplicitous demands. Salem wanted them to understand that he knew the score. His handling agents had told him all about how making tapes, *gathering evidence*, was the way the FBI squeezed somebody like him—someone who wanted to limit his role to *gathering intelligence*—into becoming a witness. Once there was a tape, Salem bluntly surmised, he would have no control over what the Bureau did with it. For all he knew, they could play it for Nosair or El-Gabrowny in an effort to get them to confess. If they did that, or if they used the tape in any similar way, the terrorists would know he had cooperated. Salem would then need protection. The government would have the leverage it now lacked to force his hand.

Feeling double-crossed, Salem decided to play chicken with the Bureau. Sure, he'd agree to record a meeting with Nosair—but only if he could do the recording himself, no other copies of it were made, and he got to keep the tape after playing it for the agents to prove he was telling the truth. After all, Salem chided, if the agents were really being straight with him, this plan should be acceptable to them. They would get the confirmation they claimed to need, yet he could maintain his independence.

No deal, said the agents. Dunbar and Napoli told Salem that this was not an acceptable compromise because their procedures required the preservation of recordings made at their direction. Salem rolled his eyes—he knew the agents had already once declined to preserve the couple of tapes he had told them about. From his perspective, the FBI could bend its precious rules if it was important enough to get the information, and now it was a lot more important to the FBI than it was to him. If his conditions were not met, he flatly said, he would have no part of any recording.

From their perspective, though, the agents were not just protecting a rule but a principle: The FBI runs informants, not the other way around. It had not been the fault of the new supervisors, Dunbar and Crouthamel, that Salem had been steered so badly. It was their responsibility, though, to impose much-needed order on the chaos, and they intended to do it. They were also not as invested in Salem and the investigation as the agents who had worked with the informant for months.

In their detachment, the impending terrorist threat became more of an abstraction than a reality. Salem had been talking about bombing for months, but there had been no bombing—mostly, there had been a lot of talk. No evidence of explosives on hand, no detonators, no safehouse. Sure, there was now a gun, but there are a zillion illegal gun transactions—an obliterated serial number doesn't compute to a terrorist plot. Even if Salem was accurately reporting what he was hearing, how real was this? And then there was this whole, foggy Egyptian intelligence angle: Was Salem some sort of Mubarak plant? Was he trying to make the radicals seem more dangerous than they really were to please masters back in Cairo? The sly, untamable informant seemed to be more trouble than he was worth—and the more recalcitrant he became, the greater the temptation to rationalize that maybe the threat had been wildly overblown.

Thus came the pièce de résistance: Dunbar asked whether Salem would submit to a polygraph to demonstrate his good faith.

Sounds like a reasonable request, all else having failed. Except . . . it would mark the *third time* Salem was subjected to a lie detector test.

As the prosecutor who would eventually have to present Salem as a witness, and as a government lawyer who had spent years investigating and trying fairly complex cases, polygraphs are my bête noir. There are, admittedly, settings in which the technique is useful. On the whole, though, they are the lazy man's approach to investigation, and it roils me that the FBI, especially on the national security side of the house, is so quick to resort to them.

For one thing, they are unreliable–that's why they're generally inadmissible in court. It always bothered me that, as the government's lawyer, I would be in the courthouse arguing that lie-detector results shouldn't be considered, while, at FBI headquarters across the street, an agent was surely suggesting that someone or another be put on the box to get to the bottom of a case. The standard legal argument, a very good one, is that polygraphs are as much a measure of anxiety as truthfulness. A cool liar can beat them; a nervous-nellie may signal deceptiveness even if he's telling the truth.

The polygraph procedure, moreover, is counterintuitive. In the judicial process, an appellate court is never permitted to reverse a case on credibility grounds. The reason is simple and sound: the jury got to observe the witness's demeanor; the appeals court sees only a cold transcript of the testimony. Lawyers, judges, and purported experts have no special province when it comes to truth-telling. Ordinary people using their common sense are just as suited to figure it out. That's how we get through life. But not so with lie-detector tests. The trained polygrapher who talks to the subject, asks the questions, observes the body language, and records the results is permitted only to give a preliminary assessment. No examination is considered final until it has been reviewed by top experts at FBI headquarters. Truth-telling–the ability of a human being to perceive, recall, and relate reality accurately–is thus stripped of all nuance, as if it were an unadorned physical fact that could be measured like body temperature.

Finally, when a witness has been polygraphed, the truth-seeking process that is supposed to be on trial is distorted. As already noted, the *result* of the test is inadmissible. But the *fact that the test was administered* is often considered fair game. The jurors hear that the FBI so suspected the witness that a lie-detector test was ordered, but you don't get to inform them if the witness passed. The subliminal message: you ought to doubt this guy because people who knew him better than you do were worried he was a fraud.

I'll concede, there are settings where the test is a necessary evil. In true emergencies, there is no time to conduct a real probe—you need your best quick answer, even if it is no substitute for searching analysis. And polygraphs make sense for background checks before we give someone a national security clearance. In that context, even if they reveal more about anxiety than veracity, it is worth finding out why people are anxious before we give them access to the crown jewels. But for a prospective witness, particularly when there is time to test his story by careful investigation, a polygraph is very damaging. In law enforcement, the idea is to put your best foot forward, not shoot yourself in it.

The Salem polygraphs, in any event, were infuriating. The first two times, early in the investigation when there was no intention of using him as a witness, the administering polygrapher found Salem credible, but headquarters, much later, changed the result to inconclusive. The final time, assertedly done to corroborate his reports about terrorist activity, was hairraising. Polygraphers are supposed to create a tranquil setting to minimize the likelihood of anxiety and a false reading. On Salem's last test, however, the polygrapher engaged in an argument with the informant, raising his temperature. Then, once the examination started, the informant, incredibly, was grilled not on bombing plots—the information we needed to corroborate—but on whether he was an Egyptian spy . . . under circumstances where he had already told the agents he was talking to Egyptian military intelligence authorities, where the agents had encouraged him to keep those communication lines open, and where his Egyptian connections had no bearing on whether jihadists were planning to blow New York City into Kingdom Come.

Egypt should have been a sensitive subject for Salem—he, of course, knew he had lied to the agents about bravely trying to save Sadat's life. Thus it is no surprise that the polygraph was suggestive of possible deception. The exam did nothing, however, to shed light on the terror plot. Meanwhile, Salem took umbrage at being asked to take the test at all, at the manner in which it was administered, and at the sense of betrayal and heavy-handedness in the push to make him a witness. It's hard to feel too sorry for him: He had misled the agents about his background. Even allowing for his well-founded security concerns, it was a tad rich for him to become indignant over being asked to tape Nosair given that he was already taping everyone under the sun and lying about it.

All that, though, was far afield from the main event. Jihadists were planning to murder, massively. Salem was the government's only window on their activities. The FBI was clearly not reviewing its files. It was conducting no surveillance of El-Gabrowny. It was not monitoring the people traveling to Attica to meet with Nosair—people like Abouhalima, Salameh, and Ayyad. And it would be months before the Bureau would stir itself to seek a national security wiretap on the Blind Sheikh—a brief one, not closely monitored, that was actually shut down a few days before the World Trade Center bombing.

Salem became convinced, not unreasonably, that the FBI wanted him to fail the polygraph—that once he refused to do things the Bureau's way, the brass decided they wanted an excuse to cut ties with him. Such a conspiracy theory might seem far-fetched if the Bureau had had a Plan B: a set of responsible investigative steps it would take to compensate for the loss of its only informant. It didn't.

Salem told the FBI he was through, and the Bureau told him he was no longer wanted. He was written off as a mendacious Egyptian spy. No one, I believe, really thought he had made the whole thing up. The agents working most closely with him for eight months thought he was reporting accurately—their supervisors, who were new, were the skeptics. He certainly hadn't made up the gun he had just received from Shinawy. He hadn't refused to tape Nosair; he had been willing to do it as long as he got to keep the tape. And had he really been an Egyptian plant here to fabricate trouble for the Blind Sheikh, he would certainly would have made up a much better story—thus far, other than the Mubarak solicitation, his information about Abdel Rahman was sketchy at best. Furthermore, though he had had every opportunity to do so, he had not claimed to see explosives in anyone's possession. The portraits he was drawing of most of the players were restrained. He had been told about ominous "underground people," but he didn't claim to have identified them yet.

Still, when he was terminated, it was as if the last eight months had never happened. The government lost his access to the battalions of Islam, and soon lost its interest in the battalions of Islam, as if they, too, had never actually happened.

The battalions of Islam couldn't have been more real.

⏳ Chapter 14

No Indication?

THE STORY OF THE WORLD TRADE CENTER BOMBING is familiar lore. The depth of the tragedy in our failure to prevent it is not, which speaks volumes about how little we've learned through the years of radical Islam's terror spree and how little we really want to know.

A determined and largely successful public relations effort has minimized the threat confronting the nation when Salem was ejected from the investigation in July 1992. It has been spearheaded by the FBI, which, for example, fed a 2002 congressional probe the nonsense that, when Salem was terminated, "there was no indication of the magnitude of the attack [jihadists] were planning or that they intended to kill thousands of Americans."[1] For what it's worth, I find this assertion particularly offensive since I had been the lead prosecutor when the United States proved in court–in an *FBI case*–the flaring-red indications that, by July 1992, jihadists intended to kill thousands of Americans. They were palpable, not just from what was derived by Salem's undercover work, but from the trove of evidence seized at Nosair's home (describing bombings and the targeting of skyscrapers and buildings of political significance), and from the Blind Sheikh's incendiary rhetoric and record, of which government was well aware–as we've seen, it was not for nothing that he was on the terrorist watch-list when he moved from Sudan to Brooklyn in 1990.

Moreover, even if one were inclined, as the Bureau apparently has been, to cinch up the blinders and pretend that all we had was the intelligence developed by Salem–conveniently skipping over, for example, the Nosair evidence that went ignored–the stubborn fact remains that El-Gabrowny told the informant the group was looking for high-explosives and sophisticated detonators, not Molotov cocktails. Over the years, law enforcement officials have insisted to the media that Salem was "only" asked to build "pipe bombs," intimating that it's unfair to suggest they were on notice that anything as horrifying as the World Trade Center bomb was contemplated. It's a distortion that, in any event, misses the point.

During the course of his discussions with the jihadists, Salem was indeed asked about pipe bombs–he was asked about a lot of different bomb types. As the training and the seizures from Nosair's home elucidated, jihadists had an abiding interest in varying explosive concoctions. That does not, however, mean the bombing campaign on the drawing board when Nosair was terminated was a pipe bomb plot. Pipe bombs don't require high-power explosives or detonators imported from a war-zone like Afghanistan. When Salem was terminated, the plan, which was still evolving, called for twelve bombs of a not-yet-determined type. It called for the murder of a state judge and a high-profile local legislator. Abdel Rahman, moreover, was already heralding Hezbollah's 1983 Marine barracks bombing as a model. Even if you buy the twaddle that there was "no indication" the attacks being planned would have been of WTC-bomb "magnitude," it is incontestable that the rampage could easily have killed many, many more people than the seven murdered in the actual World Trade Center bombing.

Missing Islam and Thus Missing the Point

With or without Salem as a source, the failure to pursue the investigation aggressively cannot be justified. It was monumentally irresponsible. Still, the excuses made for not doing so, which persist even after 9/11, are alarming because they betray an enduring misconception of what the actual threat was, and is, and what a proper response should look like. The question is not whether Abdel Rahman, Nosair, El-Gabrowny, or anyone else told Salem: "We're going to bomb the World Trade Center." It is what the body of intelligence amassed by that point would suggest to competent investigators and analysts. It is what that intelligence should tell the American people about what our enemies seek to accomplish, and why.

The terrorists were not about a single bombing or bomb campaign. Their leader, the Blind Sheikh, was pressing for jihad aimed at fulfilling religious duties to punish the United States for interfering in the affairs of Muslim countries and to establish Allah's law in America, as well as anyplace else where it did not reign supreme. There was constant emphasis on the need for training–not just explosives experimentation, but guerrilla tactics for assassinations and other operations. The goal was a domestic version, in the heart of radical Islam's principal nemesis, of exactly the game-plan al Qaeda has pursued in Afghanistan and elsewhere. The long-range plan was to build the capacity of a jihad army: battalions of Islam trained to unleash a continuing stream of terror operations, variant in kind.

In building that capacity, moreover, both mosques and fundraising were critically important. Money, obviously, would make it possible to underwrite training, materiél, transportation, and related expenses. Mosques were used as depots for weapons as well as safe-havens for terror plots and other criminal conspiracies. The mosques and Islamic centers were identified: Farooq and Abu Bakr in Brooklyn and Salaam in Jersey City were cauldrons of fundamentalist Islam. You are allowed to believe anything you want in America. If you choose to believe the deity, like the moon, is made of blue cheese and requires the occasional human sacrifice, we don't imprison you for it. We do, however, get to worry . . . and watch.

No one is entitled to immunity from suspicion for his dangerous beliefs. Fundamentalist Islam is a dangerous belief system. It reliably breeds a certain percentage of jihadists. Anyone going in and out of fundamentalist mosques was of potential intelligence interest. That means we need to care about what fundamentalist Islam is, and we need to know which mosques are proselytizing it. It doesn't mean you get arrested for what's going on between your ears or for what you believe God commands. But it most certainly does mean you should be a person of interest to the authorities, someone we have reasonable grounds to believe could pose a threat. It is simply delusional to think there is no correlation between what a person believes and how he is likely to act–as delusional as it is to think there is no correlation between Islam's doctrinal summons to violence and Islamic terrorism.

It would have been preferable to leave Salem in place, even if he refused to make recordings. If a criminal case were not in the cards—and that would by no means have been a given in 1992 if the agents had not suffered from Salem myopia—so what? In general, the FCI division did not do criminal cases anyway. If Salem had been kept in place, he might eventually have changed his mind about becoming a witness. He certainly did after the World Trade Center bombing. Even if he never had, though, the priorities for the JTTF should have been to stop any bombing from happening, to identify any potential bad actors, and, if possible, to develop evidence about any potential plot. Salem could have been of immense help in achieving those goals. That's not Monday morning quarterbacking; it was obvious at the time.

Moreover—and this is the crucial point—the absence of Salem did not mean either the absence of the threat or the absence of other available investigative techniques to assess the threat and build a criminal case, assuming prosecution was to be the method of choice for neutralizing the threat. Investigators had more than enough information at their disposal to seek either criminal or national security eavesdropping warrants in July 1992: for Nosair's visiting lounge at the prison; for the telephones and homes of people like Abel Rahman, El-Gabrowny, and Shinawy; and for mosques that were being used for criminal meetings, weapons storage, and incitement to violence.

Further, even if one factors in the mystifying failure to analyze the Nosair search evidence and allows that this made it less likely wiretaps would have been authorized, there was still plenty of good old-fashioned police work to be done. Physical surveillance cried out to be targeted on the major subjects implicated by Salem's undercover investigation; telephone, banking, and business records could have been subpoenaed and analyzed; efforts could have been made to penetrate the group with another informant or an Arabic-speaking undercover agent—even understanding that there was a scarcity of such agents at the FBI and the NYPD. Opportunities were there to infiltrate such undercover operatives in suspect mosques where recruitment for paramilitary training was ongoing. These steps would have led to the minimal amount of corroboration that would have been needed to get eavesdropping orders based on Salem's investigation.

"Neutralizing the Cell"

What you don't do is nothing, which essentially is what the FBI and JTTF did once Salem was removed. Perhaps the most hapless rationalization of all is the mantra that, in September 1992, investigators really "tried to neutralize that cell," as one agent put it in a 2003 interview with *U.S. News & World Report*, "by showing them we had been on to them for four years."[2]

After the deep involvement Salem had had with jihadists for eight months, he clearly needed a credible cover story for leaving the investigation—it would not have been conducive to his health to tell El-Gabrowny and Nosair that he'd had a falling out with the FBI. So his now former handlers came up with one. After the scheduled early July trip to Attica was postponed at the last moment, Salem contacted El-Gabrowny and explained that an emergency involving a crucial supplier to his jewelry business had arisen. For the sake of supporting his family, he had no alternative but to travel to Spain to resolve the crisis. El-Gabrowny appeared to accept the explanation and no doubt communicated it when he went to visit Nosair on July 18.

This, at best, was a temporary measure. Salem wasn't going to stay in "Spain" forever. The jihadists in Brooklyn and New Jersey were going to continue to call him and wonder why he'd suddenly dropped out of sight. Thus in late September, two months after the informant and the FBI had parted ways, the agents came up with a plan that would, they hoped, serve three purposes: give Salem a plausible reason to withdraw permanently, provide the investigators with some useful intelligence, and unnerve the plotters in the hope that this would dissuade them from following through with any bombing plans. They persuaded the U.S. Attorney's office to issue grand jury subpoenas seeking fingerprints and photographs (that is, mug shots) of many of the people who had been identified in the course not only of Salem's undercover work but during the Calverton training back in 1989.

Thus subpoenas were issued for Ibrahim El-Gabrowny, Mahmud Abouhal-ima, Mohammed Salameh, Nidal Ayyad, Ahmed Abdel Sattar, and several others, including Salem.

Subpoenas compelling production of fingerprints and photographs are a common law enforcement tactic. In an undercover investigation, for example, they are often employed when matters have stalled and agents are no longer concerned about going overt–allowing the subjects to know they are being watched. The tactic sometimes induces suspects to become nervous and make a mistake, such as evincing consciousness of guilt by making sudden flight arrangements, or reaching out for the aid of accomplices who've heretofore managed to remain anonymous and insulated. Subpoenas also provide a good opportunity to interview conspirators. That is because people subpoenaed for fingerprints and photographs do not always retain counsel and do not generally report to a grand jury room in the courthouse; the subpoenas direct them to comply by proceeding to the FBI's offices, where prints and pictures are to be taken.

In this instance, Salem's handling agents tried to intimidate the jiha-dists. When the day for answering the subpoenas arrived, the investiga-tors plastered the walls with some of the old evidence they'd gathered, prominently including the photographs from Calverton–the same pho-tographs that, according to Peter Lance, former agent Jack Cloonan (the Ali Mohamed case agent) claims no one at the FBI knew about until he (Cloonan) dug them out in 1996. The plan was to convey to the conspira-tors that the JTTF knew exactly who they were, had been watching them like hawks for years, and realized what they were up to.

It was, to put it mildly, a staggering display of naïveté. Government refused, then as now, to consider that there might actually be a nexus between Muslim teaching and terrorist activity. Consequently, a rudimen-tary fact seems to have escaped the agents' attention: the rambling lot they had called in to discourage were *jihadists*. Their revolutionary aim was to overthrow the system. No one ever thinks that will be done without resis-tance–that's why it's *jihad*. Harassment from the authorities comes with the territory. Further, the raison d'être of jihadism is to establish Allah's law because it is the higher law. The FBI's not-so-subtle message that "we know you are violating our laws" was irrelevant to these people. Their point in establishing Allah's law is that our laws are offensive to them. Telling them you know they are transgressing offensive laws is, for them, a compliment, not a form of intimidation.

But let's leave ideological implications aside and just deal with what the JTTF empirically knew. When the jihadists realized they were being surveilled at Calverton, what happened? Did they get in their cars and drive away? No, of course not. They marched over, boldly pounded on the FBI van, and challenged the agents for harassing them while they, as a group of pious Muslims, practiced their faith by blasting AK-47s at shooting gallery targets. After that, there had been the scuffle at JFK airport involving Sheikh Azzam, in which assault charges were dropped when Muslims claimed discrimination. The group's leader, the Blind Sheikh, had been permitted to enter and remain in the United States despite a career of inciting violence. And how had Nosair killed Kahane? He walked up to him in a room full of people and blew him away. He had to expect there was a very high probability that he would get caught, but it didn't stop him from acting—and then, with the acquittals, he'd gotten away with the worst of it. The people the JTTF was trying to unnerve were the very people who worshipped Nosair for what he did and for whom the acquittals were an additional sign that they had nothing to fear from American law enforcement—a Higher Power was with them.

And if all that wasn't crystal clear enough, there was the jihadists' manner when they came in to comply with the subpoenas: provocative defiance. They settled on a rendezvous point beforehand and marched to the FBI's office in solidarity. Bravado was their calling card. Abouhalima, in particular, sneered memorably. He and his cohort weren't intimidated in the slightest, and why should they have been? They didn't need pictures on the walls to realize the FBI had been watching them—they had confronted the FBI back when the pictures were being taken. El-Gabrowny, as the agents well knew, had told Salem he was certain he was being monitored, which was why he turned the television volume up when he spoke to confederates and why he said he wouldn't keep explosives in his home. Shinawy went out of his way to conduct meetings and gun transactions in the safety of mosques because he worried that police were watching.

The subpoenaed men, moreover, were not morons. They had been talking about bombing and murder. They figured: if the FBI is really "on to" you, if it actually has evidence that people are conspiring to bomb and kill, then it makes arrests. It doesn't bring plotters in for a photo-op. To a logical terrorist, a subpoena under these circumstances was encouraging, if not empowering. The one thing it was not was intimidating.

The only subpoena recipient who seemed unnerved by the experience was Salem, for whose benefit the exercise was undertaken. He did not trust the government any longer, and in his paranoia wondered if the agents were turning the tables on him—setting him up to be portrayed as one of the bad guys if, as he thought was certain, a terrorist attack finally happened. On the other hand, he needed to break ties with the jihadists and knew that his timidity, in the face of their aggressiveness, would make him look weak in their eyes—look like someone who was frightened by the law enforcement attention and might thus be weak enough to break down and tell the authorities what he knew. He needed a cover story to get out, but this one made him feel perilously estranged from both the agents and the terrorists. Once the session at the FBI was over, though, he went along with the program. He met with El-Gabrowny and Sattar, told them he believed, based on what the FBI had told him, that he was being closely monitored, opined that it would be best for all concerned if he disappeared until the heat was off, and undertook to do precisely that.

Unfortunately, Ramzi Yousef was already here.

Released on His Own Recognizance

It is almost uncanny that the ultimate "underground people," Ramzi Yousef and Ahmed Ajaj, arrived in the United States just as Salem and the FBI divorced. Like most of this excruciating story, their coming is a tale of lost opportunities. They arrived at JFK International Airport direct from Pakistan on September 1, 1992. Yousef's appearance, in particular, belied the later speculation that he might have been an undercover Iraqi operative.[3] Spies make a point of trying to blend in, to avoid calling undue attention to themselves. When Yousef deplaned, costumed in a silk suit, muslin flounces, and slip-on cloth shoes, he stuck out like a sore thumb. He then did just what an Iraqi agent with skads of other false identification would never do: He presented an Iraqi passport . . . for which he did not possess a required visa authorizing entry into the United States. In a word (well, actually, two words), amateur hour.

Ajaj, his traveling companion, presented a bogus Swedish passport. Searching his luggage, agents found six bomb-making manuals which were extensively annotated with Arabic translations (and which included the formula for the complex urea nitrate bomb ultimately composed by Yousef and deployed by conspirators at the World Trade Center). Ajaj was so patently suspect that immigration authorities denied entry and detained him.

Remarkably, Yousef, whose true name is Abdul Basit, was permitted to enter the United States despite blatant clues that he was traveling with Ajaj. To board the flight, Yousef had used a first-class pass issued to "Azan Muhammad"–the same name found on two documents seized from Ajaj. Yousef also possessed an identity card which bore his photograph but was issued in the name "Khurram Khan," the very pseudonym under which Ajaj was traveling. The immigration agents knew he was a wrong number. Yet, the team investigating Yousef and the team investigating Ajaj did not compare notes until it was too late. After a brief detention, Yousef was released on his own recognizance based on his meaningless representations that he would reside in Houston, Texas, and appear as directed for an immigration hearing. Instead, Yousef made a bee-line for Jersey City, headquarters of the Blind Sheikh–whom he knew, whose apartment he was in phone contact with, and who was regularly calling a phone number in Pakistan that was scribbled on one of Ajaj's bomb manuals.

Almost immediately, Yousef hooked up with Mohammed Salameh. Over the next six months, they used a series of small Jersey City apartments to build the World Trade Center bomb–with the help of Mahmud Abouhalima, Nidal Ayyad, and others–while remaining in phone contact

with Ibrahim El-Gabrowny and the Blind Sheikh. The JTTF missed it, however, because they weren't investigating Salameh, Abouhalima, Ayyad, El-
Gabrowny, and Abdel Rahman. They had brought most of these jihadists in
for an ineffectual brush-back pitch—the subpoenas. They had overlooked
that this tactic was highly unlikely to have any lasting *in terrorem* effect
with these particular characters and that the group's goal was not, in any
event, a single, isolated bombing plot. Even if the agents actually believed
they had unnerved the jihadists (and it is hard to fathom how they could
have), these were still jihadists and worthy of a lot more attention.

On September 6, only days after Yousef's arrival, El-Gabrowny visited
Nosair at Attica. Two weeks later, on September 20, Nosair spoke with his
wife in a prison call that was recorded but went unnoticed. Defiantly, and
ominously, he dismissed the subpoenas he'd heard the FBI dropped on his
associates. As his wife struggled to calm him down, Nosair blurted, "What
will happen in New York, God willing, it will be . . . because of my prayers.
So let them fight believers."

"Allah," Nosair foretold, "will protect us and harm them."

Salameh and Yousef initially took up residence in a small apartment at
251 Virginia Avenue, but later also used as bombing safehouses an apartment at 34 Kensington Avenue, another at 40 Pamrapo Street (where, following the bombing, agents found the walls stained with blue spots, acid
burns on the door handles, and splotches on the ceiling), and one at 65
Baldwin Avenue, where they foolishly stored chemicals, including danger-
ously volatile nitroglycerine, in a refrigerator.

From November 1992, through the World Trade Center bombing
on February 26, 1993, Salameh, Yousef, Abdel Rahman, Abouhalima,
Nosair, El-Gabrowny, and Ayyad were in almost constant contact. We now
know that because phone records were subpoenaed . . . after the bombing.
Regrettably, agents were not tracking any phones in real time. A couple
of examples of this frenetic activity elucidate how valuable it might have
been to have targeted key players for wiretapping—or, at the very least, pen-
registers, which do not monitor the actual telephone conversations but at
least apprise investigators about who is calling whom, when, and for how

long, valuable intelligence frequently used to establish the probable-cause necessary for a wiretap.

By late November 1992, for example, the phone contacts were coterminous with measures obviously geared toward assembling a powerful explosive. In the early afternoon of November 29, El-Gabrowny, keeper of the prodigious funds raised for Nosair's defense, was twice called from a Salameh/Yousef safehouse. The next day, November 30, Yousef, identifying himself as "Kamal," paid City Chemical Corporation $3615 in cash for chemicals and empty drums. That same day, Salameh, using false identification, rented a storage locker in Jersey City. Yousef's order from City Chemical was then delivered to the storage facility.

Emad, Please Call

On December 6, El-Gabrowny visited Nosair at Attica. That night, his home was called from a Salameh/Yousef safehouse. On December 9, calls from that safehouse went to Ayyad, Abouhalima, and El-Gabrowny. Abouhalima called El-Gabrowny the following day. Then, on December 11, the Blind Sheikh called El-Gabrowny in the morning and received a call from the Salameh/Yousef safehouse in the evening—right after the safehouse had been in touch with Abouhalima. The next morning, three times within the space of a half-hour, Abdel Rahman called the Pakistan number that had been written on one of Ajaj's bomb manuals—a number also frequently called by Yousef. Then, a combined four times, Abdel Rahman and someone at the Salameh/Yousef safehouse sought out Abouhalima. Abouhalima then phoned El-Gabrowny before calling the Blind Sheikh right back. Later that day, Abouhalima was again called from both Abdel Rahman's apartment and a Salameh/Yousef safehouse.

The jihadists at this point were clearly having a problem getting the explosive mixture right. Ajaj's manuals, recall, had been seized. Thus another missed opportunity: The plotters decided to turn for help to Salem, whom they knew as an explosives expert—but he was out of the investigation and, since the agents were unaware of the feverish communications and chemical purchases, there was no interest in reviving his undercover role. On the morning of December 19, Abouhalima called El-Gabrowny in an effort to reach Salem. Three minutes later, Abouhalima called Salem's residence, leaving a message imploring Salem to get in contact.

Consistent with his instructions, Salem reported the call to the agents but avoided getting further involved, refraining from calling Abouhalima back. Later that same day, Abouhalima purchased Hodgdon smokeless powder from a New Jersey gun shop.

Soon, Abouhalima took his problem to Siddig Ali. They met in a car, and after swearing Siddig to secrecy, Abouhalima explained that he needed help testing explosives–writing, rather than speaking, to avoid law enforcement monitoring (would that there had been any). Siddig agreed, and consulted both Hampton-El and an Egyptian named Abdo Haggag, who lived in the Blind Sheikh's apartment building and who later became a government witness. By the time Siddig got back in touch with Abouhalima, however, the problem had already been worked out.

As the jihadists continued to work with chemicals and burn up the phone lines, they would occasionally take time out to make the day-long trip to Attica for consultations with Nosair. After making arrangements with El-Gabrowny, Abouhalima made the journey on January 2, 1993, along with his brother Mohammed and his friend Mohammed Hassan Abdou. After the bombing, Mohammed Abouhalima recounted to Salem that they had been extremely cautious, taking pains to lean over to Nosair and whisper in each others' ears even though they were conversing in Arabic, a language apparently unfamiliar to those around them.

"We Must Be Terrorists . . . and Shake the Earth Under Their Feet"

On January 16, Abdel Rahman, who had been in constant contact with the bombers, appeared in Brooklyn for an event given the catchy title of the "Conference on Solidarity with Bosnia/Herzegovina . . . on the Inevitability of Jihad as the Solution of our Problems and for the Frightening of the Enemies of God." He thundered to the crowd that "God has obliged us to perform jihad," and that the "battalions of Islam and its divisions must be in a state of continuous readiness . . . to hit their enemies with strength and power." He continued:

> If those who have the right [to have something] are terrorists then we are terrorists. And we welcome being terrorists. And we do not deny this charge to ourselves. And the Quran makes it among the means to perform jihad for the sake of Allah, which is to terrorize the enemies of God and our enemies too. . . . Then we must be terrorists and we must terrorize the enemies of Islam and frighten them and disturb them and shake the earth under their feet.

As if that were not clear enough, the Blind Sheikh also reminded the assemblage, "The enemies at the foremost of the work against Islam are America and the allies."

By now, it having dawned upon them that allowing Abdel Rahman to set up shop in the United States was an egregious error, federal authorities were actively seeking to deport him. As the Blind Sheikh fought the deportation, capitalizing on America's friendly asylum laws, the FBI finally obtained a national-security wiretap on his home telephone–a wiretap that, by operation of law, was shut down right before the World Trade Center bombing because efforts were not made to renew it. The interceptions demonstrated that the Blind Sheikh was tight-lipped on local matters–after all, he could summon trusted subordinates for face-to-face consultations. Still, he remained the emir of an Egyptian terror organization, and two of his sons, who ultimately became members of al Qaeda, were enmeshed in the global jihad. To manage matters overseas, telephone communications were a necessity. Though he spoke guardedly, the eavesdropping provided tantalizing insight into how valuable a longer, more assiduous monitoring effort might have been.

On February 16, for example, "Mohammed" from Pakistan, addressing his emir as "your eminence," reported to Abdel Rahman that "the brothers carried out an operation" in Manfalout, Egypt, against four tourist buses and five police cars, resulting in "shooting [that] lasted for almost one hour."

"What are the results," Abdel Rahman asked.

"The brothers," Mohammed replied, "returned safely, thank God. The other side suffered heavy losses."

On February 23, Abdel Rahman instructed "Khaled" in Pakistan to tell a group leader to move forward with an unspecified operation, asserting, "What answer does he want? I mean . . . they are committed and all. They should just carry out, and that is it."

Khaled then asked, "Do you command us with anything else from this end?"

"The boys," he replied, referring to his two sons, should be sent to Abdel Rahman "since you are unable to do anything for them or assign them any work."

Khaled interjected, "You agree that they are to be assigned any work?"

Of course, Abdel Rahman responded, "any work that could be considered jihad" whether inside or outside Pakistan.

Two days later (the day before the World Trade Center bombing), "Adel" called to report that fighting had broken out in Mogadishu between American forces and Somalis. The Blind Sheikh wanted to know only one thing: were any American casualties?

"Two marines were hit."

"Okay," the Blind Sheikh answered. "That's enough. That's good."

Final bombing preparations were, by then, complete. Two weeks earlier, on February 13, Salameh had paid a final visit to Nosair at Attica, listing his residence as El-Gabrowny's Brooklyn apartment, the address on his driver's license. A few days later, after he and Ayyad had conducted a final surveillance of the World Trade Center's underground garage, Salameh used the same license to rent a ten-foot Ryder cargo van, paying the required $400 deposit in cash.

That Ryder van was carrying the bomb that exploded in the underground garage a few minutes after noon on Friday, February 26, 1993.

⧗ Chapter 15

Aftermath

THERE IS A WIDE EMOTIONAL GULF between fearing that a terrible thing will happen—even being certain that it will happen—and having it actually happen. Consistent with the complexity of his character, Emad Salem was simultaneously stunned, enraged, frightened, and opportunistically excited by the bombing of the World Trade Center.

Stunned because it was stunning. The breathtaking audacity of the attack shocked the nation and the world, but struck home profoundly for someone who had been deeply entwined in a bombing plot with committed terrorists.

Enraged because it was enraging . . . and, from his perspective, eminently preventable.

Frightened because the attack underscored his personal peril on two fronts. First, if the jihadists with whom he'd been involved had carried out the operation—and he was certain they had—it dramatically underscored that they were deadly dangerous. This did not bode well for someone who had abandoned them and who, they knew, had information that would be helpful to the authorities. Salem had continued to get occasional phone calls from El-Gabrowny and his brother Mohammed (who had accompanied Salem on one of the Attica trips). Indeed, the El-Gabrowny brothers had even come to see him when Salem was briefly hospitalized for a cardiac condition—though Salem's wife had been present the entire time, so the visit was brief and did not touch on jihadist activity. The former informant had also received the call out of the blue from Abouhalima in December. But he had tried to maintain a cordial distance, and though he thought he had nothing to fear from El-Gabrowny, he continued to worry about what the other jihadists made of his abrupt disappearance from the scene.

Second, hailing as he did from Mubarak's police state where sudden disappearances were not unheard of, Salem felt at great risk that the FBI might try to silence him—by prosecution or even murder. In his paranoia, he believed he was the only person outside government in a position to reveal publicly the devastating truth that law enforcement—and, principally in his mind, the FBI—had extensive prior knowledge of a bombing plot and failed to take action, with the result that many people had been killed and injured.

And, finally, Salem was excited. He was itching to get back in the spy business. Much of the urge was calculated—it would be an opportunity to assuage the jihadists with an ostensible show of support, while wheedling from the agents some useful admissions that they had failed to listen to him. Nevertheless, Salem was also irresistibly drawn to the bright light of public controversy, no matter how much it endangered him and his family. It was his make-up. The full-court press was now on to "solve" the bombing. He was sure he'd already solved it, and in his lingering bitterness, he wanted it known that he had been right all along, and that the FBI—which had betrayed, distrusted, and ignored him—had been tragically wrong.

He would soon get his chance. Though initial reports about the explosion in lower Manhattan speculated about an accident caused by transformer or power line problems, the FBI's peerless forensic alacrity, applied full-bore, established almost instantly that a bomb had been detonated.

Flight, Fright, and Fortune

Meanwhile, as Yousef bolted from the country, Salameh returned to the rental company about two hours after the blast to file a fraudulent report that the van had been stolen at a New Jersey shopping mall. He demanded the return of his $400 deposit. No, he was told. The company was very sorry but it would not pay without a copy of the police report Salameh falsely claimed to have filed. The chagrined Palestinian laid low for a few days but was anxious to have the money back before making further moves. On March 1, he returned to the rental company and angrily tried, without success, to bamboozle a clerk into giving him the $400.

In the interim, Abouhalima was making his escape plans. He and his brother Mohammed sought out their friend Siddig Ali, who had connections with Hassan al-Turabi's de facto government in Sudan. Siddig broke out in the jihadist battle cry *Allahu Akbar!* (God is greatest!) when Abouhalima explained that he had carried out the great bombing operation and needed to flee pronto. He promised that safe harbor was available in Sudan, and wrote letters of introduction to facilitate Abouhalima's flight. The Egyptian immediately booked a one-way trip to Jeddah, Saudi Arabia, planning to head from there to Khartoum a few days later. Mohammed Abouhalima and Siddig took him to airport, whence he departed on March 2.

Ayyad felt safe enough to keep working at Allied Signal in New Jersey, but he kept in touch with El-Gabrowny. By now, the *New York Times* had received the claim of responsibility letter, subscribed "LIBERATION ARMY[,] FIFTH BATTALION," which had been written on Ayyad's computer and mailed before the bombing. Explaining, in echoes of the Blind Sheikh, that the group had acted "in response for the American political, economical and military support to Israel, the state of terrorism, and to the rest of the dictator countries in the region," the jihadists warned:

> *OUR DEMANDS ARE:*
>
> 1 *Stop all military, economical and political aids to Israel.*
> 2 *All diplomatic relations with Israel must stop.*
> 3 *Not to interfere with any Middle East Countries [sic] internal affairs.*
>
> *IF our demands are not met, all of our functional groups in the army will continue to execute our missions against military and civilians [sic] targets in and out of the United States. This also will include some potential Nuclear targets. For your own information, our army has more than hundred and fifty suicidal soldiers ready to go ahead. The terrorism that Israel practices (which is supported by America) must be faced with a similar one. The dictatorship and terrorism (also supported by America) that some countries are practicing against their own people must also be faced with terrorism.*

The American people must know that their civilians who got killed are not better than those who are getting killed by the American weapons and support.

The American people are responsible for the actions of their government and they must question all of the crimes that their government is committing against other people. Or they—Americans—will be the targets of our operations that could diminish them.

We invite all of the people from all countries and all of the revolutionaries in the world to participate in this action with us to accomplish our just goals.

WHEN ANYONE TRANSGRESSES THE PROHIBITION AGAINST YOU TRANSGRESS YE LIKEWISE AGAINST HIM.

The *Times* reported its receipt of the letter to the FBI.

The Bureau's bomb technicians, in the interim, had determined that the epicenter of the blast had been the Ryder van, pieces of which were indicative of being blown from the inside rather than, as with the hundreds of other damaged vehicles, from the outside. From the mountains of rubble meticulously screened, they were able to unearth a shard on which the vehicle identification number was engraved, enabling them to trace the van to the rental company . . . and to Salameh.

Thus when Salameh called yet again on March 4 to ask about his deposit, the agents were ready. Posing as rental company employees, they told Salameh to come on in and get his money. After providing a ludicrous description of how the van had been "stolen," Salameh was placed under arrest. His pocket litter contained keys to the storage locker and bombing safehouses, where enough chemicals to get rolling on several new bombings remained stashed. In one of the safehouses, furthermore, agents found what appeared to be a passport photo of Nosair as well as a booklet entitled, *The Ideological and Legitimate Perspectives for the Islamic Group*, the writing of which had been "supervised by the Honorable Dr. Omar Abdel Rahman."

In the shell-shocked atmosphere of the time, Salameh's arrest ignited a global media frenzy. Hearing the initial reports on the radio, Salem instantly decided to go into investigator mode. Firing up his recording equipment, he called El-Gabrowny to ask what was going on. El-Gabrowny, clearly anxious to get off the phone, said he'd check and let Salem know later.

Break-Out

Shortly afterwards, with great cause to be concerned, El-Gabrowny was fidgeting outside his Brooklyn building when a team of JTTF agents blew by him in raid jackets. El-Gabrowny hesitated momentarily, then hustled back toward the building in the direction of the agents. When two of them stopped him from reentering, announcing that they had a search warrant for his home, El-Gabrowny became belligerent, finally smashing both agents with his elbows. Never a good idea. He was firmly restrained and cuffed.

The jihadists had obviously believed any tell-tale bombing evidence would be destroyed in the explosion. El-Gabrowny, however, had much more to be concerned about. Salem had told his handlers that plans were being made to break Nosair out of Attica, that El-Gabrowny had tried to discourage them while the appeal was underway, but that Nosair was extremely dissatisfied with that tack, putting enormous pressure on his cousin to act forcefully. Upon arresting him, the agents realized that El-Gabrowny had clearly gotten the message–it was yet another thing that their informant had gotten right.

In El-Gabrowny's pocket was an envelope bulging with five passports issued by the government of Nicaragua, bearing photos of Nosair, his wife, and their three children, each assigned a false name–"Victor Noel Jafry" (Nosair), "Ninfra Jafry Calderon" (Mrs. Nosair), and their children "Jaime Marcos Jafry," "Jorge Marcos Jafry," and "Maria Marco Jafry." The envelope also contained five fraudulent Nicaraguan birth certificates with names matching the phony passports, as well as Nicaraguan driver's licenses issued to "Mr. and Mrs. Jafry." In looking to Nicaragua to help the jailbreak, Nosair and his helpers had chosen well. Replacement birth certificates were easy to come by because of the 1972 earthquake that destroyed many government records in Managua. Once fraudulent birth records had been obtained, it was an easy matter for a corrupt paralegal to complete the necessary forms to obtain the passports, Nicaragua being a country that didn't require a personal appearance for such accommodations. The driver's licenses were due to expire in 1996–about two years before Nosair could have been released in the highly unlikely event he had been required to serve only the minimum seven-plus years on his sentence. A jail-break scheme was afoot, and Nosair's old pal Salameh had clearly been in on it– the photo on the phony Nosair passport matched the one found among his belongings at one of the bombing safehouses.

During the 1992 undercover operation, Salem told the agents Nosair had urged his confederates to get stun-guns for terror operations, opining that if only he'd had one on the night of the Kahane murder, he'd have gotten away. In El-Gabrowny's home, the agents found two recently purchased stun-guns. They also seized Kahane coroner's photos–plainly the ones Salem had claimed El-Gabrowny showed him at the 1992 dinner when they'd first discussed bombing. El-Gabrowny's home was also replete with other gems, such as Nosair's recorded diatribe about returning to the jihad; an answering machine tape containing "important" messages from Salameh and Ayyad; and a robust collection of jihadist literature, including *The Forgotten Duty*, the infamous Sayyid Qutb-inspired manifesto by Abdel Rahman's old friend Muhammad Faraj, the Egyptian Islamic Jihad icon. It seemed quite relevant and natural to sieze such booklets from a terrorist who was acting on them–there was no Patriot Act to guide us, but neither the agents, nor I, nor anyone in what was then the Clinton Justice Department ever worried that we were chilling anyone's right to read or that librarians' unions would march on our offices in protest.

As the day's events unfolded, Salem remained riveted to the television. Like rapid fire, press reports about Salameh's arrest were superseded by breaking news that El-Gabrowny had been nabbed in Brooklyn. Salem immediately called the Abu Bakr Mosque, reaching Shinawy, who confirmed that El-Gabrowny had been arrested. As Salem tried to strike up further conversation, the elder curtly rebuked him. "I am not going to talk about any of this," he snorted. "We are not going to talk about things like this now."

Salem then called Sattar, the man El-Gabrowny had called the "next champ," who was also serving as the Blind Sheikh's closest personal aide—and would later function as his paralegal at trial. Sattar had not seen Salem in some time, but explained that he believed Salem was a "target" of investigators, adding that he had thus told Mohammed El-Gabrowny to keep Salem at a distance. "Our contacts have been exposed and you see what is happening," the chagrined mailman groused. "So we are trying to keep our contact, what? Limited. I mean for the time being."

Next, Salem telephoned Mohammed El-Gabrowny, who conceded that his brother Ibrahim had been caught with passports he had been holding for Nosair—against Mohammed's repeated advice.

The passport seizure, of course, made abundantly clear that Nosair was a severe escape risk. State prison authorities were alerted and promptly moved their high-profile inmate from Attica's general population to the maximum security "Special Housing Unit." Nosair was characteristically defiant. "If the devil leaders of New York State think placing me in SHU will end the war, they are wrong," he railed to a guard. "This," he presciently promised, "is only the beginning."

The Insurance Policy

To outside appearances, the arrests of Salameh, El-Gabrowny, and Nidal Ayyad, who was also picked up on March 4, showed an investigation moving at break-neck speed. In reality, it was not nearly brisk enough. Yousef had fled, as had Abouhalima and two of their lesser known helpers, Abdul Rahman Yasin and Eyad Ismoil. Yasin, an American of Iraqi descent, had been seen around the bombing safehouses and grabbed by the FBI in Newark the same day Salameh and El-Gabrowny were arrested. Little was yet known of him, though—certainly not enough to charge him. Unlike Great Britain, Israel, and other countries with extensive histories of combating domestic terrorism, the United States has never seen fit to permit a reasonably brief period of preventive detention while the authorities sort things out to ensure that people colorably suspected of being mass-murderers are not permitted to flee or, worse, turned back onto the streets. In America, suspects must be either charged with violating the law or released, period. The use of legal devices such as "material witness" arrest warrants to justify brief periods of incarceration are essential but controversial–as demonstrated by their use in the frantic post-9/11 period. No thought was given to such tactics in 1993.

Consequently, Yasin was released. On a quick appraisal, he had seemed like a cooperative witness, and he promised to remain available for additional questioning as needed–just like Ramzi Yousef had promised to stick around for his immigration hearing. Naturally, he caught the first available plane out of the country, eventually landing in Iraq. By the time evidence was developed to prove that he was a real player, recruited into the plot by Yousef, it was way too late–he was given safe harbor for a decade by Saddam Hussein's regime and has never been found. Ismoil had also helped build the bomb, but that was not discovered until forensic analysis of the safehouses revealed his fingerprints, leading to other confirming proof. By then, he too was long gone, to his native Jordan. It would be years before he was extradited and brought to justice.[1] What common sense suggests experience was bearing out: there was no substitute for human intelligence, for an informant on the inside who could expose the conspirators in real time.

John Anticev and Louie Napoli were crushed by the news of the World Trade Center bombing and the picture emerging in the aftermath: namely, that it had been executed by the same group of Muslim radicals they had been investigating since 1989, and that the group was threatening additional acts of terror. Putting aside their personal sense of frustration and failure, they realized that Salem could be an invaluable asset if he were willing. It would surely be a lot better to have him as an ally than a hostile witness. They convinced their superiors that he should be reactivated. In the then-prevailing leave-no-stone-unturned urgency, there was no dissent.

In early March, Anticev called Salem, who agreed to come in, feigning reluctance . . . but somehow finding it within himself–actually, about bursting out of his skin—to brag that he had already gotten some valuable information from Sattar, Shinawy, and Mohammed El-Gabrowny. In his own mind, the informant was already back on the team. A lot of the attraction, though, was the chance to capitalize on the agents' remorse. As he continued to worry that they might be setting him up, he covertly wired himself, determined to turn the table on his handlers.

The meeting began disastrously. Every fiber of Salem's paranoid being stood on edge as he was escorted through the FCI unit's squadroom. On the wall, big as day, the agents had inexplicably left hanging a chart that appeared to be a compilation of bombing suspects *and that included Salem's picture*. This, Salem was certain, was exactly the prosecution scenario he feared. The agents were going to frame him, and when he tried to tell the story of how he had tried to help the government, the FBI would smear him as a terrorist who would say anything to avoid life-imprisonment. As his mind raced, the informant nearly exploded in palpitations.

Anticev tried to pacify him, sputtering that Salem was absolutely not a suspect. And he wasn't. What looked to the unknowing observer exactly like a chart of suspects was actually a vestige of the naïve intimidation plan the agents had tried six months earlier—when they subpoenaed numerous jihadists and tried to scare them off any ongoing bombing plot by brandishing old investigation photos. Sadly, the chart was more useful after the bombing than it had been before. In any event, Salem's image had purposely been included back then as a ruse to give him credibility with the real suspects. Anticev, who truly was bearing the weight of failure like a cross, was completely sincere. Salem seemed to accept the explanation, but he retained doubts. With the 1993 bombing a potentially huge embarrassment, he simply couldn't believe the FBI was, as he saw it, advertising on its walls what it had known about but not acted on in 1992. The cynic in him kept whispering, "It's a set up."

He was even more determined to protect himself. Agreeing to take a walk with the agents away from the charged atmosphere in their office, Salem expertly steered the conversation to the past, inducing Anticev and

Napoli to concede he had provided them extensive information prior to the bombing.

Although there was little dispute that Salem had informed them that jihadists were scoping out "symbolic targets," Napoli peremptorily denied Salem's assertion that he had specifically identified the World Trade Center (in addition to the Empire State Building, Grand Central Station, and other landmarks) as a potential attack site. Salem dropped the subject in the face of Napoli's unflinching tone. He always, however, took the position that he had heard Nosair, in particular, talk about such particular targets, and that the agents had either failed to ask him about it or, more likely, failed to write down what he had told them. For their part, his handling agents, who grudgingly liked him (at least a lot of the time) and thought him an invaluable source, were adamant that he reported no specific targets other than Judge Schlesinger and Dov Hikind.

I never resolved this controversy. It was certainly plausible that Salem had reported it. The notes seized from Nosair's home in 1990, which Salem didn't know about, spoke of symbolic targets—skyscrapers and buildings of political significance. The agents, moreover, did not debrief Salem often enough, and compounded that problem by an inane system in which Nancy Floyd, who knew the least, wrote most of the reports. Anticev and Napoli were, shall we say, economical note-takers: Salem would, for example, spend untold hours meeting jihadists, traveling to Attica and back, and the like, and these investigative bombshells would rate but a few handwritten lines on a pad—lines that became even more sparse when Anticev went on medical leave at a critical juncture in spring 1992. The mere fact that something wasn't recorded by the JTTF hardly meant it hadn't happened—numerous significant occurrences were proved beyond peradventure even though they'd never made it into the agents' notes.

On the other hand, the mere fact that Salem said something had happened—especially something he had a huge personal stake in—didn't mean it had. In the end, our prosecution team scoured hundreds of pages of conversation transcripts, notes, and reports; spoke to scores of witnesses; and carefully studied tapes Salem made at the FBI's direction in spring

1993–tapes in which he often recapitulated the events of 1992 in front of terrorists like Siddig and Hampton-El, who were in a position to correct him had he been lying. All of this evidence was powerful corroboration of just about everything Salem had told the agents before his July 1992 expulsion from the investigation. Yet nowhere was there any indication that the World Trade Center had been specified as a target to Salem in 1992.

Nevertheless, just as Salem had anticipated, the agents admitted that if the Bureau had only listened to him, the bombing might never have happened. Thus, although the informant had failed to prise the "World Trade Center" jackpot out of his handlers, he had succeeded in eliciting, on tape, the concession he saw as his insurance policy. Now, the FBI of his feverish, conspiratorial imagination would not be able to frame him for the bombing. As long as he had this recording, he was safe. In a very personal way, he realized why the FBI had so wanted him to make tapes. Regardless of reality, if it wasn't on tape, it didn't happen. But if it was on tape, it was powerful proof.

The agents carefully broached the subject of re-introducing Salem as an undercover informant, moving the conversation to a subject more comfortable for them: Mahmud Abouhalima. He had tried to reach out for Salem back in September. Anticev acknowledged Salem's report of the contact but now, with Abouhalima missing, the agents wondered whether Salem had preserved the message. Salem coyly responded that he wasn't sure because, after all, he had "a hundred of tape"–he'd need to check. The agents did not pursue this provocative suggestion. They assumed he was talking about answering machine tapes, not recorded conversations, and that, in context, "hundred" was a figure of speech (as in "I've got a hundred things to do today"). Even if they had other suspicions, they quickly dismissed them: The last thing they wanted to do was reopen the matter of forcing Salem to surrender tapes–the issue that had precipitated their acrimonious parting seven months earlier. Tapes aside, the informant had agreed to see what he could do to help on Abouhalima, and his help is what the agents wanted.

Emad Salem was back in the game.

⌛ Chapter 16

Spy Games

THE MARCH 1992 APPREHENSION OF World Trade Center bomber Mahmud Abouhalima in Egypt proved to be a case of almost comical intrigue. As usual, Salem was in the middle of the high-jinks. But it shaped up as a true battle of *two* wannabe spies, thanks to the Blind Sheikh's neighbor and nemesis Abdo Mohammed Haggag, another in the endless parade of Egyptian oddballs to stride across our canvas.

Haggag was a strong-willed young man, an ardent Abdel Rahman admirer who began to have his doubts about the cleric as he came of age—like many green adults who begin to question the passionate black-and-white of their youthful enthusiasms. Unlike most Egyptians inclined to fundamentalism, Haggag found himself . . . in America—with a decent job and a world of possibilities. Suddenly the jihad did not seem so appealing. Haggag seamlessly found himself, well, evolving. Maybe jihad wasn't really, you know, jihad. Maybe there really was something to this "greater" and "lesser" stuff—that revisionist construction that Western apologists tout as part of Islam's incandescent beauty.

In fact, reinventing jihad is the transition phase from the darkness to the light. Many people who enter this stage, leave Islam entirely—grasping, finally, that they cannot live within its precepts. Others become "moderates" and "reformers," hopeful that the precepts can be ignored, reinterpreted, not taken so seriously, or flat-out repealed. Still others, like Haggag, become Sufis—identifying themselves spiritually and culturally as Muslims but taking on the gleam of "mysticism" which, near as I can tell, means, "Hey man, I don't do the jihad thing."

Haggag had been overjoyed, sort of, when the heralded emir of jihad moved in next door. But familiarity bred contempt. As he got to see Abdel Rahman up close and personal, the bigger-than-life image crashed into the grittier reality. Sheikh Omar was an operator, a conniver, and a man given all too easily to what one might delicately call the tug of earthly temptations. Worst of all, Haggag learned as he helped the blind man here and there around the house, Abdel Rahman was the most reprehensible kind of hypocrite: Railing against America by day, yet, behind the scenes and out of his fawning public's view, petitioning for U.S. asylum to avoid being deported to some Islamic country.

Offended, and riding the wave of his youthful indignation, Haggag resolved to expose the old fraud. Secretly, he began writing what he was sure—no doubt based on watching American television—would be the definitive, unauthorized biography: The Lies of Sheikh Omar Abdel Rahman. True, he may not have been the most suitable raconteur—having once earned $3000 for trying to torch a company in an insurance fraud scam. But that small matter, he reasoned, was just Haggag's personal business, while exposing Sheikh Omar was about the future of Islam. Growing older, more confident, and more assertive, Haggag sharply questioned the Blind Sheikh about his private practices and his counterintuitive asylum application—a matter of no small sensitivity to the Honorable Dr. Word of Truth. Unaccustomed to such insolence from the riff-raff, Abdel Rahman began to deride Haggag as a bad Muslim. Aware that this sort of innuendo had not ended well for Mustafa Shalabi, Haggag decided to hedge his bets. He continued to be a member of the community and tried to strike an entente cordiale with the emir . . . but he also contacted the Egyptian government and agreed to spy for them.

So now, with Mahmud Abouhalima on the loose, Haggag was snooping around for the Egyptians while Salem was back in business for the FBI. Resuming his informant role, Salem went to the Abu Bakr Mosque a few days after the March 4 arrests and learned from Sattar and others that Abouhalima had fled to Saudi Arabia. Simultaneously, Haggag was learning the same information from his friends Siddig Ali and Mohammed Abouhalima, who added the tidbit that Mahmud's ultimate destination was Sudan.

Then Mahmud Abouhalima made two fateful mistakes. First, he decided to make a quick detour to his native Egypt before heading south to Sudan. Second, he told his brother Mohammed about it. Like Tinkers-to-Evers-to-Chance, this news made its way from Mohammed-to-Siddig-to-Haggag . . . and on to Egyptian intelligence, which unceremoniously grabbed Abouhalima and detained him in one of Mubarak's not-exactly-built-to-ACLU-standard prisons.

Had it not been for Salem, it's a good bet Mahmud might have been there for a long while. He was well known to the Egyptians as a top aide of the abhorred Blind Sheikh. But before anyone learned the Egyptians had snatched him, Salem happened to run into Mohammed Abouhalima in a mosque. Mohammed regaled the informant with the story of Mahmud's flight and mentioned, in passing, that Mahmud had decided to cool his jets in Egypt for a few days rather than heading straight to Sudan. Salem immediately reported this development to Anticev. As a result, the United States officially contacted the Egyptian government to request its assistance in the apprehension of Abouhalima—not knowing that the Egyptians had already apprehended Abouhalima and were interrogating him . . . shall we say, without Miranda warnings. Under the circumstances, the Egyptians decided the better part of valor was to ship him forthwith to face prosecution in New York. Thus, it is fair conclude that Abouhalima is serving a life sentence today thanks to Haggag, but he is alive and serving it in America, after a full and fair trial, thanks to Salem.

How Dare You Call Me a Terrorist!

Abouhalima's plight would prove a major part of Abdel Rahman's undoing. He had been kept abreast of Abouhalima's travels and was furious to hear about the arrest. Nevertheless, while scouring under the radar to determine how his trusted aide had been betrayed, Sheikh Omar's public face was part indignant "moderate" and part aspiring comedian in need of better writers. When news of Abouhalima's apprehension in Egypt broke, he was on a fundraising jaunt through California. There, he granted an interview to the late Bernard Shaw—as long as the CNN anchor agreed to address him as "the respected Doctor Sheikh Abdel Rahman."

Though he'd spent years chiding his adherents not to shy away from the label "terrorist," the respected Doctor Sheikh rebuked Shaw over the indignity of the media's "accusing me of being a terrorist" and, through that, "accusing Islam of terrorism." Categorically denying that he knew Nosair, Salameh, and Ayyad, three of his most stalwart followers, the celebrated *Word of Truth* author groused that the World Trade Center bombing had "shake[n] me deeply." Islam, you see, "hates aggression." It did not, he elaborated, countenance attacks on personal property or public buildings. Why, Muslims who come to a place like the United States, he assured viewers, were deemed by Islamic law to make a sacred "oath and covenant" that they would accept the laws and live peacefully.

War is deceit. When fundamentalist Muslims fight it, the only rule is expedience. Lies are made to be told, and convenants to be broken. "If thou fearest treachery from any group, throw back [their covenant] to them, [so as to be] on equal terms," the Qur'an instructs.[1] If Abdel Rahman decided the jihad would be advanced by lies–by telling an American television audience exactly the opposite of what he'd been telling Muslim throngs in mosques and conventions–then lies it would be. And now he really poured it on.

Do you, Shaw asked, urge violence against the Egyptian government?

"I say the truth," the cleric dodged before launching into a diatribe against Mubarak.

So, Shaw pressed, do you rouse ordinary Egyptians to revolt against President Mubarak?

"No, no, I do not call people for any violence."

The mendacious cleric seemed proudest, though, of his deflective comic approach. Shaw pointed out that there were reports Mahmud Abouhalima had "been a driver and personal assistant for you during the last several years."

"Do you know him," the anchor continued, "and, if so, do you know where he is today?"

"I don't know him and I don't know where he is," came the reply. Then, with a smile and that sense of humor he sometimes flashed between calls for bombings and decapitations, the sightless cleric pointed out, "And I did not have a car so that he can drive it for me!"

It was a performance as bizarre as it was foolish. Abdel Rahman had a long, lavish record of calling for violence and the overthrow of Egypt's secular regime. Moreover, it was no secret that Abouhalima had been the Blind Sheikh's closest lieutenant. Wholly apart from Nosair's recordings of the intimate Abouhalima/Abdel Rahman conversations (which investigators did not yet realize they had), the Sheikh, upon relocating to America, had moved close to Abouhalima's Brooklyn home so the latter could cater to him. The two had even opened a joint bank account, with Abouhalima handling most of the transactions to spare his emir the trouble. For Abdel Rahman to deny the relationship was like denying he was breathing. It was the sort of careless bombast he could recover from in Egyptian society, where his unquestioned mastery of the established state religion caused even the mega-powerful to tread lightly. But the spell did not carry over to America even if CNN and others might be persuaded to call him "the respected Doctor Sheikh." Though very far from being one, he looked and sounded like an idiot.

And he looked even worse—especially in front of his ultimate jury of New Yorkers—as he vainly regaled subordinates with what he delusionally perceived as his deft handling of Shaw. After the bombing, the government was once again authorized to conduct national-security wiretapping on Abdel Rhaman's phone. Thus, when he returned home a few days later, he was intercepted chuckling as he recounted the CNN episode for an Albanian underling: "They told me he was your driver. I told them: 'Do I have a car?'"

Still feeling his oats an hour later, he asked an unidentified friend, "Did you watch the CNN?"

No, the friend hadn't seen it yet, but had heard "the tactic you did with them was good."

"He told me," Abdel Rahman cackled, "Do you know Mahmud Abouhalima, and his location and things? He was your driver? . . . I told him, 'Do

I have a car to have a driver?'"

What a scream!

Nevertheless, when the laughter died down, Abdel Rahman was dismayed to learn that many of his followers were grumbling over the sudden dissonance between his public comments and private directions. "Mohammed," calling from Pakistan on March 20, gently prodded him to stop publicly denying he was the Islamic Group's emir. For "the brothers in Egypt . . . who are working," he reported, these disavowals were demoralizing. "I mean, your honor," Mohammed beseeched, "especially regarding questions that touch on the work, or concern your eminence as the emir and stuff, it is better to give general answers than specific ones."

Clearly annoyed, Abdel Rahman countered that no one should be troubled since they had "agreed . . . we don't say that I am the emir," and that direct answers about jihad would be avoided by simply repeating, as often as possible, the peremptory non-response that the Islamic Group was "anyone who follows the truth." Abdel Rahman promised to "talk his way around the issue" in the future, but found it hard to believe that his underlings were so "foolish" as not to realize what he was doing.

The conversation with Mohammed from Pakistan was also extremely interesting for reasons that eluded us until years later. It marked what, for U.S. prosecutors and agents, was the first mention of al Qaeda. It was fleeting, and we missed it. The Blind Sheikh's conversations were all in Arabic, and we got English translations–hundreds of them. We wouldn't learn the underlying Arabic words unless there was a pressing reason to ask. In reporting to Abdel Rahman about terrorist attacks in Egypt and the closing of paramilitary camps, Mohammed made a fleeting allusion to "the base," the English rendering of al qaeda. The term meant nothing to us at the time, appearing to be a cryptic reference to one of the camps, not, as now seems clear, to Osama bin Laden's enterprise.

"The brothers" had fought government forces in Asyuit, Mohammed informed his emir. Considering his next moves, the Blind Sheikh asked, "I tell you what, are there any camps that are still operational?"

"No," Mohammed answered. "I mean, there's only our own thing"–an apparent reference to an Islamic Group training camp.

But, the emir asked, "is there one—I mean, for example, if there are people who want to train or come to Pakistan? That's no good?"

Mohammed replied that no, it wasn't good. All of the camps had been closed, "even the base"—that is, *al Qaeda*. There was nothing available at the moment, "except for special situations."

"Fine," Abdel Rahman deadpanned, "This is a special situation."

Underscoring the Blind Sheikh's centrality to the global jihad, Mohammed replied, "If it is a recommendation from you, then there is no problem"—adding, for good measure, that there would be "no problem" if his "eminence" sent "a special situation."

The Informant Meets the Terrorist Right to Counsel

By the time Abdel Rahman returned from California, Salem had already spent nearly three weeks working his way back into jihadist circles. He was helped immensely by the very visible role he appeared to be taking in support of El-Gabrowny's defense. But when he began having conversations about a public relations strategy with Bill Kunstler, who had jumped in to represent El-Gabrowny right after the arrest, Salem's handling agents—who didn't know much of anything about criminal procedure—were told they had to pull Salem back. Pressing the intelligence-gathering effort was crucial, but no one wanted to jeopardize the prosecution of those already arrested for bombing the World Trade Center.

The modern interpretation of the Sixth Amendment right to counsel is another disturbing complication of using the criminal justice system as a counterterrorism weapon. As Nosair and others have made manifest, committed jihadists are not stopped from planning atrocities by arrest and prosecution. Nevertheless, under American law, once a person has been charged and has counsel, the government may neither attempt to interrogate him about the case without his lawyer's permission nor interfere with his lawyer's development of defense strategy.

The proscription against interrogation does not just apply to prosecutors and investigators; it means the government may not use an undercover informant to elicit incriminating statements covertly from a charged defendant. The proscription thus gets very complicated. Technically, it only applies to crimes that have already been charged, not new crimes the defendant may be in the process of committing. But bar associations and federal courts, which tend to elevate the rights of criminals over the demands of national security, are forever pushing the envelope under the rubric of the attorney-client privilege—arguing (and in a few aberrant cases, holding) that the government should be barred from adducing statements not only about concretely *charged crimes* but about anything that might conceivably be considered within the highly elastic ambit of the *lawyer/client relationship.* In other words, if the attorney and client agree that the lawyer is representing the client on "any matter related to the government's ongoing investigation," it is claimed that the Sixth Amendment bars the government from using an informant to determine whether the charged terrorist defendant is planning any new terrorist acts. Under this theory, the terrorist and his lawyer, not the public interest, determine the proper bounds of an investigation.

For the most part, the law does not go this far, but the government must always tread carefully—eliciting statements or defense strategy in violation of the Constitution can result in suppression of evidence, disqualification and ethical reprimand of prosecutors, and, potentially, the dismissal of perfectly valid charges based on due process considerations. And yet, not allowing an undercover informant to continue dealing with a charged defendant can blow the informant's cover, endanger him, and undermine an important national-security investigation. If, say, Salem had flatly refused to meet with El-Gabrowny once he was charged, El-Gabrowny—with the help of astute counsel—might well have begun suspecting Salem was a government plant who was shying away from him post-indictment for fear of compromising the government's case.

All of this might make sense if a defendant were charged, for example, with stock fraud and then suspected of committing new frauds while under indictment. If the government were to keep its informants away, the worst thing that could happen is new frauds might go undetected. By contrast, in a terrorism case, an indicted defendant may order and plot new mass-murder attacks. Yes, it is obviously important that such a terrorist get a fair trial and be convicted. It's a lot more important, however, that new terror strikes be prevented.

In this instance, it could have been an enormous problem, but it wasn't. Salem deftly disentangled himself from El-Gabrowny's defense by going directly to the Blind Sheikh. The informant explained that he wanted to support all of the arrested "brothers" but was concerned that this might draw renewed attention to himself, leading the agents to make a case against him based on his 1992 (ostensible) bombing activities. Abdel Rahman agreed that it would be wise for Salem to distance himself, and that the informant could show his support in less suspicious ways—like contributing money to the defense of Salameh who, unlike the other defendants, did not have lots of family in America to support him. Salem took out $50 on the spot, which the Blind Sheikh instructed him to give to Sattar for Salameh.

Meanwhile, Salem made himself useful in other ways. Given his language skills and physical prowess, he was occasionally pressed into service as the Blind Sheikh's translator and driver. Early that spring, for example, he brought Abdel Rahman to a New Jersey mosque and translated for English speakers while the emir spoke in support of Hamas—though the informant was not invited to stay when several unidentified Palestinian men came back to Sheikh Omar's apartment for an après-jihad confab.

Salem also convinced the jihadists that he knew how to detect eavesdropping devices and wiretapped telephones. He brought his "equipments" for "sweeping" to the homes, cars, and meeting places of several top figures, including the Blind Sheikh, Siddig Ali, and Sattar. Sattar, Salem reported, had even confessed that, once he'd heard about Salameh's arrest, he had "run home right away" and "cleaned up everything." Sattar later asked Salem's advice about whether there was a way to clean chemicals off the body so that no residue was left behind. Salem, who actually didn't have a clue, suggested that he try some vinegar.

I Flinch . . . and a Terrorist Escapes the Net

I've never been one to say, as the old saw goes, that if I had it to do over again, I'd do it the same way. There are always things that could have been done better, mistakes that could have been avoided. That is not to say that I have many regrets—the bad judgment calls that haunt even years later. I have a few, though, and one of them is Ahmed Abdel Sattar.

He was the Blind Sheikh's top operative—certainly once Abouhalima was put on ice. That made him a major player, among other things, in helping Abdel Rahman run the murderous Islamic Group. In the summer of 1993, months after Salem had returned to the investigation, we had to sort out who should be indicted. Sattar was on the bubble. We knew—I knew—he was a terrorist. El-Gabrowny had told Salem he was the jihad's "next champ" after Nosair; Salem had reported his involvement in discussions about killing "Leon," the Kahane activist jihadists had grappled with at Nosair's trial; and he had made damaging admissions to Salem, strongly suggesting his complicity in the World Trade Center bombing. We also learned, again through Salem, that he was using his government job—maddeningly, he worked for the U.S. Postal Service—to try to determine where John Anticev lived, causing us great concern for the agent and his family.

The problem: None of it was on tape. It was all based on Salem's testimony with no convincing corroboration. If he had helped mix the World Trade Center bomb, as he had surely been in a position to do, no fingerprints or other physical evidence tied him to the key bomb locations. And we could not prove, beyond Salem's say-so, that he had conspired to harm Leon, Agent Anticev, or anyone else.

We were also already taking on a dozen defendants, which can make for a circus of a trial. Salem was a very troublesome witness. Strategically, we thought it essential to be able to look the jury in the eye and say that, while the informant's testimony made sense, we were not asking jurors to convict anyone based on his unsupported word. On that score, the indictment of El-Gabrowny on terrorism charges was already a close call: no evidence other than Salem's testimony directly put him in a bombing conspiracy. But with El-Gabrowny, there were compelling circumstantial strands—phone records showing him in constant communication with the World Trade Center plotters while the bomb was being built, seizures from his home, phony Nosair passports. This proof undergirded Salem's account. With Sattar, there was nothing like that. If charged, his case would rise or fall based on Salem's word.

It was my call. Mary Jo White, our intrepid U.S. Attorney, had also been a terrific line prosecutor earlier in her career. She knew the case as well as any boss could know the case, but this decision was of the sort of judgment that, within the bounds of reason, has to be made by the person closest to the evidence. I was that person. She would have supported me either way. The rest of the team would have accepted my judgment. If I had said, "Let's go get him," we'd have done our best with no recriminations. Sattar was in the drafts of the indictment right up until the eve of going to the grand jury.

I flinched.

I took him out. I thought the case was strong enough to convict, but I worried that if we put the jury in the stark position of having to convict or not based squarely on Salem, and if the jury had then decided Salem wasn't sufficiently credible, that rationale could spill over to the jury's consideration of other defendants. Maybe they'd decide to acquit El-Gabrowny or even the Blind Sheikh; maybe it would snowball to the benefit of defendants who were buried by the other evidence. I calculated that Salem would look a lot stronger overall, that his flaws would seem less consequential, if he didn't appear to be make-or-break.

It was a bad call. I had a reputation for being aggressive, being willing to try tough cases—and this case was going to be tough no matter what. Letting Sattar off the hook, though, was a mistake. It might have been the right thing for the case—although, in hindsight, I'm not sure that was true either. It was certainly the wrong thing for the country, for our national security. We probably would have convicted him. Though nothing is certain, I underestimated how strong a witness Salem would be. Sattar seemed to be everyplace in the evidence even though there was no smoking gun, and we later learned that Salem actually did have a tape: the brief conversation after El-Gabrowny's arrest on March 4, when Sattar fretted to Salem, "Our contacts have been exposed and you see what is happening." Not exactly a full confession, but maybe enough to have put it over the top.

It's a judgment I'd love to defend. The problem is: I don't buy the defense. I didn't pull the trigger, and a terrorist remained on the loose for an extra decade, until he was finally indicted and convicted for helping Abdel Rahman run his terrorist organization from jail. There's no evidence that Sattar did anything to harm Americans in that time-frame, but there's also no way to be sure.

I was not the CIA turning a blind eye to the Arab-Afghans, or Chief Borelli labeling Nosair a "lone, deranged gunman," or the FBI rationalizing that maybe Salem was lying about everything. I wasn't engaged in self-delusion. I knew Sattar was evil and that he would be a continuing threat—maybe even to me personally—if we left him out there. I just decided that other interests were more important and rationalized it by the all too facile excuse that you can't get everybody—in every case involving a large-scale conspiracy, you have to draw the line someplace. But the irony: while trying to protect the case, I probably did it more harm than good. Because Sattar was not charged, he was available to function, in front of the jury, as the Blind Sheikh's paralegal. Everyone was able to see that, even as Salem testified about Sattar's complicity in a terrorist conspiracy, there was the mailman/paralegal/terrorist walking about, free as a bird. It was a reminder to the jury, day after day in a nine-month trial, that even we were skeptical about our main witness.

As a Sovereign District alum, I'm proud to say that, ten years later, a stellar team of prosecutors from our office cleaned up the Sattar problem I'd left unaddressed. They should never have had to.

☒ Chapter 17

Siddig Ali Takes Center Stage

SIDDIG IBRAHIM SIDDIG ALI WAS TIRED of being on the jihad's B-Team.

Young, handsome, bright, and an articulate speaker of English and Arabic, the Sudanese native was known and liked by Hassan al-Turabi's circle, giving him an entrée with the diplomats assigned by the National Islamic Front to Sudan's United Nations mission in New York City. That gave him the pedigree and skills to be a useful confidante and translator for Sheikh Omar Abdel Rahman, to whom he made bayat, the pledge of undying loyalty. Nevertheless, he wanted to do more. He wanted to be a hero.

He longed, for a time, to be another Nosair, at whose New York State trial he was a fixture at the beck and call of his friends Ibrahim El-Gabrowny, Ahmed Abdel Sattar, and the Abouhalima brothers. He had been on the cusp of recruitment into the bombing conspiracy in 1992 when a July trip to visit Nosair had been postponed at the last minute–and then seemed to fizzle as Salem walked away and the FBI served a flood of grand jury subpoenas. He was brought into the periphery of the World Trade Center bombing plot in December 1992, when Mahmud Abouhalima asked him for help testing various explosive compounds. But, after taking too much time to consult with the renowned mujahid "Doctor Rashid" (Clement Hampton-El) and his friend Abdo Haggag, he got back to Abouhalima too late–the conspirators already had their answer and didn't seek further help from Siddig.

What could he do to achieve the glory he thought was his destiny? The answer, obviously, lay in training. His emir, the Blind Sheikh, stressed that without it, nothing truly worthwhile could be accomplished. Thus in autumn 1992, Abdel Rahman encouraged Siddig to team up with Doctor

Rashid in running a paramilitary camp the latter was establishing in rural Pennsylvania. Under the arrangement, Hampton-El, financed by Islamic militants overseas, set up the facility; Siddig selected the recruits, with Abdel Rahman's approval.

As Siddig later explained to Salem, "Our goal was that these people get extensive and very, very, very good training, so that we can get started at anyplace where jihad was needed." At the time, the plight of the Bosnian Muslims was a prominent concern, and much was made of the possibility of sending trained warriors to Bosnia–in the mold of Al-Kifah's support of the jihad in Afghanistan. Siddig made it clear, however, that the preparation was not limited to Bosnia–indeed, none of the participants ever went there. The goal was to be ready "to do anything," including "over here" in the United States. Echoing his emir, he stressed the need "for people to be ready for action" wherever action was needed.

Hampton-El took steps to secure detonators and "clean" guns–though he made the mistake of seeking them from Garrett Wilson, an undercover agent of the U.S. Naval Investigative Service. He told Wilson he envisioned training a group in "commando tactics": "sentry neutralization techniques," bomb identification, Navy SEAL training, Israeli police tactics, and the like.

The effort started up in earnest in October 1992–continuing until the World Trade Center bombing, when Hampton-El and Siddig shut it down due to stepped-up government surveillance. While it ensued, trainees traveled to the Pennsylvania woods on occasional weekends, though sessions were also held in the more conveniently located (but thus less secure) Lincoln Park, near Jersey City. Mahmud Abouhalima, then busy building the World Trade Center bomb, declined to go, opining that Siddig and Doctor Rashid were not taking adequate precautions against law enforcement monitoring. He was right: the FBI learned about the training thanks to Wilson and managed to get some surveillance photos. Nevertheless, Abouhalima's brother Mohammed attended, as did Haggag and a number of Sudanese associates Siddig was molding into a terror cell: Tarig Elhassan, Amir Abdelgani, and Amir's cousin, Fadil.

The Mubarak Murder Plot

Siddig hoped to have them do a lot more than train. His antipathy for the Egyptian regime, like his emir's, intensified after Abouhalima was arrested and returned to the United States. He told Haggag the time was ripe to "execute the desire of the Sheikh" for Mubarak's demise. Haggag–who, of course, was secretly cooperating with Egyptian intelligence–first suggested that this was crazy-talk. It would be nigh impossible, he said, "a suicidal operation." Not so, according to Siddig. He had learned Mubarak was scheduled to visit the United States toward the end of March. He'd arranged to get information about the Egyptian president's itinerary from Ahmed Yousef, a deputy consul stationed at Sudan's UN mission. Sure enough, Haggag recalled, when Siddig called Yousef a few days later, the diplomat was already trying–not yet successfully–to get the Mubarak information, though he admonished that such matters should be discussed in person at the mission, not over the telephone.

Yousef subsequently advised Siddig that Mubarak would be staying at the Waldorf Astoria. Siddig scouted the location and sketched an assassination plan on a scrap of paper, which, after displaying it to Haggag, he crumpled and ate. He anticipated needing two taxis (some of his Sudanese associates were cab drivers), which could more readily park near the hotel without being disturbed. At the appropriate time, the assassination team–trainees from the Pennsylvania camp–would spring into action, first deploying hand grenades to distract and disable the sentries, then firing machine guns at the vehicle carrying the Egyptian president. Because the terrorists were trained, and because they considered themselves a "cell" under his leadership, Siddig opined that it was unnecessary to alert them until the last minute. He and Haggag would hold the plan closely to preserve operational security. Amir Abdelgani later confirmed for Haggag that he didn't need to know about operations ahead of time–"I am willing. I am ready to do anything he wants."

Toward the end of March, with the post-World Trade Center heat still intense, Siddig and Haggag arranged a rendezvous with Hampton-El on Court Street in Brooklyn. After satisfying themselves that they were not being followed, they retreated to a quiet parking lot, where Hampton-El reminded Siddig that they were supposed to be keeping their distance at the moment. Siddig explained that he wouldn't have bothered Doctor Rashid if the matter at hand were not "an emergency." "Brother," he elaborated, "there is an Islamic operation, and we need a group of submachine guns and grenades, and a group of pistols." On Siddig's assurance that the operation had been approved, Hampton-El promised to get back to him in a few days. There was no question that the mission was authorized: as Abdel Rahman later told Haggag when they discussed Mubarak, "Depend on God. Carry out this operation. It does not require a fatwa."

Haggag passed information about the plot to his Egyptian intelligence contacts. As a result, the New York leg of Mubarak's U.S. trip was cancelled. Before that happened, though, a federal agent called Haggag, asking to meet him. Startled, Haggag went to the Blind Sheikh, who told him "nothing comes from these people except evil." At Abdel Rahman's direction, Haggag consulted Bill Kunstler's partner, Ron Kuby, who, with Haggag's approval, declined the requested interview.

Haggag, however, met with the FBI anyway, at the suggestion of an alarmed and curious Siddig, who told him it would be wise to find out what the FBI knew. Haggag met with agents who didn't ask him about Mubarak—they wanted, instead, to talk about the Pennsylvania paramilitary training. Nevertheless, Haggag took the opportunity to burn everyone: Declining to cooperate with the agents but falsely telling Siddig that the FBI had grilled him about the Mubarak plot. Haggag, secretly, was desperate to neutralize the murder conspiracy without calling attention to himself—he figured it was far better for him if it looked the plan had been foiled by the Americans, whom he obviously hadn't warned, than the Egyptians whom he had.

Siddig was stunned. He had not even revealed the target of the "Islamic operation" to his trusted friend Hampton-El. His only discussions had been with Haggag—there having been no need to seek additional approval from Abdel Rahman for an effort to kill Mubarak. Insightfully, Siddig surmised that Haggag might be setting him up to be labeled an FBI informant, and was probably lying–that he hadn't really spoken to the FBI but had just lost his nerve. The pair argued bitterly, with Siddig vowing there would be a "next time" which Mubarak would "not be able to escape [because] . . . you will not be with me at all." He contacted Hampton-El to cancel the munitions order, warning him to "watch out" because the plan might have been compromised.

"An Operation . . . at the Military Places"

By April 1992, the frustrated Siddig found himself frequently in Salem's company. Both of them were at the Blind Sheikh's beck and call. This presented Salem with a key opportunity. Siddig's initial anger at Haggag was fading. He wanted to believe that his friend had not betrayed him, and it led him to speculate that the downfall of the Mubarak plot may have been the FBI eavesdropping on their conversations. Understanding that Salem had the capacity to detect monitoring devices, he asked the informant to sweep his residence and check his telephone. Salem was happy to comply.

The two got to talking, and Siddig complained bitterly that the Muslims, even with hearts in the right place, could seem to get nothing right– the stupidity of Salameh in going back for his van rental deposit being a classic case, the unraveling of what he described as his recent conspiracy to murder Mubarak being yet another. Salem, seeing he had a live one, egged him on. Siddig related that he controlled a group of men who had undergone paramilitary training and were willing to take on dangerous jihad missions. Salem, too, had been looking, he said, for the right opportunity: a well-planned, disciplined jihad operation. He'd be honored to sign on to Siddig's team.

Feeling confident, the Sudanese cut to the chase: "Can't we conduct an operation over here," he asked, "at the military places?"

Siddig observed that in both Manhattan and Brooklyn there were U.S. armories, each of which served as both a "gathering point for reserve officers," and a "depot for ammunition and weapons." The feasibility of getting inside such an installation would require study, he conceded. His cell, though, combined with Salem's expertise in bomb construction, gave the initiative some hope of success. Salem agreed, and the two resolved to speak again after giving the matter more thought.

Siddig was wisely concerned about jumping in too fast with Salem, whom he had seen here and there for over a year but did not know well. He thus consulted Ali Shinawy at Abu Bakr mosque. Shinawy acknowledged that some people wondered about Salem; Shinawy, however, said he'd always found Salem trustworthy and committed to the cause.

Salem, meanwhile, also needed to double back. He had agreed to reenter the investigation to help solve the World Trade Center bombing which, he remained convinced, should never have happened. Now, however, things were taking a dramatic turn. The bombing already seemed to be solved, but there were plenty of other potential terrorists in the Blind Sheikh's orbit. Several of them, Siddig the most obvious but hardly alone, had training (either in the U.S. or overseas) and seemed anxious—perhaps emboldened by the World Trade Center attack—to conduct jihad operations in America.

These jihadists had to be stopped, he thought. He was in a unique position to stop them. From what Salem could detect, the FBI did not have a lot of other options. There appeared to be few, if any, Arabic speaking agents who could go undercover as he was doing—if there were, he'd have met them. But, he wondered, what about his personal safety? What about the risk to his new wife and children? His family in Egypt? He was not yet certain the government could be trusted at all, and if he waded in deeper, he would soon have to trust them regarding everything.

In the end, the FBI made his choice simple—not easy, but simple. Under no circumstances was 1992 going to be repeated. The government badly wanted Salem's cooperation, but the right ground rules needed to be set from the start this time. Salem must agree to become a cooperating witness, to make tape-recordings at the direction of the FBI, and to testify in any resulting cases. At the conclusion of the undercover investigation, he and his family—including family in Egypt—would be relocated under new identities, they would have protection from the United States Marshals'

Witness Protection Program for as long as his cooperation was needed, and he would be rewarded generously for the sacrifices, in addition to being compensated for any financial losses.

No figure was agreed to, no contract yet formalized. Not then. It was a good faith promise. Salem was leery. But he was also invested. He wanted to avoid another World Trade Center attack, and he craved the thrill that addicted him to spy work. But every bit as much as Siddig, he longed for the chance to be the hero of his grandiose imagination—to measure up to his fantasies, to be the Emad Salem who really did take a bullet for Sadat.

Salem signed on.

So did I.

⌛ Chapter 18

Recruited for the Jihad

THE SOUTHERN DISTRICT HAS ALWAYS BEEN a 24/7, year-round operation. Young prosecutors with their federal agents, City and State police,
office investigators, paralegals, support staff, and interns can be found
scurrying the halls any time after about 5 a.m.–sometimes earlier if the late
night before never ended.

Trials have hard schedules. Voluminous appellate briefs and legal
memoranda for the District Court have fixed deadlines. Indictments must
be filed in accordance with time-frames fixed by the federal Speedy Trial
Act. Very little else, however, works with the predictability of a normal
work-day. In fact, there is nothing normal about the work-day, which usually goes at least twelve hours, often much longer–eating up weekends and
holidays, consuming your life. It has to be that way. Crime does not work
nine-to-five either. Key events in investigations happen at all hours of the
day and night. Witnesses have to be interviewed when they are available–
and if cooperating endangers them, that can make for some quirky times
and places. If a federal judge says, "Trial next Monday," or "motion papers
by next Friday," there is no work-a-day formula for complying with that–
you kiss your family goodbye and do whatever has to be done so the United
States is ready to proceed when the gavel comes down.

Even allowing that controlled chaos is standard, the spring of 1993 was
unusually frenetic and dramatic. The World Trade Center bombing, virtually next door to our office, still reverberated weeks later. I was the chief
of the General Crimes Unit, the training ground for brand-spanking-new
Assistant United States Attorneys, and the ranks were unusually thin due to
one of government's periodic hiring freezes. Nevertheless, two of my best

new prosecutors—Michael Garcia, who, a dozen years later, would be named United States Attorney by President Bush, and Lev Dassin, whom Mike would make his Criminal Division Chief—had been poached to work full-time on the bombing investigation. I couldn't complain. Nearly a decade earlier, I'd been grabbed—as a paralegal about to be minted a lawyer—to be the all-purpose newbie on the "Pizza Connection" case, which, at seventeen months, turned into the longest federal criminal trial in American history. It had been an incomparable learning experience, and I was convinced (as I still am) that a mega-prosecution, in which you're in the trenches with the best veteran AUSAs and every issue under the sun arises, was the best way to make good prosecutors.

It was an era of dramatic change. The new administration in Washington meant a change of parties for the first time in a dozen years. President Clinton had seized the moment to name Janet Reno the U.S. Attorney General, the first woman ever to hold the position. It had only been two weeks since she'd been confirmed, but virtually all of the nation's ninety-three U.S. Attorneys were about to be fired so the Democrats could put their own stamp on federal law enforcement. The headwinds in New York strongly suggested that we, too, were about make history with the appointment of Mary Jo White as the first woman to hold the storied post of United States Attorney for the Southern District of New York. To put it mildly, she would not be a token hire.

That was the state of play at about 8 a.m. on March 25 when I walked across the third-floor bridge to the courthouse with another AUSA, Alexandra Rebay, who'd started in the office shortly after I had and was now chief of the Senior Narcotics Unit, which handled investigations of international drug cartels. We were headed over to the chambers of U.S. District Judge Louis J. Freeh, the legendary former FBI agent and federal prosecutor who had been my boss and mentor on the Pizza Connection case, and who'd been placed on the bench by President George H.W. Bush in 1991. Unbeknownst to us at the moment, President Clinton would make him Director of the FBI in a few months. Right now, however, he had far more significant business to attend to.

He was going to marry us.

In the Sovereign District, it's very hard to keep a secret—at least a romantic secret—but we'd managed to be very discreet since we'd started dating the previous summer. We had told no one we were getting married except Louie, which was sort of unavoidable under the circumstances. I thought I'd be content to keep it that way forever if I could. In fact, after the short but wonderfully simple ceremony—Louie in a ceremonial robe and his excited clerks looking on as our witnesses—we figured on just going about our day, Alexandra off to her early meetings, me to argue a case that morning before the U.S. Court of Appeals for the Second Circuit. But once it was done, and we were married, it felt so right, as it has every day for the last fifteen years, I thought I'd burst.

As I pulled my notes together to run back to the courthouse for the appellate argument, my friend Jim Johnson—with whom I'd tried a gut-wrenching case the year before, involving a drug gang's vicious attempted murder of an undercover New York City cop—poked his head into my office. I told him my "guess what I did this morning" story. Alexandra 'fessed up to a couple of confidants, too. By mid-morning, the news was all over the place—Assistants date all the time, but usually lots of people know it's going on and the first news you hear of it is not typically that they got hitched in the courthouse and went back to work.

It became a joyous day in what is a very insular, self-consciously unique community. Our interim U.S. Attorney, Roger Hayes, invited the whole office to his library for a gracious, impromptu toast. Scores of AUSAs and staff packed in to cheer and wish us well. It was one of those rare moments of unmitigated happiness. For Alexandra and me, it was about the rest of life. For our small, proud "Sovereign" society, though, it was a welcome respite, if only for a few minutes. It had been a month since a bombing by jihadist terrorists had rocked our world, and this seemed like the first time in an eternity that the wheels had stopped.

Then it ended and they went back to spinning. Double time.

New marriage was far from the only tectonic shift under my feet. For three years, my ex-wife and I had been sharing custody of our son, then six.

The most awful thing about failed marriages and kids is that there's no way to make it right. I had no intention of being an every-other-weekend father. Nevertheless, joint custody, which seems so noble and admirable ("Look at them, they're putting aside their differences for the sake of the children"), turns out to be more about the parents' self-esteem than the kid's mental health. Children need stability, a big part of which is sleeping in the same bed every night. They need to know both their parents love them and are there for them, but they also need to know where home is. I wanted home to be with me—not as a trophy but because at that point, between the two of us, I was in a better position than my ex-wife to make home work. Hard as it was for her, she'd finally agreed in early 1993. Andy IV, named after my dad (still my hero thirty-six years after his passing), moved in full-time with Alexandra and me that spring—in the Bronx, where we were the top floor of a two-family home in Throggs Neck.

New Era

Life was finally settling down. I was as happy as I'd ever remembered being. Strangely, though, I was a little bored at work, notwithstanding the fact that I worked in the world's most interesting place. I had been very excited back in 1992 to take the General Crimes chiefdom. Nothing was more important to perpetuating the office's traditions than training the new prosecutors. The office has an ethic, a way of doing things that gets passed to each new generation, and the gestalt, the sum of the office's performance, hinges directly on how those values get instilled in each new individual member.

I grew to be fond of Otto Obermaier, the U.S. Attorney in the early 1990s, but I perceived that things had changed for the worse since the era of Rudy Giuliani, the U.S. Attorney who had hired me in the eighties. There was less emphasis on rooting out the bad guys; more emphasis on deferring to the bench and having cordial relations with the defense bar. There was more academic training about what we were doing, and less doing it. I'm all for training, but I believe the courtroom—doing actual cases, dealing with concrete problems, not being afraid to make inevitable mistakes—is the best classroom. If I was a good boss, and most of my charges seemed to think so, it was only because I'd been permitted to make every mistake imaginable . . . twice. When I gave sage advice, it was generally because I had a battle scar from back when I wasn't such a sage.

Getting along with the judges is also important. We, however, weren't just young lawyers who needed to know their place among the most esteemed members of our profession. We were officials of the executive branch. We were *peers* of the court, carrying out a constitutional function, enforcing the nation's laws, that was crucially different from the equally important—but not more important—role of the judiciary. We were there to represent the public on whom criminals prey; the judges were there to make sure the accused criminals got a fair shake from the public. Those are very distinct responsibilities.

The whole idea of checks-and-balances is that the branches are expected to be in tension. It is that, not the goodness of mankind, on which we rely to keep government officials honest. When disputes happen, it's often because everyone is doing his job properly, not because the prosecutor or the judge is out of line. I thought we'd lost that sense since Rudy left. When it came to the judges, I thought the office had become a bit too much like the Catholic school of my youth, where the nun clobbered you for some seeming indiscretion and then, once you got home, your parents clobbered you because the nun had clobbered you.

I wanted to be a General Crimes chief in the mold of Barbara Jones, now a terrific judge in the Southern District. She had been the first chief I had worked for as a prosecutor (in the Organized Crime unit because I was assigned to the Pizza Connection case), and was the gold standard for how to train, encourage, and inspire new Assistants. I wanted to push these tyro-AUSAs to get themselves into court, to be thoughtful and respectful but forceful and unafraid of error in a job where error is unavoidable and paralysis is the inexcusable sin.

Once in the job, though, I was disappointed. There were only a half-dozen AUSAs—not like the classes of a dozen or more that were typical in years past. Instead of the forty or fifty cases I'd been expected to handle as a new AUSA, my charges were carrying well over a hundred each. It was all they could do to stay above water. Besides the two new AUSAs we'd lost to the World Trade Center investigation, the Southern District now had a satellite office in White Plains which my unit was expected to help staff (which I thought was a terrible idea until . . . I was asked to run the White Plains Division my last five years in the office, at which point it suddenly seemed like a great idea). And worst of all, the federal sentencing guidelines, instituted in the late 1980s, had changed the very nature of the job.

Intended to bring more predictability to sentencing by reducing judicial discretion and thus, among other things, making plea bargaining less of a crapshoot, the guidelines had turned criminal cases into as much an exercise in accounting as investigation. Overwhelmed AUSAs were spending less time in court and more time on dry number-crunching–points for exacerbating role, points for mitigating role, points for acceptance of responsibility, obstruction, breach of fiduciary duty, criminal history categories, base offense levels, downward departures, on and on it went with its mind-numbing tabulations and charts. It was a new vocabulary and a dramatically more abstruse way of approaching a case.

The approach I'd been taught in the pre-guidelines days was basically to tell the defense lawyer, "Either your client eats Count One or I'll see you at trial"–leaving the defendant with the choice of pleading to one charge and taking his chances with the sentencing judge, or going to trial on the whole indictment and risking convictions on multiple counts with the likelihood of much more jail time. That simpler, better world was now gone. And unlike the old days, when a case was pretty much over when the judge imposed sentence, it seemed like guidelines cases never ended. When AUSAs were not calculating guidelines metrics for plea-agreements, they were writing briefs about those calculations. And every time a court or the sentencing commission would make a decision that altered the guidelines some way, a flood of habeas corpus petitions would rain down from long-ago defendants in faraway prisons who wanted the benefit of the new rules.

I had expected to teach people about trying cases. Instead, I'd come in every morning to a stack of guidelines stipulations. I had to sign off on all of them. And how could I complain? My newbies had been in the office until one or two o'clock in the morning cranking out the stips just so they'd have a chance to get through the next day's pile. I loved my troops, and I'm very proud of what good prosecutors and friends they became. But it was not the job I'd imagined when I took it. I was beginning to think my useful time as a prosecutor was at an end.

Most people stay in the office around four years. I was in my eighth, with two years as a paralegal and several years with the Marshals Service before that. I wasn't sure I wanted to start with another brand new U.S. Attorney—my fifth. I knew Mary Jo White's reputation as a boffo Southern District Assistant, and I'd been grudgingly impressed as hell the only time I'd dealt with her—on the opposite side of a turf fight over a big organized crime case when she was Deputy U.S. Attorney in the Eastern District, right across the bridge in Brooklyn. I thought she'd be a very strong U.S. Attorney, but I wasn't thrilled at the idea of another new transition. Maybe it was time to move on.

That was what I was thinking, anyway, when Gil Childers and Henry DePippo walked into my office and shut the door.

Duty Calls

Gil and I were old pals. When I had worked on Pizza, Gil had been a young Kings County Assistant District Attorney who was assigned to our office to work on the famous mafia "Commission Case" against the bosses of the five New York crime families. Rudy Giuliani then had the good sense to bring him completely into our fold. Gil and I had grown up in the office together. And I'd liked Henry from the moment I'd met him upon being asked, as a senior AUSA, to second-seat him in one of his first three trials, as is our custom. The case had pled out at the last minute, but I'd been impressed by his manner and his brain—he was an unassuming regular guy, a big sports fan like me, but crackerjack smart and unruffled by the pressure of litigation in a way that seemed beyond his years. Gil and Henry were now deputy chiefs of the entire Criminal Division, which meant they were my neighbors on the Seventh Floor. One of the deputies' major tasks was to help the General

Crimes chief train the young'uns. Still, much as I liked them, Gil and Henry had lately been exactly zero help to me. They were leading the prosecution of the World Trade Center bombers, and their major "contribution" to my life in recent weeks had been to steal Mike Garcia and Lev Dassin from my already strapped unit. When they walked in, I got a knot in my stomach—anticipating that they wanted yet another AUSA.

They did.

Gil and Henry had indicted Mohammed Salameh, Mahmud Abouhal- ima, Nidal Ayyad, and Ahmed Ajaj for bombing the Twin Towers. They had drawn Judge Kevin Thomas Duffy, and he was determined to push the case to trial by the late summer—whirlwind speed for a case of such significance and complexity. Judge Duffy was obviously intent, however, on making a point about the capacity of the American justice system to deal with a ter- rorist attack on the United States—firmly, fairly, and with due dispatch. This was not going to get off track or become a kangaroo court. Ibrahim El-Gabrowny's case was more complicated. There was, they explained to me, evidence that he'd been involved in the bombing plot, but he'd only been indicted so far on charges arising out of the phony Nosair passports and his assault on the agents who'd come to execute the search warrant at his home.

The other El-Gabrowny evidence couldn't be revealed right now. A shiver went through me as Gil and Henry explained that the World Trade Center might just be the tip of the iceberg. Poker-face is not my speed—my face goes red like the light behind a hockey goal. My pulse was pounding under my jaw and it was an effort to maintain the same mien as they elabo- rated that we'd had an undercover informant into El-Gabrowny last year. The same guy had been reactivated by the bombing, and now it looked like the same group of Muslim fanatics (as I conclusorily thought of them then), led by this maniac Blind Sheikh in Jersey, was planning another terrorist operation that might rival or surpass the World Trade Center attack in its deadliness.

Gil, Henry, Mike, and Lev had been working pretty much round-the- clock for two months, trying to manage the indicted case involving what truly was the crime of the century (if one looks at the bombing as a crime) while concurrently managing the investigation of something that might be just as cataclysmic, but which we had a good chance of stopping if it was done right. They couldn't keep doing both. They needed to get ready for trial and hand off the ongoing investigation to someone capable of running it. That someone had to be a lawyer with whom they could work effectively because this was the jihad and it was going to take a long time.

They wanted me.

I was dumbfounded. Not so much to be asked–if the shoe had been on the other foot, Gil and Henry would be among the first lawyers I'd had turned to, so I wasn't surprised that they'd come to me. There was no template for prosecuting international terrorism, but the closest analogue we did have was international organized crime, and that had been my specialty. I was a natural person to ask. No, what staggered me was the magnitude of what I'd heard. Less daunted than enraged that these terrorists, who had already ravaged my country and my city, were hellbent on killing even more of us, many, many more of us, all in an effort to extort us into submitting to their agenda–which, at the very bottom of my learning curve, I then thought of as strictly a political agenda.

I pretended that I'd think about it, but there was no question I was going to do it. Gil and Henry were smart enough to know that and gracious enough to say they'd wait a bit for me to come back to them. There were added enticements. El-Gabrowny's case had been assigned to Judge Michael B. Mukasey–whom, I am glad for the country's sake, we now know as U.S. Attorney General Michael B. Mukasey. I didn't know Judge Mukasey well back then. I'd second-sat one young AUSA in a short trial before him–that was it. He was, however, the very model of what a judge ought to be: smart, quick, thoughtful, eminently fair, and in control–if you were in front of Judge Mukasey, you were made to know you were in federal court doing serious business. If we could make the bigger case on El-Gabrowny and other terrorists, he'd be the judge, which by itself was reason to sign on.

Plus, Gil and Henry had told me they'd already recruited Rob Khuzami to work on the case. Rob was a little older than me, but my junior in the office because he'd worked in private practice for a few years first. Thus, though I'd been asked to second-seat him in one of his first trials, I was more like a potted plant because he was already a very polished litigator. We were contemporaries and easily became friends. It was one of the few "second-seat" assignments that felt more like a collaboration than a clinic, and I was delighted at the prospect of partnering up on what promised to be an experience that would change our lives.

Most of all, though, I was worried about the effect on my son's life. Taking this on would mean a lot of time away, when he most needed me at home. He had already been through more than enough upheaval for any six-year-old, and this would be a cataclysm. A terrorism case would not only mean I was on duty all the time, and that I'd need to skip around the country interviewing witnesses whose lives were in danger. It would mean our own security would be an issue—and would become even more of an issue, months down the road, when we got reliable information that the jihadists were talking about having me killed.

That meant stepped-up protection for Alexandra, Andy, and me. I wasn't fazed by it. Terrorists are trying to kill everyone, so when you hear they want to kill you, it's not such a stretch. For me, it was like a badge of honor—if I was getting under their skin, it was because I was effective, and they knew it. Security is hardest on a protected prosecutor's family, not on the prosecutor himself.

Doing a big case is like being asked to pitch in the seventh game of the World Series. If you want to be a prosecutor—and that was all I ever wanted to be since hearing the stories of my grandfather's halcyon days at the Bronx DA's Office—this is what you were put on the planet for. It's the calling. Like the pitcher, you're too busy and too focused to deal with the fanfare. You've got the game—it's everybody around you who has to live with the anxiety. Security is intrusive, which is not a comfortable way to live. But for Alexandra and me, who were in law enforcement and dealing with violent people, it wasn't scary. The problem was that it would frighten a six-year-old kid who'd already been through a rocky time and who shouldn't have needed to be escorted to the first grade by federal agents just so his dad could play big-time lawyer.

I was lucky. I have a wonderful, patriotic family that pulled together to make life work. My mom and my five siblings made sure Andy felt like he was home whether I was there or not. I have a tireless, unflappable wife who not only took the burdens of home off my shoulders but, as she moved on to become chief of the office's Appeals Unit (the lawyer for the lawyers), she became the legal adviser to both our team and Gil and Henry's. It meant we never put the case down, but it also meant I never felt like it was spinning out of control, no matter how complicated and contentious it became. And I have a very fine son, who should have had a lot more of my attention, but who grew to be proud of what I was doing and to understand why I had to do it.

I agreed, of course, to take over the case. It was three years of insanity and faithful service. But I was just a lawyer, not a soldier. I did my bit to face down a jihad, not a crime-spree. It hardly seems right, though, to call it a sacrifice. It was the highest honor of my life. It was what I owed my country. And it was a pittance compared to what our men and women in uniform are asked to pay every day of this war.

⌛ Chapter 19

The Landmarks Plot

By early May 1993, Siddig and Salem had worked out their arrangement: Siddig would direct violent operations, supplying people and explosives in addition to directing where and when bombs would be detonated; Salem would provide technical information necessary for bomb construction, but would have no participation in deploying explosives. Siddig was running the cell and had the connections. As an informant, Salem's challenge was to draw them out into the light while appearing to help them make war on America.

On May 7, Salem officially began making undercover tapes under the supervision of Agent Anticev and Detective Napoli. These tapes were our case. They were both devastating evidence and a frightening window into radical Islam.

Upon meeting Salem that day, Siddig explained that he had decided to target the United Nations complex rather than one of the armories. He had been studying the armories, and saw they were sometimes used for public flea markets, suggesting to him that a bombing would not do much to destroy U.S. munitions. By contrast, the UN was the tool through which the United States operated a "new government which rules the world," promulgating resolutions oppressive to Muslims everywhere–proving, one is constrained to observe, that there isn't much rational about the jihadist world view.

The contemplated attack had a practical side to go with its symbolism. Siddig explained that he had contacts in the Sudanese government mission who would help them obtain the credentials necessary to drive a vehicle laden with explosives into the complex without detection

"You Are Not Far From Us"

The strike would be carried out by his "cell," which is how he viewed the men—mainly Sudanese with a couple of Egyptians, he told Salem—who had undergone paramilitary training in Pennsylvania. Henceforth, they would refer to the UN as "the big house" and the bomb to be built as a *hadduta*, the Arabic word for "fairy tale."

Abdel Rahman, Siddig recounted, had already approved the plan, calling it not merely permissible but "a must" and "a duty." "Of course," the Sudanese native stressed, "the Sheikh is not going to stand on podiums" calling for a bombing attack on a specific target. That was not his way of doing things.

Siddig thus encouraged Salem to speak directly with Abdel Rahman about the plan, but cautioned that operations had to be broached with extreme caution due to the stifling surveillance. One had to be very careful in his apartment, which might well be bugged. More importantly, in speaking with the Blind Sheikh, phrasing should be broad enough to convey the question effectively but sufficiently elliptical to give Abdel Rahman deniability about details and tactics. For example, Siddig suggested, it would be better to ask, "What is the Islamic rule . . . in killing the leadership of the infidels," than to refer specifically to bombing the United Nations. Abdel Rahman was their emir, others depended on him for guidance, and thus it was their responsibility, Siddig stressed, to keep him above details and active involvement.

Salem attempted to draw Siddig out concerning the reasoning behind the World Trade Center bombing. Why kill civilians? Salem said he'd been wrestling with whether this was justifiable in Islam. Siddig agreed it was a vexing question which he had discussed a length with "the brothers." All agreed, he expounded, that it was forbidden to make the main point of a strike the wanton killing of "Muslims, children and women, the unarmed and [noncombatants]." A state of war, however, altered the usual rules. Fighting a war was a holy obligation, and the war, as a practical matter, could not be prosecuted without such casualties. Thus, the World Trade Center attack should not be seen merely as an effort to kill civilians; rather, it was "to hit the economy" that was the enemy's lifeblood, and to serve for the future as "a message that 'you are not far from us, anytime we want you, we will get you.'"

Salem had suggested to Siddig that bomb construction be carried out in a safehouse, and offered to scout potential locations. This was critical to the FBI. Hanging over the investigation was always grave concern about maintaining control. The Bureau remained extremely nervous about the prospect that, despite its best efforts and Salem's infiltration, the bombing would happen anyway and the FBI would be blamed. There was still deep distrust of Salem. The FBI wanted any explosive components to be in a setting it controlled–so that even if all the players hadn't yet been identified, we had the raw materials in our sight at all times.

When they met again a few days later, Siddig told Salem consideration needed to be given to whether a safehouse would be needed for longer than the one-month timeframe they'd been discussing. He explained that he had other plans in mind: Not just the UN but another attempt on President Mubarak, who was now scheduled to visit New York in September; and, returning to Nosair's old hit-list, strikes against the Jewish Defense League, which Siddig believe maintained a training camp in Upstate New York, and on Assemblyman Dov Hikind in Manhattan.

More importantly, the still simmering rage over Abouhalima's arrest had spawned another target for consideration: The Jacob K. Javits Federal Building on Duane Street in lower Manhattan. This is the headquarters for the FBI's New York Field Office. It was also the first place where Abouhalima had been brought after being surrendered to the Americans. Siddig added that he had surveilled the location late at night and found only a few potential obstructions: a single police car and a police booth on one side.

"If you get in from here, it is so easy," he said. "How sweet it is dealing with them. We take the police down and everything." More study was needed though, because they would want a daytime attack. They were not looking merely to do financial damage. It was murdering the agents that would hearten "Muslims all over the world."

Now that the plan was up and running, Siddig wanted to make the pilgrimage to Attica, despite the fact that Nosair was under tighter scrutiny since jail-break evidence had been found during El-Gabrowny's arrest. On May 21, he and Salem made the long trip. They spent several hours meeting with Nosair, which Salem could not record since the discovery of a taping device by prison authorities would have blown the investigation. Although they were secluded in a high security unit and speaking in Arabic, Nosair wanted to speak with each man individually, and they whispered, leaning over a divider.

Nosair was already pleased. He had heard about the paramilitary camp Siddig began with Hampton-El the previous year. Nonetheless, he did not agree that it was a propitious time for bombing the UN or other targets. Instead, he opined, now was the time to use the skills honed in training to snatch important officials who could then be ransomed for his release and that of the World Trade Center bombers. Nosair had been giving the matter much thought and had two kidnapping targest in mind: former President Richard M. Nixon and former Secretary of State Henry Kissinger. It was they, after all, who had initially portrayed Muslims as "a great danger . . . in the future." Here again, Nosair was echoing the Blind Sheikh, who often contended that America's interference in Middle East affairs had been set in motion by Nixon, who, according to Abdel Rahman, had insisted that America must remain a presence in the region "to demolish the Islamic awakening in any of these countries." Nosair advised that, in excuting these kidnappings, they should remember to remove the victims' clothing since, he believed, prominent figures like Nixon and Kissinger carried transmitters because of concerns about abduction.

Siddig promised to think about this proposal and to extend Nosair's warm regards to Sheikh Omar. After consulting Abdel Rahman, however, he concluded that Nosair's kidnapping plan was impractical. At this point in his life, he explained to Salem, Nixon "doesn't have any decision making" authority. "Even if we take him, kill him, so what? He doesn't have any influence in the country." They resolved to concentrate on the bomb-ings.

"Inflict Damage on the American Army Itself"

The investigation's most critical moments, and Salem's most daring performance, occurred during the late evening of May 23, 1993, when the informant decided to take up Siddig's suggestion that he consult directly with the Blind Sheikh. There were several other men in the cleric's apart-ment when Salem asked to speak privately with Abdel Rahman. Sheikh Omar agreed, but insisted they move themselves into the kitchen "away from the monitoring" he was sure American intelligence had installed in his living room.

There was monitoring, but it was not in the living room; it was in Salem's briefcase. From time to time, Salem would be hugged just a little too long or patted just a little too familiarly. He knew people were checking him for wires. But for some reason, there was never much mind paid to the briefcase he always carried—the one containing the recording device.

To pave the way for what he was about to do, the informant cleverly appealed to the Blind Sheikh's gargantuan vanity. He said he'd asked for a private session because he wanted to make *bayat*, the pledge of loyalty, to Abdel Rahman. He proceeded with a lugubrious promise to hold Sheikh Omar as his unquestioned emir and to follow his guidance in all endeavors. Abdel Rahman seemed pleased, green-lighting the informant to go on to his next subject.

But when that subject turned out to be the fact that he and Siddig were planning to "do a job," the Blind Sheikh cut him off, saying, "Go visit Mahmud. Ask him about Siddig. That's it. Go visit Mahmud."

Salem protested. It was not a good idea to visit Mahmud Abouhalima right now—such such a visit might be used against Salem after "we do some-thing."

"Wait" on doing something, the Shiekh insisted. "Visit Mahmud and ask him about Siddig. Ask Mohammed Abouhalima about Siddig. Ask Mohammed Abouhalima, 'what did your brother say about Siddig?'"

Abdel Rahman knew there was a traitor in his ranks and now, thanks to the machinations of Abdo Haggag, suspicion had fallen on Siddig. But though Siddig was guilty of many things, betrayal was not one of them. Haggag was the culprit. Haggag had secretly been cooperating with the Egyptian authorities. When they interrogated Abouhalima in Egypt, they thus knew to grill him about asking Siddig for bomb-construction help during the World Trade Center plot. Abouhalima reasonably deduced that Siddig must have been a mole for the Egyptians. In reality, though Siddig had not confided in the Egyptians; unbeknownst to Abouhalima, he had confided in *Haggag*, who had promptly passed the information on to the Egyptians. Evaluating what they knew–the Egyptian interrogation, the compromise of the Mubarak plot, and the fact that the FBI knew about the Pennsylvania training–the Blind Sheikh and Abouhalima had added two-plus-two and come up with five. It was an understandable error, but an error nonetheless. Abdel Rahman was not completely convinced that Siddig, whom he had always liked and relied on, was the traitor. But he was worried about it, and he was warning Salem.

Salem, though, knew that Siddig was almost certainly not a traitor–the FBI would not be directing him to make tapes on an informant. He also realized he might never get such an opportunity with Abdel Rahman again, just the two of them in close quarters. In fact, it probably wouldn't be long until someone from the living room interrupted them. He needed to think fast.

The informant countered that it was inconceivable Siddig could be a traitor. After all, they were "preparing for a big deed." Abdel Rahman conceded that this might be true, but Salem, he said, would lose nothing by at least speaking with Mahmud's brother, Mohammed. Siddig's infidelity had not been established, but Salem should at least ask Mohammed, "What is the incident that arose your doubts?" Further prodded by Salem, the emir of jihad revealed his awareness of the Abouhalima/Siddig meeting in the midst of the Twin Towers bombing plot: "Because Mahmud is saying, 'I did not tell anyone at all except Siddig, and I told him in a certain automobile.'" That, the Blind Sheikh related, is "what was reported to me."

Salem continued to plead Siddig's case, pointing out that it was difficult to believe him a traitor when he was the one "doing actual work" rather than pushing others forward to be compromised. The Blind Sheikh allowed that this was true, conceding that nothing had been proved and Siddig might well be loyal.

The two then had the following exchange in hushed whispers, Salem gently holding his briefcase near the sightless cleric's face, careful not to let it sway even slightly lest his sharp ears pick up the creaking sound, yet praying that no one would barge in and tell Abdel Rahman what he was doing:

> Salem: I wish to know in regards to the United Nations, do we consider it the house of the devil? Because my strike is a devastating one and not a screw-up one like the one that took place at the Trade Center. We are preparing for something big, something big if God is willing, that will bring it upside down. So is this considered *halal* [licit] or *haram* [illicit]?
>
> Abdel Rahman: It is not *haram*, however, it will be bad for Muslims.
>
> Salem: Not *haram*, however, it will be bad for Muslims, we do it or–?
>
> Abdel Rahman: No.
>
> Salem: Forget it.
>
> Abdel Rahman: Find a plan, find a plan . . . to inflict damage, inflict damage on the American army itself. But the United Nations . . . will be a disadvantage for the Muslims. It will harm them deeply.
>
> Salem: So, forget about the United Nations?
>
> Abdel Rahman: No.
>
> Salem: We keep it in the Army.
>
> Abdel Rahman: Yes. Keep it eh–You all think of something else, because the United Nations–they will consider it to be the center of peace, and that Muslims are against peace, and will create a difficulty

and will disturb the Muslims' being.

Salem then explained that Siddig was also considering the FBI's New York headquarters for a strike.

"Wait for a while," replied the Blind Sheikh. "We will talk about this later. Slow down a little bit." It was important, he emphasized, that such an operation be planned carefully. "Are you paying attention," he asked before his chilling wind-up: "The man who killed Kennedy was training for three years."

"No, no, we will do a good job," Salem replied.

"Okay," Abdel Rahman answered, "May God make things easy for you."

The Blind Sheikh had been his usual slick self. The UN bombing was permissible . . . but tactically unwise. Siddig was an informant . . . or maybe he wasn't. Of course, Abdel Rahman's major function was to pass on the Islamic propriety of an action–if he had said *haram*, that would have been the end of it. As long as it was *halal*, tactics were a side issue, and one he generally wanted to stay out of.

No matter what happened, though, we now had him, on tape, soliciting a bombing of United States military installations. Moreover, Sheikh Omar would never be able to claim that Salem had put words in his mouth. Bombing the American military was entirely the cleric's idea. As far as I was concerned, we had a case on Abdel Rahman now. We'd have to fight for it, and there would be a lot of resistance, but the real crime would be to shrink from doing what cried out to be done.

Not surprisingly, Abdel Rahman was suffering jihadi's remorse the next day when Salem drove him to an appearance. When the informant tried to bring up the UN again, Abdel Rahman curtly cut him off, saying he did not want to talk in a car and adding that he wasn't happy about having talked about it in his apartment either.

Later, Salem told Siddig the Blind Sheikh had said the UN strike was permissible, but was a bad tactical idea because it would cast Muslims in a bad light. Siddig expressed surprise, "But with me, he wasn't, um–according to my conversation with him there was no problem."

Siddig, who had more regular access to Abdel Rahman than Salem did, asserted that he would refrain from bombing the United Nations if Abdel Rahman were truly against it. But for now, "the work will increase," he said, noting that he had already put some of his men on alert, and begun efforts to obtain needed information about the United Nations complex from his sources in the Sudanese embassy. And indeed Siddig (whose phone was now being tapped by the FBI) had spoken with Ahmed Yousef, telling the diplomat, "May God grant you the ability to repulse the enemies–the ones who are here. Because we're ready, we are watching the situation. . . . Strong conspiracies are being weaved in the darkness." Yousef, as if directly speaking to the American people, warned: "We are not going to prevail by outnumbering you, but rather God's wrath is focused upon you."

Drawing Out the Cell

By the end of May, the FBI had obtained a "safehouse"–a garage in Queens for Salem to urge as the base of operations. The Bureau installed hidden cameras and microphones. The installation was never the coup that it should have been–the young agents assigned to operate the controls from a remote, windowless location which was squalid and just hellish in the approach of what would be an unusually hot summer, often did not know how to manipulate the cameras and shift microphones so the optimal one was activated (rather than all of them, which created indecipherable echo). Salem, however, was virtually always on the scene at the necessary times with his trusty briefcase. We continued to have phenomenal audio, though the video left much to be desired.

For his part, Siddig was also moving forward on the explosives and man-power fronts. He had met with Hampton-El, who was trying to obtain some grenades they might need in carrying out bombing operations, as well as the sophisticated, pliable explosive C-4. Doctor Rashid's only concern was that Siddig had consulted with the Blind Sheikh and gotten a fatwa. As long as he had, Hampton-El would do what he could to help and said he did not need further details.

On May 27, Siddig brought Salem to the Medina Mosque in lower Manhattan to meet two of his cell members, Amir Abdelgani and Fares Khallafalla. The four men proceeded to the safehouse where they tested a timing device and sat down to hash out the current state of planning. Siddig explained that he had been conducting surveillance of the FBI's office and was finding it a daunting target, which they would likely "want to put . . . aside for a while until we plan it." Still, in addition to the UN, he had now settled on two additional targets: the Lincoln and Holland Tunnels.

The mission, he urged, was imperative. Before the World Trade Center bombing, "the one billion Muslims in the world [had not seen] any action which strikes America." Abdelgani agreed that America would "decrease" as they continued to hit it. Yes, Siddig, concurred, it was important to keep hitting it. But it was also important to avoid a "negligible" attack. He wanted a strike that people would not "forget tomorrow"–one that would "paralyze the economy." No action, he assured, would be taken without Sheikh Omar's approval, since a fatwa was necessary "when you do anything which is basically unlawful" and which would be wrong unless the "mission is under the flag of God and his Messenger."

To better convey his plan, Siddig sketched it on a piece of cardboard as he went along. All three bombings would be executed on the same day, five minutes apart:

> Practically, we will do the big house [code for the UN], but theoretically there are three. The big house, I will take care of it. I and with, I'll see who. . . . There will be five minutes between each of them. Boom! God, the whole world! And after five minutes, the people, uh–Boom! "God, God, God, is it believable!" And that's it, there is nothing more. Then, boom! This will drive the whole world crazy, this will make all America on stand-by.

The men began conducting surveillance of the targets the following day. As they drove through Manhattan's Diamond District, Abdelgani snickered that it should be added to the target list since it would be "like hitting Israel itself." The tunnels they saw as easy marks; by contrast, as they drove by the FBI's offices, Siddig pointed out the various difficulties–wistfully noting that it remained his "favorite target." Meanwhile, the Sudanese diplomats had promised to contribute license plates assigned to the Qatar embassy. They would not be able to get the consul's actual car for the UN attack, Siddig reported. The cell would need to acquire a Lincoln Continental–the preferred vehicle of third-world diplomats–and make certain the bomb could fit in it. The bombs for the tunnels, on the other hand, could be housed in vans. Siddig believed he would probably turn to a "criminal" friend of his, Wahid Saleh, for help with stealing cars. Unlike rentals, stolen vehicles could not be traced back to the plotters.

When the Blind Shiekh called him later, Siddig explained that he had been on "a very important errand" about which he would "tell your Honor, God willing, when I see you later." First, though, he needed to bring Salem to meet with Doctor Rashid.

"Boom! Five Minutes Apart!"

The session with Hampton-El in Brooklyn was extraordinary in ways that transcended the new round of terrorism that was in motion. Hampton-El had been importantly involved in the 1992 bomb plot, before Salem left the investigation. Now, in the course of this two-hour 1993 meeting, on tape and in English so an American jury could listen to Hampton-El's own words, he confirmed Salem's version of 1992 in important particulars, right from the start: "You know, we talked about some things already," he told Siddig, referring to Salem. The informant later jumped in, saying, "Remember, we go back a year ago, I started a project and you and brother Ali Shinawi. We met and we talked." Fearing this would unnerve Hampton-El, Siddig interrupted, admonishing, "Don't mention names, brother, there's no need to mention names." Hampton-El was kindly, though, and cut to the bottom line: "Let me just say . . . we haven't talked in a while, but there's a whole lot we discussed previous."

The informant had been removed from the investigation because he wouldn't make corroborating tapes. We now had a participant corroborating him. Now, 1992 could no longer be dismissed by defense lawyers as

Salem's word against El-Gabrowny's.

Siddig, who had been outraged to learn that he might be under suspicion as an informant, was particularly gratified to learn that the highly respected Doctor Rashid had spoken up in his defense. He'd angrily rejected rumors about his friend and training partner Siddig. He'd reminded people such talk could get a person killed and should be avoided in the absence of "proof, proof, proof, proof."

As the conversation turned to present needs, Salem adroitly weaved in the past. When Siddig indicated that bombing components were their main requirement, Hampton-El asserted, "The detonator is very important," prompting Salem to remind him of their June 1992 meeting, when Hampton-El had said ready-made bombs were "available." The elder statesman replied that this was because, back then, he had sources with "C-4's, . . . M16s, AKs, everything. Detonators, bulletproof vests, they had everything." Unfortunately, the FBI had since arrested his suppliers, but he was not without hope. On "the detonators," he said he would "speak to this one brother and if he's not able to do it himself, then I'll be the middle man. Then I'll go see some people to get the detonators. . . . I'll get as many as possible."

More at ease, Siddig mentioned that one target was the United Nations. Hampton-El brightened. Such an operation, he recalled, had once been "one of my projects."

"This project you talking about," he continued, "this takes a lot of courage, man." Careful planning, he advised, was the key:

> I wanted to stress that, I said it three times, I said if this takes until next year . . . very important to be patient, because, number one, you want to be successful. And . . . Allah is not going to let it happen until it pleases Him. He wants to make sure that you think about all of everything you're doing. . . . What would be fantastic is to do it and leave them in a ball of confusion not knowing who did it.

Salem asked about the going rate for grenades. They'd cost fifty to a hundred dollars apiece, replied Hampton-El. "For the time being," the informant elaborated, "I need three hand grenades so I can take the detonators out of it." Hampton-El was incredulous, "That's the only reason you need them, is to get the detonators?" When the informant nodded, Hampton-El countered, "Let's see if we can get some detonators without putting you in jeopardy. Because that's dangerous."

Hampton-El continued to highlight the need for careful planning, but he very much liked the notion of multiple strikes in quick succession. Target "structure symbols," he recommended, and then "something else simultaneously happens someplace else. . . . When that happens, simultaneously, something is happening at the same time someplace else." This, Siddig enthusiastically exclaimed, was exactly the plan. Compared to the UN, the Lincoln and Holland Tunnels would be a "lot easier, lot simpler," Siddig added. Emphasizing the point with the sound of snapping fingers, he predicted the tunnels would "break like straws. Boom! Five minutes apart!"

"The Path to God Is Obvious"

Siddig and Salem went directly from Hampton-El's Brooklyn safehouse to the Abu Bakr Mosque, where the Blind Sheikh was expecting them. Instructing Salem to keep his distance, Siddig huddled with Abdel Rahman in a corner. The emir was livid that Salem had approached him about the UN plot in his home. Siddig became equally angry–mainly because the Sheikh was upset, partially because, though he'd encouraged Salem to consult the Sheikh, he'd also cautioned him to steer clear of the apartment. Siddig, glaring at the informant while the animated cleric groused, finally motioned Salem to approach. With Abdel Rahman by his side, Siddig berated Salem for violating the rule against talking about operations in the Blind Sheikh's home.

With the message conveyed, Abdel Rahman could afford to be kinder. Noting that Salem was "dear, a friend and a brother," Sheikh Omar slipped easily into the egoist's penchant for discussing himself in the third person:

The Sheikh must remain a front for the Muslims–distant from all these matters. They should not even be talked about with me. Are you paying attention? Are you paying attention? I mean–meaning let me just be for *dawa* [the call to God] and be as a front for the Muslims. And challenge them without, without feeling any apprehension.

Sheikh Omar had this whole nod-and-a-wink method worked out, and here was Salem spoiling the party. At this point, there had been more than enough nodding: Abdel Rahman was fully aware that Siddig was preparing a bombing campaign. Now was the time for winking: "May God straighten your path. The path to God is obvious. Whoever wants to make a good work for God, the path before him is obvious. It does not need any consultation or anything. The path to God is clear." Didn't Salem get the program? By giving the Sheikh deniability, jihadists got the benefit of a religious injunction to "challenge [our enemies] and wipe the floor with them," yet "we"– meaning, the imperial *we*–"can talk." The Blind Sheikh wanted to jab a stick in America's eye, yet be protected by America's First Amendment: he wanted to let the jihadists know it was open-season without rendering himself liable for any resulting attacks. It was a beautiful arrangement . . . if people like Salem would just let it be.

Siddig was not the only underling to be read the riot act. A few days later, Sattar informed the Blind Sheikh that Salameh had called from jail and was "upset." That was enough for now, though. Sattar said he would refrain from further details until he could meet Abdel Rahman face-to-face in the safety of the mosque.

⧗ Chapter 20

Planning the End Game

It was early June and the finish line was finally in sight. An FBI agent brought Gil Childers and me to a hotel in Manhattan. It was the first time I laid eyes on Emad Salem.

He burst in the door with Detective Louie Napoli. The hotel had been chosen so Emad would have a chance to explain it away on the off chance anyone saw him. Given the stage we were at in the investigation, it probably would have been unwise in any event to bring him to our office or the FBI's. It was clearly out of the question now, though, with Siddig and Amir Abdelgani unpredictably going out on scouting trips, occasionally surveilling the the Bureau's building to determine whether it would be possible—by starting a diversionary fire down the block on Broadway or shooting the lone federal police officer standing guard near one of the entrances—to get a bomb in or at least near the garage. If the jihadists observed Salem coming in or going out of the FBI's office, the investigation would be over and he would likely be killed. It was not a risk we could run.

High Wire Act

Emad was bundle of nervous energy: talking a mile a minute even though he didn't know us, eyes darting, continually checking his phone and his omnipresent briefcase. He was clearly under great stress. Besides his jitters, it was impossible not to notice that he kept pressing the fingers of his right hand against his heart. I wasn't certain whether he was still worried about his cardiac health or just wanted us to think he was, to underline how fully he was putting himself on the line. I asked him how he'd been feeling and he said, appreciatively but dismissively, that he was fine. I silently fretted though—he was either really in discomfort or performing, and neither possibility boded well.

The other thing that stood out is how badly he wanted to be regarded and treated like an agent rather than a civilian. He was certainly invested in the investigation more than any witness I'd ever seen before.

Salem was obviously excited and pleased that we seemed headed toward a successful conclusion. There would undoubtedly be several arrests—we didn't yet know how many. As long as Siddig kept relying on Salem rather than freezing him out and turning to someone else, there would be no terrorist attack, not this time. We were a little concerned as Emad explained that Siddig was starting to get angry at all the questions he was asking—and, indeed, I'd have been even more concerned if I had seen transcripts of their conversations, which wouldn't happen until translations were done, many months down the road. The informant pushed Siddig very hard for information and went out of his way in conversations with him and others to mention names and recap history. It would make for great evidence as long as he got away with it; but much later, I often found myself wincing as I read it. Real terrorists don't like anyone who talks too much. They kept Salem around because he was useful, but as time went on he grated on them. He talked too much, and he was lucky to have gotten out alive.

Emad was worried, too. While he was out in his undercover role, he was able to shove aside anxieties about his family's security. With us now, he was thinking about it and about how drastically life would change within the next couple of weeks. When we took the case down and swept up the terrorists, he would suddenly go from anonymity to renown: The government informant who had prevented the indescribable horror that might have occurred if Siddig had turned for assistance to someone other than him—or, as Bill Kunstler would claim, the "agent provocateur" who concocted the whole thing to play on our fears and anti-Muslim bias. It would be a startling transformation. Life as Emad previously knew it would be over.

My presence at the meeting was thus significant for two reasons: I'd be working with him for a long time to come, so it was important that we get to know each other and, hopefully, hit it off. More salient at the moment, though, I also had witness security experience as a Deputy U.S. Marshal, unlike most prosecutors and investigators. It was too early to bring the Marshals into the mix—the active investigation was not yet over, Salem was appropriately concerned about meeting any new people (each additional one cut in on the secret was a risk to blow the whole thing and thus a danger to him), and it was no sure thing yet that he'd go for the WitSec program, which is a very difficult life. I was there to begin talking to him, with some authority, about what life would soon be like, underscoring that we were grateful for what he was doing, capable of protecting his family, and fully committed to doing just that.

Family concerns aside, Salem wanted to show Gil and me how smart he was—certainly smarter than a couple of prosecutors, the FBI, and everyone else. But a lot of that seemed contrived, as if taking shots at the FBI and the government in general was a schtick. He was clearly fond and respectful of Napoli . . . even as he suggested, with Louie sitting right next to him, that he, Emad Salem, was the only one in the investigation, maybe in the world, who knew what he was doing.

What got Emad genuinely excited, though, was recounting his der-ring-do with the Blind Sheikh in the kitchen. He actually seemed pleased that the Sheikh and Siddig had given him grief about it in the days after it happened. It confirmed for him what a good spy he was—and it was des-perately important to him to be a good spy. Abdel Rahman was a clever, cunning icon, and Salem had gotten him to do something he didn't want to do: talk in an accountable way. Salem made a point of asking us and the agents whether the tape was clear and whether it had been properly secured as evidence. He lit up as he described the event—as if he were transported there all over again. I hadn't heard the tape yet. It was in Ara-bic, so I wouldn't have understood it anyway. Yet, when I did finally hear it (with the help of a translator), I knew it would be devastating evidence: the sinister whispering and the patent bile in Sheikh Omar's voice when he recommended bombing the *American* military. Even without being able to speak a word of Arabic, jurors would listen to that tape and their hair would stand on end.

It was a short get-together. Salem would soon be meeting Siddig again. As we broke he stressed that he had one demand. He understood that the situation was fluid. We were still trying to identify players and could not tell him when we'd swoop in and make arrests–hopefully, catching terrorists in the act of constructing bombs in the safehouse. The only thing he wanted was to get a call ahead of time, even if it was only a few minutes ahead of time, alerting him that the take-down was about to happen. He would, he said, make an excuse to step out and get some coffee or something. But under no circumstances was he to be arrested, put down, placed in cuffs, and dragged out. He was adamant.

Weirdly so, I thought. Most undercovers *want* to appear to be arrested. It allows an informant to be whisked away as a fellow "defendant" in the eyes of the bad guys–meaning hours elapse before they realize who the mole is, and by then he's long gone. No threats and catcalls right there on the spot–something undercovers are sensitive about, it being no easy thing to deceive people, even evil people, specifically for the purpose of getting close to them, befriending them, so you can betray them. I could tell from our brief conversation that Salem and the FBI were not warm and fuzzy–though they seemed positively brotherly when they weren't consciously pushing each other's buttons. What I didn't yet know, of course, was that Salem so distrusted the Bureau, even as he worked intimately with agents day after day, that he was still not convinced it wasn't a set up. In his mind, an "arrest" might really be an arrest.

Agents and Prosecutors

By now, our most significant targets–Abdel Rahman, Hampton-El, and Siddig–were all on tape making very damning statements. Two of Siddig's confederates, Amir Abdelgani and Fares Khallafalla, had been lured out into the open. Still, there was much work to be done. Hampton-El had weapons and explosives suppliers; they hadn't been identified and we wanted to find them. Siddig also had other underlings he said were ready and willing to conduct terrorist attacks, and it was important to find out who they were. The Sudanese UN mission was clearly a problem, and we wanted to know how pervasive the threat was. Most crucially, as we wound down, I was already worried about the law.

Terrorism was far from unknown in the United States before the World Trade Center bombing. Other than during the Civil War, however, its incidents had never before been frequent or existentially threatening. As a result, the legal system circa 1993 was woefully unprepared for radical Islam. Our investigation was already elucidating some gaping weaknesses—weaknesses that counterintuitively penalized investigators for foiling plots.[1]

For example, a *successful* bombing could be punished with a term of life imprisonment and, once capital punishment was revived under federal law in the mid-1990s, by execution if the bombing had caused any deaths.[2] The criminal code, however, contained no specific provision for bombing *conspiracy*. Therefore, if a group plotted a bombing but was interrupted by effective law enforcement, the plotters had to be charged under the catch-all federal conspiracy statute, which punishes an agreement to violate any criminal statute with a maximum *five-year* penalty.[3] Such a term was grossly insufficient for a conspiracy to slaughter tens of thousands of people.

There were a few other legal remedies, but these, too, were unduly limited and problematic. Federal law, for example, made it a crime to *attempt* to carry out a bombing, which at least provided another charge against unsuccessful plotters.[4] But the penalty was paltry: a maximum of ten years' imprisonment, and, as with conspiracy, no requirement that the judge impose any minimum term of incarceration at all. One assumed any judge would hammer a would-be mass-murderer, but you couldn't be sure.

Worse, attempt law created an absurd tension between public safety and prosecution. Proving attempt requires the government not only to show that the plotters agreed to commit the crime at issue (here, bombing) and took some preparatory measures, but also that those measures amounted to what the law calls a "substantial step" toward the accomplishment of the crime. The difference, however, between "mere preparation" (which is insufficient) and a "substantial step" (which is required to establish guilt) is a murky legalism – made more ambiguous back in 1993 because the leading case on attempt, which was not a model of clarity, came in the context of an attempted *bombing*.[5]

The tension here was manifest. Because prosecutors must fear that purposeful actions to carry out a bombing could be construed by a court as "mere preparation" rather than a "substantial step," their incentive is to let the conspirators go forward until the last possible second in order to bolster the chances of conviction. Public safety, however, strongly counsels against this approach. If the investigators lose control of events, which can easily happen when dealing with organizations whose operations are by nature secretive, massive loss of life can result.

With safety pitted against courtroom evidentiary hurdles, we were smack in the age-old square-off between prosecutors and agents. I was well familiar with this dance, and it was why the Bureau and I intermittently adored and despised one another–a not unfamiliar modus vivendi for cops and prosecutors, headstrong types from often diverse backgrounds whose missions are a tense mixture of competing agendas and mutual dependency.

Agents know the world, the flesh-and-blood divide of good guys and bad guys. They are typically not graduated from the nation's top schools, but the best of them, and there are many, are achievers with a curious bent of mind and a winning way with people. Those assets gel into a practical education not available at the top schools. Agents are also dedicated lifers. Many have military or police department backgrounds (gone are the days when most FBI agents were trained lawyers or accountants). They tend to be athletic, married with children, and active in their suburban neighborhoods–enclaves likely to be a long diurnal commute from frenetic Manhattan. They come to the Bureau (like young men and, increasingly, young women come to the NYPD) expecting to serve the public for over twenty years before retiring still young enough to take on some cognate (and better paying) private security gig.

The FBI, though, is a regimented bureaucracy. Risk-taking–especially risks that could redound to the detriment of the Bureau's public reputation, which is just as assiduously tended today as it was under J. Edgar Hoover–

is not encouraged. The independent thinkers tend to stick out. The truly astute ones choose their battles carefully and can move up the ladder. The rest either learn to conform or have very bumpy careers raging against the machine.

Prosecutors—in the Southern District, at least—are nearly the opposite. Young, brash, with Ivy League (or comparable) diplomas, and fresh from either a coveted judicial clerkship or a brief but well-compensated tenure as an associate at a white-shoe New York law firm, they are predictably steeped in active idealism, abstractions, and process. Law enforcement, however, is about real life. Real life doesn't conform to antecedent rules of process and maddeningly defies our abstract notions of it. And for those who frequently know very little of the world, idealism can have a rough time coping with the revelation that virtually all one's defendants turn out to be, well, guilty. That's not how their law professors said it would be. Assistant United States Attorneys are thus drawn to their agents the way raw recruits are drawn to their drill sergeant: the flinty veteran who has long known the truths they are just discovering.

But only so far. For where the Bureau can be stifling, the ethos of the Sovereign District is creativity—to strive for the next in a cross-generational line of groundbreaking cases, a goal for which the expanding and ever more complex corpus of federal law presents endless possibilities. Plus, AUSAs are not lifers. In New York, unlike much of the country, they tend to be city dwellers who stay less than five years before moving on to something much more lucrative. Especially in their first years, they are frequently single with no life but the job—and, as it is the world's greatest job, they work it with unrestrained gusto.

Inevitably, this divergence of type is exacerbated by inherent distinctions between the objectives and functions of cops and prosecutors. Prosecutors always want more evidence. Agents want to close the case, make arrests, and move on to the next thing. Prosecutors have a great interest in the investigation, but agents are in charge of it. The U.S. attorney can suggest, but it is the FBI that decides what to look into and how many resources to devote. The FBI consults with the district U.S. Attorney's Office on strategy, and it must take the prosecutor's guidance when it seeks to employ the court's processes (such as wiretaps, search warrants, or the grand jury) in furtherance of an investigation. But while the probe ensues, the agents call the shots. Prosecutors take the wheel only when charges are filed and matters turn to apprehending suspects, returning indictments, and preparing for trial.

Not surprisingly, the metrics by which agents and prosecutors are judged–or, certainly, by which they were judged before September 11, 2001, when federal law enforcement, at least nominally, moved from a prosecution to a prevention paradigm–reflect these distinctions. Agents are measured by arrests and the number of investigations they close out. Prosecutors are judged by convictions and the attendant legal controversies to be won along the way–arguments often involving esoterica seemingly remote from the criminal transaction at issue. Agents, as a result, have a powerful incentive to wrap matters up quickly, obtain the usual guilty pleas (by which well over 90 percent of criminal cases are disposed), and move on to the next set of suspects. Prosecutors, to the contrary, want to collect more evidence and refute all conceivable defenses before they have a chance of being made. Agents are content to win 3-2 and play every day; prosecutors want to win 100-0, maybe once or twice a year.

Agents fume that prosecutors are insecure solipsists: forever complicating the simple. They don't seem to care that the cops–instead of analyzing the ninth set of phone records or interviewing the tenth bank teller from a robbery that is on videotape–could be out catching more crooks. Prosecutors, similarly, grouse that agents are rube cowboys, clueless about the legal nuances of complex crimes like racketeering, money-laundering, and fraud; they cut corners in blithe ignorance of how some defense shark will go about dismantling the case. Agents, needless to say, are plenty worldly enough to know that, this being New York, in a year or two, today's know-it-all, twenty-something prosecutor will *be* the defense shark raking them over the coals.

This dynamic was the root of my love/hate relationship with the FBI. In many ways, I was more like an agent than the typical prosecutor. I spent a little over a year while I was in law school working as a paralegal in a big law firm. Other than that, I'd been in government. I had never worked as a lawyer in private practice and never clerked for a judge. I was a law-enforcement guy, and I'd now been at it longer than most of the agents with whom I worked. Unlike most AUSAs, I looked at myself as a lifer—as much of one as the agents were. And as a Deputy Marshal, even though I was very young, I worked with agents and their witnesses, whom we were protecting. It was an invaluable reservoir of experience to draw on when I later became a prosecutor with my own case agents and high-strung witnesses.

Don't get me wrong. There's an invisible divide between lawyers and agents. You're on one side or the other, and I was definitely on the lawyer side. But I liked, understood, and sympathized with my agents more than most prosecutors. I was able to get them to do things to help cases by explaining why it was in their interest rather than dictating to them in the imperial "because I know the law and you don't" manner they sometimes get, and bristle at, from young AUSAs.

There was a flip side, though. Because I understood where they were coming from, I had less patience for bullshit. When they said public safety demanded that the investigation be brought to a close *this instant*, I didn't feel like a twenty-something who needed to defer to their better judgment on investigative matters—I thought, as long as we were in control, which we clearly were, there was no need to shut down the case while we still had lots of work to do. We argued about that incessantly. Later, when they found out Salem had taped agents and the brass suddenly decided he should be cavity-searched before my debriefings of him—to "ensure the safety and security" of the agents, of course—I went nuts. Petty vindictiveness, I ranted, was making my job impossible—listening to Salem decry the FBI for three hours not being my idea of an effective debriefing about the facts of the case. I didn't buy the *safety and security* nonsense and got into a near brawl with one of the brass when, having lost my temper, I suggested that maybe if he trained his agents not to say moronic things, he wouldn't need to worry about who was taping them.

It isn't always obvious, but I love the FBI. The Bureau does many things wrong, but there's no human institution that doesn't. Unlike most, the FBI is filled with patriots who truly want to serve and protect our nation. I've spent my years out of government continuing to defend agents when I think they're right (which is the vast majority of the time) and to fight in the arena of ideas so they are given the tools they need to protect us—as well as the benefit of the doubt they need if they are to become effective intelligence professionals who can stop bad things from happening rather than investigating them after people have been killed. When we've fought, it's been in the family. Like lovers' quarrels.

Suffice it to say there was a lot of love toward the end of the investigation.

⌛ Chapter 21

"These Projects Are a Duty!"

IN THE FIRST WEEK OF JUNE, Siddig recruited Tarig Elhassan into the plot, explaining that he was the most dedicated of all the cell members. Siddig was becoming concerned about financing the operation, which would require explosives, detonators, the purchase of stolen cars, continued rental of the safehouse, and firepower—grenades and high powered guns—for protection during the execution of the bombings. He decided to reach out to Mohammed Saleh in Yonkers. Saleh, Siddig explained, was a Palestinian who "loved the jihad very much," worked with Hamas to help kill Israelis, and was friendly with Hassan al-Turabi, "the leader of jihad in Sudan."

He brought Salem to Saleh's home in Yonkers, where the Palestinian owned a couple of gas stations. Upon learning that they were in need of funds for jihad, Saleh, who knew Siddig was close to the Blind Sheikh, asked, "Are these jihad subjects for here or for Egypt?"

The "projects," Siddig assured him, were "here" in the United States and were "military."

Saleh exclaimed, "These projects are a duty!"

Saleh related that his associates often complained that while "we hear about jihad in Egypt and Bosnia," great opportunities were being wasted in America. Weapons, for example, were easily available here. Saleh conceded that he had been having difficulty obtaining "night radar" (that is, night vision goggles) for "some brothers of Hamas's young men." Beyond that, though, even "assassinations" were easy in the United States—he had told his associates "if you do not have the willingness to do these deeds, it is very easy to rent hired hands in New York." He was surprised and annoyed that UN Secretary General

Boutros Boutros-Ghali, "this son of a dog" whose office was in Manhattan, had not yet been murdered—adding that "when he went to Somalia, they should have killed him there," since it would have been "very easy" in light of the "young men . . . very good quality Somalis" he knew, having met them at a Hamas convention in Oklahoma City.

Saleh agreed that it was essential to "prepar[e] the young men" to assert "force to scare the enemy of God and your enemy." "Faith in God," he stressed, "must be followed by action," and he was prepared to contribute "in any, any way . . . be it materially or physically or intellectually."

Siddig unfolded the plan for him and underscored that much thinking had already gone into it, including consultation with the "*Mujahida*"—the Islamic authority for jihad. Salem took this as an opening to blurt that "the Sheikh" was "the emir of jihad," prompting a livid Siddig to chastise him, yet again, for unnecessarily mentioning names. To make the point emphatically, instead of orally telling Saleh the proposed bomb targets, he wrote them down on a small notepad, instructing the informant to eat the paper once Saleh had read it.

Siddig told Saleh, "No one knows about this matter except the brothers involved in its execution, the great emir, and God." Guns and explosive powder were needed, but money was the main cause "keeping us behind now."

"No, God willing, it is available," Saleh responded. "I shall press my capabilities," he promised.

Other jihadists were pressing their capabilities as well. Khallafalla bought two more timers on Canal Street, so there was now one for each prospective bomb. He assured Salem that the entire cell would contribute if it was necessary to extend the lease on the safehouse since the plan was not coming together as quickly as they'd anticipated.

"Doctor Rashid," meantime, was calling around to promising explosives sources, including Mustafa Assad—who had been identified as a willing bomber by Nosair and Shinawy back in 1992. On the morning of June 17, Hampton-El met with Siddig and Salem at the Farooq Mosque in Brooklyn. As usual, much time was spent beatifying the militant life, with Hampton-

El once again showing off his war wound and calculating that "one hour of jihad is worth 80 years of prayer."

When the conversation turned back to the bombing plot, however, he made passing mention of something critical–something that would control the course of our investigation, and take the wind out of my sails as I tried to cajole the agents into to letting the investigation continue. Very soon, Hampton-El said, he was planning to leave for the Philippines, to fight alongside Muslim insurgents there. Siddig expressed an interest in going, too, but only after completion of the "mission" that was underway. He reminded Hampton-El that three detonators were still needed–or, at least, a block of enough C-4 that Salem could divide into three. Hampton-El expected an answer imminently.

Hampton-El was one of our most important subjects. If he went to the Philippines, that would be the last we'd ever see of him. Yet, if we arrested him, that would be the end of the investigation. Due process requires that an arrested person be informed of the basis for the charges against him. The only basis for charging Hampton-El was the evidence Salem had gathered. Arresting Hampton-El would necessitate blowing Salem's cover, and therefore we'd need to arrest everyone. I wasn't even sure we had enough proof to make out an attempted bombing yet. From here on out, the investigation would be a tension convention: hoping things would move along faster–more evidence of a concrete "substantial step" to further the plot–but with one eye on Hampton-El, ready to take the case down if he made a move to leave.

"Islam Is Inevitably Coming" with "Cities in Baths of Blood"

Siddig and Salem proceeded from the Farooq Mosque directly to Abdel Rahman's apartment, where they were to be the translator and bodyguard, respectively, at an afternoon press conference the Blind Sheikh had called. Abdel Rahman had told them he planned to warn the West, and especially Americans, about the dire perils of backing the Egyptian regime. Before the media arrived, they spent considerable time preparing, Abdel Rahman cataloguing Mubarak's sundry alleged predations. "Europe and America," the Sheikh planned to admonish, "will have to face the consequences of what Mubarak is doing because they are the ones who are supporting him with financial power and moral support."

Agreeing with Siddig that the object was to "threaten" the United States, Abdel Rahman then articulated the warning he would issue later that afternoon–when he'd be surrounded by the assembled media while flanked by Siddig and Salem, whom he knew to be preparing a largescale bombing siege of Manhattan:

And finally we mention these following facts.

> Number one: The series of death sentences and carrying them out, will yield the cities in baths of blood. The first who will be drowned in it is Mubarak and his gang.

> Number two: The determination of the Muslim youth only increased as a reaction to those policies and they became more steadfast.

> Three: The issue of abolishing the Egyptian regime, for the Muslims, is an imperative ordained by the Islamic law.

> Four: The Egyptian regime has chosen the road of the no return. It is crumbling. There is no question about it. It's only a matter of a short period of time.

> Five: The West has to deal with the realities of the moment and know that Islam is inevitably coming. And the Islamic Group, which represents the groups of the Muslims in Egypt, is the only force which will crush the tyranny and injustice.

> Six: There is no escape from confronting this regime. Mediation or negotiation is useless.

Later, when the press arrived, the Blind Sheikh was asked the question he'd anticipated about the World Trade Center bombing. He gave the rehearsed answer: he rejected aggression, and it was, of course, illogical that he and others would "target or harm" the place where they had chosen to live. Siddig did the translating, promising to "uphold the security of America."

When the media left, Abdel Rahman summoned Haggag to his apartment and presided over an extraordinary trial–a confrontation between Haggag and Siddig over which one of them was an real informant . . . recorded, naturally, by the real informant, Emad Salem. Haggag asserted that everything in which Siddig was involved was known to the FBI, adding that this was not just his view but that of the "brother . . . in captivity," whom everyone trusted implicitly. Cutting Haggag off before he could mention Mahmud Abouhalima by name, Sheikh Omar directed him to stick to the subject of his own interaction with Siddig. But that "subject"–the Mubarak plot–was not one fit "to be mentioned here in the house," Haggag countered. Yet, such concerns did not stop him from returning to an even more unfit topic: Abouhalima's report that he'd been interrogated by Egyptians about his pre-World Trade Center bombing consultation with Siddig "regarding dangerous matters at certain locations."

Fuming, Siddig furtively described that meeting with Mahmud as "the very special matter and which the Sheikh knows of, I had told him about it. He knows about it and there is no reason discussing it here." Haggag and Siddig then remarkably tried to outdo each other, and impress the emir, regarding which of them more wanted to murder Mubarak–squabbling over who had really been the architect of the plot and who had ruined it.

Siddig correctly inferred that Haggag was lying about being grilled by the FBI over the Mubarak plot–speculating that Haggag had been sought out for an interview due to the Pennsylvania training, not Mubarak, and that Haggag had falsely told Sheikh Omar he'd been questioned about Mubarak because he'd gotten cold feet. Siddig was wrong in his supposition that the FBI must have learned about the paramilitary camp by Haggag's phone; but he reasonably intuited that if the FBI truly had an informant in the Mubarak plot, it would have let the conspiracy play out. After all, he pointed out–much as I had recently been urging the Bureau–with better evidence the government could have "dragged us all down, right and left . . . including our honorable Sheikh."

Moreover, Siddig very persuasively argued that he had been with "the captive brother" right up until the latter's flight. If Siddig had really been an informant, Abouhalima would have been arrested right there and then— a point even Haggag had to admit cut in the Sudanese man's favor.

Still, Haggag maintained that he had other information at his disposal— information he declined to go into because the "time" was not right. His sudden reticence exasperated Abdel Rahman, who pointed to areas of his apartment he was sure were bugged and asked whether Haggag really thought he could "expose more than what has already been exposed." "Is there anything else," he scoffed, "more dangerous than the already mentioned ones?"

Haggag stubbornly demurred. The Blind Sheikh then ruled that Haggag had made "false accusations" against Siddig. Outraged, he inveighed the Sheikh's destruction of Haggag's "hope for any collective Islamic work" in the United States. He began shouting about the scathing biography of Abdel Rahman he was writing. Finally, he stormed out of the apartment, leaving the Blind Sheikh smirking at Haggag's reference to "collective Islamic work"— as if Haggag had ever been willing to do "anything" for the jihad. The emir chastised Siddig for enlisting such a shallow person in his activities "without even seeking a consultation." Siddig was relieved, but duly apologetic: "All of this is wrong on my part. This is the one whom we trusted." Sheikh Omar decreed that Haggag would "never sit with me again."

"Get Me My Lawyer — That's What's So Beautiful about America"

With the clock ticking on Hampton-El's departure, coupled with his lack of success in obtaining detonators, Salem egged things along by suggesting to Siddig that it would be possible to build less sophisticated but equally effective "ANFO bombs" (made of ammonium nitrate and fuel oil). The concept pleased Siddig, who drafted Khallafalla to accompany him on a fertilizer run to a nursery in lower Manhattan. In the interim, Siddig had also recruited Victor Alvarez ("Mohammed the Spanish") into the plot.

Alvarez accompanied Amir Abdelgani to assess the prospects for purchasing stolen cars on the black market.

Siddig convened several of his troops–Elhassan, Khallafalla, Alvarez, and Amir Abdelgani–at the safehouse on the evening of June 19. While they discussed the three bombing targets and the errors made by the World Trade Center bombers in the placement of their explosive, Siddig got a call from Hampton-El, who had just received the bad news from Mustafa Assad that his detonator sources had come up empty. Doctor Rashid said he was still searching and would keep trying. Khallafalla, meanwhile, vigorously urged Siddig to turn to Mohammed Saleh for the fuel oil needed for ANFO bombs. Elhassan chimed in that he, too, was making progress: consulting an engineer about not only the tunnels but also the George Washington Bridge, reckoning the points in each structure where bombs would do maximum damage.

On June 21, Siddig purchased fifty-five-gallon steel drums for mixing explosives and reached out to his "criminal" friend Wahid Saleh for help obtaining stolen cars. Elhassan, meanwhile, reported that his George Washington Bridge initiative was running into problems: "The operation of blowing it up would do nothing because the bridge is a suspension bridge. The cables which connect it are very strong and the center column is the base for all other cables. You have to demolish the center column, that's it." Though he was getting a bit nervous that the engineer was wondering why he wanted all this information, Elhassan had arranged for them to meet in person.

Back at the safehouse again that evening, the jihadists talked about future operations they hoped to carry out if the present bombing plot went well. In addition to the George Washington Bridge and the Federal Building, Siddig, Amir Abdelgani, and Elhassan discussed scouting a U.S. military base on Staten Island–which Siddig apparently sensed might be a more promising target than the Manhattan armory he had surveilled back in the spring.

The plotters then engaged in a breathtaking conversation, castigating the United States with the exception of the one thing they really liked about our nation: the criminal justice system.

The discussion was forced by Elhassan, who had lingering doubts about Alvarez's commitment–especially whether he had the courage to withstand the pressure of interrogation if he were arrested. Gazing deeply into Alvarez's eyes, Siddig sternly explained that the bombs would soon be ready, and that perhaps Alvarez should flee to Puerto Rico once the stolen cars had been obtained. Siddig reasoned that Alvarez, unlike the others, was an American citizen: "You understand, brother, for me, for him, no problem. No problem. For you? It's your country. You understand?"

Joined by Elhassan, he warned Alvarez that there would be immense public outcry following the bombings, prompting police to use "every tactic," including torture, to break suspects, and to press aggressively for cooperation. "They'll get you, your mother, your sister, family. They will tell you, 'We're gonna put them in jail.' They will say, 'You know what? You did it. We know you did it. But, if you tell us who else, we'll let you go. Sign the paper.'"

Alvarez would have only two choices. "Number one you talk," begging to be released and handing up "Muslims, terrorists." The "second choice" was the "hard" but rewarding path of praying for the strength–"Oh Allah, make me strong. Let them cut me to pieces!" It was the path of defiantly chanting, "There's no God but Allah." To anneal him in fortitude, Siddig promised that if Alvarez were in jail, he would not be abandoned. After all, Alvarez need only look around him, that very day in that very safehouse, to see that the World Trade Center bombers had not been abandoned:

> What happens? The trial is gonna come. They gonna find you guilty. You're already guilty. "You pig"–for being Muslim. But your brothers outside work for you. Now, we will, *insha Allah* [God willing], free Mahmud, Nidal, all of them, *insha Allah, insha Allah!*

Inspired, Elhassan added, "The people must understand America has to change. . . . They have to understand American can break down, can come down. That's it." The simpler Alvarez was agreeable . . . albeit less than riveting: "The American people, they're getting the idea, they know, that the Jewish people is the one that keep influencing them."

Choosing America as an enemy was not, however, without its advantages. Amir Abdelgani advised his confederates that, if arrested, "Nobody talk until seeing his lawyer."

"You understand," Siddig echoed. "Tell them, 'I don't know. I'm not talking to you. Bring my lawyer.' Never talk to them. Not a word. 'My lawyer'—that's it! That's what's so beautiful about America."

Take Down

Following Khallafalla's suggestion, Siddig turned to Saleh, who agreed to supply fuel oil. Amir Abdelgani and Siddig drove a van to one of Saleh's service stations in Yonkers, where Saleh instructed one of his employees to pump fuel into the fifty-five-gallon drums they were hauling. Fearing that he would clean them out, Saleh agreed to store the drums, allowing Siddig to send people back to get more fuel and the drums the next day.

June 23 was full of frenetic activity—the last such day. Hampton-El continued talking about his imminent flight to the Philippines and the possibility of bringing Siddig with him. It was take-down time.

Siddig and Doctor Rashid agreed to meet the following morning to discuss their plans, but the latter told Salem he still had "some flyers out" for detonators, because "this is a duty. I'll continue the efforts and hopefully Allah will open the door up for us." Siddig and Salem then drove to Alvarez's Jersey City apartment building. Alvarez came down with an Uzi semi-automatic rifle and barrel extension, which he had promised to supply. After complimenting him, Siddig instructed Alvarez to be at the safehouse that evening.

Meanwhile, Siddig agreed with Amir Abdelgani that the latter's cousin, Fadil Abdelgani, a veteran of the Pennsylvania paramilitary training, should be brought into the fold. The Abdelganis proceeded to drive to Saleh's service station in Yonkers, obtaining more fuel oil and loading the barrels into their van, which they promptly drove to the Queens safehouse.

After leaving "urgent" messages, Siddig finally reached his stolen car connection, Wahid Saleh, who agreed to meet him at 10 p.m. In the interim, he brought Salem on what they anticipated would be a final surveillance of the tunnels. As Siddig drove, Salem trained a video recorder on various spots inside and outside the tubes. As they passed a "Hazardous Materials" checkpoint outside the Holland Tunnel, Siddig motioned to the manned police booth and stated, "I am carrying disasters for him. If only he knew what I have in store for him, he'll go crazy."

Amir and Fadil Abdelgani brought the drums to the safehouse, meeting Siddig and Salem there. Fadil was still unsure of participating further in the plot, explaining that he had to go make an *Istikara* prayer–seeking divine intervention to guide a decision. Remaining with Salem in the safehouse, Amir said he was confident Fadil, who had left with Siddig for the Medina Mosque in Manhattan, would come fully on board. Siddig, meanwhile, broke off to meet Wahid Saleh, taking him to the safehouse. This unsettled Amir, who distrusted Wahid. He grabbed the Uzi and brandished it, while Siddig, taking this cue, warned Wahid, "He who betrays is severely punished by Allah." "Just talking about" what was about to happen, Siddig cautioned, "could put us in prison for life, believe it." Wahid got the point, and indicated he would need about four days to get Siddig all the necessary cars.

It was well after midnight. Having evidently gotten the green-light from Allah, Fadil Abdelgani returned to the safehouse with Alvarez and Elhassan. As Salem busied himself at a work table, adjusting timers, Siddig, Elhassan, Alvarez, and the Abdelganis began mixing fertilizer and fuel in the drums. The FBI's cameras rolled, catching the scene for posterity.

At 2 a.m., without any warning to the informant (though agents had spoken with him only a few hours earlier), a S.W.A.T. team descended on the safehouse along with a phalanx of JTTF agents. The scene was loud and the show of force quite intentionally intimidating, as is the practice in such raids. All of the jihadists were apprehended at gunpoint. Salem, too, was forced to the floor and subdued, screamed at not to move, guns pointed at his head.

He was ostensibly placed under arrest, the one thing he had vehemently insisted was not to happen to him. The circumstances made the truth inescapable: the raid had been planned for days . . . and the government, including me, had not trusted him with the details, even as he put his life on the line.

⌛ Chapter 22

Don't Deport Him, Indict Him

I THOUGHT THE UNDERCOVER INVESTIGATION WAS TENSE. It was a day at the beach compared to what followed.

Salem was apoplectic. Unlike the jihadists–now, "the defendants"– who were merely shocked by the raid, Salem had been aware it would eventually happen, had been in a high state of anxiety over it (and everything else), and was obsessed about his health in any event. The "arrest," frightening and enraging him, convinced him that he was having a heart attack, meaning he had to be hospitalized rather than whisked immediately to the safehouse–for security, not bombing–that we had arranged for him. All hell was breaking loose and he was swearing up and down that he would never lift a finger for the government again.

I felt badly, but not *that* badly. There is a limit to how many battles you can fight; there is a point at which pushing the FBI becomes interfering with the FBI. In the closing weeks, I had lobbied heavily to keep the investigation going–with unfailing and essential support from my new boss, Mary Jo White, the Southern District's new U.S. Attorney, who was proving to be every bit the powerhouse we'd hoped for. Much of the FBI brass did not like the delay, but they deferred. When the flight talk started, however, I had to back off–the agents were absolutely right that we couldn't let Hampton-El (and maybe even Siddig if he got hinky enough) leave the country. Better a somewhat weaker case than a strong case with no defendants. But any chits of influence that were mine to play had to be spent on the case. Lobbying the Bureau to accede to Salem's request to be given a heads-up about the take-down would have been obnoxious. The agents knew Salem better than I did, I assumed they had their reasons not to trust him (which they did), and my area of expertise for these purposes was the law of attempt–I don't do S.W.A.T. or presume to tell the FBI how to do it. They had their plan. That wasn't my business. I cared about how evidence got preserved and about ensuring that any interrogations complied with the law so that, on the off chance we got any confessions, they'd be admissible. Beyond that, the take-down was the agents' call. As it happened, everyone except Saleh followed Siddig's earlier directions: Get me "my lawyer." Saleh did not confess, but he made ludicrous false statements that were very valuable at trial.

In the run up to the arrests, Rob Khuzami and I, with the help of the bombing case team, had been crazed writing complaints and search warrants, steeling ourselves for the media frenzy when it was publicly revealed, on June 24, that associates of the indicted World Trade Center bombers had been planning to blow up the UN and the Lincoln and Holland Tunnels–in addition to targeting FBI headquarters, U.S. military installations, and other sites. I didn't have a lot of time to worry about Salem's well-being, but I began worrying a lot upon learning his "arrest" may have provoked a serious cardiac episode. It hadn't–but he had clearly been under enormous stress.

Stress, it seemed, was the order of the day. I had had big cases before, but the histrionics attendant on this one were like nothing I'd ever experienced. The media always needs a bumper sticker–I think I started seeing "You Decide–2008" about five minutes after the close of the 2006 elections ("You Decide–2006"). This was the same thing. Before settling on the "Day of Terror" or the "New York City Landmarks Plot," they played for a while with the "Bridges & Tunnels Plot"–a label I still hear from time to time even though the evidence of any concrete plan to blow up the George Washington Bridge was scant. Press folk, meanwhile, found us everywhere. There were no respites anymore, not for months. For my mental health, I held on to a gig I had teaching trial advocacy at my alma mater, New York Law School, the next semester. It wasn't exactly a holiday, but it was an oasis because it had nothing to do with the case . . . or so I thought until I was cornered by a network news producer at the end of class one night. As about a zillion press people had already learned, there was nothing I could tell him that wasn't already on the public record. It never stopped them from asking . . . and asking.

Some of it, I confess, was a lot of fun. I was like a broken record saying "no comment," which is the government's default position after the initial burst of publicity when arrests are made. One day, though, we had a court appearance—one of our first before Judge Mukasey—that I had been worried about but that ended up going well. Rob and I got into the courthouse elevator with a few other people, including a very attractive woman who was a reporter covering the case for a major news organization. I had not been a good interview to that point, but feeling my oats at that moment as the big muckety-muck lead-prosecutor-with-the-biggest-case-on-planet-earth-thank-you-very-much that I was, I looked at her and playfully said, "I'll take your questions now." She stared right back and said, "I just have one: Does Rob Khuzami ever have a bad hair day?"

In all the years I've known him, I don't think he has. Rob is one of those smart, good-looking guys that you want to kill as your own hair falls out and you put on another ten pounds.

My hair was falling out by what seemed like the bushel as the summer of 1993 wore on. The main reason was the Blind Sheikh. He hadn't been charged.

Resistance

With few exceptions, the operatives who had been apprehended in the World Trade Center bombing and the subsequent plot to bomb the UN and the tunnels were the lowest of low-level terrorists. Recruited because of their radical fervor, many of them had had training and were certainly capable of doing great harm. But they weren't leaders; people like Victor Alvarez and Fares Khallafalla could follow rudimentary directions, but they were never going to *plan* terror attacks. Taking such actors out was important—terrorism doesn't happen without the foot soldiers. It would do little, however, to address the real threat: the ringleaders with the capacity to inspire, order, and design terror attacks—those who could recruit, maintain, and direct the foot soldiers. To make a real impact, those were the players who had to be neutralized.

In this instance, we had a real shot. Solid proof and good fortune had combined to put the top terror leader in our grasp. The Blind Sheikh had been allowed to slip the noose several times in Egypt, and the result had been acts of terror and the recruitment of countless jihadists under his influence. We had a chance to put a stop to that—at least as much as you could hope to neutralize him without killing him, there being no death penalty offense with which to charge him. I thought it was a very good chance. The evidence of his belligerence toward the United States was abundant. He was on tape calling for strikes against our armed forces. Yes, it would be a challenge to find charges that would both fit our evidence and overcome inevitable First Amendment protests against the purported stifling of religious conviction and political dissent. But that wasn't the half of it.

There was resistance in our government to charging him. People in the intelligence and foreign policy communities worried about upsetting Muslims and rousing global jihadist opposition, at the cost of provoking more terrorist attacks on American interests and potentially destabilizing important American alliances in the Islamic world. I thought this was just preposterous. I had no doubt that we might face more terrorist attacks. The more I learned about Islamic fundamentalism, the more I understood that jihadists despised us out of a sense of religious duty. And that was the real point: they would attack us whether we prosecuted the Sheikh or not. Forbearing would, by far, be the worse option. What terrorists thrive on is weakness. What has a chance of getting through to them is steely conviction. If we didn't prosecute Abdel Rahman after what he'd done, we would not only look and be weak; we would be allowing him to set up shop someplace else—knowing that he was an influential anti-American zealot calling for attacks against the United States. That was unacceptable.

There was also the problem of the FBI. Many there didn't see a pressing need to prosecute the Blind Sheikh. As they saw it, four terrorists had already been apprehended for carrying out the World Trade Center bombing. The forensic evidence tying them to the attack was compelling. And no matter how atrocious a bombing may be as a matter of *history*, as a *crime* it's just a single-transaction offense. Proving it requires no complex, multi-faceted historical conspiracies, no trips down memory lane, no need to delve deeply into time and space and motives. Furthermore, the follow-up Landmarks plot seemed like a piece of cake—the FBI had wired up Salem and the safehouse, and as a result we had jihadists on tape—describing their plans, conducting surveillance on their targets, and building their bombs. Therefore, proponents of this view maintained, we could do two very narrow, straightforward cases: one on the World Trade Center bombing, and one on the Spring 1993 plot with Siddig, Hampton-El, and the other arrested defendants.

Why did we need to get into the past? Why get into all that business from 1989 through 1992? The 800-pound gorilla in our midst was left unsaid but never unnoticed: Why get into the paramilitary training (showing we'd known about the bombers for years), the Nosair search evidence (that hadn't been analyzed), and Salem's initial undercover work (proving that we'd had an informant into the jihadists months before the World Trade Center bombing and let him go without doing responsible follow-up investigation)? Why paint ourselves as incompetents just to firm up an otherwise questionable case against an aging, blind preacher with a host of health problems who couldn't aim a rifle or construct an explosive? Why not just deport him and call it a day?

For once, it could be said that our law enforcement and national security communities appeared to be on the same page—because this was lunatic stuff from both of them. Even if it had arguably been the right thing to do, and it wasn't, there was no conceivable way to draft narrow charges that would bleach away the past and spare everyone's embarrassment. Salem was an integral part of the spring 1993 bombing plot. How he came to be involved with Siddig and the rest would have to be explained at the trial, and that couldn't be done without proving how he had infiltrated Abdel Rahman's jihad army way back in 1991. Lush details about the earlier infiltration peppered his conversations with Siddig and Hampton-El, among others. The story, warts and all, was going to come out no matter how cleverly we sculpted the indictments. It would be a lot better—and do us a lot prouder—if we told that story ourselves.

More to the point, Abdel Rahman richly deserved to be prosecuted. Walking away from a case on him would also mean walking away from El-

Gabrowny and Nosair, as to whom proving the past history would also be crucial. That would have been unforgivable. These were dangerous men, jihadists targeting the United States for terrorist attacks. Deporting the Blind Sheikh, limiting El-Gabrowny's prosecution to the false passports and minor assault on the search agents, and contenting ourselves with the state sentence Nosair was already serving (which could conceivably have resulted in his release on parole by 1998) were not options if the safety of Americans was to be our compass. With Abdel Rahman in particular, outsourcing to another country a profound national security peril we were in a position to neutralize ourselves would have been a betrayal of government's first responsibility: the protection of the governed.

Reaching Back to the Civil War: Seditious Conspiracy

Unquestionably, finding the right charge was going to be a challenge—and not just for the case against the Blind Sheikh. Many of our defendants were not implicated in the World Trade Center bombing. The evidence against Abdel Rahman on that attack was there, but it was very circumstantial. Absent that, we were left with a bombing conspiracy and a far from air-tight attempted bombing—sentencing exposure of no more than fifteen years, quite possibly only five, and, at the court's discretion, as little as zero. We needed a charge that would add some punch to the penalties and be a vehicle for relating the historical conspiracy: the entire evolution from the Sheikh in Egypt to the Sheikh in New York City, with all the paramilitary training, murders, and plots in between.

As a seasoned organized crime prosecutor, my first impulse was RICO—the Racketeer Influenced and Corrupt Organizations Act.[1] This was an innovation of the early 1970's that was instrumental in the Justice Department's dismantling of the once mighty American mafia, which today is a mere epigone. Rather than focusing on individual offenses, RICO made it a crime to be a member of an "enterprise" (such as a mafia family, a violent drug gang, or even an ostensibly legitimate entity, like a corporation or a political organization) which committed the myriad violations of law that come under the umbrella of "racketeering activity" —an extensive list that includes many crimes (including bombing) that are hallmarks of terrorism.

RICO had some potentially major advantages. Conviction ordinarily carried a potential penalty of up to 20 years, and the penalty could be extended up to life imprisonment (or, later, death) if any of the underlying "predicate" crimes committed by the enterprise carried such a penalty—such as Nosair's murder of Meir Kahane.

Especially in 1993, however, RICO also presented difficulties. Legally, the federal courts were concerned about the wide net the statute potentially cast, and thus construed it in ways designed to limit its scope. Among these was to require proof that the charged enterprise have an "economic purpose." This made RICO a suspect option in terrorism cases. It was not an insuperable hurdle: fundraising was a big part of Abdel Rahman's business, and it was key to underwriting the paramilitary training that made terrorism go. But this is different in kind, not just degree, from the sorts of RICO enterprises familiar to American courts. Mafia families are in it for the money; their *raison d'être* is to earn revenue through criminal activity. Not so terrorist organizations, the atrocities and attendant crimes of which are motivated by jihadist beliefs. As it happens, booty is a big part of Islamic fundamentalism, but that gets into religious doctrine, which courts and Americans recoil from doing.

The U.S. Supreme Court reversed the economic purpose line of cases in 1994,[2] but clearing this *legal* underbrush did not remove the *strategic* impediments to using RICO. For conviction under RICO, the law requires proof that each defendant be shown to have committed at least two "predicate" crimes. This can be a problem when charging those at the top echelon of terror networks, such as the Blind Sheikh. He, in fact, did occasionally participate in operational details of plots, but his role, principally, involved giving the jihad enterprise structure and purpose, inspiring the field commanders and foot soldiers who planned and carried out missions, and providing them with the necessary Islamic validation for those attacks. Here, there was no question Abdel Rahman was the most important member of the enterprise, but when it came to specific acts like the World Trade Center bombing, the Kahane homicide, or even the Spring 1993 bombing plot (which he shrewdly said was a bad idea even as he approved it), satisfying the "proof beyond a reasonable doubt" standard would be much more difficult. Not impossible, but difficult.

More saliently, prosecutors want to be on offense, not defense, especially against the lead defendant. Sketchy evidence of participation is a tactically poor position to assume during a jury trial. It leaves the prosecution in the uncomfortable posture of explaining why, if the terrorist leader really is the focal figure we allege he is, there is comparatively little evidence that he actually carried out any terrorist operations.

If RICO had been the only game in town, I'd have been willing to run with it, although whether the Justice Department would have is open to question. There was, however, no need to go there. Poring over the statute books, I found another option—a controversial one, but one that was apt to the task. It was a Civil War-era law that criminalized "seditious conspiracy"—a confederation to wage war against the United States.[3] This, of course, was *exactly* what the militants had formed. Crucially, the statute prescribed a penalty of up to twenty years' imprisonment. If we used it, it would mean all our defendants would be looking at thirty-five-years' imprisonment—not enough, in my mind, for what they were planning to do, but enough time to neutralize them for the rest of their able-bodied-terrorist years.

Notwithstanding the fact that seditious conspiracy was a perfect fit, it was not 1862 anymore. Civil-liberties thinking had evolved—I would say, metastasized—a great deal since then. Bringing such a charge was certain to create an uproar in the academy and in other Left-leaning bastions of privacy and defendants' rights activism, like the ACLU. I worried about their potential influence over the new Clinton Justice Department, more than I would have with a politically conservative, national security-oriented administration. Law enforcement is thankfully apolitical when it gets down to cases, but it is unavoidably political when it comes to enforcement policy. After all, a president's leanings in this area are a big part of what we vote on.

In the abstract, of course, the lines between vitriolic political opposition, advocacy of revolution, and actually plotting violence can indeed be blurry. Nevertheless, in the brute reality of terrorism, the divides are readily discernible. Far from portending a threat to core freedoms of speech, association, and religious exercise, a worthy seditious conspiracy prosecution can serve to uphold our civil order—the order that is vital if our fundamental liberties are to flourish. In any event, these considerations were sure to spark spirited debate. That inured to the advantage of those who did not want to charge the Blind Sheikh.

In the summer of 1993, I was very concerned that those people were getting the upper hand. We initially did not arrest the Blind Sheikh on criminal terrorism charges. But it was obvious—at least to the Southern District—that we couldn't just leave him out there while the rest of government dithered over what to do. Finally, sanity prevailed to the extent that it was agreed he should be detained on immigration violations, which were then the subject of drawn-out litigation over his asylum claim. I was depressed that even such a commonsense step seemed an uphill battle. Nevertheless, it did produce one of my favorite moments of the entire case.

Abdel Rahman was holed up in a Brooklyn mosque. There were concerns that he might cause a riot. We assembled what we thought were all of the relevant agencies at a big conference room in the FBI's office: NYPD, the Southern District U.S. Attorney's Office, INS, the FBI, of course, and probably a few more I can no longer remember. There were about forty people in the room when, finally, official word came from Washington that Attorney General Reno concurred in our assessment that the Blind Sheikh should be placed in immigration custody. At that point, there started a movement to dispatch some police and federal agents to go grab him. But the New York INS representative protested—he needed to make a call first.

The rest of the room fell stunned. Why, with the Attorney General of the United States having spoken, did INS now think someone else needed to be consulted? Well, because Abdel Rahman was a *New Jersey* immigration case, and INS had sent its *New York* guy to the meeting.

"You don't understand," he puttered, "his case belongs to Jersey."

"Yeah," countered Ray Kelly, New York City's no-nonsense Police Commissioner, "but the streets belong to me."

The Blind Sheikh was arrested. There were no riots. And, as the New Yorker I will always be, I was very glad, years later, when my City had the good sense to bring Commissioner Kelly back for a second stint in the job he was born for.

The Real Trial

Nonetheless, the rest of the news was not so encouraging. Immigration remand is not a stop-gap. Immigration is a body of law with its own procedures and deadlines. If a person is going to be deported, he is essentially supposed to be sent back to the last place he was before he came here (Saudi Arabia in the Blind Sheikh's case), the nation of which he is a citizen (Egypt), or someplace else willing to take him, provided sending him there does not violate some U.S. treaty obligation. By beginning deportation proceedings, we were thus inadvertently causing a problem for Saudi Arabia—a Wahhabist hotbed where, on the one hand, jihadist elements would no doubt want the great emir and, on the other hand, the House of Saud—which prefers to export its terrorists—would want no part of him. It was potentially destabilizing.

If the Saudis said no, that would next place Egypt in the hotseat. Of course, if Mubarak's regime had wanted Sheikh Omar back, it would not, in 1990, have escorted him out of the country in the first place. Meanwhile, Abdel Rahman's old friend Gulbuddin Hekmatyar was now Prime Minister of Afghanistan, and he began making public statements that nothing would please him more than to roll out the red carpet for Sheikh Omar.[4] If that happened, the emir of jihad would be right back in business—an incorrigible threat to the United States operating with the blessing of an anti-American jihadist regime. And, if Afghanistan couldn't land him, there was always Turabi's Sudan, where perhaps Sheikh Omar could join Siddig's diplomat friends Ahmed Yousef and Siraj el-Din from Khartoum's UN mission—each of whom the State Department was soon to banish from the United States for conspiring with our defendants to bomb the UN complex at Turtle Bay.[5]

As all this was unfolding, public reports started circulating that the Clinton administration had quietly squeezed Mubarak to request Abdel

Rahman's extradition. Thus the *New York Times* related on July 7, 1993:

> Egyptian officials are angry that Washington has shifted responsibility of any prosecution of the sheik to Cairo, because the American authorities detained him on immigration charges instead of charging him with a crime. "Once the cleric became too much of a liability," an Egyptian official said, "rather than arrest him they decided to let him leave the United States a free man unless, they told us, we agreed to make an extradition request. This is another example of American ineptitude."
>
> State Department officials said that under American law, Mr. Abdel Rahman, who is appealing an expulsion order, could leave and seek refuge in a third country that would support his militant goals, including the overthrow of the Egyptian Government. The only way to counter such a departure, American officials said, was a formal extradition request by the Egyptian Government, which was delivered to the United States Ambassador, Robert H. Pelletreau, by Foreign Minister Amr Mousa on Sunday.
>
> The anger expressed by Egyptian officials over American actions regarding the sheik represents a growing alienation between the two allies, especially as the Clinton Administration places greater emphasis on human rights issues and the establishment of democratic governments.[6]

I was livid beyond description. "The only way to counter" a departure to a third country where Abdel Rahman could set up shop absolutely *was not* "a formal extradition request by the Egyptian Government." *It was to indict him in the United States.* We had a strong case. I was confident that we would convict him if we were just permitted to present it. And every day we didn't charge him, we were running the risk of weakening our hand. People would say, and many would assume, that we didn't really believe we had the goods on the Blind Sheikh—that we charged him because we were afraid of an international incident . . . an international incident, or a series of them,

I thought we would needlessly be provoking by not stepping up to the plate and filing the indictment we had been scrubbing for weeks.

There are two reasons the right thing got done—two reasons the Blind Sheikh was finally indicted in August 1993 for seditious conspiracy, bombing conspiracy, attempted bombing, solicitation to attack U.S. military installations, and solicitation as well as conspiracy to murder Egyptian President Mubarak. Their names are Mary Jo White and Janet Reno.

I sketched out the legal argument with Rob and Alexandra for why we'd convict him—which we ultimately did, on every count. I also lobbied the FBI's New York Office. The late Jim Fox, then head of the office, and Bill Gavin, his deputy, were not crazy about the case. But to their credit, they maintained an open mind and grasped, when it was laid out for them, why it was inconceivable to construct narrow cases that would not get into all the embarrassments attendant to Salem's initial infiltration. I could not convince them to support the case, but they agreed not to oppose it and convinced Floyd Clark, then the acting FBI Director, to remain neutral.

Mary Jo, Rob, and I then conducted what essentially was a two-day trial of the Blind Sheikh before the Justice Department's top brain trust, which was being lobbied by those in the intelligence community and the foreign service who were opposed. I groused to Mary Jo that if we could just get this guy in front of twelve New Yorkers, *insha Allah*, we'd clean his clock—having to persuade Main Justice was a much tougher chore. But it was a valuable exercise to go through, in the Justice Department's finest tradition. Attorney General Reno and her advisers wanted to make sure we had satisfactory answers to the hard questions about the law and the evidence. They grilled us—me in particular—about seditious conspiracy, in a way that prepared me for all the tough questions the defense lawyers, Judge Mukasey, and Court of Appeals would ask down the road. But the clincher was Mary Jo, who capped things off with a brilliant summation: A concise, between-the-eyes account of what this man had done, who he was, and what we'd be inviting if we shirked from our duty. The kind of presentation that left me thinking, "God, I wish I had said that."

After hearing all the advice, Attorney General Reno was very strong, dismantling the arguments for not going forward. Patently, there was energetic opposition in the Administration and even in pockets of her own Department. She faced it down. I had my share of disagreements with the Clinton Justice Department. In particular, the beefed-up regulations it imposed in 1995 to impede national security agents from communicating with criminal investigators and prosecutors–the infamous "wall"–was a travesty that would ultimately destroy any chance we may have had to thwart the 9/11 attacks. On the Blind Sheikh, however, Janet Reno could easily have taken the coward's way out. She stood firm. And she never wavered in both her confidence that we would get the job done and her conceit–one I no longer share but still solemnly respect–that bringing our enemies to heel in the full flower of the criminal justice system was imperative if we were to be the America to which we aspire.

Coming back home from Washington that day was the proudest I'd even been as a lawyer. We'd needed to perform at our best, and we had. We would be able to get the Blind Sheikh before those twelve New Yorkers. To be sure, my sense of pride was diminished by my sense of reality: we had been helped immeasurably by the immigration debacle which left indictment looking as though it was merely the best of a bad set of options. In my mind, though, we should have won on merit regardless of the political landscape. And now that Justice was done, justice would be done.

⏳ Chapter 23

The Salem Tapes

Trial lawyers come in all shapes, sizes, and decibel levels. The bad ones are bad at just about everything. The good ones, however, tend to have different strengths. There are superb orators, outstanding tacticians, excellent writers, deft cross-examiners, etc. There are a few who master all the skills, but there is none who lacks the most necessary attribute of all: good antennae.

I've got them. I can usually sense a problem a mile away. It's odd because it doesn't carry over into other areas of my life. In my personal affairs, I miss many things I should get, and I am often surprised when I shouldn't be. But for whatever reason, put a box around a situation, tell me it's a legal problem, and even if some folks are groping around in the dark, it's sometimes as if I've got those night-vision goggles Mohammed Saleh was trying to get for all those wonderful "young men" down at Hamas. My trial lawyer antennae have served me well. Sometimes they have also gotten me into trouble. With Emad Salem, they did both.

I went to see him on Sunday, June 27, 1993, after the most wrenching, exhilarating and exhausting week I'd ever had as a prosecutor. We had taken the case down in the wee hours of Thursday morning and tucked the still smoldering Emad and his family in a safehouse in New Jersey, under the protection of the FBI. It was no longer safe for him in Manhattan, where he lived, and we hadn't given him notice about the arrests, so his household goods were still in his apartment. His wife was angry, his children were confused and upset, his sister in Egypt was being harassed by fundamentalists, his name and photograph were pasted on every newspaper in the world, and there is no good word to capture how furious he was. He knew he couldn't go home, and the last people on earth with whom he wanted to be were agents of the FBI, which, he concluded had used him then screwed him. He had simmered down some when I spoke with him briefly after the raid. He had a mercurial nature, though, and with all the anxieties pressing on him, he ebbed and flowed from promising complete cooperation to threatening total recalcitrance.

Along with Rob Khuzami and Lev Dassin, I wasn't there to debrief him that Sunday. There would be plenty of time for that in the months ahead. But it was important that he understand we were now in a new phase of the investigation. I already knew enough of the background to appreciate that many of his problems with the Bureau stemmed from a failure to communicate effectively at the beginning of their relationship. We weren't going to have that situation again—not if I could help it. So while we needed to talk about his health as well as his concerns over protection, relocation, and financial compensation, the critical thing was to arrive at an accurate understanding of what we could expect from each other during what promised to be a very protracted pretrial phase given the large number of defendants and voluminous discovery that would take many months to translate into English.

It was a long conversation, and I was taken aback by the depth of his paranoia. Emad feared that the FBI, while protecting him, might try to kill him. He was, he reasoned, the only person outside law enforcement who knew the Bureau had foreknowledge that might have prevented the World Trade Center bombing. By eliminating Salem, the FBI could avoid the public obloquy that would surely result. Unfolding his conspiracy theory, Salem made the most fleeting of references to having an "insurance policy." My antennae for some reason told me he was likely talking about something more than selling his story to the media, which is what he'd seemed to be driving at. I suspected he was hoarding something tangible that he thought could be used for blackmail purposes.

I wanted to know what it was. A prosecutor can't play ostrich. There is nothing worse than an explosion at trial—especially a terrorism trial. Such metaphorical explosions can lead to acquittals, enabling jihadists to get back to work on the real ones. If there were landmines out there, we needed to know now. Confronting Salem, though, was not a good idea. He felt he had been treated alternatively like a criminal and a child. I wanted to get off on the right foot, and that meant treating him like a man—a man who, though cynical, was smart, had done incredibly heroic work, and had impressed me from the first time I met him a few weeks earlier as singularly invested in the case.

I explained that, however things may work in Egypt, the United States doesn't kill people over the possibility of embarrassment. Hell, embarrassment is the default condition of government. Moreover, we had already crossed the Rubicon as far as his pre-bombing infiltration of the jihad army was concerned. The Sheikh was not yet charged, but by arresting the other defendants we had necessarily taken on the obligation to provide them with generous discovery of the government's intelligence files. By making him a witness, we had ensured that the whole story was coming out, no matter what happened.

In a last point, appealing to his cunning nature, I posited that there was a big difference between embarrassing and bad—a lesson the defendants would learn at the eventual trial. Yes, it was embarrassing that we had had an informant who might have helped us stop the bombing but had failed to exploit the opportunity. We were surely going to sustain a hit for that— although that hit would now be mitigated by the fact that we had also, thanks to Salem, prevented attacks that would have killed many more people than died in the World Trade Center strike.

Still, as far as concerned the case—the thing Salem cared about most deeply—this was not bad. Why? Wouldn't the jury be upset? No, I explained. The only logical way Salem's infiltration and extraction in 1991-1992 could be embarrassing was if the defendants were guilty of the conspiracies with which we intended to charge them. If the Sheikh's people hadn't bombed the Twin Towers, there was nothing to be embarrassed about; if they had, we might be *embarrassed*, but they were *guilty*. It might be very tempting for the defense to play the embarrassment card—nothing appeals to defendants and their lawyers as much as watching government witnesses squirm.

But while that might be uncomfortable for me to sit through (it was), they'd lose and we'd win in the long run. A trial is about the long run, not the fleeting peaks and valleys.

This grabbed Salem. He certainly wanted to see the Bureau get what he thought was its comeuppance. But the case, not the comeuppance, was his primary concern. The notion that he could have it both ways hadn't seemed to occur to him. Now, we'd shifted his focus from what was embarrassing as a matter of public relations to what was critical for purposes of a successful prosecution.

I tried to tap into the protectiveness he felt about the case. We can live with any embarrassment, I explained. We can't live with not knowing all the significant facts. That was the kind of thing that destroyed cases and wasted everyone's hard work. If he was hiding something that would affect the case, he had to tell us what it was.

He did.

Salem had been keeping secret tape-recordings at his apartment. At first, he just described recording the agents' admissions that he had provided them with information before the Twin Towers attack. Soon, though, he dilated on the home recording system. *All* the conversations were taped, though nothing was filed away systematically. When he was done with a tape, he'd nonchalantly put it aside, usually in a box. Sometimes he re-used old tapes (and thus recorded over what had gone before); sometimes he may have lost or discarded tapes. Nevertheless, he did not intentionally keep or get rid of particular recordings. He did not have an accounting of what was on the tapes. He was sure he had tapes of the agents. But there were lots of tapes and it was certain that other people had been recorded too: defendants, potential witnesses, the informant's wife and children, their friends and acquaintances—anyone who'd been in contact with the Salem home.

Legally, different government disclosure duties apply depending on whether recorded statements have been made by defendants, co-conspirators, agents, ordinary witnesses, or non-witnesses. But that was a side issue. As a practical matter, my conclusion came instantaneously: we had to get the recordings as soon as possible, and preserve them. Even without having heard them, I knew they'd be controversial and potentially damaging, but we couldn't pretend they didn't exist or suggest to Salem that, since the government had never taken physical custody of them, they were technically his to keep or discard as he saw fit.

Predictably, the tapes became fodder for a motion to dismiss the indictment based on alleged "outrageous government misconduct." And after the trial, when I was called to testify for several hours about my role in acquiring them, I confessed that I'd been "utterly unconcerned" about whether they were discoverable, testimony out of which the defense lawyers tried to make some hay—chutzpah of a high order on their part.

As I elaborated for the court, I wasn't concerned about whether we had a legal obligation to get the tapes because I didn't think my opinion would matter. As a technical legal proposition, they may not have been discoverable. Salem was an informant but he was not "the government," and we hadn't told him to make the tapes. Moreover, they were not, strictly speaking, in our possession; they were in Salem's. The government is generally required only to turn over relevant evidence that is *in its possession*.

That kind of analysis, however, was for law school exams. I was in the real world, where a real court would not likely have been deterred by such niceties. Almost any judge would have ordered us to acquire the tapes and disclose them. Or, worse, if we had tried a "not in our possession" dodge, the defense would inevitably have found out about the tapes and persuaded the court to issue a subpoena for them. If that happened, it was possible that the defense would have the tapes and we wouldn't; defense lawyers could have used them to impeach Salem's testimony and I, in self-inflicted ignorance, would have no way of preparing him or rehabilitating him—a disaster. So, leaving the law aside, common sense dictated that we get the tapes and find out what was on them before trying the case. That way, neither side would be sandbagged, the outcome discovery rules are designed to accomplish.

It would have been stupid to do anything else. And once I made that decision, the tapes were guaranteed to be preserved and disclosed so defendants could use them—which they did to a fare-thee-well. I had *acted* to ensure the terrorists' due process rights whether I was duty-bound to do so or not; yet, at the post-trial hearing, their lawyers wanted to quibble over whether my description of my motives reflected a sufficiently lofty sense of duty. My sense of duty is what protected everyone's interests—theirs and ours.

I told Emad that the rules required the government to provide defendants with various kinds of recorded statements. The judge, I explained, was very likely to view Salem's tapes as our obligation to preserve and reveal to the defense—even though he had made and kept them without our knowledge. The whole case, I stressed, could go down the tubes if we failed to do that. Emad understood. He clearly appreciated being reasoned with like an adult, and agreed with surprisingly little fuss to give us the tapes.

That agreement turned out to be the easy part. Actually getting the tapes was something else again.

The Search . . . and the Blow-up

Salem expressed two concerns. First, he wanted a solemn commitment from me that recorded conversations having nothing to do with the case (but which might identify his friends and family to the terrorists) would not be disclosed in discovery. It pains me to say that, after being very critical of the agents for having made Salem a promise (of no testimony) they were not in a position to make, I made the very same mistake. I gave Salem my word that conversations unrelated to the case would be withheld. I should have told him I would try my best. In fact, the court ordered some of them disclosed, and others were disclosed in violation of a protective order when a defense expert—who was authorized only to examine the physical tapes—made copies of some of them.

The second issue was dicier. Emad did not trust the FBI. So he demanded an assurance that the Bureau would not have an opportunity to destroy the tapes. I promised that once we had the tapes, he could personally inventory them and a duplicate set would be made for him forthwith. That seemed easy enough. But the tricky part was: how to get the tapes so this could be done? Who would retrieve them?

I broke the news about Salem's tapes to the FBI. Needless to say, the brass and the agents were not pleased—Salem had double-crossed them, ignored their instructions not to tape (which were meant for his benefit since he didn't want to be a witness), left the investigation over an insistence that he wouldn't tape when he was taping anyway, and intentionally deceived his handling agents by wiring up against them as if they were criminals. But everyone understood—at least most of the time—that that was water under the bridge now. We needed the tapes and we needed Salem. If he refused to cooperate, we'd be without his assistance in reviewing and translating hundreds of hours of recordings he'd made under the agents' direction, the crux of our case. We had to try to make this work.

Salem's repeated complaint was that he'd been treated as if he were a criminal. He thus did not want agents to search his home as if they had a warrant for a crook's house. Initially, he insisted that he would go back to his home, under the agents' protection, to retrieve the tapes. But that was out of the question because of the security situation—his Manhattan apartment building had become a curiosity to terrorists and media. For the same reason, Emad's Plan B, namely, sending his wife to get the tapes, was also a non-starter.

Several FBI officials understandably argued that these proposals showed Salem to be unreasonable and untrustworthy. They grumbled that I should just go to court and get a search warrant—a proposal I thought unreasonable on their part. It would have shot into another galaxy of fury someone whose continuing cooperation we needed, someone who had gratuitously volunteered the existence of the tapes.

Finally, we arrived at an agreement that the FBI could enter Salem's apartment provided that Agent Nancy Floyd, whom he did trust, was present for the search. I also promised Emad that his home would not be ransacked. I did not, however, ask Salem how many tapes there were (what he had said indicated he had no idea) nor where in his home they were located. I expected him to work out those details with the people who were going to do the search. I would have offered to go myself, but prosecutors don't go on searches—it turns them into witnesses, which can disqualify them from the role of lawyer in the case.

To avoid any screw-ups, the FBI dispatched its top lawyer in New York, Jim Roth, a tough but fair Irish son-of-a-gun I tangled with a lot, but grew to like and appreciate over the years. Along with Nancy, Jim decided to bring along one of his underlings, FBI Agent Lynn Harris. In the meantime, the moody informant was back in his helpful frame of mind, telling the agents that, as long as the FBI would be going to his home anyway, there were other things there that might be useful: faxes that Siddig had written and directed to Salem to send in an effort to get financing, and the carpenter's nails that El-Gabrowny, back in 1992, had suggested using in bomb construction.

Thus, by the time Jim left to search for the tapes, he understood he was also to look for facsimiles and "nondangerous bomb making paraphernalia." Emad, however, had privately asked Nancy to pick up some clothes and jewelry. So, while Salem said he didn't want his place ransacked, he was now giving the FBI cause to look here, there, and everywhere. To make it a perfect snafu setting, the FBI had Salem sign a consent-to-search form. The form mentioned only the tapes, not the other items, but didn't limit the locations to be searched. Salem didn't limit the areas to be searched because he didn't know where everything was. But Floyd didn't know about the consent form, and thought the FBI's authority was limited to a chair in Salem's bedroom where he'd told her he thought the tapes were–even though he had asked her to retrieve other items which weren't in the chair. Roth correctly understood that he was permitted to look everywhere, but just for the tapes, faxes and "paraphernalia." Your government at work.

At Salem's apartment, the three agents went first to the bedroom where a number of tapes were found. Although there was no full-blown search, Roth moved throughout Salem's apartment, opening and closing closets and drawers. This got Floyd upset, and they carped at each other. Near Salem's desk, Roth found the faxes and what appeared to be three telephone answering machines, from which he withdrew tapes. As Floyd opened drawers of the desk to search for Salem's jewelry, Roth saw additional tapes and took them as well. He also saw a stack of photographs. He wanted to take them, but Floyd insisted they shouldn't be touched. Jim thus called the FBI office, where I was waiting with Carson Dunbar, the agent in charge of FCI. Carson relayed Jim's conclusion that Emad was in possession of photographs that might compromise FBI investigative techniques. I agreed that any such photographs must be seized–even as I sighed and steeled myself for what was certain to be Salem's next eruption.

I now knew there was going to be trouble, so I raced to the New Jersey safehouse to try to prevent Salem and the FBI from killing each other. The three search agents got there very soon after I did. Emad was brought to our conference room. There, I made the first in a series of errors–allowing him to huddle privately with Floyd before I could speak with him. As a result, the first thing he heard was that Roth had snooped around his whole apartment (which, of course, was what Jim was supposed to do, though Nancy made it sound sinister) and had seized photographs over her objection. Salem flew into a rage, screaming that all agreements were off and that he would no longer cooperate with the government. And that was the pleasant part.

Things went downhill as Roth, who was doing a slow burn over Floyd's insubordination and Salem's histrionics, tried to complete a written inventory and put his initials on each of the fifty-five seized tapes–which he would have done in an orderly way at his office had I not insisted that the tapes be brought directly to Salem, as I had promised. Emad, in his anger, reached over and randomly grabbed a handful of the cassettes that were spread out on a table. Jim reached across, put his hand on Salem's, and told him sternly not to touch anything yet. Emad warned Jim to remove his hand if he knew what was good for him.

To appreciate this tableau, understand that Salem was a muscular martial arts black-belt in the throes of a tantrum. The agents in the room were armed and high-strung. I, though equally alarmed, was very much unarmed–and though perhaps wearing a black belt, decidedly not one. Yet, I had somehow brilliantly inserted myself physically in between Emad and Jim. And as Salem railed about suing the FBI for violating his constitutional rights, I recalled that even a minor assault on a federal officer is a felony–so we were now brewing the lovely prospect of competing lawsuits.

But at the brink, Jim thankfully released Emad's hand. The informant slammed the tapes on the table but didn't try to take them again. I was relieved–but too relieved. In the tense aftermath, I neglected to make sure Roth initialed all of the tapes. He didn't. This omission meant defense lawyers would later be able to claim that the tapes we'd gone to such trouble over were not the "real" ones Roth had seized.

The photographs, of course, had caused all this fuss. I demanded to see them–something I shouldn't have done in front of Salem, but I had lost my temper, too. When I looked at them, I blew a gasket. There was nothing in them that had the remotest possibility of compromising any FBI investigative techniques. Salem had taken some pictures of the bombing safehouse and of himself in it. He was planning to write a book about his adventures. The government, meanwhile, was never going to use that location again– the terrorists themselves had roamed around in it for weeks, and soon, when our evidence became public, the whole world was going to have similar photos. The "compromise" business was sheer nonsense: the Bureau was peeved at Salem; they couldn't complain about the tapes, so they were making a mountain out of the molehill that was the innocuous photos. My blood was boiling, and I made a point of directing that the photos be given back to Salem, who triumphantly threw them into his briefcase and slammed it shut. In effect, I had lost my cool, embarrassed the agents in front of Salem, and rewarded his tantrum–the trifecta!

Wait a second, though. Sure, the photos were innocuous. But then, while it was foolish for Roth and Floyd to have turned them into grist for a controversy, it also made no sense for Salem to have gone off the deep end over them. Was he a lunatic?

No. Much later, when things had calmed down, Salem explained to me that he'd photographed his wife . . . in the altogether. He believed–incorrectly, as it turned out–that these nude photos were in the same stack of pictures Roth had found. He was thus enraged that Roth had taken them, and then became even angrier upon not finding them in the stack. He jumped to the conclusion that Roth must have ogled them before leaving them behind.

What can I say? It wouldn't be the Blind Sheikh case if there weren't a bizarre twist at the bottom of a pointless controversy.

Blunder

In the heat of the argument, Salem taunted the agents that they were not as smart as they thought they were, and that they had missed several things in his apartment. I decided to ignore that for the time being–Salem, after all, was in no position to go back to his apartment so if he wasn't bluffing there'd be time later to deal with whatever else he was hoarding. Meanwhile, I told him that, though I felt his pain, nothing we had talked about at the outset had changed: the government still had legal disclosure obligations. Salem, however, angrily threw back at me my commitment to disclose only those tape recordings that were material to case; recordings of a personal nature, I'd committed, were to be returned to him.

I had, indeed, given him my word on that. I was hoping we would have time to sort through the tapes carefully–I had promised him a duplicate set so he'd be pacified while we went through the originals. But now he was saying he wouldn't cooperate anymore and wanted back, right now, any personal property that was unnecessary for the case.

I then made a fateful blunder: I gave in. I directed that the tapes were to be checked right away. Those known to contain any conversation with either agents or subjects of the investigation would be surrendered to the government regardless of what else was on them. Those Salem believed contained only his family's personal conversations or other irrelevant matters (music, for example), or as to which the contents were uncertain, would be set aside for review by Salem and an FBI interpreter. Based on that review, any tapes pertinent to the case were to be kept by the government; all other tapes were to be returned to Salem.

Roth argued that this was mistake. The tapes had been lawfully seized– we didn't owe Salem the original tapes, at least not at this point, and he should have been content with the duplicates as a show of good faith. Jim was right . . . about the narrow legal status of the tapes. But it wasn't that simple. I was the government official who had negotiated Salem's consent for agents to enter and search his apartment in his absence–he had wanted to go himself, I hadn't let him, and I had promised the place wouldn't be ransacked (as Floyd was saying it had been). In the rush of events, I hadn't been told about the consent form. So my credibility was on the line, under circumstances where I didn't believe the representations I'd made to Salem had been carried out.

On the other side of the ledger, Salem had risked his life interacting with very dangerous people over a long period of time. I thought we owed it to him to respect that, and it was in our interest to do so since it was already manifest that he'd be a critical trial witness. Any chance of getting accurate and thorough testimony hinged on being able to debrief him exhaustively. With this latest imbroglio, I was worried that he would demand to leave the place where he was under protection. He wasn't under arrest. He was a volunteer and we couldn't prevent him from leaving. If he left, though, he might flee or be killed–and arresting him as a material witness didn't seem to me like a great strategy for persuading him to cooperate again.

Plus, the real concern here was whether he'd manipulate or destroy any tapes we let him keep–in the event the court deemed those tapes relevant at some future point. I thought it was highly unlikely that would happen. Salem had been the one who told us about the tapes. He could easily have concealed them from us with an eye toward manipulating or destroying them later if that's what he'd wanted to do. But he hadn't. He had made clear that the case was so personally significant he'd give us anything in his possession that would help. I thought if we could just get beyond the heat of the moment, I'd be able to persuade him to surrender not only the tapes but any other relevant items. I also thought that, as long as he stayed in our custody, he'd have neither the ability nor the incentive to destroy evidence, so there was no upside in exacerbating the dispute at this moment. Moreover, if properly carried out, the procedure I imposed would have assured us of obtaining any discoverable tape.

And it might have worked if I had stayed. But it was already very late Tuesday night and I still had a lot to do to get ready for court proceedings and other case-related matters the next day. When you arrest a bunch of terrorists, as we had five days earlier, there is a lot going on. So once I was satisfied the tape review procedure was in place and everyone had calmed down, I left. Naturally, this being the Blind Sheikh case, the procedure was not carried out properly. It was hurried and slipshod. Salem immediately identified thirty tapes as having to be surrendered to us. That left twenty-five tapes for review, which should have taken a couple of days. Instead, Salem and the FBI interpreter spent less than two hours spot-checking them, at the end of which Salem was permitted to keep eighteen tapes.

As I drove back to the City, my anger dissipating after another heated argument with FBI officials—who were still more upset that Salem had taped his handling agents than about anything else—I began to have deeper tactical misgivings about what I'd done. I was an experienced prosecutor, yet I'd made a rookie mistake. Criminal trials are always about the dead and the missing. Defendants don't need to prove they are innocent; all they need to do is create doubt about the provenance of the government's case. The best defense lawyers expertly suggest that if only the unavailable witness or the lost piece of evidence were here, the jury would know the "true" story. The dead and the missing are reservoirs of doubt because they can say or be anything the active defense-lawyer imagination claims they are—and who is to prove otherwise?

If we had tapes from Salem and gave them back to him, it would undoubtedly be claimed that they were the "exculpatory tapes," the ones that would have proved defendants were entrapped or agents corrupt. It wouldn't matter if there had really been nothing on them but old Beatles tunes—their disappearance would be the smoking gun that undermined the whole case. If we had these irrelevant tapes in hand, we could easily show any such suggestion was absurd; but if we surrendered control of them to Salem, the jury would just have to take our shifty informant's word for what was on them—an untenable position for us.

Within the next day or so, I was informed that Emad had been given some tapes back, and that the atmosphere was far more benign. We had, gingerly, asked him to start reviewing some of the recordings he'd made under the Bureau's direction. The work was good for him, and he was back on board. So I phoned him and explained that it might well hurt the prosecution if the government could not account for all of the tapes. It had, I admitted, been a bad mistake on my part not to tell him that on the night of the search. No arm-twisting was necessary. When he wasn't in orbit over some problem, real or imagined, Salem always locked in and got the point. He immediately agreed to give the eighteen tapes back, and promised that once he had access again to his household goods, he'd go through them and make certain we had everything that might conceivably be relevant.

Because of the threats against his life after the public revelation that he had infiltrated the Blind Sheikh's network on behalf of the United States, the Salem family had to be relocated fourteen times in the ensuing two years. Emad's household goods, to which he didn't get access until months after the arrests–when U.S. Marshals thought it was safe enough to bring the family back to their apartment for a day to pack–trailed behind the moves haphazardly. True to his word, however, Salem went through them and eventually found other tapes, notifying us and turning them over to agents each time. He sent me through the ceiling by making new tapes, of his ex-wife, even after all the hullabaloo, but he dutifully gave us those as well.

Nevertheless, the damage was done. The defense at trial–particularly, on behalf of Mohammed Saleh and Fares Khallafalla, who were cooked and should have had no defense–used Salem's personal tapes to portray him as shady and manipulative. Every random overdub when he had thoughtlessly flipped from one tape to another was portrayed as a sinister scheme to splice and dice conversations to distort their meaning. The eighteen tapes became the "missing" tapes, even though we had gotten them back. I had allowed Salem to have control of them for a couple of days, and, before doing that, I'd failed to make sure Jim Roth initialed and dated them. In effect, I gave the defense lawyers all the ingredients they needed to claim Salem had swapped the "real," "exculpatory" tapes–the tapes that purportedly proved entrapment–with different, irrelevant cassettes.

And, ladies and gentlemen, if he manipulated his own tapes, why wouldn't he manipulate the tapes he made under the government's supervision? How do we know he didn't swap those tapes too? So it went, for weeks. And when Salem's personal tapes and the bungled handling of them were not being used to challenge the integrity of the recordings that formed the core of our case, they were being used to suggest the FBI—embarrassed by its failure to stop the World Trade Center bombing—had conspired with Salem to entrap the Blind Sheikh and these very nice Sudanese men, who were somehow misled into believing they were mixing explosives in Queens as a training exercise in preparation for killing Serbs in Bosnia, not Americans in New York.

At one point in the trial, as one lawyer after another groused theatrically about my supposed recklessness in handling Salem's tapes, Judge Mukasey pointed out that it was passing strange to hear such an allegation made about the guy who made sure the lawyers got the tapes in the first place. Lynne Stewart, the Blind Sheikh's lead counsel, retorted that "no good deed goes unpunished."

It was one of the few things she said at trial with which I agreed.

Our wonderfully diligent jury of sensible New Yorkers rejected all the fanciful theories of entrapment and dark corruption. Yet the Salem tapes and the fact that he was paid over a million dollars—both as a reward and to compensate for his family's financial losses—probably added two months to the nine-month trial. It also required months of pretrial and post-trial litigation, in which the terrorists sought to have the charges dismissed, and their convictions for waging war against the United States reversed, over the gross due process violations purportedly committed by the FBI and your amanuensis. And, of course, it landed me in the witness box for about four hours of grilling. I can attest that it is a lot easier to ask the questions than to answer them.

I didn't enjoy talking about the tapes fiasco. Though there were no good options, it still rankles, all these years later, that I didn't handle it better. I did, however, enjoy being able to defend myself. I was gratified, moreover, when Judge Mukasey gave the misconduct claims the back of the hand, and when, upon review, the United States Court of Appeals for the Second Circuit not only did the same but added, "The prosecutors conducted themselves in the best traditions of the high standards of the Office of the United States Attorney for the Southern District of New York."

Still, it's worth remembering that, for the most part, Salem's personal tapes were entirely irrelevant to the World Trade Center bombing, the Landmarks Plot, the murder and abduction plots—the terrorist siege against our country. If American lives are to hinge on the prosecution of terrorists vested with the full protections of the criminal justice system, it is alarming to consider the dross that can be the difference between success and failure.

⌛ Chapter 24

Trial and Error

No DESCRIPTION CAN DO JUSTICE TO how intense, rewarding, and pre-posterous a terrorism trial is. The patina of danger and death hang over the proceedings. It is a thrill and a source of patriotic pride to observe the world's greatest legal system grant the full flower of due process to our committed enemies and see them, nonetheless, brought to heel. It is, fur-ther, a counterintuitive absurdity to observe the world's greatest legal sys-tem grant the full flower of due process to our committed enemies, with the result that we can neutralize only minute percentage of them while surren-dering boatloads of intelligence to make the rest of them more efficient at killing us.

The Blind Sheikh case, *United States* versus *Omar Abdel Rahman, et al.*, took about nine months to try, beginning with jury selection in the first week of January 1995 and ending on October 2. For shorthand, the case was called *Abdel Rahman* rather than *Rahman* because the latter is an Arabic word for God–though, under the circumstances, I confess to having been more worried about *United States* v. *God* being presumptuous than offen-sive. We started with twelve defendants, but Siddig Ibrahim Siddig Ali pled guilty to all charges just as the evidence started to be presented in February, and Wahid Saleh (whose cameo role was to provide stolen cars for bomb placement) pled guilty to a single count of bombing conspiracy well into the trial. The ten remaining defendants who went all the way to verdict were all convicted.

Those are the dry facts. They don't come close to telling the story.

Trials are won every bit as much outside as inside the courtroom: The countless, sleepless hours of interviews, research, memoranda, study, and travel. In one of those "trials of the century" that happen every few years, this is magnified. In a case that actually is the trial of the century, it enlarges geometrically. We were extraordinarily fortunate, however, to be up to the challenge. That's largely because, as Rob Khuzami and I were drowning in paper and cantankerous witnesses through 1993, our boss, U.S. Attorney Mary Jo White, had the good sense to have Pat Fitzgerald join the trial team. Fitz and I have been friends for close to twenty years. He is now famous (or, depending on whom you talk to, infamous) as the special prosecutor on the Valerie Plame Wilson leak investigation. More significantly, though, he is the best lawyer, with the sharpest, quickest mind, I have ever seen. Since coming on board our case, he had done more to combat the scourge of jihadist terror than any civilian government official in American history.

The Southern District is a deservedly storied office. The team assembled for the Blind Sheikh trial was as good as any the office ever sent to federal court. It is the greatest honor of my professional life to have been a part of it. I'm proud to have been the lead prosecutor, but the distinction is purely nominal. Someone has to be the lead. I was the most senior, so that someone was me. But there wasn't a hierarchy. It was a partnership. The "Three Musketeers" the Blind Sheikh called us. We had different, complementary strengths, and that made for extraordinarily good chemistry.

We were all detail-oriented, but in different ways. I was the big picture guy—the theory of the prosecution was mine and I worked very hard to build an unassailable legal framework for it, making certain it embraced all the disparate jihadist acts we sought to prove. Rob took ownership of the most difficult block of the evidence, the Kahane homicide proof, and built it into a juggernaut. The way we'd planned the case, the time-bomb was always Salem—we didn't know if he'd do well or implode. To prevail, we needed the Kahane evidence to go in well at the beginning. Planned out like a game, the idea was to be ahead by the time we got to Salem, take our hits with him, and then get to our tapes to pull ahead again, with Fitz blending in a powerfully concise presentation of the World Trade Center bombing.

The key, though, was Kahane. If that didn't go well, we'd be behind and the defense would have momentum going into Salem. Thanks to Rob, it was never close. From the very beginning of the trial, Nosair was radioactive—revealed as a cold-blooded murderer whose profoundest wish was to get back to the jihad. He sat there that way, just a few feet from the jury, for the next seven months. By the time Salem hit the stand, we were way ahead, and because he ended up being a great witness, we were able to endure all the squirm-in-your-seat moments involving his misadventures with the FBI.

Pat was the engine that made it go. I took charge of the daily legal challenges, Fitz managed the evidence. In every big trial, someone must be on top of the game plan—the "order of proof"—knowing where we are, what we've already established, what we are laying the groundwork to show, what we can cut or need to add because the defense did or didn't do what we'd anticipated, and whether we've proved every element of every offense charged against every defendant. It is a dizzying task in a nine-month, ten-defendant trial on a lengthy indictment. Fitz steered us masterfully. By doing so, moreover, he was able to give a summation that is still talked about in the courthouse thirteen years later—a meticulous, relentless, three-day sledgehammer.

He also did the thing I couldn't do: prepare Salem for the onslaught that would be weeks of cross-examination. I did a good job suiting Emad up to testify. But, with a central witness in a big case, especially one as complex and stressed as Emad, the job of the prosecutor responsible for presenting his testimony is a lot about pumping him up, reassuring him that he is up to the task. That prosecutor can't then be the one to rip into him in mock cross-examination. Mock cross needs to be every bit as nasty and demeaning as it will be in the courtroom with experienced defense lawyers. If the prosecutor responsible for presenting the witness tries to do it, it can rupture the relationship and send the witness reeling.

Mock cross was more critical for Salem than any witness I'd ever encountered. He had to be taken down several notches. It was crucial to his self-image that he was not a criminal; he was a volunteer and a hero. But he had also been lying about his exploits in Egypt for years, had perjured himself about it in state court, and had given false statements to the agents about it. He didn't want to admit it. He was, moreover, so cocky, so certain he was smarter than everyone else, he figured he could outwit any lawyer who tried to corner him.

Prosecutors tend to be poor cross-examiners. They are builders, not wrecking crews. Direct examination, crafting the narrative, is their skill. Defense lawyers, who by contrast are often lousy story-tellers, are the scintillating cross-examiners. Pat Fitzgerald, like Louie Freeh and a handful of other prosecutors, is the rare exception. He is a Hall of Fame cross-examiner. After about an hour with him, I wondered whether Emad might even confess to torching the Hindenburg. I knew for sure we'd never again hear about his daring attempt to save President Sadat; that we would be able to lay all his prior deceptions before the jury, rather than be surprised or accused of hiding them; and that Salem appreciated, in a way he never had before, the magnitude of the damage he'd done to his credibility by gratuitously lying under oath about a non-issue in a fender-bender case. In any event, the defense had at Salem for about five weeks and never shook him. Again, it was because of the work done outside the courtroom.

You Can't Cross-Examine a Tape

If I had a strategic coup in the case, it was the design of Salem's examination. He had weeks of recorded conversations with jihadists in the throes of planning a heinous bombing campaign against the United States. The defense's expectation was, as in most tape cases, that I would offer the tapes into evidence during the testimony of the witness who had participated in the conversations (in this case, Salem), and then go through them with him so he could set the stage and recount to the jury crucial details—the meaning of any coded language, who was doing what as the conversation ensued, and any important gestures or actions that are not reflected in a cold transcript.

I had a different idea. Our tapes were very strong evidence and I thought the gist could be understood without need of much explanation. Plus, I was worried that Salem might get destroyed on cross-examination. If that had happened, and if I had examined him in a way that suggested our tapes could not be understood without his explanation, I feared the jury would decide that rejecting him meant our tapes should be rejected too. So I decided not to ask him about most of the conversations. Essentially, he would just give a general overview of the events of late 1991 through spring 1993. That was plenty.

This strategy hamstrung the defense lawyers in two critical ways. First, they couldn't cross-examine Salem on a damaging conversation without first, themselves, presenting the damaging conversation to the jury. Basically, the price of beating up on the informant included forcing the lawyer to show that the client had been involved in a terrorist conversation–I didn't just let them knock down our story; to knock it down, they had to help tell it, which no defense attorney ever wants to do.

Second, once Salem was finally off the stand, we then presented the conversations to the jury without interruption. You can only cross-examine a witness. You can't cross-examine a tape. The conversations, harrowing discussions about murdering innocent people, were often lengthy. The defense lawyers had to sit on their hands day after day, unable to interrupt the flow, while the jury heard conversation after devastating conversation. The effect was that Salem got to tell the story once, in overview, then our tapes got to tell it again, in seamless, gory detail. Some of the defense lawyers told me afterwards, grudgingly, that it was the most frustrating experience they'd ever had trying to attack a prosecution.

We were also fortunate and privileged to have Judge Mukasey presiding. It is an oddity of history that the Blind Sheikh trial began around the same time as the zoo known as the O.J. Simpson murder trial, and it ended on Sunday, October 1, 1995, two days before the Simpson verdict. In fact, the day after our jury convicted all the defendants, we were in the midst of an office discussion about whether I should appear on ABC's *Nightline* to debate the case with Abdel Rahman's lawyer, Lynne Stewart, when Ted Koppel's producer called to say, "Never mind." Judge Lance Ito had announced that the verdict in the Simpson case would be revealed the next day. Our case didn't have the same media appeal. We weren't on TV–cameras are not permitted in federal court trials–and we didn't have sex and race and the glove that didn't fit. We just had a clash of civilizations and a jihad army waging war against the United States, the beginnings of a rampage against our nation that persists to this day.

The most regrettable thing about the coincidence is that the Simpson case and its self-absorbed personalities became the image of what many Americans think a trial looks like. It wasn't. And the image of what a trial should look like was being played out across the country, in our Manhattan federal courtroom. It was presided over by a man who epitomized judgment, work ethic, and fairness. If I could, I would try to improve on the Court of Appeals' assessment. I can't:

> The trial judge, the Honorable Michael B. Mukasey, presided with extraordinary skill and patience, assuring fairness to the prosecution and to each defendant and helpfulness to the jury. His was an outstanding achievement in the face of challenges far beyond those normally endured by a trial judge.

President Bush has had to make many tough decisions in his two terms. Naming Michael Mukasey Attorney General of the United States was not one of them—though it will surely be remembered as one of the best.

Defeating the Ali Mohamed Defense . . . and Ali Mohamed

Still, for all the allure and the memories of the courtroom, it is the work done outside the courtroom that makes the courtroom work. For me, besides all the brief writing, legal jousting, and preparing scores of witnesses, including Salem, that meant dealing with the al Qaeda terrorist, Ali Mohamed.

We prosecutors didn't really know who Ali Mohamed was until Nosair's top lawyer, my friend Roger Stavis, brought him to our attention. We had handed over discovery that mentioned him—materials seized from Nosair after the Kahane homicide—but we hadn't taken much notice of them. Roger, however, had an imaginative defense to the seditious conspiracy charge: Nosair could not have been complicit in a terrorist war against the United States because he was actually an ally of the United States in the CIA-backed mujahideen war against the Soviets in Afghanistan. This defense had a lot of problems—not least that the Soviets announced they were leaving Afghanistan in 1988 and were out by early 1989, which was about the time our conspiracy was getting started; and that Nosair killed Kahane and plotted bombings in New York City between 1990 and 1993, activities that didn't seem to have much to do with fighting the Soviets.

Leaving those obstacles aside, the linchpin of Nosair's gambit was to hoodwink the jury into believing that Ali Mohamed was a CIA operative who came to the New York area to train potential mujahids for Afghanistan—that is, that Nosair was not in a jihad army against America and all infidels, but rather in an American-supported militia against Communism. Alas, Ali Mohamed was not a CIA operative when he dealt with Nosair; the documents Mohamed brought to New York were unclassified and stolen, not "top secret" components of a CIA training effort; and there was lots of evidence that the Blind Sheikh's concept, strongly supported by Nosair, was to fight America.

This defense never had a prayer. I always believed the real thought behind it was to complicate the case with classified information issues. If a defendant can show classified information may be relevant, and if the government doesn't want to reveal it, and if the judge bars or limits its admission, then the defendant has a colorable appellate claim that his conviction should be reversed. Here, however, the CIA spoiled the fun by declassifying enough information about its role in Afghanistan that Nosair was able to get his entire defense in—he couldn't credibly claim anything relevant was withheld.

Still, while trying to make some hay from all this, Roger also subpoenaed Ali Mohamed as a trial witness. I, therefore, had to interview Mohamed because I needed to get to the bottom of what classified information issues his testimony might entail (the law requires questions about the admissibility of classified information to be resolved prior to trial). As it shook out, the more investigation I did, the more stunned I became . . . finally concluding that Mohamed was probably a terrorist who'd been operating right under our noses. The interview thus became an important part of our continuing investigation—the jihad was not going to end with our trial.

So there I was in that Santa Barbara conference room in December 1994, face-to-face with Osama bin Laden's bodyguard and highly capable confidant. I learned a few very important things. First, I had no need to be concerned that his testimony would help Nosair. What he said about Nosair has never been made public. Suffice it to say, however, that I had an obligation as the government's lawyer to disclose to the defense any information in our possession that was exculpatory. No disclosures were required after my interview of Ali Mohamed.

Second, Mohamed was very close to Osama bin Laden, about whom we had just started to hear. Mohamed explained that he had been asked by Mustafa Shalabi to move bin Laden from Afghanistan to Sudan. Mohamed was also very forthright about his fundamentalist beliefs, including the inevitable triumph of Islam. He didn't come out and say triumph *through jihad*, but he spoke impeccable English and I felt I understood what he meant. At the time, I had never heard of al Qaeda and understood bin Laden to be a possible financier of terrorism who may have given El-Gabrowny twenty thousand dollars for Nosair's defense fund. It was not until much later that I learned Mohamed had told FBI agents in California that bin Laden ran an organization called al Qaeda which, according to the way Mohamed minimized it at the time, was building an army that might be used to overthrow the Saudi government.[1]

The aforementioned Peter Lance alleges that I instructed Mohamed to disappear rather than honor Nosair's trial subpoena;[2] argues that I am one of a cabal of corrupt and incompetent government operatives, led by Pat Fitzgerald, who allowed Mohamed to run rampant until, finally, he helped bomb the U.S. embassy in Kenya; and speculates that I may have given Ali Mohamed crucial intelligence information that he shared with al Qaeda.[3] It's a toss-up which of these slanders is the most lunatic.

Lance's unimpeachable source for the subpoena claim is none other than the convicted terrorist Ibrahim El-Gabrowny, who claims Mohamed told him, "Mr. McCarthy advised Ali Mohamed to ignore the subpoena's order and not to go to testify on Nosair's behalf and that Mr. McCarthy will cover up for him regarding that."[4] Yes, sounds just like something I would say. Why, one might wonder, did counsel for Nosair and El-Gabrowny never come close to hinting that I did such a thing, much less file a motion to have their clients' convictions overturned? Obstruction of justice, after all, is a serious offense, and never more serious than when committed by a government official. They didn't make the allegation, of course, because they well know it never happened.

I had a long record as a prosecutor of complying with federal discovery rules, even when (or, actually, especially when) information was harmful to the government's case. No one should get a medal for that; those are the rules and we are expected to follow them. I am the prosecutor who gave Nosair's lawyers the Ali Mohamed evidence. Just as I am the prosecutor who went out and got Salem's private tapes so they could be disclosed. The Salem evidence stood to be both highly consequential and damaging to our case. To the contrary, with due respect to Roger, his Afghanistan theory was risible—a rare combination of something both absurd on its face and offered despite the fact that, even if believed, it doesn't help. I was never worried about it in the slightest. Once he'd been steamrolled by the Kahane proof, Nosair was a dead-man-walking. I had nine other defendants to worry about—and on the remote chance that Nosair might have beaten the seditious conspiracy count, he would have been convicted and sentenced to life imprisonment on the murder and attempted murder charges. I wouldn't obstruct justice on principle, but I imagine that for those who stoop to it, there might be some self-interest involved.

Ali Mohamed was not called to testify because Roger didn't try to call him. He subpoenaed him, but didn't try to get him to the stand. If he had tried, and the court had directed me to help, I would have. It never happened. And it never happened for two very good reasons: First, Nosair was better off with Ali Mohamed missing. Contrary to Lance's shoddy account, our jury learned in depth about Ali Mohamed. Based on this information, Nosair's dubious defense was best served by gingerly floating the fuzzy possibility that the mysterious Mohamed might have been a CIA operative who recruited Nosair into an American-supported Afghan expedition. Roger is a very capable defense lawyer, and this, not surprisingly, is exactly what he did. Had Mohamed taken the witness stand, the trial balloon would have been harpooned.

Second, it is virtually certain that Ali Mohamed would not have testified even if Roger had made a real effort to bring him in. I base that assessment not on anything Mohamed said to me but on two decades' experience as a prosecutor. Mohamed had a very live Fifth Amendment privilege against self-incrimination, so he would not have had to testify unless he wanted to. He knew (just as Roger knew) that the government regarded him as an unindicted co-conspirator, and thus that any statements he made could be used to help build a case against him. Further, his testimony would very likely have publicized the fact that he had offered himself to the FBI as an informant. While that may (or may not) have been just what the al Qaeda deputy Ayman Zawahiri wanted him to do, it would not have sat well with many other terrorists.

That goes to Lance's second, inane conspiracy theory. Pat Fitzgerald and I did not allow Ali Mohamed to run wild and then cover it up; we are the ones who put a stop to his career. I raised holy hell when I got back to New York City after meeting with Mohamed. The trial was about to start, but I took time I didn't have to make it known to the appropriate government officials that I strongly suspected Mohamed was a terrorist, that the FBI should be investigating him rather than allowing him to infiltrate as a source (as he had tried to do at the CIA and as he did do in the army); and that if the FBI was going to use him it needed to keep close tabs on him— otherwise, you know what they say: *imagine the liability*.

Lance is grossly misinformed . . . or worse. Yes, it's true the embassy was bombed in 1998 and Mohamed was not prosecuted for the bombing conspiracy until after that. There's just one small problem. What Mohamed did to contribute to the bombing was done *in late 1993*, before I ever met him—perhaps before I'd even heard of him. Indeed, virtually all of his meaningful activity on behalf of al Qaeda took place before I met him. It was between 1990 and 1994 that he was: training terrorists in

Afghanistan; escorting Zawahiri on two trips to the United States; transporting bin Laden to Sudan; creating the al Qaeda cell in Kenya; scouting American, British, French and Israeli targets for attacks; training bin Laden's bodyguards in Sudan; and arranging security for a meeting between bin Laden and Hezbollah's top terrorist, Imad Mugniyah (after which Hezbollah and Iran began providing al Qaeda and Egyptian Islamic Jihad with training and weapons).[5]

After I had the FBI contact him in Kenya to come in for the interview in late 1994, he reported the contact to al Qaeda. He was promptly instructed not to return to Nairobi.[6] Essentially, al Qaeda got leery of him, believing that American authorities were watching him; perhaps they were also concerned that he might be telling us more than he should. For whatever reason, Mohamed's useful career as an al Qaeda operative ended when I interviewed him. He wasn't arrested because we didn't have a case on him yet—the things he admitted to in his guilty plea allocution were not learned until years later. But I am the one who raised alarm bells about him in 1994, and Pat Fitzgerald is the one who pursued him after that, ultimately nailing him. The fact that that didn't happen until after the embassy bombing doesn't mean he was allowed to run wild, right under the government's nose, throughout that time. For much of it, he was out of the country, and, at least to my knowledge, there's no evidence of any terrorist act committed by him after 1994.

The one significant thing he did do for al Qaeda, in 1995, was to pass along the so-called "list of unindicted co-conspirators" that we disclosed to the defense lawyers at the start of the Blind Sheikh trial. Some explanation of such lists is in order. For very sound reasons, the Justice Department generally does not permit prosecutors to name uncharged persons and entities in indictments. Americans don't want people smeared. The government should not make allegations unless it is prepared to charge and prove them publicly. For defendants who are charged in a big conspiracy case, however, knowing only the names of other formally charged defendants is not enough to prepare a defense. Federal conspiracy law is very prosecutor-friendly. The government need not charge that someone is a member of a conspiracy in order to use that person's out-of-court statements against the defendants who are charged. The prosecutor need only show some evidence that the person may be a member of the conspiracy. It's thus important that defense lawyers know not only who has been charged but who else the government believes may be in on the conspiracy–after all, the statements of such people may be the difference between conviction and acquittal. Therefore, federal discovery law often requires the government to list for defense counsel the names of all the people it believes may be involved.

One instantly realizes this is valuable intelligence to have. Some people on the list may be totally innocent and the government just hasn't yet done enough investigation to figure that out. For example, terrorist defendant A calls person B very often. Does that make B a terrorist? Well, he might be one, but he might also just be the pizza delivery man. Unfortunately, in 1994, all we had heard about Osama bin Laden was that he might be a terrorist financier; we had woefully insufficient evidence to charge him, and even if we had had better proof, he was overseas and we had no practical way to get him here. He was thus an unindicted co-conspirator–and was, in fact, on our list. He was on the government's radar screen, but we couldn't indict him at that time. Think, though, how valuable that would be for bin Laden to know. If you are he, you say: "Maybe the government has an informant in my inner circle. Maybe I should use a different phone. Maybe I should stop having meetings in my usual places because they might be bugged."

Ali Mohamed obtained a copy of the coconspirator list and faxed it from California to bin Laden's secretary (and now-convicted terrorist), Wadih el-Hage, in Kenya, for hand-delivery to bin Laden. There were about 200 names of persons and entities on the list. We gave it to terrorist defendants as we were bound by law to do. Mohamed ended up with it, and ran it up al Qaeda's chain of command. Lance speculates that maybe I am the one who gave Mohamed the list in early 1995. Why? It's hard to follow, but he claims Mohamed called me on December 22, 1994, which, apparently, is also a day he called el-Hage. And . . . ? What does that have to do with the co-conspirator list that wasn't sent to our defense lawyers until over a week later? Lance doesn't say. He just cavalierly tosses out the possibility that maybe I gave it to him.

The truth is, I have no idea how Mohamed got it. I can't deny that Mohamed may have called my office on December 22, 1994. He may even have spoken with me, although calling my office in those days usually did not mean getting me—I was a little busy. I don't ever remember talking to him on the phone, but I do remember hearing from agents on at least two occasions around the January 1995 start of our trial that he was angry: Once because I was not moving quickly enough to get him reimbursed for the travel expenses he had laid out to come to our interview (a few thousand dollars which I admit I wasn't tripping over myself to send to someone I strongly suspected was a terrorist); and once because he had learned his name was on the co-conspirator list.

In any event, I feel validated in the decision not to be interviewed by Peter Lance for his very strange book. He will have to content himself with the crack sources on whom he chooses to rely for scurrilous allegations, such as Ibrahim El-Gabrowny. If, however, one wants to know why al Qaeda got such valuable intelligence from the United States during our trial and the several other terrorism prosecutions of the 1990s, the blame lies with the entire convoluted notion of treating national security threats as if they were ordinary criminal cases.

⚏ Chapter 25

None So Blind . . .

On the Fourth of July in 1997, the United States submitted one of the longest briefs ever filed in the appeal of a criminal case: a 650-page opus I wrote to defend the convictions and lengthy sentences in the Blind Sheikh case—terms that sent Omar Abdel Rahman and Sayyid Nosair to prison for life and all the remaining defendants for between twenty-five and thirty-five years. Early the next year, I argued the case in an extraordinary two-day session before the United States Court of Appeals for the Second Circuit. When I walked out the door of that majestic courtroom on the seventeenth floor of the grand old U.S. courthouse of Foley Square, I thought I was done with the jihad.

As it turned out, I was no more done with it than radical Islam was done with our country. I would later end up in Nairobi, in day after heart-rending day interviewing victims whose lives had been destroyed in 1998 when al Qaeda—using Ali Mohamed's five-year-old plan—bombed the U.S. embassy there. Not all that long afterwards, I joined the ranks of my brothers and sisters in law enforcement in the unspeakable horror that was the aftermath of September 11, 2001. Sleepless nights became desperate sleepless weeks trying to prevent a reprise, simultaneously struggling to transform a reactive culture into a pre-emptive culture.

Those missions persist. They are bound, however, for frustration and failure if we continue to avert our eyes from hard truths about the limits of the justice system and the perils inexorably posed by Islam.

Law Enforcement and National Security

It is a critical error to conflate the vastly different realms of domestic law enforcement, by which government keeps internal order, and national security powers, by which government protects the American people against external threats from both hostile nations and international terror networks. It is a cheery commonplace to claim that we live in an "international community." The truth is far from that. There is no such thing as a global body politic, all members adhering to the same laws and recognizing the same authorities. To the contrary, the domestic realm and the international realm have always been and will always remain fundamentally different in kind, and they implicate quite distinct species of executive power.

Terrorism prosecutions confound that distinction. A counterterrorism strategy that places too much reliance on them thus has numerous harmful consequences. It shifts national-security (as opposed to police) functions from the ambit in which executive discretion to respond to threats is necessarily broad to the ambit in which executive action is heavily regulated and the federal courts, by performing their ordinary functions, actually empower our enemies.[1]

In law enforcement, as former U.S. Attorney General William P. Barr has explained, government seeks to discipline an errant member of the body politic who has allegedly violated its rules.[2] That member, who may be a citizen, an immigrant with lawful status, or even, in certain situations, an illegal alien, is vested with rights and protections under the U.S. Constitution. Courts are imposed as a bulwark against suspect executive action; presumptions exist in favor of privacy and innocence; and defendants and other subjects of investigation enjoy the assistance of counsel, whose basic job is to put the government to maximum effort if it is to learn information and obtain convictions. The line drawn here is that it is preferable for the government to fail than for an innocent person to be wrongly convicted or otherwise deprived of his rights.

Not so in the realm of national security. There, government confronts a host of sovereign states and sub-national entities (particularly international terrorist organizations) claiming the right to use force. The executive is not enforcing American law against a suspected criminal but exercising national defense powers to protect our country against external threats.

Hostile foreign operatives acting from without are generally not vested with rights under the American Constitution; their confederates acting within our country may or may not have at least some constitutional rights, depending on their immigration status (permanent resident aliens are generally considered "U.S. persons" but not those in lesser status) and the threat environment of the time (for example, whether the nation is at war and whether such wars involve threats to the homeland). In either event, regarding hostile foreign operatives as if they were full-fledged American citizens charged with ordinary crimes can have disastrous consequences. The galvanizing concern in the national security realm is to defeat the enemy, and, as Bill Barr puts it, "preserve the very foundation of all our civil liberties." The line drawn here is that government cannot be permitted to fail.

Terrorism prosecutions create the conditions for failure, and thus for more terrorism. To begin with the most obvious point, criminal prosecution, by itself, is a grossly inadequate response to the military challenge of international terrorism. For example, while the actual size and expanse of the al Qaeda network is the subject of dispute, it is clear that in the eight years between the World Trade Center bombing and 9/11, the international ranks of militant Islam swelled, and its operatives successfully attacked U.S. interests numerous times, with steadily increasing audacity and effectiveness. Cumulatively, in an age when weapons of mass destruction have become more accessible than ever before, militant Islam may actually pose an existential threat to the United States. At a minimum, it constitutes a formidable strategic threat. And in any event, this threat is manifestly more menacing than such quotidian blights as drug trafficking and racketeering, which a strong society can afford to manage without forcibly eradicating. Simply stated, international terrorism is not the type of national challenge the criminal justice system is designed to address.

Yet during the eight years between the bombing and the destruction of the Twin Towers, the virtually exclusive U.S. response was criminal prosecution. This proved dismally inadequate, particularly from the perspective of American national security. The period resulted in less than ten major terrorism prosecutions. Even with the highest conceivable conviction rate of 100 percent, *less than three dozen terrorists* were neutralized—at a cost that was staggering and that continues to be paid, as several of these cases remain, all these years later, in appellate or habeas-corpus litigation.

Stopping fewer than three dozen terrorists is a patently insufficient bottom line in dealing with a global threat of such proportions. Nonetheless, equally alarming from the standpoint of what may reasonably be expected from criminal prosecutions, the system could not have tolerated many more terrorism cases. The trials take years to complete, the appeals take even longer, and there is the obvious problem of securing courthouses, jail facilities, and trial participants throughout the United States.

Of equal salience, prosecution in the justice system actually increases the threat because of what it conveys to our enemies. Nothing galvanizes an opposition, nothing spurs its recruiting, like the combination of successful attacks and a conceit that the adversary will react weakly. For militants willing to immolate themselves in suicide-bombing and hijacking operations, mere prosecution is a provocatively weak response. Put succinctly, where they are the sole or principal response to terrorism, trials in the criminal justice system inevitably cause more terrorism: they leave too many militants in place and they encourage the notion that the nation may be attacked with relative impunity.

Moreover, Ali Mohamed's transmission of the co-conspirator list from the Blind Sheikh trial is just a single indication of a gargantuan problem: prosecutions in the criminal justice system arm international terrorist organizations with a trove of intelligence, including information that identifies intelligence methods and sources, thus further improving their capacity to harm Americans. Under discovery rules, the government is required to provide to accused persons, among many other things, any information in its possession that can be deemed "material to preparing the defense."[3] Moreover, under current construction of the *Brady* exculpatory evidence doctrine, the prosecution must disclose any information that is even arguably material and exculpatory,[4] and, in capital cases, any information that might induce the jury to vote against a death sentence, whether it is exculpatory or not (imagine, for example, the government is in possession of reports by vital, deep-cover informants explaining that a defendant committed a terrorist act but was a hapless pawn in the chain-of-command).[5] The more broadly indictments are drawn, the more revelation of precious intelligence due process demands–and, for obvious reasons, terrorism indictments tend to be among the broadest.[6] The government must also disclose all prior statements made by witnesses it calls,[7] and, often, statements of even witnesses it does not call.[8]

This is a staggering quantum of information. When, moreover, there is any dispute about whether a sensitive piece of information needs to be disclosed, the decision ends up being made by a judge on the basis of what a fair trial dictates, rather than by the executive branch on the basis of what public safety demands.

Finally, the dynamic nature of the criminal trial process must be accounted for. The discovery typically ordered, of necessity, will exceed– often far exceed–what is technically required by the rules. The rules, after all, define the bare minimum, disclosure beneath which risks reversal of the case on appeal. As already noted, terrorism trials are lengthy and expensive. The longer they go on, the greater is the public interest in their being concluded with finality. The Justice Department does not want to risk reversal and retrial, so it tends to bring close questions of disclosure to the presiding judge for resolution. The judge, in turn, does not wish to risk reversal and, outside the ambit of classified information, judges are never reversed in our system for ruling against the government on a discovery issue. (Because of double jeopardy principles, the government gets no appeal if a defendant is acquitted.)

Thus, the justice system's incentives press on participants to disclose much more information to defendants than what is mandated by the (already broad) rules. These incentives, furthermore, become more powerful as the trials proceed, as the government's proof is admitted, as it becomes increasingly clear that at least some of the defendants are probably guilty, and as the participants become even less inclined to put much-deserved convictions at risk due to withheld discovery–even though making legally unnecessary disclosures runs the risk of edifying our enemies, a risk that, though seemingly intolerable, is inchoate and thus easier to rationalize.

The burdens of post-trial litigation factor in here as well. Virtually *any* information that emerges post-trial but which was not disclosed at trial will become grist for a new trial claim based on allegedly "newly discovered evidence."[9] While most of these claims are frivolous, they are almost always resource-intensive–frequently coming years later and forcing the prosecutor's office (and sometimes the court) to assign new personnel who must master these voluminous records in order to demonstrate why the newly revealed information would not have made a difference in the outcome of the trial.

It is freely conceded that the disclosure of this bounty of government intelligence is routinely accompanied by judicial warnings: defendants may use it only in preparing for trial and may not disseminate it for other purposes. To the extent classified information is implicated, disclosure is also theoretically subject to the constraints of the Classified Information Procedures Act.[10] Nevertheless, and palpably, people who commit mass murder, who face the death penalty or life imprisonment, and who are devoted members of a movement whose animating purpose is to damage the United States are going to be relatively unconcerned about violating court orders (or, for that matter, about being hauled into court at all). As underscored by al Qaeda's receipt of the co-conspirator list from our trial, the congenial rules of access to attorneys, paralegals, investigators, and visitors make it a very simple matter for accused terrorists to transmit what they learn in discovery to their confederates–and we know that they do so.

The justice system's discovery requirements also endanger national security by discouraging cooperation from our allies. As illustrated by the recent investigations conducted by Congress, the Silberman/Robb Commission, and the 9/11 Commission regarding pre-9/11 intelligence failures, the United States relies heavily on cooperation from foreign intelligence services. This is particularly true in areas of the world from which threats to American interests are known to stem and where our own human intelligence resources have been inadequate. It is vital that we keep that pipeline flowing. Clearly, however, foreign intelligence services (understandably, much like our own CIA) will necessarily be reluctant to share information with our country if they have good reason to believe that information will be revealed under the generous discovery laws that apply in U.S. criminal proceedings.

Finally, there is a profound but often undetected corrosion of our justice system when we force the square peg of terrorism into its round hole. My belief that we oughtn't treat terrorists as criminals, far from being caused by disdain for the rigorous demands of civilian due process, reflects instead an abiding reverence for our system's majesty. Treating jihadists as if they were U.S. citizens accused of crimes and presumed innocent reduces the quality of justice Americans receive from their courts.

Islamic militants are significantly different both in make-up and goals from run-of-the-mill citizens and immigrants accused of crimes. They are not in it for the money. They desire neither to beat nor cheat the system, but rather to subvert and overthrow it. They are not just about getting an edge in the here and now—their aspirations, however grandiose they may seem to us, are universalist and eternal, such that pursuit of those ends is, for most jihadists, more vital than living to see them attained. They are a formidable foe, and, as noted above, the national security imperatives they present are simply absent from the overwhelming run of criminal cases.

As a result, when we bring them into our criminal justice system, we have to cut corners—and hope that no one, least of all ourselves, will discern that along with the corners we are cutting important principles. Innocence is not so readily presumed when juries, often having been screened for their attitudes about the death penalty, see intense courtroom security around palpably incarcerated defendants and other endangered trial participants. The legally required showing of probable cause for a search warrant is apt to be loosely construed when agents, prosecutors, and judges know denial of the warrant may mean a massive bombing plot is allowed to proceed. Sensitive intelligence that is relevant and potentially helpful to the defense—the kind of probative information that would unquestionably be disclosed in a normal criminal case—may be redacted, diluted, or outright denied to a terrorist's counsel, for to disseminate it, especially in wartime, is to educate the enemy at the cost of civilian and military lives.

Since we obdurately declare we are according alleged terrorists the same quality of justice that we would give to the alleged tax cheat, we necessarily cannot carry all of this off without ratcheting down justice for the tax cheat–and everyone else accused of crime. Civilian justice is a zero-sum arrangement. Principles and precedents we create in terrorism cases generally get applied across the board. This, ineluctably, effects a diminution in the rights and remedies of the vast majority of defendants–for the most part, American citizens who, in our system, are liberally afforded those benefits precisely because we presume them innocent. It sounds ennobling to say we treat terrorists just like we treat everyone else, but if we really are doing that, everyone else is necessarily being treated worse. That is not the system we aspire to.

Worse still, this state of affairs incongruously redounds to the benefit of the terrorist. Initially, this is because his central aim is to undermine our system, so in a very concrete way he succeeds whenever justice is diminished. Later, as government countermeasures come to appear more oppressive, it is because civil society comes increasingly to blame the government rather than the terrorists. In fact, the terrorists–the lightening rod for all of this– come perversely to be portrayed, and to some extent perceived, as symbols of embattled liberal principles, the very ones it is their utopian mission to eradicate. The ill-informed and sometimes malignant campaigns against the Patriot Act and the National Security Agency's terrorist surveillance program are examples of this phenomenon.

In sum, trials in the criminal justice system don't work for terrorism. They work for terrorists.

Confronting Islam

And withal, our trials have been a priceless elucidation of alarming truths. A trial is a crucible like no other. Political correctness and sloganeering melt away. A jury is not a body of academics, activists, or politicians. Jurors are ordinary people with a weighty, accountable responsibility. They have to be told a story that comports with reality or they won't convict the person whose fate lies in their hands. A trial is not an exercise in rhetoric or spin. You don't get to make blithe pronouncements—that terrorism has nothing to do with Islam, that jihadists are a bare fringe distorting the true faith, or that terrorists acted because of poverty, alienation, or, needless to say, Israel—and have everyone nod politely or cheer piously. You actually have to prove things beyond a reasonable doubt. You have to depict the world as it is, not as we wish it were. We find out what people really did and why they really did it.

What we learn is that all our chest-thumping pronouncements about the "true Islam" and how terrorists are not "true Muslims" are a triumph of hope over experience. What do we, in the West, really know about the *true Islam*? What have we allowed ourselves to learn?

The Blind Sheikh never testified at his trial. I wasn't that surprised. This is not Egypt. He was not going to convince twelve New Yorkers that God had ordered their City savaged so Allah's banner could be raised. I also knew he had his public to think about. It would have been a tad uncomfy for the *Word of Truth* author to be asked lots of questions about another of his writings—the petition in which he asked the United States, the head of the snake, to grant him asylum so he could avoid being sent to some less suitable Islamic country.

Nevertheless, I still had to prepare in case he decided to take the stand in his own defense. And, consistent with what our government had been assuring the American people since the Twin Towers bombing, I sat down to plot a cross-examination that would expose him as a fraud—a charlatan who was twisting and perverting Islamic doctrine toward barbarous, evil ends. To be sure, Islamic theology was his turf, not mine. I was not fool enough to think I could debate him on it. But if what we in the United States government were saying was true—and I was simply certain it had to be—surely there must be three or four narrow points on which I could nail him. Islam, after all, is a religion of peace, no? Indeed, a decade later and in the midst of a war brought on by serial jihadist attacks, Secretary of State Condoleezza Rice—at the now (of course) annual *Iftaar* dinner the State

Department holds to mark the end of Ramadan—officially promoted Islam to the "religion of *love* and peace" (emphasis added).[11]

There was nothing. I pored over hundreds of pages: speeches, writings, recorded conversations. Nowhere could I catch him. I supposed I could debate him—a debate I would lose—over whether his was the best interpretation of what Islam commanded. He could not, however, be credibly disputed on his representation of religious tenets. Were there benign Islamic scriptures he omitted? Sure. But that didn't change the inconvenient fact: when he cited threatening scripture, he wasn't distorting it. The passages said exactly what he claimed they said.

It got worse. The defense case in our trial went on for two months—extremely extensive for a criminal trial. As it unfolded, numerous Muslims were called to the stand. They were what we'd call "moderates," and, on the whole, I believe they really were peaceful, well-meaning people, summoned to testify that they had never heard Sheikh Omar call for violence against America. Every now and then, though, a question of religious doctrine would come up, and they would demur. Those sorts of questions, you see, were the purview of the great imam.

This made not a bit of difference to the trial—Abdel Rahman had incontestably called for brutal strikes so many times that it was irrelevant whether these apparently nice people had gotten the word. What was jarring, however, was that they were nice people and yet they were ready to defer, on matters of importance in their faith, to the homicidal maniac sitting in the corner of our courtroom.

Islam is a dangerous creed. It rejects core aspects of Western liberalism: self-determination, freedom of choice, freedom of conscience, equality under the law. Don't think so? Try as a non-Muslim to enter Mecca or Medina. You can't. They are closed cities. Our "allies," the Saudi government, the keepers of Wahhabist tradition, bar non-believers. Meanwhile, our top "moderate" ally in Iraq, Grand Ayatollah Ali Sistani, instructs the faithful that non-Muslims should be considered in the same category as "urine, feces, semen, dead bodies, blood, dogs, pigs, alcoholic liquors," and "the sweat of an animal who persistently eats [unclean things]." Not long ago, he issued a fatwa decreeing not merely that homosexuality was "forbidden" but that those who engage in it should be "punished, in fact, killed. The people involved should be killed in the worst, most severe way of killing."[12] Then there's the new Afghanistan, which, like the new Iraq, is now operating under a Sharia-infused constitution that the State Department helped write. In 2005, an Afghan man was subjected by his country to a capital trial. His offense: apostasy. He had committed the unforgivable crime of converting from Islam to Christianity. He was saved from the death penalty only by international outrage—and even then, the court let him off the hook by pretending he must have been suffering from mental problems (why else would anyone possibly renounce the Religion of Peace?). He had to be whisked out of the country for his own safety.

A catalogue of such incidents could fill another book. As they occur—terror attacks, murders, and riots over, for example, French efforts to enforce the civil law, Dutch theatrical depictions of Islam's subjugation of women, Danish cartoons, apocryphal tales of Qur'ans flushed down American toilets, a teddy bear being named "Mohammed" by a Sudanese grammer school class, and other indignities real and imaginary—we shake our heads and avert our eyes. We move quickly on, never stopping to consider what it all means—except, of course, for those among us who, in their self-loathing, ponder what *we* must have done to cause such offense.

We pronounce 9/11 the work of a few fringe terrorists who have "hijacked" a religion of love and peace. We throw billions in military hardware at the Saudis—home to fifteen of the nineteen hijackers—as they underwrite Hamas and fill U.S. madrassas with anti-Western, anti-Semitic bile. We target billions more at Fatah, the Palestinian creation of terror master Yasser Arafat (which to this day maintains its own terrorist militia, the al-Aqsa Martyrs Brigades), in the hope that it will make peace with an Israel it is committed to obliterating. We prop up a new Iraqi "democracy" dominated by Shiite fundamentalists who draw ever closer the Islamic Republic of Iran—the nation whose official motto is "Death to America." And all the while at home, as radical Islam paints its targets on our cities, we fret about profiling and are repulsed by the very thought that matters of doctrine and culture could be any of our concern—even a doctrine that rejects our way of life and a culture unwilling or unable to suppress the savage element it breeds wherever it takes hold.

Islam is like fire. For the majority of Muslims who would reject, reform, or tacitly ignore its combustible elements, it is a force for good: a source of comfort, a guide to dignity and the life honorably lived. But for countless others—not a fringe, but tens of millions over whom the majority is bereft of influence—it is a conflagration waiting to happen. We are the realm it would engulf. And there is always a Blind Sheikh ready to light the fuse.

We can open our eyes and see it. Or not.

Notes

Chapter 2

1   See, e.g., Jonathan B. Tucker (Editor), *Toxic Terror—Assessing Terrorist Use of Chemical and Biological Weapons* (MIT Press 2000): John V. Parachini, "The World Trade Center Bombers (1993), " Chapter 11, p. 188 (http://cns.miis.edu/research/World Trade Center01/pdfs/toxter11.pdf).

2   *Final Report of the National Commission on Terrorist Attacks Upon the United States ("9/11 Commission Report")* (Norton 2004), pp. 14-46.

3   The World Trade Center attack alone was the entire focus of three trials and figured prominently in others. Four defendants were convicted in the first (1993) and two in the second (1997). One of the latter pair, bombing mastermind Ramzi Yousef, was also convicted with two others in the so-called "Bojenka" trial (1996) involving a conspiracy to bomb U.S. airliners in mid-flight over the Pacific. Meanwhile, a dozen defendants, including the Blind Sheikh, were convicted in 1995 of seditious conspiracy involving the World Trade Center bombing, the New York City landmarks plot, and several other crimes. Another defendant, the brother of one of the World Trade Center bombers, was convicted in 1996 of being an accessory after the fact. Six defendants were indicted, and five convicted, in connection with the 1998 bombings of the U.S. embassies in East Africa. The sixth, a high-ranking al Qaeda member named Mamdouh Mahmud Salim, never faced trial for the embassy bombing because, during the trial preparation phase, he tried to murder a prison guard during an escape attempt, shoving a shiv into the guard's eye. He pled guilty to that attempted murder in 2002. The attempted bombing of Los Angeles International Airport in connection with the Millennium observance produced three convictions. That computes to a total of 29 defendants. It is noteworthy that the Khobar Towers bombing in Saudi Arabia (killing 19 members of the U.S. Air Force) and the U.S.S. *Cole* bombing in Yemen (killing 17 members of the U.S. Navy) did not even spur arrests or indictments prior to 9/11, much less any more aggressive governmental response.

Chapter 3

1   Bernard Lewis, *Islam and the West* (Oxford University Press 1993), p. 155; Ibn Warraq, *Why I Am Not a Muslim* (Prometheus Books 1995) (2003 ed.), p. 279 (quoting Ignaz Goldhizer, *Introduction to Islamic Theology and Law* [translated by Andras and Ruth Hamori] [Princeton 1981], pp. 162-63).

2   Joseph Schacht, *An Introduction to Islamic Law* (Oxford/Clarendon Press 1982), pp. 69-71; Robert Spencer, *The Politically Incorrect Guide to Islam (and the Crusades)* (Regnery 2006), p. 38.

3   Schacht, *An Introduction to Islamic Law*, p. 73.

4   Lawrence Wright, *The Looming Tower* (Alfred A. Knopf 1996), pp. 57, 138; see also Fawaz A. Gerges, *The Far Enemy—Why Jihad Went Global* (Cambridge University Press 2005), p. 100. As Wright recounts, Abdel Rahman is said to have tartly rebuked the younger Zawahiri, reminding him that the sharia also forbids a prisoner from being emir. Wright further describes how the rivalry between Abdel Rahman and Zawahiri, who ran competing (though at times cooperating) Egyptian terror organizations, became especially heated when they accused each other of treachery while jockeying for leadership positions in Afghanistan during the 1980s. Following the Blind Sheikh's conviction and sentencing to life-imprisonment, however, Zawahiri joined Osama bin Laden in vowing revenge if he died in American custody. See, e.g., "Inside Al-Qaeda: a window into the world of militant Islam and the Afghani alumni" (*Jane's* Sept. 28, 2001 ed.) (http://www.janes.com/security/international_security/news/misc/janes010928_1_n.shtml).

5   Bernard Lewis, *The Middle East: A Brief History of the Last 2,000 years* (Scribner 1995), pp. 97-99.

6   Ibn Taymiyyah is widely regarded as a theological eminence. See, e.g., Schacht, *An Introduction to Islamic Law*, pp. 63, 72. For a decidedly contrary view, see Stephen Schwartz, *The Two Faces of Islam* (Anchor Books 2002, 2003), pp. 60-62.

7   Robert Spencer, *The Truth about Muhammad—Founder of the World's Most Intolerant Religion* (Regnery 2006), p. 8.

8   Spencer, *The Truth about Muhammad*, pp. 89-90.

9   Spencer, *The Truth about Muhammad*, pp. 47-58; Warraq, *Why I Am Not a Muslim*, pp. 34-65.

10   Schacht, *An Introduction*, p. 115 & n. 1; Spencer, *The Politically Incorrect Guide to Islam (and the Crusades)* (Regnery 2006), p. 24.

11   Serge Trifkovic, *The Sword of the Prophet—Islam: History, Theology, Impact on the world* (Regina Orthodox Press 2002), pp. 37-54; Spencer, *The Truth about Muhammad*, pp. 89-145.

12   Andrew Bostom, "The Sacred Muslim Practice of Beheading," *FrontPage Magazine* (May 13, 2004) (http://www.frontpagemag.com/Articles/ReadArticle.asp?ID=13371).

13 Annemarie Schimmel, *Islam—An Introduction* (State University of New York Press 1992), p. 35.

14 Marc Sageman, *Understanding Terror Networks* (University of Pennsylvania Press 2004), pp. 1-2.

15 Sageman, *Understanding Terror Networks*, p. 2.

16 Sageman, *Understanding Terror Networks*, p. 2.

17 Emmerich de Vattel, *The Law of Nations*, Book II ("Of a Nation Considered in Its Relations to Others"), ch. IV, sec. 49 (1758) (Joseph Chitty ed. 1852) (available at the Constitution Society's website, http://www.constitution.org/vattel/vattel_02.htm) (accessed Nov. 20, 2007); see also, Richard Samuelson, "U.N.-Natural Law" (Claremont Institute Aug. 31, 2006) (http://www.claremont.org/blogs/blogid.4572/blog_detail.asp).

18 Sageman, *Understanding Terror Networks*, p. 2.

19 Daniel Benjamin and Steven Simon, *The Age of Sacred Terror—Radical Islam's War Against America* (Random House Trade Paperback 2003), pp. 54-55.

20 Benjamin & Simon, *The Age of Sacred Terror*, p. 55 & n. (citations omitted).

21 Bernard Lewis, *The Middle East*, p. 233.

22 Ibn Warraq, *Why I Am Not a Muslim*, p. 12.

23 See Andrew Bostom (editor), *The Legacy of Jihad—Islamic Holy War and the Fate of Non-Muslims* (Prometheus Books 2005), pp. 125-26 (collecting Qur'anic verses commanding warfare).

24 Bostom, *The Legacy of Jihad*, pp. 136-37, quoting the Sahih Bukhari Collection of Hadith, Vol. 4, bk. 52, nos. 42 & 48.

25 Bostom, *The Legacy of Jihad* (Ibn Taymiyya, "Al-Siyasa Al-Sharriya"), p. 165 (quoting Sura 2:193 and 8:39).

26 Bostom, *The Legacy of Jihad*, pp. 168-69

27 Bostom, *The Legacy of Jihad*, p. 166; Benjamin & Simon, *The Age of Sacred Terror*, pp. 48-50.

28 Benjamin & Simon, *The Age of Sacred Terror*, pp. 52-54.

29   Amir Taheri, *Holy Terror* (Adler & Adler 1987), pp. 226-27; Warraq, *Why I Am Not a Muslim*, p. 12.

30   Sayyid Qutb, *Milestones* (Ch. 4, "Jihaad in the Cause of God") (Mother Mosque Foundation, Cedar Rapids, IA, 1993), pp. 57-58, 59-60; see also Bostom, *The Legacy of Jihad*, pp. 233, 235.

31   Qutb, *Milestones*, pp. 60, 75; see also Bostom, *The Legacy of Jihad*, pp. 235, 246.

32   Qutb, *Milestones*, pp. 58-59; see also Bostom, *The Legacy of Jihad*, p. 234.

33   Qutb, *Milestones*, pp. 61-62; see also Bostom, *The Legacy of Jihad*, p. 236.

34   Qutb, *Milestones*, pp. 63; see also Bostom, *The Legacy of Jihad*, p. 237; see also Benjamin & Simon, *The Age of Sacred Terror*, pp. 64-66.

35   The passage, Sura 2:190-91, continues: "[B]ut fight them not at the Sacred Mosque, unless they first fight you there; but if they fight you, slay them. Such is the reward of those who reject faith."

36   Qutb, *Milestones*, p. 61; see also Bostom, *The Legacy of Jihad*, p. 236; and Wright, *The Looming Tower*, p. 47 (Khomeini: "Yes, we are reactionaries, and you are enlightened intellectuals: You intellectuals do not want us to go back 1,400 years. . . . You, who want freedom, freedom for everything, the freedom of parties, you want all the freedoms, you intellectuals: freedom that will corrupt our youth, freedom that will pave the way for the oppressor, freedom that will drag our nation to the bottom.")

37   Qutb, *Milestones*, p. 61; see also Bostom, *The Legacy of Jihad*, p. 236.

38   Qutb, *Milestones*, p. 64; see also Bostom, *The Legacy of Jihad*, p. 238.

39   See also Sura 5:50 ("Do they then seek after a judgment of (the Days of) *Jahiliyya*? But who, for a people whose faith is assured can give better judgment than Allah?"); see also, e.g., Suras 3:154, 33:33.

40   Qutb, *Milestones*, pp. 71-75; see also Bostom, *The Legacy of Jihad*, p. 243-46; and Benjamin & Simon, *The Age of Sacred Terror*, pp. 64-66.

41   Wright, *The Looming Tower*, p. 16.

42   See, e.g., Federation of American Scientists Intelligence Resource Program, Report on the Muslim Brotherhood (http://www.fas.org/irp/world/para/mb.htm) (accessed June 27, 2007); see also Steve Coll, *Ghost Wars: The Secret History of the CIA, Afghanistan, and Bin Laden, from the Soviet Invasion to September 10, 2001* (The Penguin Press 2004), p. 112.

43 Wright, *The Looming Tower*, p. 25. Consistent with the arc of his thought, Qutb, too, saw liberal democracy as a form of repression because it effectively imposes on people "the servitude to other men." Qutb, *Milestones*, p. 61; see also Bostom, *The Legacy of Jihad*, p. 234.

44 Benjamin & Simon, *The Age of Sacred Terror*, pp. 61-62.

45 Wright, *The Looming Tower*, pp. 28-30.

Chapter 4

1 Benjamin & Simon, *The Age of Sacred Terror*, p. 68.

2 John K. Cooley, *Unholy Wars: Afghanistan, America and International Terrorism* (Pluto Press 1999), pp. 40-44; Benjamin & Simon, *The Age of Sacred Terror*, p. 76; Wright, *The Looming Tower*, p. 56. On apostasy, see, e.g., Sura 4:89 ("They would have you disbelieve as they themselves have disbelieved, so that you may all be alike. . . . *If they desert you, seize them and put them to death wherever you find them*") (emphasis added). To the extent there is interpretive gloss on Qur'anic apostasy passages, most authoritative are the Hadiths – the traditions and admonitions of Mohammed and his companions. According to Abdullah Ibn Abbas, Mohammed's cousin and among the most influential educators in both Sunni and Shiite traditions, the prophet's instructions in this regard were quite clear: "Kill him who changes his religion." Indeed, the only credible dispute in Islam about apostasy pertains to the nature of the penalty – beheading or some different method of execution. Robert Spencer (editor), *The Myth of Islamic Tolerance* (Prometheus Books 2005) (Ibn Warraq, "A General Overview of Apostasy"), pp. 428-31.

3 Nevertheless, for a perceptive assessment of the eerie consonance of Sayyid Qutb's thought with that of Karl Marx, see Theodore Dalrymple, "There Is No God but Politics" (*New English Review* May 2007 ed.) (http://www.newenglishreview.org/custpage.cfm?frm=7240&sec_id=7240); see also Steve Coll, *Ghost Wars*, p. 112 (recounting Qutb's call for a "Lenninist approach to Islamic revolution").

4 Benjamin & Simon, *The Age of Sacred Terror*, p. 76; Cooley, *Unholy Wars*, p. 30.

5 Center for Defense Information Report, "Al-Gama'a al-Islamiyya–Islamic Group" (Dec. 2, 2002) (http://www.cdi.org/terrorism/algamaa.cfm); Gilles Kepel, *Muslim Extremism in Egypt* (University of California Press 2003) (first published as *The Prophet and Pharaoh* (Al Saqi Books 1985)), pp. 207, 255.

6 Spencer, *The Truth about Muhammad*, p. 98; compare Annemarie Schimmel, *Islam—An Introduction* (State University of New York Press 1992), p. 70 (noting that in early Islam, "conversions [to Islam] were not even deemed desirable because the special taxes on *dhimmis* were a boon for the treasury").

7   Sura 8:41 ("And know that out of all the booty that ye may acquire [in war], a fifth share is assigned to Allah—and to the Messenger, and to near relatives, orphans, the needy, and the wayfarer . . ."); see also Sura 8:69 ("But now enjoy what ye took in war, lawful and good").

8   Kepel, *Muslim Extremism in Egypt*, pp. 71-102; Gerges, *The Far Enemy—Why Jihad Went Global* (Cambridge University Press 2005), pp. 7, 12; Benjamin & Simon, *The Age of Sacred Terror*, pp. 70-71.

9   Benjamin & Simon, *The Age of Sacred Terror*, p. 71; Kepel, *Muslim Extremism in Egypt*, pp. 81-85, 100-02.

10   Benjamin & Simon, *The Age of Sacred Terror*, p. 76; Kepel, *Muslim Extremism in Egypt*, pp. 192-204 (translating *The Forgotten Duty* as *The Hidden Imperative*).

11   MaryAnneWeaver, "Blowback" (*TheAtlanticMonthly*May1996)(http://www.theatlantic. com/issues/96may/blowback.htm; and http://s3.amazonaws.com/911timeline/1990s/ atlanticmonthly0596.html); see also Wright, *The Looming Tower*, pp. 95-97.

12   Mary Anne Weaver, "Blowback"; Benjamin & Simon, *The Age of Sacred Terror*, p. 99; Wright, *The Looming Tower*, pp. 95-97, 101-03; United States Treasury Department Designation of Maktab al-Khidmat/al-Kifah as a Terrorist Entity (Sept. 23, 2001) (http:// www.ustreas.gov/offices/enforcement/key-issues/protecting/charities_execorder_- 3224-i.shtml).

13   Cooley, *Unholy Wars: Afghanistan, America and International Terrorism*, pp. 43-44.

14   As Daniel Benjamin and Steven Simon point out, jihadists were enraged over not only Sadat's recognition of and peace treaty with Israel, but a 1979 domestic program, said to be inspired by Sadat's wife, the upshot of which was to increase the legal prerogatives of women, or, as the jihadists saw it, to undermine the ability of men to control their wives, in flat contradiction of the Qur'an. Benjamin & Simon, *The Age of Sacred Terror*, p. 74.

15   As the Second Circuit U.S. Court of Appeals incisively put it in 1999, rejecting the appeals of Abdel Rahman and his co-defendants, "as a cleric and the group's leader, Rahman was entitled to dispense 'fatwas,' religious opinions on the holiness of an act . . . sanctioning proposed courses of conduct and advising . . . whether . . . acts would be in furtherance of jihad[,]" however, his "role . . . was generally limited to overall supervision and direction . . . as he made efforts to remain a level above the details of individual operations." *United States* v. *Abdel Rahman*, 189 F.3d 88, 104 (2d Cir.), *cert. denied*, 528 U.S. 982 (1999).

16   Cooley, *Unholy Wars: Afghanistan, America and International Terrorism*, pp. 40-41; Gerges, *The Far Enemy*, p. 5; see also Alison Mitchell, "U.S. Accused Sheik Last Year of Inciting Violence in Egypt) (*New York Times* July 27, 1993) (http://select.nytimes.com/ search/restricted/article?res=F00612FE345F0C748EDDAE0894DB494D81) (report-

ing that an October 1992 report by the State Department's Bureau of Human Rights and Humanitarian Affairs had "established beyond any doubt' that Mr. Abdel Rahman told the assassins of the Egyptian President Anwar el-Sadat that it was Islamic law to eliminate a leader who did not rule by God's precepts").

17   Benjamin & Simon, *The Age of Sacred Terror*, p. 84.

18   Benjamin & Simon, *The Age of Sacred Terror*, pp. 82-83.

19   Johannes Jansen, *The Dual Nature of Islamic Fundamentalism* (Cornell University Press 1997), p. 124; see also Perspectives on World History and Current Events, "Muhammad abd al-Salam Faraj–Founder of *Jama'at al-Jihad*, the group that killed Anwar Sadat" (http://www.pwhce.org/faraj.html) (accessed June 29, 2007).

20   Gregory M. Davis, "Islam 101" (*Jihad Watch* March 13, 2007) (http://www.jihadwatch. org/archives/015638.php).

21   Gerges, *The Far Enemy*, pp. 5-7; Benjamin & Simon, *The Age of Sacred Terror*, p. 84.

22   Annemarie Schimmel, *Islam–An Introduction*, p. 63.

23   Spencer, *The Truth About Mohammed*, pp. 103 & ff.; see also University of Southern California, *USC-MSA Compendium of Muslim Texts*, Hadith Collection *Sahih al-Bukhari*, Vol. 4, Bk. 52, No. 269 (http://www.usc.edu/dept/MSA/fundamentals/hadithsunnah/ bukhari/052.sbt.html#004.052.269). On *A Word of Truth*, see Gerges, *The Far Enemy*, pp. 5-7 & nn. 18, 26-27, citing Dr. Omar Abdel Rahman, *A Word of Truth: Dr. Omar Abdel Rahman's Legal Summation in the Jihad Case* [in Arabic] (no publisher and no date).

Chapter 5

1   Mark Riebling, *Wedge: How the Secret War between the FBI and CIA Has Endangered National Security* (Osprey Productions1994) (Touchstone 2002 reissue with a new epilogue).

Chapter 6

1   Weaver, "Blowback"; Rohan Gunaratna, *Inside al Qaeda–Global Network of Terror* (Columbia University Press 2002), p. 24; Edward A. Gargan, "Where Arab Militants Train and Wait" (*New York Times* Aug. 11, 1993) (http://partners.nytimes.com/library/ world/africa/081193binladen.html?Partner=PBS&RefId=Eutttn-uFBqv); Editorial, "Jihad and the Loss of Sovereignty" (*Daily Times* of Pakistan Dec. 25, 2003) (http:// www.dailytimes.com.pk/default.asp?page=story_25-12-2003_pg3_1).

2   Wright, *The Looming Tower*, p. 100.

3   Weaver, "Blowback."

4   Weaver, "Blowback"; Wright, *The Looming Tower*, p. 100; see also Steve Coll, *Ghost Wars*, pp. 49-50.

5   See generally Evan Kohlmann, *Al-Qaeda's Jihad in Europe: The Afghan-Bosnian Network* (Berg Publishers 2004); see also, e.g., Anthony Shadid, "Battle-tested Afghan war veterans at core of group targeted by U.S." (Associate Press Aug. 21, 1998) (http://www. chron.com/disp/story.mpl/side2/1055650.html).

6   At an early stage of the deportation proceedings that were aborted when the Blind Sheikh was indicted, the Egyptian media reported that President Mubarak had claimed Abdel Rahman was a CIA operative, a report that was later retracted, although that did not stop it from being repeated publicly. Chris Hedges, "U.S.-Egypt Ties Are Strained In Detention of Islamic Cleric" (*New York Times* July 7, 1993) (http://select.nytimes.com/search/restricted/article?res=F00617FC3F5F0C748CDDAE0894DB494D81). Playing off these rumors, a New York attorney for Abdel Rahman also speculated at the time that there might have been a CIA connection. Douglas Jehl, "C.I.A. Officer Signed Visa For Sheik, U.S. Says" (*New York Times* July 14, 1993) (http://select.nytimes.com/search/restricted/article?res=F00613F83 C5B0C778DDDAE0894DB494D81). At the same time, however, Montasser al-Zayyat, one of Abdel Rahman's Egyptian lawyers, warned that if the cleric were extradited to Egypt it "could 'set off a wave of violence' against American interests around the world." Joseph B. Treaster, "Lawyer Says Sheik Plans Fight Against Extradition" (*New York Times* July 6, 1993) (http://select.nytimes.com/search/restricted/article?res=F0061FF9385F0C758CDD AE0894DB494D81). More to the point, the Blind Sheikh himself, however, never claimed any relationship with U.S. intelligence in the years between his arrest in July 1993 and the imposition of a life sentence in January 1996. See also Steve Coll, *Ghost Wars*, p. 87 (detailing the lack of contacts between the CIA and Osama bin Laden).

7   U.S. Dept. of State, "Did the U.S. 'Create' Osama bin Laden? Allegations that the U.S. provided funding for bin Laden proved inaccurate" (Jan. 14, 2005) (http://usinfo.state. gov/media/Archive/2005/Jan/24-318760.html).

8   This was true from the very beginning of American intervention. As National Security Adviser Zbigniew Brzezinski wrote in a top-secret memo to President Jimmy Carter within days of the 1979 Soviet invasion, "Our ultimate goal is the withdrawal of Soviet troops from Afghanistan. Even if this is not attainable, we should make Soviet involvement as costly as possible." Steve Coll, *Ghost Wars*, p. 51; see also U.S. Dept. of State, "Did the U.S. 'Create' Osama bin Laden?"

9   Sageman, *Understanding Terror Networks*, p. 57; for more on Wali Khan Amin Shah, see, e.g., Maria A. Ressa, *Seeds of Terror—An Eyewitness Account of Al-Qaeda's New-*

est Center of Operations in Southeast Asia, (Free Press 2003); Rohan Gunaratna (Editor), *Combating Terrorism* (Marshall Cavendish Academic 2005) (Andrew C. McCarthy, "Anti-Terrorism Law: The American Experience"), ch. 11, p. 256.

10   Sageman, *Understanding Terror Networks*, p. 57.

11   See, e.g., Murad Batal al-Shishani, "The Rise and Fall of Arab Fighters in Chechnya" (*The Jamestown Foundation* Sept. 14, 2006) (http://jamestown.org/docs/Al-Shishani-14Sep06.pdf), pp. 2-6; Schacht, *An Introduction to Islamic Law*, p. 73; see also Benjamin & Simon, *The Age of Sacred Terror*, at pp. 170-71 (discussing Salafi fundamentalists who endorse jihad in principle but oppose it in present practice, which is a useful contrast to the discussion in Murad Batal al-Shishani's essay, cited above, of Salafi jihadists, such as al Qaeda terrorists, who, in addition to revering Islam's first generations, both urge and practice jihad).

12   See, e.g., Sageman, *Understanding Terror Networks*, pp. 56-58; see also id. at 38, 45; compare Steve Coll, *Ghost Wars*, p. 120 ("CIA officers in the Near East Division who were running the Afghan program also embraced Hekmatyar as their most dependable and effective ally").

13   *United States* v. *Omar Abdel Rahman, et al.*, No. 93 Cr. 181 (S.D.N.Y.), Transcript 14,357-58 (1995).

14   9/11 Commission Final Report, p. 56.

15   U.S. Dept. of State, "Did the U.S. 'Create' Osama bin Laden?," citing Peter Bergen, *Holy War, Inc.: Inside the Secret World of Osama bin Laden* (The Free Press 2001, 2002), pp. 64-66.

16   Lorenzo Vidino, *Al Qaeda in Europe—The New Battleground of International Jihad* (Prometheus Books 2006), p. 75 & nn. 12-13 citing Sageman, *Understanding Terror Networks*, and Marlena Telvick, "Al Qaeda Today: The New Face of the Global Jihad" (*PBS Frontline Special* Jan. 2005) (interview with Marc Sageman) (http://www.pbs.org/wgbh/pages/frontline/shows/front/etc/today.html).

17   Andrew Marshall, "Terror 'Blowback' Burns CIA" (*The Independent* Nov. 1, 1998) (http://s3.amazonaws.com/911timeline/1990s/independent110198.html).

18   Bergen, *Holy War Inc.,* p. 70.

19   Michael A. Ledeen, *The War Against The Terror Masters* (Truman Talley Books, St. Martin's Griffin 2002 & 2003), p. 37.

20   The State Department not only cites CIA officials regarding the arrangement but also

quotes extensively from Brigadier Mohammad Yousaf, who ran the ISI's Afghan Bureau and was thus responsible for Pakistan's covert aid to the Afghan mujahideen. Surprisingly, State further relies on none other than Ayman al-Zawahiri, al Qaeda's number two, for the proposition that the United States dealt directly with the Pakistanis, not the Arab-Afghans. U.S. Dept. of State, "Did the U.S. 'Create' Osama bin Laden?," citing and quoting Mohammed Yousaf and Mark Adkin, *The Bear Trap: Afghanistan's Untold Story* (L. Cooper Publishing 1992), p. 81, and the serialization of Zarqawi's biography in *Al-Sharq al-Awsat*, Dec. 3, 2001 (Foreign Broadcast Information Service (FBIS), GMP20011202000401).

21   Bergen, *Holy War Inc.*, pp. 71-73.

22   9/11 Commission Final Report, p. 134.

23   See, e.g., Testimony of Dr. Thomas Fingar, Deputy Director for Analysis, Office of the Director of National Intelligence, to the House Armed Services Committee ("Fingar Testimony") (July 11, 2007) (http://armedservices.house.gov/pdfs/FC071107/Fingar_Testimony071107.pdf), p. 7; David E. Sanger and Mark Mazzetti, "Cheney Warns Pakistan to Act on Terror" (*New York Times* Feb. 26, 2007) (http://www.nytimes.com/2007/02/26/world/asia/26cnd-pakistan.html?hp); Carlotta Gall, "Pakistan Link Seen in Afghan Suicide Attacks" (*New York Times* Nov. 13, 2006) (http://www.nytimes.com/2006/11/13/world/asia/14afghancnd.html?).

24   Associated Press, "Analysts: al Qaeda back to pre-9/11 strength" (*USA Today* July 11, 2007) (http://www.usatoday.com/news/washington/2007-07-11-us-terror-threat_N.htm?csp=34).

25   Associated Press, "Analysts: al Qaeda back to pre-9/11 strength."

26   Fingar Testimony, p. 3.

27   Associated Press, "Analysts: al Qaeda back to pre-9/11 strength."

28   Sanger & Mazzetti, "Cheney Warns Pakistan to Act on Terror."

29   Jim Lobe, "Bush-Musharraf Alliance Under Growing Attack" (Inter Press Service News Agency July 12, 2007) (http://www.ipsnews.net/news.asp?idnews=38516).

30   Fingar Testimony, p. 8.

31   Chidanand Rajghatta, "Bush Backs Pak-Taliban Deal" (*Times of India* Sept. 8, 2006) (http://timesofindia.indiatimes.com/articleshow/1971329.cms).

32   Transparently straining not to criticize Musharraf, President Bush gritted, "I don't read it that way," when asked if the truce hadn't given safe-haven to jihadists. Remarkably, the Presi-

dent added the Pollyannaish surmise, "What [Musharraf] is doing is entering agreements with governors in the regions of the country, in the hopes that there would be an economic vitality, there will be alternatives to violence and terror." Rajghatta, "Bush Backs Pak-Taliban Deal." In mid-2007, by which time the Pakistani regime had entered several such truces, key findings of the National Intelligence Estimate (NIE), publicly released by the U.S. Director of National Intelligence, conceded that al Qaeda had "regenerated key elements of its Homeland attack capability" thanks to its new "safehaven in the Pakistan Federally Administered Tribal Areas (FATA)." NIE, "The Terrorist Threat to the US Homeland" (July 2007) (http://www.dni.gov/press_releases/20070717_release.pdf). With his regime in jeopardy and jihadist elements spreading beyond the territories ceded in these truces, Musharraf declared martial law in November 2007. See, e.g., Stanley Kurtz, "Al-Qaedastan–Grim possibilities for Pakistan" (*National Review Online* Nov. 5, 2007) (http://article.nationalreview.com/?q=YzU2MTVlN2E2MmJmOWRjYjVkMjQ4ODI5NWR jZTJmOTU=); Bill Roggio, "The Second Coup–'Pakistan is on the verge of destabilization'" (*The Weekly Standard* Nov. 4, 2007) (http://www.weeklystandard.com/Content/Public/Articles/000/000/014/315gqklr.asp).

33 Carlotta Gall, "Pakistan Link Seen in Afghan Suicide Attacks" (*New York Times* Nov. 13, 2006) (http://www.nytimes.com/2006/11/13/world/asia/14afghancnd.html?) (reprinted at http://www.iht.com/articles/2006/11/13/news/afghan.php).

34 Ben Leapman, "4,000 in UK trained in terror camps" (*Daily Telegraph* July 15, 2007) (http://www.telegraph.co.uk/news/main.jhtml?xml=/news/2007/07/15/nterr215.xml).

35 Philip Johnston, "Bomb plotters 'directed from the mountains'" (*Daily Telegraph* May 31, 2007) (http://www.telegraph.co.uk/news/main.jhtml;jsessionid=1DX2HS4SOEWPVQFIQ MFCFFOAVCBQYIV0?xml=/news/2007/05/31/walqaeda131.xml) .

36 Philip Smucker, "Ethnic group in Pakistan faces attacks by jihadists" (*Washington Times* July 9, 2007) (http://washingtontimes.com/apps/pbcs.dll/article?AID=/20070709/ FOREIGN/107090057/1001).

37 Smucker, "Ethnic group in Pakistan faces attacks by jihadists."

38 Sageman, *Understanding Terror Networks*, p. 57.

39 Fingar Testimony, supra, p. 8; see also, Jane Perlez, "Aid to Pakistan in Tribal Areas Raises Concerns" (*New York Times* July 16, 2007) (http://www.nytimes.com/2007/07/16/ world/asia/16pakistan.html?_r=1&ref=world&oref=slogin).

40 Weaver, "Blowback."

41 Andrew C. McCarthy, "Benazir Bhutto: Killed by the Real Pakistan" (*National Review Online* Dec. 27, 2007) (http://article.nationalreview.com/?q=MTExNmE0MzY3YjBlY WEwZDkzOThkMWJiM2JmZGQ2NDE=).

Chapter 7

1   9/11 Commission Final Report, p. 56; see also, e.g., Steven Emerson, *American Jihad—The Terrorists Living Among Us* (Free Press 2002), pp. 127-58; Gunaratna, *Inside al Qaeda*, pp. 3-8; Wright, *The Looming Tower*, 102-03; Benjamin & Simon, *The Age of Sacred Terror*, pp. 99-100.

2   Steven Emerson, *American Jihad—The Terrorists Living Among Us* (Free Press 2002), pp. 129-31.

3   Sageman, *Understanding Terror Networks*, p. 3.

4   Emerson, *American Jihad—The Terrorists Living Among Us*, p. 135 & précis to the Introduction; see also, e.g., id., p. 132 ("Azzam also made clear that Afghanistan would be used as a training ground where Muslims from around the world could receive preparation for taking the jihad to their respective regions: 'The Palestinian youth came here to Afghanistan, *and also non-Palestinians*, and they were trained, and their souls became prepared, and the paranoia of fear disappeared, and they became experts. *Now every one of them returns . . . ready to die.*'") (emphasis added).

5   9/11 Commission Staff Monograph on 9/11 and Terrorist Travel, Ch. 3, "Terrorist Entry and Embedding Tactics, 1993 to 2001" (Aug. 21, 2004) (http://www.9-11commission.gov/staff_statements/911_TerrTrav_Ch3.pdf) ("9/11 Commission Monograph"), pp. 50-51; Douglas Jehl, "C.I.A. Officers Played Role in Sheik Visas" (*New York Times* July 22, 1993) (http://select.nytimes.com/search/restricted/article?res=F0061EFF3F5C0C718EDDAE0894DB494D81).

6   See, e.g., Reuel Marc Gerecht, "The Sorry State of the CIA—and why it's unlikely to improve" (*The Weekly Standard* July 19, 2004 ed.) (http://www.weeklystandard.com/Content/Public/Articles/000/000/004/299qznfy.asp?pg=2).

7   See, e.g., Robert I. Friedman, "The CIA and the Sheik—The Agency Coddled Omar Abdel Rahman, Allowing Him to Operate in the U.S. Now This Unholy Alliance Has Blown Up in Our Faces" (*Village Voice* March 30, 1993) (available at http://www.libertyforum.org/showflat.php?Cat=&Board=news_history&Number=294518825).

8   Jehl, "C.I.A. Officers Played Role in Sheik Visas."

9   9/11 Commission Monograph, pp. 50-51.

10 9/11 Commission Monograph, p. 50; see also Steven A. Camarotta, "How the Terrorists Get In" (*The Public Interest* Fall 2002) (available at http://www.cis.org/articles/2002/sacpiarticle.html); Douglas Jehl, "C.I.A. Officer Signed Visa for Sheik, U.S. Says" (*New York Times* July 14, 1993) (http://select.nytimes.com/search/restricted/article?res=F00613F83C5B0C778DDDAE0894DB494D81).

11 Douglas Jehl, "Flaws in Computer Check Helped Sheik Enter U.S." (*New York Times* July 3, 1993) (http://query.nytimes.com/gst/fullpage.html?res=9F0CE0DD163AF930 A35754C0A965958260&sec=&spon=&pagewanted=print); see also, e.g., Camarotta, "How the Terrorists Get In"; Jehl, "C.I.A. Officer Signed Visa for Sheik, U.S. Says"; Jehl, "C.I.A. Officers Played Role in Sheik Visas."

12 9/11 Commission Monograph, p. 50.

13 INS was a Justice Department agency. In the various reshufflings following the 9/11 attacks, it was shifted to the new Department of Homeland Security and renamed the Bureau of Immigration and Customs Enforcement–taking on some of the enforcement responsibilities that used to be the bailiwick of the U.S. Customs Service.

14 9/11 Commission Monograph, p. 50.

15 Jehl, "C.I.A. Officers Played Role in Sheik Visas."

16 Damra was indicted in 2003 for procuring his American citizenship by fraud–specifically, by materially omitting from his 1994 application, inter alia, his affiliation with MAK, his ties to the Palestinian Islamic Jihad terrorist organization, and his prior calls for violent attacks against Jews. *United States* v. *Fawaz Damra*, Indictment No. 03 Cr. 484 (N.D. Ohio 2003) (available at: http://news.findlaw.com/hdocs/docs/terrorism/ usdamrah121603ind.html). He was convicted in June 2004, stripped of his U.S. citizenship, and ultimately deported to the West Bank. See, e.g., Robert Spencer, "Jurors see video of Ohio Imam Damra fund-raising, introducing al-Arian" (*Jihad Watch* June 17, 2004) (http://www.jihadwatch.org/archives/002263.php) (quoting from Associated Press); Amanda Garret, "Prelude to Terror–How Damra misled FBI" (*Cleveland Plain Dealer* Sept. 16, 2004) (http://www.cleveland.com/damra/index.ssf?/damra/ more/1095334425278000.html); Associated Press, "Cleveland Muslim Leader Convicted of Lying about terror ties, Deported" (Fox News Jan. 5, 2007) (http://www.foxnews.com/story/0,2933,241857,00.html).

17 Affidavit of FBI Special Agent Anne E. Asbury in support of defendant's arrest *United States* v. *John Philip Walker Lindh* (E.D.Va Jan. 15, 2002) (http://www.usdoj.gov/ag/ criminalcomplaint1.htm), paragraph 6; Jason Burke, "Hijacking suspect was bin Laden bodyguard" (*The Guardian* Sept. 30, 2001) (http://observer.guardian.co.uk/waronterrorism/story/0,,560729,00.html); see also Wright, *The Looming Tower*, p. 141 (on the role of Zawahiri in establishing the Farooq ["Farouk"] camp near Khost).

18 The other pillars are: professing the oneness of God and the prophethood of Mohammed, fasting during the holy month of Ramadan, and the pilgrimage to Mecca required at least once of all Muslims reasonably capable–from the perspective of health and financial condition–of fulfilling it. Schimmel, *Islam–An Introduction*, pp. 34-42.

19   Emerson, *American Jihad*, pp. 129-30; Gunaratna, *Inside Al Qaeda*, p. 101.

20   Emerson, *American Jihad*, pp. 129-30.

21   See, e.g., Council on Foreign Relations Backgrounder on al Qaeda ("How big is al-Qaeda? It's impossible to say precisely, because al-Qaeda is decentralized. Estimates range from several hundred to several thousand members") (http://www.cfr.org/publication/9126/ alqaeda_aka_alqaida_alqaida.html#5); Memorial Institute for the Prevention of Terrorism Group Profile on al Qaeda (estimating strength at 50,000 members) (http://www. tkb.org/Group.jsp?groupID=6); GlobalSecurity.org analysis, conceding that al Qaeda's decentralized structure renders precise knowledge of its size impossible (http://www. globalsecurity.org/military/world/para/al-qaida.htm).

22   On bayat, see, e.g., *United States* v. *Ali Abdelseoud Mohamed*, Complaint Affidavit of FBI Special Agent Daniel Coleman in Support of Arrest Warrant (September 1998) (available at http://intelwire.egoplex.com/2006_09_28_exclusives.html) ("Mohamed Complaint"), p. 6.

23   See also Mohammed ElShafey, "My Life with al Qaeda: A Spy's Story" (*Asharq Al-Aswat* Dec. 18, 2006) (http://www.asharq-e.com/news.asp?section=8&id=7375); Gregg Jones, "Bin Laden's proud alums: Graduates of al-Qaida camps say U.S. too late to stop Islamic militancy" (*Dallas Morning News* Nov. 5, 2001) (http://www.hvk.org/articles/1101/85. html).

24   See, e.g., McCarthy, "Negotiate with Iran?," quoting 9/11 Commission Final Report, p. 61.

25   See, e.g., Bill Roggio, "Somalia's Terror Camps" (*Counterterrorism Blog* July 2, 2006) (http://counterterrorismblog.org/2006/07/somalias_terror_camps.php) ("In 2002, a confidential report indicated Somalia contained 17 known operational terrorist training camps. . . . The environment in Somalia is said to compare to that of Afghanistan during the heyday of the Taliban. Terrorists from Afghanistan, Pakistan, Chechnya, Iraq and the Arabian peninsula are said to be flocking into Somalia to staff the camps or enter training. Camps are said to be training recruits to employ improvised explosive devices (roadside bombs or IEDs.").

26   See, e.g., Combatant Status Review Tribunal Hearing ISN 10016 for Zayn al Abidin Muhammad Husayn (more commonly known as "Abu Zubaydah," a high-level al Qaeda detainee) (March 27, 2007) (http://www.defenselink.mil/news/transcript_ISN10016. pdf), p. 16 (Zubayda observing that Ahmed Ressam–who attempted to bomb Los Angeles International Airport in 1999 in connection with the Millennium observance–could not know all the inner workings of even the camp he attended, Khalden, because he was "only a student, a trainee. He don't know the big picture.").

27   See, e.g., Gunaratna, *Inside Al Qaeda*, p. 8 (between 10,000 and 110,000 from 1989 to October 2001); El Shafey, "Inside the Jihad: My Life with al Qaeda–A Spy's Story," (tens of thousands); Jim Lacey, "Assessing al Qaeda–It's not what you think" (*National Review Online* Aug. 25, 2004) (http://www.nationalreview.com/comment/lacey200408250834.asp) (between 20,000 and 100,000); BBC News, "Al-Qaeda camps 'trained 70,000'" (BBC Jan. 4, 2005) (German intelligence estimate of 70,000); see also Stephen Hayes, "Saddam's Terror Training Camps: What the documents captured from the former Iraqi regime reveal—and why they should all be made public" (*The Weekly Standard* Jan. 16, 2006 ed.) (http://www.weeklystandard.com/Content/Public/Articles/000/000/006/550kmbzd.asp) (2,000 terrorists per year, including some tied to al Qaeda, trained at Iraqi Regime's camps at Samarra, Ramadi, and Salman Pak between 1999 and 2002).

28   Title 18, United States Code, Sections 951 through 970.

Chapter 8

1   See, e.g., Carl Campanile, "Osama's Sheik–Lynne's Man Fueled 'War': Feds" (*New York Post* Oct. 8, 2004).

2   *United States* v. *Ahmed Abdel Sattar*, Indictment S1 02 Cr. 395 (S.D.N.Y. 2003), pp. 9-10.

3   *Sattar* Indictment, p. 8.

4   *Sattar* Indictment, p. 9.

5   Andrew C. McCarthy, "Lynne Stewart & Me–Justice and Sadness" (*National Review Online* Feb. 15, 2005) (http://article.nationalreview.com/?q=OGFkNjA4YTJkY2ZhN2YyY2U5OGMwZTY1OGU2NTk4MTI=).

6   Serge F. Kovaleski and Hassan M. Fatah, "A Surgeon's Trajectory Takes an Unlikely Swerve" (*New York Times* July 3, 2007) (http://www.nytimes.com/2007/07/03/world/europe/03doctor.html?_r=1&oref=slogin).

7   Peter Lance, *Triple Cross* (Regan 2006).

8   In March 1998, once the appeal in the Blind Sheikh case was concluded, I left the Southern District intending to be a private lawyer and writer in Connecticut. Within a few weeks, though, I accepted an appointment as an associate Independent Counsel on the investigation of former Clinton Administration HUD Secretary Henry Cisneros–to write the government's pretrial briefs, not to try the case. The venture into private life and independent-counsel dabbling proved very temporary. In February 1999, I returned to the Southern District to run its satellite division in White Plains, New York, for five years.

9   Lance, *Triple Cross*, pp. 15-16.

10   Benjamin Weiser, "U.S. Ex-Sergeant Linked to bin Laden Conspiracy" (*New York Times* Oct. 30, 1998).

11   *United States* v. *Ali Abdelseoud Mohamed*, Complaint Affidavit of FBI Special Agent Daniel Coleman in Support of Arrest Warrant (September 1998) (available at http://intelwire.egoplex.com/2006_09_28_exclusives.html) ("Mohamed Complaint"), p. 5.

12   Wright, *The Looming Tower*, p. 49.

13   *United States* v. *Ali Mohamed*, No. S (7) 98 Cr. 1023 (S.D.N.Y.), Guilty Plea Transcript (October 20, 2000) (Andrew C. McCarthy one of five prosecutors representing the United States), p. 26.

14   Wright, *The Looming Tower*, p. 179-80.

15   Benjamin Weiser & James Risen, "The Masking of a Militant: A special report—A Soldier's Shadowy trail in U.S. and in the Mideast" (*New York Times* Dec. 1, 1998); Weiser, "U.S. Ex-Sergeant Linked to bin Laden Conspiracy."

16   Weiser & Risen, "The Masking of a Militant: A special report—A Soldier's Shadowy trail in U.S. and in the Mideast" (*New York Times* Dec. 1, 1998); James Risen, "C.I.A. Said to Reject Bomb Suspect's Bid to be a Spy" (*New York Times* Oct. 31, 1998).

17   See, e.g., Committee for Accurate Middle East Reporting in America (CAMERA), "Timeline of Hezbollah Violence" (July 17, 2006) (http://www.camera.org/index.asp?x_context=2&x_outlet=118&x_article=1148); see also Andrew C. McCarthy, "Negotiate with Iran?—How many more Americans do they need to kill before we get the point?" (*National Review Online* December 8, 2006) (http://article.nationalreview.com/?q=N2ViM TQ1NTllMjAxZDVmNjg3ZjIyMWRlMWU5OWE3N2M=).

18   Lance, *Triple Cross*, pp. 15-16.

19   Lance, *Triple Cross*, pp. 15-16; see also Wright, *The Looming Tower*, p. 180.

20   Weiser & Risen, "The Masking of a Militant"; Wright, *The Looming Tower*, p. 180; Lance, *Triple Cross*, p. 16.

21   Weiser & Risen, "The Masking of a Militant."

22   Weiser & Risen, "The Masking of a Militant."

23   Weiser & Risen, "The Masking of a Militant." In 1995, the *Boston Globe*, relying on anon-

ymous sources, reported that Mohamed had been admitted to the United States through the assistance of the CIA's Operations Directorate, a claim that Lance repeats. Lance, *Triple Cross*, p. 17, citing Paul Quinn-Judge & Charles M. Sennot, "Figure Cited in Terrorism Case Said to Enter US with CIA Help Say Defendants Trained by Him" (*Boston Globe* Feb. 3, 1995); see also Wright, *The Looming Tower*, p. 180 (claiming that by the time the CIA added Mohamed to the terrorist watch-list, Mohamed "was already in California on a visa waiver program that was sponsored by the agency itself . . . to shield valuable assets or those who have performed important services for the country"). I do not believe this story is true, though I cannot prove it. Based on what I learned, what has been reported (including by Lance's better informed source, former agent Jack Cloonan), and what we know from the State Department's 1993 investigation into the deplorable deficiencies in the system for watch-listing terrorists during the 1980s and 1990s–the same deficiencies that allowed the Blind Sheikh to travel freely and ultimately emigrate to the United State–I credit the conclusion that the issuance of Mohamed's visa was the result of incompetence, not anything more diabolical than that. Mohamed had not performed any services for the United States; quite the opposite. His first order of business upon arriving in the U.S. was to marry an American citizen (something he wouldn't have needed to worry about if his ability to remain in America had been guaranteed by the CIA), and, more to the point and as further discussed, infra, the Agency rejected him when he attempted to re-establish contact in 1989.

24 See, e.g., Richard H. Shultz Jr., "Showstoppers–Nine reasons why we never sent our Special Operations Forces after al Qaeda before 9/11" (*The Weekly Standard* Jan. 26, 2004 ed.) (http://www.weeklystandard.com/content/public/articles/000/000/003/613twavk. asp); Andrew J. Budka (Major, USMC), "Low-Intensity Conflict and the Marines–A Seabased Solution" (Marine Corps Command and Staff College, May 15, 1989) (http://www.globalsecurity.org/military/library/report/1989/BAJ.htm) pp. 7-8.

25 Weiser & Risen, "The Masking of a Militant."

26 Weiser & Risen, "The Masking of a Militant"; Wright, *The Looming Tower*, pp. 180-81.

27 Weiser & Risen, "The Masking of a Militant."

28 Mohamed Complaint, p. 9.

29 Weiser & Risen, "The Masking of a Militant."

30 Lance, *Triple Cross*, pp. 34-35.

31 Weiser & Risen, "The Masking of a Militant"; Wright, *The Looming Tower*, p. 181.

32 Weiser & Risen, "The Masking of a Militant." According to Peter Lance, Jack Cloonan, the retired agent who had the ticket on the FBI's investigation of Mohamed in the 1990s,

told him that Mohamed "planned an operation against the Spetznaz . . . and killed a bunch of them," and that Mohamed claimed the two belts had been "taken off two Spetznaz commandos whom he'd personally ambushed." Lance, *Triple Cross*, p. 44.

33   Weiser & Risen, "The Masking of a Militant."

34   Lance, *Triple Cross*, p. 44.

35   See, e.g., Norville de Atkine, "Why Arabs Lose Wars" (*MERIA Journal* March 2000 ed.) (http://meria.idc.ac.il/journal/2000/issue1/de-atkin.pdf), arguing that the "perpetual ineffectiveness" of Arab armies is rooted in Arab culture's distinctive lack of individual freedom and initiative.

36   Wright, *The Looming Tower*, pp. 180-81.

37   Weiser & Risen, "The Masking of a Militant."

38   Weiser, "U.S. Ex-Sergeant Linked To bin Laden Conspiracy."

39   Lance, *Triple Cross*, p. 39.

40   Lance, *Triple Cross*, p. 51.

41   Lance, *Triple Cross*, p. 49, n. 31, which appears id., p. 498.

42   For an excellent discussion of al Qaeda's formation, see Wright, *The Looming Tower*, pp. 131-37.

43   Weiser & Risen, "The Masking of a Militant."

44   Weiser & Risen, "The Masking of a Militant."

45   Mohamed Complaint, pp. 7-8.

Chapter 9

1   It is a mistake to refer to the PLO as "secular" as many in the foreign policy establishment are wont to do. The PLO, now superseded by the Palestinian Authority, was an amalgam of Palestinian liberation organizations which incorporated Islamic, secular, socialist, and Arab nationalist movements. The impulse to label as "secular" the PLO and, particularly, Arafat's primary base within it, Fatah, is transparently to build a case–an arrantly counterfactual case–that Fatah is "moderate" and worthy of American support because it might someday evolve into a western style democracy living side-by-side in peace with Israel, as contrasted with the incorrigible and unabashedly jihadist Hamas. In point of

fact, Fatah is secular only by comparison to Hamas. It is propelled by jihadist rhetoric and theory (especially regarding the religious duty to "liberate" Jerusalem), has a decades-long history of terrorism, and, far from being "moderate," maintains its own terrorist wing, the al-Aqsa Martyrs Brigades. See, e.g., Andrew C. McCarthy, "Our Terrorists Are Better Than Your Terrorists–Supporting Fatah, the Bush administration makes a deal with the devil" (*National Review Online* June 21, 2007) (http://article.nationalreview.co m/?q=MDg2NTNkOTM0ZjI5ZTEzNzBjNzc4ODNjZjRhMmRlZjQ=); Andrew C. McCarthy, "The Father of Modern Terrorism–The True Legacy of Yasser Arafat" (*National Review Online* Nov. 12, 2004) (http://article.nationalreview.com/?q=MjhiMjI3NDIyM zgzY2JmMTY2YTk1NmJhYjhMWZlZjQ=).

2   See, e.g., Benjamin & Simon, *The Age of Sacred Terror*, pp. 103-04.

3   Mary W. Tabor, "Request from Sheik for Custody Release Is Denied by Court" (*New York Times* Aug. 17, 1993) (http://select.nytimes.com/search/restricted/article?res=F00610 FD3E5E0C748DDDA10894DB494D81); Memorial Institute for the Prevention of Terrorism, Profile of the Islamic Group ("al-Gama'a al-Islamiyya") (http://www.tkb.org/ KeyLeader.jsp?memID=5651) (accessed July 21, 2007).

4   See, e.g., Wright, *The Looming Tower*, pp. 142-43; Bergen, *Holy War, Inc.*, pp. 73-74.

5   See, e.g., Emerson, *American Jihad*, p. 134.

6   For a recent account tying this incident to Fawaz Damra's 2004 prosecution, see Garrett, "Prelude to Terror: How Damra misled FBI."

7   Debra Burlingame, "On a Wing and a Prayer–Grievance Theater at Minneapolis International Airport" (*Wall Street Journal* Dec. 6, 2006) (http://www.opinionjournal.com/ editorial/feature.html?id=110009348); M. Zudhi Jasser, "The Flying Imams: A Defining Moment in American Values?" (*Family Security Matters* April 6, 2007) (http://www.familysecuritymatters.org/global.php?id=870234); on CAIR, see Andrew C. McCarthy, "Singing CAIR's Tune on Your Dime–as the Bush administration squanders a trust, Democrats prepare a new 'Sister Souljaj Moment'" (*National Review Online* Jan. 2, 2007) (http:// article.nationalreview.com/?q=NjY4M2VjNmE2NmIxNzM3YjYyNTJjMjI4Y2JkOTE1YW I=).

8   Wright, *The Looming Tower*, pp. 142-44.

9   Wright, *The Looming Tower*, pp. 143-44 (describing Zawahiri spreading rumors in Peshawar on the day of the murder that Azzam was an American mole, but singing his praises at the funeral the following day).

10   Joe Milicia, "Ohio Cleric to be Deported" (Associated Press Nov. 25, 2005) (http://www. breitbart.com/article.php?id=D8E3LOTO0&show_article=1).

11   9/11 Commission Monograph, p. 62 n. 45 (citing to affidavit of Abdel Rahman filed in connection with his U.S. asylum petition).

12   9/11 Commission Monograph, p. 62 n. 45 (citing to affidavit of Abdel Rahman filed in connection with his U.S. asylum petition).

13   9/11 Commission Monograph, pp. 50-51; see also Douglas Jehl, "C.I.A. Officer Signed Visa For Sheik, U.S. Says" (*New York Times* July 14, 1993); Steven A. Camarota, "How the Terrorists Get In" (*The Public Interest* Fall 2002) (http://www.cis.org/articles/2002/sacpiarticle.html).

14   Bergen, *Holy War Inc.*, pp. 136-37; see also James C. McKinley Jr., "Islamic Leader on U.S. Terrorist List Is in Brooklyn" (*New York Times* Dec. 16, 1990) (http://select. nytimes.com/search/restricted/article?res=F30614F6355E0C758DDDAB0994D8494 D81).

15   9/11 Commission Monograph, p. 51.

16   Joseph B. Treaster, "Immigration Board Rejects Sheik's Plea for Asylum" (*New York Times* July 10, 1993) (http://select.nytimes.com/search/restricted/article?res=F0061E F93F580C738DDDAE0894DB494D81); see also 9/11 Commission Monograph, p. 51.

17   9/11 Commission Monograph, p. 51.

18   9/11 Commission Monograph, p. 51.

19   Thomas Joscelyn, "The Pope of Terrorism (Part I): Hassan al-Turabi, ally of Saddam Hussein and bin Laden's long-time friend and benefactor, is freed from jail" (*The Weekly Standard* July 25, 2005) (http://www.weeklystandard.com/Content/Public/ Articles/000/000/005/880qqeoh.asp); see also Andrew C. McCarthy, "The Sudan Connection: The Missing Link in U.S. Terrorism Policy" (*The Weekly Standard* Nov. 2, 1998 ed.).

20   Mohamed Complaint, p. 8.

21   Benjamin Weiser, "Informer's Part in Terror Case Is Detailed" (*New York Times* Dec. 22, 2000); Mohamed Complaint, pp. 8, 9; Ali Mohamed Guilty Plea Transcript, p. 27.

22   Mohamed Complaint, p. 9; see also *United States* v. *Usama bin Laden, et al.*, Indictment No. S(9) 98 Cr. 1023 (S.D.N.Y. 1999) (available at http://cns.miis.edu/pubs/reports/ pdfs/binladen/indict.pdf), p. 13.

23   Bergen, *Holy War, Inc.*, p. 137.

24 Emerson, *American Jihad*, pp. 134-35; Bergen, *Holy War, Inc.*, p. 137.

25 Milicia, "Ohio Cleric to be Deported."

26 Emerson, *American Jihad*, pp. 136-37; Bergen, *Holy War, Inc.*, pp. 138-39.

Chapter 10

1 Mark Steyn, *America Alone* (Regnery 2006).

2 The circumstantial evidence of Abouhalima's complicity was suggestive, but not compelling. By the time Nosair was federally tried (after being acquitted by a New York state jury), Abouhalima (as well as Salameh and Ayyad, who were also implicated) had already been sentenced to 240 years' imprisonment for bombing the World Trade Center. Peter Lance asserts conclusorily that the plan called for Abouhalima to be stationed in his taxi in front of the hotel, but that he was shooed away by a doorman. Lance, *Triple Cross*, p. 57. It's a plausible theory, but Lance cites no evidence in support of his offered insight into the plot's details—his guess is as good as yours. And though he contends that a freelance photographer, Shannen Taylor, saw Abouhalima get waved away in front of the Marriott, no pictures were snapped and Lance provides no indication that the photographer could actually identify Abouhalima. It bears noting that Abouhalima bore a striking resemblance to Nosair's friend Mustafa Shalabi, who was still alive when Kahane was murdered. He also had a younger brother, Mohamed Abouhalima—another friend of Nosair, later convicted for accessory-after-the-fact of the World Trade Center bombing—who looked nearly like a twin. It is, moreover, hard to believe the getaway driver in a daring murder plot would allow himself to be moved by a hotel doorman—at least not more than a few feet away from the hotel entrance. That said, it is entirely possible that Abouhalima was shunted away by traffic police, or even that he was out there, at or near a pre-arranged rendezvous point, but Nosair, in his haste, simply missed him among a passel of yellow cabs in front of a busy New York City hotel.

3 John Kifner, "Police Say Kahane Suspect Took Anti-Depression Drugs" (*New York Times* Nov. 9, 1990) (http://query.nytimes.com/gst/fullpage.html?sec=health&res=9C0CE3 DC1E31F93AA35752C1A966958260).

4 James C. McKinley Jr., "Islamic Leader on U.S. Terrorist List Is in Brooklyn" (*New York Times* Dec. 16, 1990) (http://select.nytimes.com/search/restricted/article?res=F30614 F6355E0C758DDDAB0994D8494D81).

5 Joint Staff Inquiry for the Senate and House Intelligence Committees, "Hearing on the Intelligence Community's Response to Past Terrorist Attacks Against the United States from February 1993 to September 2001" (October 8, 2002) (http://www.fas.org/irp/congress/2002_hr/100802hill.html).

6   McKinley, "Islamic Leader on U.S. Terrorist List Is in Brooklyn."

7   Chitra Ragavan, "Tracing terror's roots—How the first World Trade Center plot sowed the seeds for 9/11" (*U.S. News & World Report*, Feb. 24/March 3, 2003).

8   Kifner, "Police Say Kahane Suspect Took Anti-Depression Drugs." Nosair had been involved in an electrical accident that badly burned one of his legs and affected one of his hands. As those who trained with him and chased him down the streets of Manhattan could attest, however, he was quite ambulatory.

Chapter 11

1   Andrew C. McCarthy and Mansoor Ijaz Debate, "Can Islam Reform Itself" (Opinion-Duel.com Feb. 28, 2006).

2   Rule 16(a)(1)(E), Federal Rules of Criminal Procedure.

3   Alison Mitchell, "U.S. Accused Sheik Last Year of Inciting Violence in Egypt" (*New York Times* July 27, 1993) (http://select.nytimes.com/search/restricted/article?res=F00612 FE345F0C748EDDAE0894DB494D81).

Chapter 12

1   Ronald Sullivan, "Kahane Trial Lawyers Ordered to Prove No Bias in Juror Choices" (*New York Times* Nov. 13, 1991) (http://select.nytimes.com/search/restricted/article?re s=F20611FC3B590C708DDDA80994D9494D81).

2   This was a ludicrous concern. Based on the trajectory determined from examining the bullet entrance and exit wounds in Kahane's neck, police found a deformed copper-jacketed projectile (and resulting physical damage) in a window area of the ballroom. Also, near the doorway area where Franklin had been shot, police recovered a deformed lead projectile and a copper jacket. Among other ballistics evidence in the vicinity of the Lexington Avenue Post Office where Acosta had been shot, investigators found two deformed copper-jacketed projectiles. Ballistics testing determined that the rounds recovered from all three areas had been fired from Nosair's .357 magnum. It should, moreover, go without saying that Nosair was convicted of *coercion* and *assault* while in possession of the gun, offenses which involved the *shooting* of the gun at Kahane, Franklin, and Acosta.

3   Sura 33:9 ("O ye who believe! Remember the Grace of Allah [bestowed] upon you when there came down on you Hosts [to overwhelm you]; but we sent against them a hurricane and forces that ye saw not; but Allah sees [clearly] all that ye do"); see also *The Holy Qur'an—English Translation of the Meanings and Commentary*, revised and edited by

The Presidency of Islamic Researches, Ministry of Hajj and Endowments (Kingdom of Saudi Arabia 1410 H [1990]), p. 1241 n. 3680 (commentary on sura 33:9).

4   Ronald Sullivan, "Judge Gives Maximum Term in Kahane Case" (*New York Times* Jan. 30, 1992) (http://select.nytimes.com/search/restricted/article?res=F10615F63D5D 0C738FDDA80894DA494D81); see also Daniel Pipes, "Judges Repair the Mistakes of Juries" (DanielPipes.org May 1, 2006) (http://www.danielpipes.org/blog/599).

5   Sullivan, "Judge Gives Maximum Term in Kahane Case."

Chapter 13

1   See, e.g., Ragavan, "Tracing Terror's Roots," supra (addressing, based on interviews with law enforcement officials, the FBI's concern that the jihadists' request for Salem to build bombs, "place[d] the FBI in a legally precarious position").

Chapter 14

1   Joint Staff Inquiry for the Senate and House Intelligence Committees, "Hearing on the Intelligence Community's Response to Past Terrorist Attacks Against the United States from February 1993 to September 2001" (October 8, 2002) (http://www.fas.org/irp/congress/2002_hr/100802hill.html).

2   Ragavan, "Tracing Terror's Roots." The quoted agent is John Anticev. It is worth repeating, however, that Anticev was on an extended medical leave when Salem was terminated from the investigation. He had been Salem's principal FBI contact on the investigation; he would not have wanted Salem terminated; and the decision both to terminate Salem and to refrain from pursuing other investigative options was a supervisory call, not one made by Anticev and the other line agents, Detective Napoli and Agent Floyd. Anticev made many errors in the handling of Salem, as he has, to his credit, conceded both in trial testimony and other settings. He is not responsible, however, for the key decisions. It is noteworthy, moreover, that the too-little-too-late attempt to neutralize the cell was made after he returned to duty. It was a grossly inadequate effort, but at least it was something—which by definition makes it more than what went on in the months between Salem's ejection and Anticev's return to duty.

3   See generally Laurie Mylroie, *The War Against America: Saddam Hussein and the World Trade Center Attacks: A Study of Revenge* (Harper revised ed. 2001). Dr. Mylroie's contention that Yousef (the alias for a Pakistani man actually named Abdul Basit) may have been an Iraqi spy, rests largely on the Iraqi passport in the name of "Ramzi Ahmed Yousef" that he presented upon entering. Yousef used his Pakistani passport, in the name of "Abdul Basit," upon fleeing on the night of the bombing. Mylroie argues that

the "real" Basit family disappeared in Kuwait when Saddam Hussein's regime invaded in 1990, permitting the regime to assign Basit's identity and background to "Yousef," one of its operatives. Quite apart from the unlikelihood that a professional intelligence operative possessed of various false identities would use his authentic one upon entering the United States to carry out a terrorist attack, several people, including Yousef's codefendants, knew him as Abdul Basit both before and after 1990.

Chapter 15

1   Ismoil and Yousef were finally convicted after a joint trial in 1997. See Gunaratna, *Combating Terrorism* (McCarthy, "Anti-Terrorism Law: The American Experience," p. 256).

Chapter 16

1   Sura 8:55; see Spencer, *The Truth about Muhammad*, supra, Ch. 7 ("War Is Deceit"), pp. 111-12 (describing Allah's direction to the Prophet that treaties may be broken as necessary).

Chapter 20

1   See Gunaratna (editor), *Combating Terrorism*, Ch. 11, McCarthy, "Anti-Terrorism Law: The American Experience," pp. 252 & ff.

2   The Violent Crime Control and Law Enforcement Act of 1994 established general statutory procedures for seeking and imposing capital sentences, effectively complying with the Supreme Court's revamping, in the 1970s, of death penalty jurisprudence. The 1994 Act supplemented the few capital crime authorizations then available (mainly, for murder committed in the course of certain drug trafficking offenses) with many additional murder offenses, and more still were added in 1996. The federal offenses for which the death penalty is currently authorized generally require as a necessary element the killing of a victim, but they include a few non-homicidal offenses, such as treason and espionage. See Dept. of Justice Monograph, "The Federal Death Penalty System: Supplementary Data, Analysis and Revised Protocols for Capital Case Review" (June 6, 2001) (http://www.usdoj.gov/dag/pubdoc/deathpenaltystudy.htm), at Part I.

3   Title 18, United States Code, Section 371.

4   Title 18, United States Code, Section 844.

5   *United States v. Ivic,* 700 F.2d 51 (2d Cir. 1983).

Chapter 22

1   Title 18, United States Code, Sections 1961, et seq.

2   *National Organization for Women v. Scheidler,* 510 U.S. 249 (1994).

3   Title 18, United States Code, Section 2384.

4   Alison Mitchell, "Egyptian Cleric May Drop Fight Against Deportation" (*New York Times* August 19, 1993 (http://select.nytimes.com/search/restricted/article?res=F00616FA35 5B0C7A8DDDA10894DB494D81).

5   McCarthy, "The Sudan Connection."

6   Chris Hedges, "U.S.-Egypt Ties Are Strained In Detention of Islamic Cleric" (*New York Times* July 7, 1993) (http://select.nytimes.com/search/restricted/article?res=F00617FC3F5F0 C748CDDAE0894DB494D81).

Chapter 24

1   Mohamed Complaint, p. 7.

2   Lance, *Triple Cross*, pp. 175-76.

3   Lance, *Triple Cross*, pp. 178.

4   Lance, *Triple Cross*, pp. 175-76.

5   Mohamed Guilty Plea, pp. 27-29.

6   Mohamed Guilty Plea, pp. 29-30.

Chapter 25

1   Much of the discussion that follows is extracted from a proposal I have made for the creation of a National Security Court to handle terrorism matters. See Andrew C. McCarthy and Alykhan Velshi, "We Need a National Security Court" (John Yoo [editor] *Outsourcing American Law*) (available through the Foundation for Defense of Democracies (http://www.defenddemocracy.org/usr_doc/NationalSecurityCourt.doc).

2   Testimony of Former Attorney General William P. Barr before the House Intelligence

Committee (Oct. 30, 2003), pp. 2-3 (http://intelligence.house.gov/Media/PDFS/Testi-monyofWilliamPBarr.pdf).

3   Rule 16(a)(1)(E), Fed. R. Crim. P.

4   *Brady* v. *Maryland*, 373 U.S. 83 (1963); see also *United States* v. *Bagley*, 473 U.S. 667, 682 (1985) (concept of materiality conveys the potential to undermine confidence in the outcome); *Kyles* v. *Whitley*, 514 U.S. 419, 434 (1995) ("showing of materiality does not require demonstration by a preponderance that disclosure of the suppressed evidence would have resulted ultimately in the defendant's acquittal"); and see *id.*, at 437 (even when the prosecutor's office and the investigating agency do not know of exculpatory information, they have an obligation to seek out and disclose any such information that may be in the wider government's possession).

5   *Brady* v. *Maryland*, 373 U.S. at 87; *see also Moore* v. *Illinois*, 408 U.S. 786, 794-95 (1972).

6   A terrorist who is acquitted due to insufficient evidence is not a person who will simply return to the commission of crimes; he is a danger to return to acts of war and indiscriminate mass homicide. The incentive for the Justice Department is thus to use every appropriate means to ensure conviction. One of the most appropriate is to present elaborate proof of the dangerousness of the terrorist enterprise of which the defendant is an operative. This approach has the dual benefit of placing acts in their chilling context while expanding the scope of evidentiary admissibility (particularly by resort to liberal rules for the admission of co-conspirator statements under Rule 801(d)(2)(E) and background evidence). While focus on the enterprise greatly enhances the prospects for conviction, however, it exponentially expands the universe of what may be discoverable.

7   18 U.S.C. Sec. 3500.

8   Rule 806, Fed. R. Evid.

9   See Rule 33, Fed.R.Crim.P.; see also 28 U.S.C. Sec. 2255 (permitting collateral challenge based on alleged errors in the proceedings leading to conviction).

10   18 U.S.C. App. 3 (Pub.L. 96-456, Oct. 15, 1980, 94 Stat. 2025).

11   Secretary of State Rice, Remarks at the Annual Iftaar Dinner (Oct. 25, 2005) (Department of State Website, http://www.state.gov/secretary/rm/2005/55577.htm).

12   Andrew C. McCarthy, "Sistani and the Democracy Project–A useful measure of the divide between 'To Hell with Them' and 'Anything Goes'" (*National Review Online*, March 20, 2006) (http://www.nationalreview.com/mccarthy/mccarthy200603200816.asp).

Index